Arming the Warship

Arming the Warship

*Naval Weapons Technology
and Gunnery from the
Spanish Armada to the Cold War*

IVER P. COOPER

McFarland & Company, Inc., Publishers
Jefferson, North Carolina

Portions of this work were previously published in the *Grantville Gazette* and are used by permission. Use of released U.S. Navy imagery does not constitute product or organizational endorsement of any kind by the U.S. Navy.

ISBN (print) 978-1-4766-9499-3
ISBN (ebook) 978-1-4766-5284-9

LIBRARY OF CONGRESS AND BRITISH LIBRARY
CATALOGUING DATA ARE AVAILABLE

Library of Congress Control Number 2024044414

Front cover images: (top) diagram of a 32-pound naval cannon (Office of Naval Records and Library); (bottom) drawings of an *Iowa*-class battleship in World War II configuration (Office of Naval Intelligence)

Printed in the United States of America

McFarland & Company, Inc., Publishers
Box 611, Jefferson, North Carolina 28640
www.mcfarlandpub.com

For Lee, Louise and Jason.

Table of Contents

Preface

In 1815, a single British "Common Class" 74-gun ship of the line possessed greater firepower than Napoleon's "Grand Battery" at the Battle of Waterloo. The warship, although merely a "third rate" vessel in the Royal Navy's scheme, carried twenty-eight 32-pdrs (that is, guns firing 32-pound shot) on the gun deck, twenty-eight 18-pdrs on the deck above, fourteen 9-pdrs on the quarterdeck, and four 9-pdrs on the forecastle (Blake and Lawrence 2005, 25). That's a total shot weight of 1,562 pounds. (The 9-pdrs were sometimes replaced by carronades, which would have fired heavier shot.)

In contrast, according to the Alex Testo (2016) reconstruction for Project Hougoumont, the Grand Battery consisted of twenty-four 12-pdrs from the reserve battery and twenty-eight 6-pdrs and ten 5.5-inch howitzers from First Corps. The howitzer fired a 24-pound shell. (That's nominally a total projectile weight of 696 pounds, but add 10 percent to account for the difference between the French pound and the English one.)

The reason for the disparity may be summed up in one word: resistance. The field artillery was brought to the battlefield on two-wheeled carriages drawn by horses. The tractive force needed to pull a wheeled vehicle carrying a load is the total load (including the vehicle itself) multiplied by the coefficient of rolling friction (resistance) for the particular wheel-road combination. The resistance is the result of the deformation of the wheel and road as a result of the rolling motion, which requires energy. For wooden wheels rolling on dirt roads, it obviously is higher than for modern rubber tires on asphalt or steel train wheels on steel rails.

Naval artillery, in contrast, is brought by sea, and the effective resistance to movement is the hydrodynamic resistance. This force has two components: the "frictional resistance," which is the result of the formation of a stagnant boundary layer of water around the hull, creating shear forces as water streams by, and the "frontal resistance," which arises because the ship must push water out of its way. Buoyancy lifts the ship partially out of the water and, by reducing the draft and wetted surface area, reduces the resistance (Barthel 2021, 12).

Because of the disparity in resistance, horses towing canal boats on still water could tow forty to fifty times the weight that they could when hitched to a cart (Coulthard 2021). In the case of a sailing ship, the propulsive force is provided not by horses but by the wind, and a relatively modest wind was sufficient to give a sailing warship headway despite the weight of its armament.

This is one of many examples in which science provides insights into the limitations on military capability. And military capability, in turn, has often had a profound effect on history. In the case of naval power, this was the subject of Alfred Thayer Mahan's seminal text, *The Influence of Seapower on History, 1660–1783* (1890), and, of course, many later naval histories.

This book examines the evolution of naval armament, armor, ballistics and gunnery from a scientific and technological perspective. Each chapter is devoted to a particular aspect (e.g., gunfounding, projectiles or propellants). Within each chapter, the historical development is traced and related, where appropriate, to scientific concepts. (Much of what is said about these topics is relevant to land artillery, too, since the laws of physics don't care whether the projectile is fired from a naval gun or a self-propelled howitzer.)

Chronologically, the emphasis is on the sixteenth to nineteenth centuries, with progressively more selective attention to later developments. While the British and American navies are emphasized, there are references to the navies of other powers—notably the Spanish, French, Dutch, German, Swedish, Russian and Japanese navies. No attempt is made to comprehensively cover every ship or ammunition design; this is a "broad brush" work and thus must rely on selected examples.

This point leads to an important caveat: This book does not qualify every statement as to the applicable navy and time period, so the reader should pay attention to the date of any "period" source cited.

For the purpose of this book, "naval armament" includes "Greek fire" projectors, rockets, missiles and torpedoes, as well as the use of a ship as a projectile, but these topics receive relatively brief treatment—the emphasis is on "great guns." The aircraft carried by carriers and other vessels are not considered (that subject would require a book in its own right).

Abbreviations

AA	Anti-aircraft
BB	Battleship
BL	Breechloader
C_D	Drag coefficient
cwt	Hundredweight (112 pounds)—there are 20 cwt to a long ton (British)
fps	Feet per second
g	Gram, or gravitational acceleration at Earth's surface
GS	General Service (British, both land and sea service)
HMS	Her (His) Majesty's Ship (British)
kg	Kilograms (about 2.2 pounds)
kn	Knots (nautical miles per hour)
ln	Natural logarithm
m	Meter (about 3.28 feet)
MER	Maximum effective range
Mk	Mark
mm	Millimeter
mps	Meters per second
PBR	Point-blank range
pdr	Pounder (typically refers to the weight of shot)
psi	Pounds (force) per square inch (unit of pressure); psia (psi absolute); psig (psi gauge—zero is normal atmospheric pressure)
RML	Rifled muzzleloader
rpm	Revolutions per minute
sq	Square (area measurement)
USN	United States Navy
USS	United States Ship
VCG	Vertical center of gravity
Wt	Weight

CHAPTER 1

Big Guns at Sea

Naval Guns

To the admiral, a gun is a means of delivering death and destruction at a distance. To the scientist, a gun is a pressure vessel, in which the burning gunpowder fills the bore behind the projectile with gases under extreme pressure. And it is also an engine, which converts the chemical energy of gunpowder into the kinetic energy of a moving projectile by virtue of the expansion of those gases.

To the gun designer, it is all of these things. The gun designer must craft the gun so it can deliver a high enough muzzle velocity that the desired projectile will reach its target at the design range, and so the gun will withstand the internal pressure generated by the expected powder charge without bursting and yet be light enough to serve its purpose.

For the purpose of this book, the term "guns" refers to heavy weapons that fire a projectile that does damage as a result of kinetic energy (shot) or explosive power (shells) and are typically part of the "fixed" armament of a warship (although they may be occasionally and temporarily taken ashore). Handguns are considered here only to the extent that they introduced technology that was later transferred to artillery guns.

Artillery was used on land and at sea. Land artillery was further classified as field, siege, garrison and seacoast artillery. Because of the mobility of the ship, its artillery encompassed a large range of gun sizes, including counterparts to field, siege, garrison and seacoast artillery pieces.

The terms "gun" and "cannon" are both given several different meanings, and those meanings have changed over time. A "cannon" could have the same meaning that I have given to "gun." In the seventeenth century, it was a piece that fired solid shot and had a lower ratio of length to diameter than a "culverin." A third meaning is discussed in the next section.

Cannons, Mortars and Howitzers

By the eighteenth century, the term "cannon" meant an artillery piece intended for direct fire—that is, fire at a low angle of elevation (typically not more than 15 degrees, judging from range tables). If a high angle of elevation were needed—say, to throw the projectile over a wall or other obstacle—a mortar or howitzer would be employed.

Cannons have the longest length relative to their caliber, and mortars the shortest, with howitzers falling in between. There was only limited use of howitzers and mortars by navies.

As discussed in more detail in chapter 5, mortars were used exclusively to hurl explosive or incendiary shells, rather than solid shot. They were mostly used as siege weapons. There were small vessels specially designed to carry and fire mortars; these were used for shore bombardment. A ship could also carry mortars that could be landed and used to strike a position that was out of reach (because of shoals or enemy batteris) of the ship's guns.

Manucy (1985, 59) states that in the mid-eighteenth century, French mortars had a bore length of 1.5 calibers; English ones had 2–3 calibers. (The barrel length would probably be about a half-caliber longer.)

In the later Georgian navy, there were 10- and 13-inch mortars (Landmann 1801, 20). They were fitted into "bomb vessels" (see "Shells" in chapter 5 for their use). These mortars had barrel lengths of 56 and 65 inches, respectively (*Edinburgh Encyclopedia* 1832, "Ordnance" 805)—five calibers.

The most recent appearance of the mortar on board a naval vessel was probably on the American LCI(M) gunboats of 1944–1945. These were converted LCI(L) (Landing Craft Infantry, Large) amphibious vessels bearing three 4.2-inch "chemical" mortars (Rielly 2013, 25–26).

The howitzer was something of a compromise weapon. It could employ low- or high-angle fire, and it could fire shot or shells.

Naval use of the howitzer appears to date to the War of 1812. The British loaded 5.5-inch howitzers onto ships and landed them to attack shore targets. During the Mexican War, the American navy placed army mountain howitzers into boats for shoal water operations. John Dahlgren subsequently designed bronze 12-pdr (4.62-inch bore) and 24-pdr (5.82-inch bore) howitzers specifically for use on boats. Both boat and field carriages were provided, and in general these fired anti-personnel projectiles (shell, canister, and shrapnel) (see chapter 5). The Dahlgren boat howitzers were first used in 1856 against the Chinese (Tucker 1992).

Pedreros

Pedreros (perrières, petros, steenstruk) are stone throwers, and, because of the relatively low density of stone, they typically were of large caliber (12–50-pounders for sea service, up to 1,000-pounders for land sieges), with short barrels (4–8 calibers) and a reduced diameter (½ to ⅓ caliber) powder chamber. Because of the lightness of stone, the powder charge was small (usually one-third shot weight) and the barrel thickness reduced relative to that of cannons (Guilmartin 2003, 175–76; Manucy 1985, 37).

The reader is warned that the term *pedrero* (from Latin *petra*, "stone") came to refer to "a particular weight or shape" of gun—that is, "iron shot were fired from what was still called a stone cannon" (Oppenheim 1896, 56). The "iron-shot pedrero" still had a powder chamber whose diameter was smaller than that of the bore (Oppenheim 1913, 4:39). William Monson (1569–1643), in his posthumously published *Naval Tracts*, referred to a "cannon petro" with a 6-inch bore, and a weight of metal 3,000 pounds, firing 24.5-pound shot with fourteen pounds of powder (4:38). A quick density calculation reveals that this material must have been iron shot, not stone. Oppenheim claims that pedreros were first "adapted as an iron shot gun during the reign of Elizabeth" (4:39).

Nonetheless, Manucy says that "stone projectiles remained in use as late as 1800 for the pedrero class" (1985, 60), and these sometimes fired "baskets of stones" (68) rather than a single large one. The pedreros were also used to shoot "grapeshot made of lead balls" (Mihajlović 2014, 56).

The Parts of an Early Modern Cannon

The barrel contains a (hopefully) centered and cylindrical hole called the bore, terminating at the business end, the muzzle. The opposite end of the barrel is the breech end. The diameter of the bore is the caliber of the gun.

While the bore is cylindrical, the barrel is tapered, being widest at the breech end and narrowest at or near the muzzle. The taper is much greater for guns constructed before the late nineteenth century, and the subsequent reduction in taper is attributable to both a greater understanding of the distribution of pressure inside the bore and the development of slower-burning propellants (see chapters 4 and 9).

The more detailed nomenclature and description that follows applies, with minor variations, from the late Renaissance to the mid-nineteenth century. Beginning at the rear of the gun, we have the knob-like cascabel, which is quite a bit narrower than the barrel proper. On naval guns, initially, the breeching rope (used to arrest the recoil) was tied around the neck of this knob. Later, the cascabel was forged with an integral vertical or horizontal ring for securing the breeching ropes.

The cascabel is attached to the breech end. (The term "breech" also refers to the metal between the rear of the bore and the forward end of the cascabel.) There is a reinforcement, the base ring, at the breech end of the barrel.

Near the rear of the bore there is a cylindrical hole, the vent, that connects the bore (or a connected powder chamber) to the outside of the barrel. This opening is used to ignite the powder inside. The barrel gradually narrows as one approaches the muzzle until close to the face of the muzzle, where it swells outward slightly. The swell "gives strength to the gun at its termination to prevent the mouth from splitting from the shocks of the projectiles" (NPS19th 2022, 2). It also makes sighting easier (see chapter 8). The bore may be widened slightly at the muzzle end to facilitate loading the projectile.

The barrel has several moldings: from breech to muzzle, we have the base ring, the first reinforcement ring, the second reinforcement ring (sometimes omitted) and the muzzle astragal (NPS18th, 2015). There may also be a chase astragal. Despite the names, it appears that these features were ornamental, possibly intended to be reminiscent of the hoops of the bombard (Manucy 1985, 43).

The section from the base ring to the first reinforcement ring is called the "first reinforce," and from the first reinforcement ring to the second one is called the "second reinforce." The section from the second reinforcement ring to the "muzzle astragal" is the "chase." The "chase astragal," if present, is on the chase, near the second reinforcement ring.

The trunnions, which are side-pointing cylinders that engage the gun carriage, are typically extended from the second reinforce. As a result, the weight of the breech end is greater than that of the muzzle end, by perhaps one-twentieth the weight of the gun, and this difference is called the "preponderance" (Simpson 1862, 88).

The trunnions may be placed vertically on the lower line ("quarter-hung") or on the centerline ("center-hung") of the bore (Manucy 1985, 41). Quarter-hanging the trunnions gave an "unobstructed side sight" (for use with "quarter-sights") and

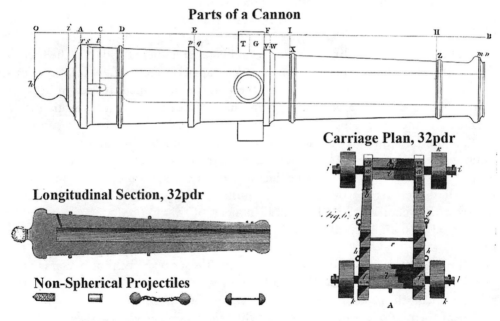

Parts of a Cannon

Longitudinal Section, 32pdr

Carriage Plan, 32pdr

Non-Spherical Projectiles

Plate V from William Falconer and William Burney's *Universal Dictionary of the Marine* (1815) shows the parts of a cannon: OA, the cascabel; AC, the breech; CD, the vent-field; AE, the first reinforce; EF, the second reinforce; FI, the chase-girdle; FB, the chase; HB, the muzzle; T, trunnions; RS, the base-ring and ogee; PQ, the first reinforce ring and ogee; VW, the second reinforce ring and ogee; X, the chase astragal and fillets; Z, the muzzle astragal and fillets. AB is considered the length of the gun (67). This diagram also shows a longitudinal section of a 32-pounder (note the variation in thickness of the metal from the breech to the bore) and the plan of its carriage (note the breeching bolts [G] for attaching the breechings that arrest the recoil; the eyebolts [H] to which the gun tackles are attached, and of course the axle trees and trucks) (68). Finally, it depicts four projectiles. From left to right, these are grape shot, canister shot, chain shot (with spherical heads) and bar shot (with hemispherical heads) (468).

diminished the recoil. However, "the strain was too great on the carriages," so guns were subsequently center-hung (Simpson 1862, 87).

Principal Dimensions

The principal dimensions of the gun barrel that are most likely to be named in historical literature are its caliber, its length, and its weight. These dimensions were often stamped on the barrel. The caliber is the diameter of the bore.

The length of the barrel is defined as the distance from the base ring to the face of the muzzle. It is *not* the length of the cylindrical bore inside the barrel, although that is likely to be only a few inches shorter than the barrel. Length may be quoted as being so many calibers rather than as an absolute number.

The gun weight is, properly speaking, the "weight of metal," not including the carriage. The thickness of the metal, and thus the exterior diameter of the barrel, varies along the length of the barrel, as discussed further in chapter 9.

Artillery Classification by Size

The smallest fixed naval weapons of the early modern period—the swivel guns— were used against enemy personnel or small boats. They could be mounted on a railing or free-standing pedestal on a ship or on a ship's boat. Some were also used by frontier forts. They fired half-pound (Lavery 2021, 52), 1-pound (Garry 2012, 48), or 1.5-pound (Skaarup 2012, 98) balls. In England, they weren't counted as "guns" for the purpose of "rating" warships because they weren't mounted on carriages.

Luis Collado divided sixteenth-century Spanish artillery into three classes: (1) long-range pieces (culverins and sacres); (2) "battering" (siege) pieces (cannons); and (3) stone throwers (Manucy 1985, 31). The artillery of the first class fired shot ranging from ½ to 48 pounds (34), and those of the second class, from 9 to 130 pounds (36). It is unlikely that the larger cannons were used on ships.

Tables 1–1 and 1–2 provide data on sixteenth- and seventeenth-century British artillery, respectively. The values given are typical, not fixed. There was no formal differentiation between sea and land artillery in this period, but the heaviest pieces are likely to have been used only as siege artillery. The lightest pieces (the shaded rows in the tables) were most likely swivel guns.

Table 1–1: Sixteenth-Century British Artillery

Gun	Shot Wt (lbs)	Bore Diam/ Caliber (ins)	Length (ft)	Powder Wt (lbs)	Gun Wt (lbs)
Cannon Royal	74 (66)	8.54 (8)	8.5	30	8,000
Cannon Serpentine	42 (53)	7		25	5,500
Demi-Cannon	32 (33)	6.4	11	18	4,000
Culverin	18 (17)	5.2	10.83	12	4,840 (4,500)

Gun	Shot Wt (lbs)	Bore Diam/ Caliber (ins)	Length (ft)	Powder Wt (lbs)	Gun Wt (lbs)
Basilisk	14 (15)	5		9	4,000
Culverin, Bastard	11 (5)	4.56 (4)	8.5	5.7	3,000
Demi-Culverin	8 (9)	4		6 (8)	3,400
Saker	6 (5)	3.65 (3)	6.83	4 (5)	1,400
Minion	5.2 (4)	3.5 (3)	6.5	3 (4)	1,050 (1,000)
Falcon	2	2.5 (2)	6	1.2 (3)	680 (660)
Falconet	1	2	3.75	0.4 (3)	500
Serpentine	0.5 (2)	1.5 (1)		0.3	400
Rabinet	0.3	1		0.18	300

(Manucy 1985, 34. The divergent values in parentheses are from James 1826, Volume 1, Appendix 2, and came in turn from Sir William Monson's Naval Tracts.)

Table 1–2: Mid–Seventeenth-Century British Artillery

Gun	Shot Wt	Caliber	Length (ft)	Powder Wt (lbs)	Gun Wt (lbs)
Cannon of 8	64	8	12	32	8,000
Cannon Serpentine	52	7.5	11.5	26	7,000
French Cannon	46.5	7.25	12	23.25	6,500
Old Demi-Cannon	36	6.75	11.25	20	6,000
Ordinary Demi-Cannon	32	6.5	10.5	18	5,600
Demi-Cannon	24.5	6	11	16	5,000
Ordinary Culverin	16.75	5.5	12	12.5	4,300
Demi-Culverin	11.75	4.5	11	9	3,000
Saker	5.25	3.75	9.5	5	1,900
Minion	3.25	3.25	8	3.5	1,100
Falcon	2	2	7	2.5	750
Falconet	1.5	2.25	6	1.25	400
Robinet	0.75	1.5	5.5	0.75	300
Base	0.5	1.25	4.5	0.25	200

(Manganiello 1994, 26. See also Norton 1628, 53; Nye 1648, chapter 34; Roberts 1672, 38–39; Seller 1691, 137–40.)

The word "cannon" is derived from Italian *cannone*, which, in the early fourteenth century, referenced an organ pipe and later came to mean a tube-shaped object generally. "Culverin" is from Latin *colubrinus*, meaning snake-like, and presumably referring to the fangs of a venomous snake. "Serpentine," of course, has a similar implication. The "basilisk" was considered the "king of serpents," possessing a lethal glance.

The word "saker" is from Arabic *saqr*, meaning "falcon," although folk etymology has associated it with "sacred." The derivation of "falcon" and "falconet" is obvious.

A "minion," of course, may be a servant or henchman of someone more powerful, and that sense transferred over to a small cannon. The word "robinet" was a "pet form" of the name Robert. However, Ffoulkes suggests that it references "the pugnacious robin-redbreast" (2011, 95). "Base" usually refers to the lowest point on a structure, or the lowest stratum of society, and the "base" is the smallest cannon in the table.

"Demi" means half, and from the table it appears that a demi-culverin threw roughly half the weight of shot as that projected by a culverin, and there is an analogous relationship between the demi-cannon and the cannon royal. The Spanish had "medio" (one-half), "tercio" (one-third) and "quarto" (one-quarter) cañons, which fired shot bearing the implied relationship to the shot weight (48 pounds) fired by the doble cañon (Manucy 1985, 36).

Guns could be specified as thicker ("reinforced," "double"), thinner ("bastard"), shorter ("cutt"), and with a tapered bore ("drake"). (The tapering was possibly for ease of loading, and an increased rate of fire [Lavery 1987, 91].)

There were also variations between gun-founders and even from gun to gun. ("Demi cannon could … vary up to three hundred weight within the same batch" [Bull 2004, 8].)

The archaic British gun naming system persisted to the end of the seventeenth century, as evidenced by John Seller's *The Sea-Gunner* (1691, 139). But in the period 1716–1725, Albert Borgard succeeded in changing the designation of cannons from fanciful names to ones referencing the weight of the shot fired. The larger sizes were 4, 6, 9, 12, 18, 24, 32 and 42 pounds (Collins, "British Cannonball Sizes"). This is, of course, closely related to the diameter of the shot and, in turn, to the caliber of the gun. Seller, for example, states that a 3-inch-diameter iron shot weighs 3.75 pounds (1691, 134).

British mortars continued to be classified even after 1715 by their caliber, and this practice was carried over to shell guns in the mid-nineteenth century. Thus, the U.S. Navy had both the 8-inch shell gun and a 64-pounder with an 8-inch bore (Dahlgren 1856, 24). Modern naval guns are identified by their caliber.

Gun Caliber

The diameter of the bore fixes the volume (and thus the mass) of the projectile if it's spherical, and it determines the proportionality of volume to length if it isn't. These in turn affect the aerodynamic characteristics of the projectile. The diameter also strongly affects how much damage the projectile does for a given impact velocity. These issues will be explored in later chapters.

While it was normal for guns to be classified by the weight of shot fired, comparing guns of different countries was complicated in that they defined the "pound" differently.

As late as the nineteenth century, manufacturing tolerances for both cannons and cannonballs were loose, so, to ensure that most balls would fit into the guns for which they were intended, the bores were deliberately made to a diameter greater than the intended shot diameter. The resulting gap, measured as either a difference in diameter or an annular area, was called "windage."

Windage allowances (see chapter 3) varied with time and place, and the greater the windage, the smaller the shot (or larger the bore). In the early nineteenth century, a "24-pounder" had a true caliber ranging from 5.8230 inches (English) to 6.1107 inches (Swedish). The French "24" actually fired 28.5-pound shot, and its "36," 43.2 (Simmons 1837, 62–63).

Gun Length

The largest seventeenth-century naval artillery were 42-pounders (British navy) or 36-pounders (most others). The former type was first used in large numbers on *Sovereign of the Sea* (1637) and thereafter was mostly used on first rates (for warship classification, see chapter 2). The demi-cannon (32-pounder) was the main British battleship gun after 1745 (Nelson 2001), but the American navy used 42-pounders as lower deck guns (Simmons 1837, 64).

Gun and projectile size grew only gradually over the eighteenth and nineteenth centuries. The 32-pdr was a popular American Civil War carriage gun, weighing 27–57 cwt and firing either 32.5-pound shot or a 26-pound shell.

The most powerful gun actually mounted on a ship in the American Civil War was a 15-inch Dahlgren, weighing 42,000 pounds. It had an 8–14-man crew and fired 440-pound solid shot or a 330-pound shell. Charges were 50 and 35 pounds, respectively (Canfield 1968; Heidler et al. 2002, 548; Symonds 2012, 35). The "muzzle of the 15-inch gun was so large it would not fit through the bored gun ports of the turret. To prevent muzzle smoke from filling up the turret and asphyxiating the gunners, Ericsson designed what he called a 'smoke box' around the muzzle that directed most (but not all) of the smoke outside the turret" (Symonds 2012, 34).

Some very large-caliber guns saw limited deployment in the late nineteenth century. These included a 17.72-inch rifled muzzleloader (RML) placed on the Italian battleships *Duilio* and *Dandolo* and the 16-inch RMLs mounted on HMS *Inflexible* (launched 1876). Nonetheless, the "standard gun caliber for battleships in most major navies in 1905 was the 12-inch" (Tucker and Roberts 2005, 830).

In World War I, newly built American battleships had 14-inch guns, and the *Iowa*-class battleships of World War II had 16-inch guns. The largest caliber naval gun ever built was the 18.1-inch Japanese type 94, mounted on the battleships *Yamato* and *Musashi* (Stille 2012, 9).

The greater the caliber of the gun, the greater its weight and cost, assuming that the ratio of length to caliber was kept the same. And armament weight affected the ship's draft and stability. So warship designers were repeatedly faced with the question of whether to "advance" to fewer but bigger guns. In addition, whether the bigger guns were needed depended on the designers' expectations as to engagement range and enemy armor protection, neither of which were truly within their control.

Long Guns

Lengths can vary, so guns are customarily identified by both weight of shot and length—for example, a 10-foot-long gun firing 24-pound shot is a "24–10."

Manucy (1985, 45) provides the lengths of the principal eighteenth-century English ship cannons, both bronze and iron. These ranged from 1.5- to 48-pounders.

The barrel (or bore) length of a gun may also be expressed relative to its bore diameter—that is, as being so many "calibers"; a "⁵/₃₈" has a bore 5 inches wide and is 38 calibers (190 inches) long.

In sixteenth-century artillery nomenclature, cannons were distinguished from culverins by their length, although both were direct-fire weapons projecting cast iron cannonballs. The culverins had long (at least 26 times caliber) unchambered bores, whereas the cannons had shorter (about 18-caliber) bores, and some early specimens had reduced diameter powder chambers (Guilmartin 2003, 175ff; Meide 2002).

According to Collado (1592), Spanish culverins had a length of 30–32 calibers. The *passovolante*, throwing a 1- to 15-pound ball, had a length/caliber ratio of 40–44 (Manucy 1985, 34). The Spanish full cannons of the same period were 18 calibers long, but the demi-cannons could reach 24 calibers and the quarter cannons 28 (36). Thus, there was actually some overlap between the culverin and cannon subtypes.

In the mid-eighteenth century, the English ship guns designed by John Muller were fifteen calibers long (Manucy 1985, 43). For early nineteenth-century English iron guns, Theophilus Beauchant (1828, 102) provides relationships outlined in Table 1–3.

Table 1–3: Length and Weight of English Iron Guns (1828)

Gun (pdr)	Length (calibers)	Length (feet)	Weight (cwt)	Gun Wt/ Shot Wt	Caliber (in)*
42	17.098	10	67	170	7.018
	16.244	9.5	65		
32	18.721	10	58	193	6.41
	17.725	9.5	55		
24	20.604	10	52	231	5.823
	19.574	9.5	49.5		
	18.542	9	47.5		
18	21.542	9.5	42	249	5.292
	20.408	9	40		
12	24.659	9.5	34	294	4.623
	23.361	9	32		
	22.063	8.5	31.5		
	19.468	7.5	29.25		
9	21.4	7.5	24.5	305	4.200
	19.9	7	23		

Gun (pdr)	Length (calibers)	Length (feet)	Weight (cwt)	Gun Wt/ Shot Wt	Caliber (in)*
6	26.2	8	22	411	3.668
	19.6	6	16.5		
4	22.4	6	22.25	343	3.204
	20.6	5.5	11.25		
3	18.6	4.5	7.25	270	3.013

Calibers from Douglas 1829, 75.

While I included the 42-pounders, William Falconer and William Burney (1815, 67) say that they were "laid aside" in 1790. It can be seen that gun lengths varied from 16 to 25 calibers.

The Beauchant table also shows a variation in length among guns of the same caliber. Cannons can have unusually long barrels to (ideally) give them extended range. A long gun might be used as bow or stern armament.

Turning to the twentieth century, the *Iowa*'s main guns were 50 calibers long. The optimal length is related to the mass of the projectile and the size and composition of the powder charge (see chapters 4 and 9).

Carronades

The cannonade, a short-barreled (hence, short-range but light) cannon throwing a heavy weight of metal for its size, was introduced into the British navy in 1779 (Chapelle 1935, 56). By 1815, carronades had become the main armament on small ships (Glete 1993, 30).

By way of explaining the carronade's popularity, consider that a Napoleonic 5.17-foot carronade firing 42-pound shot (equivalent to the heaviest gun on a Napoleonic battleship) weighed 22.25 hundredweights (cwt; each 112 pounds); a long gun of the same weight would be just a 9–7 (23 cwt) or a 6–8.5 (22 cwt). There was even a 68–5.17 carronade weighing 36 cwt; it could replace a long 12–9.5 (36 cwt) or 18–9 (39 cwt) (Ireland 2000, 47–49; Tucker 1997, 19).

The carronade was light because it was short barreled (typically only about 7 calibers in length), lacked trunnions, and had less thickness of metal to contain the blast (hence it used a smaller powder charge, one-eighth to one-sixteenth the weight of shot) (Roberts 1996, 232).

A carronade-equipped warship could throw an incredible weight of metal at an enemy—if that enemy came within range. Chapelle says that carronades were an excellent choice for a fast ship, but a poor one for a sluggard (1935, 152).

The first engagement involving the carronade was during the American Revolution, between HMS *Flora* (36 long guns and 6 carronades) and the 32-gun French *Nymphe*, in 1780. They engaged first at 400 yards (two cable lengths), and then the *Flora* closed to half the distance. The *Nymphe*, which had the larger crew, attempted to board the *Flora*, but the boarding party was defeated and she was boarded in turn (Coutts 1908, 59–67).

The British navy became quite enthusiastic about the carronade, to the point of arming some ships solely with carronades. One such ship was the frigate *Rainbow* (20 × 68-pdr, 22 × 42-pdr, 6 × 32-pdr, total shot 1,238 pounds). In 1782, it came across the 38-gun French frigate *Hebe*, whose largest gun was an 18-pounder. The captain of the *Hebe* saw the size of the trial shot that hit it (fired by a forecastle 32-pounder), decided that he was facing the early modern equivalent of a pocket battleship, fired one broadside for the sake of honor, and surrendered. In 1787, the French started making their own carronades (Tucker 1973).

However, if a ship with long guns was able to keep its distance from one armed primarily with carronades, the long guns would prevail. This difference was repeatedly demonstrated during the War of 1812 (Tucker 1997, 22–23).

Gun Weight

Some typical gun weights were given in Tables 1–1 to 1–3. Bronze guns were usually lighter than cast iron ones of the same caliber and length; steel guns had a similar advantage over their predecessors, because of steel's greater tensile strength per unit weight.

Guns designed to fire only shells (hollow projectiles) could be lighter than those firing solid shot; shells were lighter than solid shot of the same caliber—hence less powder was needed to project them, so the gun barrels could be thinner. Or, keeping gun weight the same, you could increase caliber. The Paixhans 80-pounder shell gun (1837) weighed the same as the traditional 36-pounder (Tucker 2009, 1320).

Gun Design: Basic Choices

Muzzleloading versus Breechloading

The cannon bore is a tube, open at one end (muzzle) and closed (at least at the time of firing) at the other (breech). To load a naval muzzleloader, the gun is drawn in, the bore is cleaned, the powder charge and the shot are rammed in at the muzzle end, and the cannon is run back out the gun port. A breechloader has a loading door at the breech end; this is opened, the charge and shot are inserted, and the door is closed.

A breechloader could have either an integral chamber, into which the powder and shot were placed directly, or a removable chamber (Buchanan 2006, 251ff); this chamber would be loaded with the powder and shot and then the chamber placed in the breech. The removable chamber looked somewhat like a beer mug.

The proponents of muzzleloading and breechloading have engaged in a half-millennium-long struggle for ascendancy. However, just because modern naval guns are breechloading doesn't mean that this outcome was a foregone conclusion.

The first naval cannons were breechloaders, and *Mary Rose* (1545) carried both wrought iron breechloaders and bronze muzzleloaders. In Elizabethan breechloaders, the removable chamber was wedged into the breech. Cyprian Lucar (1588) warns that the gunner "ought not stand upon that side of the piece where the wedge of iron is placed ... because [it] may through the discharge of the piece fly out and kill the gunner" (Corbett 1898, 333).

By the early seventeenth century, the main guns of a warship were all muzzle-loaders, but her swivel guns were still breechloaders.

Naval muzzleloaders usually were brought inboard for loading. According to Colin Martin and Geoffrey Parker (1999, 193), this task was done manually; "the much more efficient process of allowing a gun's own recoil to bring it inboard under the restraint of a breeching rope was not developed until well into the seventeenth century." John Smith, in *Seaman's Grammar* (1627), says, "britchings are the ropes by which you lash your Ordnance fast to the Ships side"; in light of Martin and Parker's comment, these lashings were evidently too tight for recoil-aided loading.

The longer the barrel, the less convenient it was to load it from the muzzle end, and large-caliber guns tended to have long barrels. On the *Mary Rose*, the gun crews were so cramped that it's been suggested that they engaged in outboard loading; the gunner would sit on the barrel, sticking out the gunport, to reload the piece (Konstam 2008, 40). The most obvious advantage of the breechloading system was that the gun could be reloaded from inboard while run out, which potentially increased the rate of fire.

While short-barreled carronades were easy to load, they had other problems; the flash could set fire to the rigging, and the vent fire could do the same to the hammocks hanging over below-deck carronades (Douglas 1829, 103).

For any smoothbore muzzleloader, the shot had to fit loosely in the bore, so it could be rammed down. But when fired, gas could escape around the shot and out the muzzle, and it was also difficult to keep the projectile centered as it moved down-bore.

Late in the history of muzzleloading artillery, the first problem was reduced by using a gas check (a thin disc that filled the cross-section of the bore). The first gas check was a *papier-mâché* disc inserted between the cartridge and the base of the shot, but by 1878 a copper disc was attached to the base of the projectile. This device was used with studded projectiles in rifled muzzleloaders (Carman 2015, 168). The centering problem theoretically could have been addressed with a sabot (see chapter 6), but that wasn't normally done.

The most enduring design problem with breechloaders, which had a door rather than solid metal at the breech end, was preventing gas loss at the breech. The more powerful the gun, and the greater the strength of the powder, the greater the pressure that this mechanism had to withstand.

The first successful breech mechanism was invented by William Armstrong in 1854. The vent piece (a vertically sliding block) was secured by pressure from a hollow screw. To load, this screw was loosened, the vent piece removed, and the projectile and charge inserted through the hollow. The vent piece was then replaced and the screw tightened. On the chamber side, the vent piece had a coned copper ring fitted into a coned seating (EB 1911, "Ordnance").

Unfortunately, the success was limited. "During the bombardment of Kagoshima in 1863 there were 28 accidents in the 365 rounds fired from 21 guns. On a number of occasions the vent pieces were blown from the guns. The guns were also inaccurate" (Brassington 2008).

The breech mechanism problems were probably attributable to poor handling and maintenance—"not tightening the breech screw sufficiently" or "not keeping the chamber and vent-piece ring … scrupulously clean." But there were complaints about "the difficulty of managing and manufacturing the vent-piece" (Tennent 1864, 327). Sailors were not keen on lifting the heavy vent pieces, especially if the sea was rough (Ruffell 1997, "Armstrong Gun").

Moreover, the rise of the ironclads demanded an increase in punch, and the imperfect seals of the mid-nineteenth-century breechloaders frustrated this goal. The British navy conducted comparative trials, and in 1865 the Board of Ordnance decided to switch to rifled muzzleloaders (Konstam 2018, 38).

This turnabout didn't last long. In 1879, one of the guns of the HMS *Thunderer* misfired; the misfire was undetected and the gun was reloaded, making it inadvertently double-shotted. When the gun fired again, it exploded, killing everyone in the turret. This accident couldn't have happened with a breechloader—the gun crew would have seen the unexploded charge when they opened the breech—and the British navy reluctantly abandoned muzzleloading for good (Batchelor and Hogg 1972, 11), at least regarding new construction (in 1896, out of the 45 battleships in the Royal Navy, 16 still had "heavy armaments consisting of muzzle-loading guns" [Engineer 1896, 487]).

The *Thunderer* accident provided the impetus for change, but there were other considerations at work as well. A new powder that could achieve a higher muzzle velocity had been developed. But if it was used in a muzzleloader, the shell zipped out before the charge was exhausted. In other words, the barrels weren't long enough. But if the barrels were lengthened, then recoil wasn't sufficient to bring the muzzle inside the turret for loading, so some poor soul had to venture outside the turret to reload the gun from the outside. This was actually done on HMS *Inflexible* (Watts 1994, 56)!

Normally the threads of a screw engage continuously with those of a threaded screw box. The problem with a continuous screw breech plug is that it can be time consuming to tighten and untighten.

With an interrupted screw, the threads of both are discontinuous, resulting in a screw orientation such that it can be slid into the screw box without engaging. For example, looking down the axis of the box, it might have threading from 12 o'clock to 3 o'clock, and 6 to 9. If so, then the screw in the slide-in orientation would have threading only from 3 to 6 and 9 to 12. Once inserted, such a screw would be given a quarter-turn, and then the threads would be fully engaged (Wilson 1896, 249).

The disadvantage of the classic interrupted screw was that it engaged along only half the circumference and thus, to have the same sealing strength as the continuous screw, would need to be twice as long (NAVORD 1957, 5B4). This disadvantage was largely overcome by the Welin stepped interrupted thread in the 1890s. The circumference of the screw is divided into multiple groups. Each group can further be divided circumferentially into several arcs, which progressively increase in diameter, creating a stepped pattern. On the screw, the arcs at the lowest step level are blank, and the other arcs are threaded.

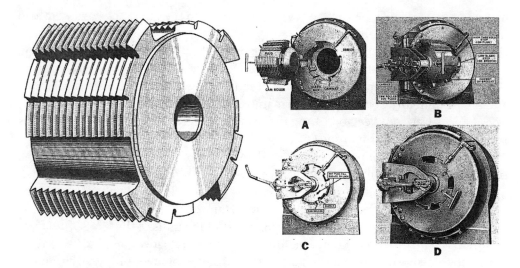

Left: The Welin-type stepped-thread plug (NAVORD 1957, Figure 5B10). Right: The Welin interrupted screw breech mechanism is closed and locked in views A–D (NAVORD 1957, Figure 5B11): (A) open position; (B) plug swinging inward (horizontally on this older mount; vertically in later models); (C) plug in closed position, "cam roller on the plug contacts a camway in the screw box," permitting rotation of the plug in the screw box; (D) plug rotated to fully locked position. In view of the weight of the plug (up to 1,400 pounds on a 16-inch gun), there might be air- or spring-powered assistance in operating the breech mechanism.

A gunner on the USS *New Jersey* (BB-62) touching the lowered breechblock (plug) of a 16-inch gun. The breech mechanism is clearly of the Welin interrupted screw type. Photograph from November 1944. Courtesy of the National Archives, NAID 520876.

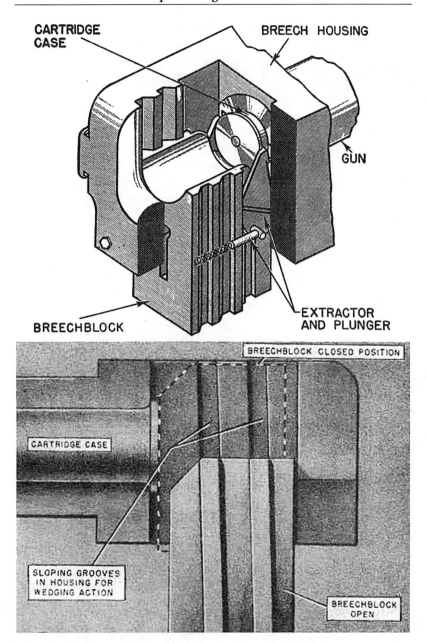

CARTRIDGE CASE

BREECH HOUSING

GUN

BREECHBLOCK

EXTRACTOR AND PLUNGER

BREECHBLOCK CLOSED POSITION

CARTRIDGE CASE

SLOPING GROOVES IN HOUSING FOR WEDGING ACTION

BREECHBLOCK OPEN

Top: Isometric view of the vertical sliding wedge breechblock in the breech housing. The block slides in the vertical grooves. Note that one face of the groove is sloped, to cause the block to wedge against the cartridge (NAVORD 1944, 4B3). Bottom: Schematic profile view, with the breechblock in the open position. The dashed line shows its closed position (NAVORD 1957, 59). Note that the cartridge case is on the right side of the block in the top illustration and on its left in the bottom one.

In the disengaged position, a threaded arc on the screw (plug) can face a threaded arc on the screw box, provided that the arc on the box is deeper so they don't engage. You slide the screw in and then turn it to engage. With three different threaded diameters, and one smooth, you have threaded engagement for 75 percent of the circumference, and with two groups, only a one-eighth turn is needed to engage. A 16-inch naval gun might develop a gas pressure of 40,000 psi, necessitating a 1,400-pound plug (NAVORD 1957, 5B4).

The Welin mechanism was one of several used by the twentieth-century U.S. Navy. Its 1937 manual also refers to, among other devices, the French and Elswick interrupted screw, the vertical and horizontal sliding wedge, the rotary/sliding wedge, and sliding bolt mechanisms (NAVORD 1937, 154–57). By 1944, all guns using bag ammunition (see chapter 6) used the Welin mechanism, and those using case ammunition, the sliding wedge (NAVORD 1944, 49–50). The latter could be implemented as a vertical or horizontal slide (NAVORD 1957).

Smoothbore versus Rifled Bore

The cannons in use prior to the nineteenth century had smoothbore barrels, which means just what it says. However, the barrel of a firearm may be rifled—given helical grooves—in order to impart a spin to a projectile. The effect would be to gyroscopically stabilize the flight of the projectile.

Rifling was introduced into small arms in the sixteenth century, as we know from a 1563 Swiss ordinance: "For the last few years the art of cutting grooves in the chambers of the guns has been introduced with the object of increasing the accuracy of fire; the disadvantage resulting therefrom to the common marksman has sown discord amongst them. In ordinary shooting matches marksmen are therefore forbidden under a penalty of £10 to provide themselves with rifled arms. Every one is nevertheless permitted to rifle his military weapon and to compete with marksmen armed with similar weapons for special prizes" (*Chamber's Encyclopaedia* 1896, 718). These, apparently, were used to fire balls, since elongated rifled projectiles reportedly were first invented by the bishop of Munster in 1662 (*ibid.*).

The first rifled artillery pieces were probably those of Giovanni Cavalli in 1846 (Kinard 2007, 222). Both rifles and smoothbores were used in several mid-nineteenth-century naval conflicts, notably the American Civil War, the Second Schleswig War, the Third Italian Independence War, and the Guano War.

Rifling was not a panacea; reloading was more difficult, and range and accuracy were not always improved. The metal ("lands") between the grooves can get worn down. In addition, during the American Civil War, rifled artillery seemed more prone to burst than muzzleloading Dahlgrens, and rifled projectiles couldn't gain range by grazing ricochet (see chapter 10). These circumstances may explain the Union navy's wartime preference for smoothbores (Heidler et al. 2002, 1046), even though in 1859, after comparative testing, the U.S. government had concluded that "the era of smoothbore artillery has passed away" (Bell 2003, 44).

After the Battle of Lissa (1866, Austria versus Italy), Wilhelm von Tegethoff, the Austrian commander, commented, "The lack of results on the part of the enemy have shown that smoothbore guns on the sea have much more value than a rifled one, since a rifle requires for best results at long range a still position, difficult to find on the sea" (Greene and Massignani 1998, 254). (But see chap. 12.)

The driving force for the adoption of rifled guns appears to have been not so much increasing effective range but their ability to fire an elongated shell, thus one carrying more explosive for a given caliber (Colomb 1898, 340ff). But it took perhaps two decades to perfect heavy rifled cannons (Bell 2003, 44), and Dahlgren smoothbore-armed Civil War vintage monitors were placed on coastal defense duty during the Spanish-American War (Deogracias 2003, 37).

Smoothbores could be converted into rifles. One could insert a rifled wrought iron tube (reducing the caliber by several inches) after reaming out the old bore to match the outer dimension of the tube (Wilhelm 1881, 374).

In order to apply spin to the projectile, it must somehow engage the rifling. With small arms, the bullet could be made of lead, which is malleable. However, there were two problems with making artillery projectiles out of lead. The first was that lead was expensive, and the second was that lead, being soft, would foul the inside of the barrel.

A number of expedients were experimented with in the nineteenth century. A lead coating on the projectile was introduced by Baron Martin von Warhendorff in the 1840s (Kinard 2007, 222). That wouldn't be as expensive as making the whole thing out of lead, but fouling would still be a problem. The British nonetheless used this system with breechloaders.

Whitworth and Lancaster made projectiles with twisted side faces to match the rifling; when mass produced, the rounds tended to jam in the bore. The Confederates used some Whitworth rifles.

For rifled muzzleloaders, one had to provide sufficient windage that the projectile could still be rammed down the barrel. One solution, proposed by Armstrong in 1854, was to provide the projectiles with studs to engage the grooves of the rifling. The engagement is reliable, but the projectile must be studded to match the twist in a particular gun, and the gun cannot have increasing twist. In addition, the grooves must be wide and deep to accommodate the studs, thus weakening the gun, whereas the studs increase air resistance to the projectile (Bruff 1903, 303).

If the studs were taller than the depth of the grooves, there would be a clearance between the main body of the projectile and the lands (the uncut portions of the bore between the grooves) (War Office 1902, 182). Unfortunately, if the studs have clearance, and there's no gas check, then gas escapes and damages the bore.

It was discovered that the copper gas check mentioned earlier not only reduced the gas loss from windage but also engaged the rifling. It was used in rifled muzzleloaders, but it was found advantageous to make the grooves shallower and more numerous than in a breechloader.

However, the most successful ploy was to place "a copper 'driving band' into a groove cut around the body of the projectile" (EB 1911, "Ammunition"). The relevant engineering considerations confronted by its developers were what material to make it out of, how thick and long it should be, whether to have one long band or several short ones, where on the projectile body to place it, and how to secure it there. The choices made, in turn, determined how well it engaged the rifling, how much wear it imposed on the bore, and the aerodynamic characteristics of the projectile.

Rifling does increase the friction between the projectile and the barrel, which can reduce muzzle velocity and also generate heat and accelerate the erosion of the barrel. Because of the problem of barrel wear, the rifling may be cut into a liner rather than the barrel proper. Then the liner may be replaced if the wear becomes excessive (Slover 2023, 138).

Chapter 2

The Ship as a Weapons Platform

As pointed out in the preface, it was easier to move a heavy load (such as guns) over water than over land. Until the invention of steam locomotives and the creation of a rail network, movement over the open sea was also, on average, faster. A sailing warship could average 100–150 miles a day (Royal Museums Greenwich 2018), whereas an artillery column would be lucky to cover twenty miles in the same period (Bond and McDonough 1916, 90). Railroads increased the speed of artillery movement, but paths that could be taken were constrained by the rail network (and rail gauge differences between different national networks), and rail movement could be interdicted by attacking the track at any point on the line of march, whereas interdiction of warships was easy only when they passed through narrow straits or at their origins or destinations.

The greatest constraint on the application of seapower was that a ship could go only where the depth of water was sufficient, and its ability to strike inland was limited by the effective range of its guns. However, that limitation has been attenuated by the development of the missile (see chapter 13).

Constraints on Warship Design

Buoyancy acts vertically upward, whereas weight (gravitational force) acts vertically downward. At equilibrium, the two must be equal. The buoyant force is the gravitational acceleration times the mass of water displaced by the submerged portion of the hull. The greater the weight of a loaded warship, the greater its draft (the depth to which it is submerged) and the greater its resistance to movement. Thus, the weight of a warship—hull, propulsion system, armament, and so on—is limited by its displacement and the maximum draft for seaworthiness. In 1671, the *Kronan* carried an armament of about 180 tons, 8 percent of its 2,300-ton displacement (Glete 2010, 572).

Table 2–1 below shows weight breakdown estimates for the 32-gun frigate HMS *Pearl* (Gardiner 1992, as quoted by Braithwaite 2009, 13) and, based in part on the *Pearl*, the 32-gun frigate HMS *Southampton* (built 1757, Appendix 3). For the latter, Braithwaite also estimated the vertical center of gravity relative to the keel, which would affect lateral stability.

Table 2-1: Vertical Weight Distribution on Warships

	Southampton		Pearl
Ship Section	*Wt, kg*	*VCG, m*	*Wt, kg*
Top Hamper	53,480	17.977	59,457
Boats	2,997	8.128	2,997
Armament	**79,350**	**6.243**	**74,625**
Ground Tackle	32,766	4.416	32,766
Hull	479,229	4.399	524,662
Stowage	237,117	2.100	152,705
Ballast	120,642	1.762	132,080
OVERALL	**1,029,000**	**4.411**	**1,002,741**

(*Stowage for* Southampton *based on six months of foreign service. Armament consists of guns, shot, powder and gunner's stores. Armament subtotal and overall total bolded for ease of comparison.*)

It can be seen that if one subtracts the weight of the hull, the armament accounted for about 14.4 percent of the total weight.

Steam power made it possible for warships to cross the oceans without worrying about the direction of the wind, but the weight of the propulsion system—the engine, transmission, propulsor (paddlewheel or screw), coal bunkers, and coal—was undoubtedly greater than that of the sailing ship (masts, yards, sails and rigging—Braithwaite's "top hamper"). When shell guns forced warship designers to add armor, that change made the allocation of weight even more difficult. Designers had to make compromises regarding weight of guns, engines, armor, and even fuel and ammunition carried.

Early Modern Warship Classification

Throughout history, warships have served a variety of functions, including participating as combatants or reconnaissance elements in fleets, escorting friendly shipping, raiding or blockading enemy shipping, and bombarding enemy coastal forts and towns. One size does not suit all purposes, so a navy will have a variety of warships, with armaments ranging from heavy to light.

In 1612, British warships were divided according to tonnage into ship royal (800–1,200 tons), middling ships (600–800), small ships (250–600), and pinnaces (80–250) (James 1826, 1:4). They were reclassified (for wage purposes) into six rates, according to crew size, in 1626: first (>300), second (250–300), third (160–200), fourth (100–120), fifth (60–70), and sixth (40–50) (5).

The 1621 Swedish naval budget divided warships into *realskepp* (regal ship), *örlogsskepp* (warship), *mindre* (small) *örlogsskepp, pinasser* (pinnaces), and *farkoster*. This scheme was abandoned after 1622. On October 6, 1633, Axel Oxenstierna proposed a new system that divided *örlogsskepp* into *stora* (large) and *rätta* (normal) and split off *minsta* (smallest) from *mindre*. A simplified version of this system was used in the 1640s through 1670s (Glete 2010, 328ff).

Naval expansion in the second half of the seventeenth century resulted in the development of rating systems based on the number of guns: "six rates in England, seven charters in the Dutch Republic, and five ranges (and *frégates légères* as a sixth) in France" (*ibid.*). One tabulation can be found in Table 2–2.

Table 2–2: Comparative Warship Classification

	British 1685	*British 1714*	*British 1802*	*French 1670*	*Dutch 1680*	*Russian 1727*	*Spanish Napoleonic*
Rate	Number of Guns						
First	90–100	100	100–120	70–120	80+	90–100	100–120
Second	64–90	90	90–98	56–70	70–78	80–88	80–100
Third	56–70	70–80	64–84	40–50	60–68	66	74–80
Fourth	38–62	50–60	50–60	30–40	50–58	54	50–60
Fifth	28–38	30–40	30–44	23–34	40–48		30–44
Sixth	4–18	10–20	20–28	8–16	32–44		?–30

(threedecks.org [British, French, Dutch, Russian]); Harbron 1988, xiv, 24 (Spanish)

I have included several later British rating schemes; you can see how Napoleonic ships of the line were expected to carry more guns than their seventeenth-century counterparts. Just to complicate matters further, the British rates were sometimes further subdivided into classes.

In counting guns, the British navy ignored swivel guns (Chapelle 1949, 92) and, in the nineteenth century, initially ignored carronades. The rating system considered only the number of guns, not the weight of the shot they threw.

From a ship design standpoint, a more important metric is the total firepower (the sum of the shot weights from all guns, in pounds).

The efficiency of the warship as a weapons platform may be expressed as the ratio of total firepower (pounds) to the ship displacement (tons), although there are difficulties when it comes to estimating displacement for pre-nineteenth-century warships (whose size was expressed in tons burden, actually a volumetric measure of cargo capacity, rather than in tons of water displaced). For the Swedish navy, it was around 0.4 in the 1630s but increased to 0.75 in 1671 (Glete 2010, 571).

In 1833, the Royal Navy changed its rating system. All three-decked ships were considered first rate. Most other ships were classified based on their "war complements": second rate (700 men and up), third rate (600–699), fourth rate (400–599), fifth rate (250–399), and sixth rate (under 250). Steam vessels were "assigned a rate at the discretion of the Lords of the Admiralty" (Miles 1841, 39).

The term "battleship" dates back only to 1794; it was an abbreviation of "line-of-battle ship." I will unabashedly use the term "battleship" anachronistically to refer to the more powerful fleet units of any time period.

Initially, ships of the first four rates were considered powerful enough to be placed in the "line of battle," which didn't exist as a battle formation until the mid-seventeenth century. But by the mid-eighteenth century fourth rates tended to be used only in backwaters (or by inferior navies). The principal battleship was the third rate, especially the Napoleonic "74." First and second rates were either flagships or relegated to home water defense.

In the early seventeenth century, the term *frigate* still had strong traces of its original meaning as a kind of war-galley. It had come to mean a sailing ship that had long, sharp lines like those of a war-galley (*fragata*); they were sometimes called "galleon frigates" to differentiate them from the "galley frigate." In English usage, these race-built sailing ships could be merchantmen or warships. The only "frigates" on the 1633 Navy List had a mere three guns and were probably royal yachts.

Pepys considered the first true frigate built in England to be the *Constant Warwick* (1646), modeled on a French privateer and bearing 26–32 guns (*Naval Encyclopedia*). By 1650, according to the Oxford English Dictionary, the term was fixed as meaning a warship, and it came to mean one with two full decks, only one of which was a gun deck. Frigates were of the fifth and sometimes the sixth rates (a sixth rate with only a single deck was considered a "post ship" or "corvette").

Frigates were used by fleets for reconnaissance; by convention, in a fleet engagement, a battleship wouldn't fire on a frigate unless the frigate had fired first. (And then the battleship would probably blow it out of the water.) They were also the ship of choice for detached service, much like late nineteenth-century cruisers or twentieth-century destroyers.

A large and diverse group of British warships wasn't rated. These ships included sloops-of-war, bomb ketches, and purpose-built fireships. In the Napoleonic period, the sloops could further be divided into ship-rigged (three masts, with or without a quarterdeck) and brig-rigged (two masts). These had up to 28 or 22 guns, respectively, and thus overlapped with the contemporary sixth rates (20–28 guns) (Blake and Lawrence 2005, 23).

It's worth noting that in the mid-nineteenth-century American navy, a sloop-of-war could be a quite powerful warship. USS *Portsmouth* (1843) had eighteen 32-pounders and two Paixhans 64-pounder shell guns.

Modern Warship Classification

In the late nineteenth century, the term "cruiser" came to replace "frigate," denoting a ship designed for scouting and commerce raiding. The "destroyer" also came into existence, and that name was short for the more specific "torpedo-boat destroyer." When submarines replaced torpedo boats as a threat to capital ships, the destroyer took on the anti-submarine role.

With the purpose of arms control, the London Naval Treaty of 1930 defined aircraft carriers, capital ships, heavy cruisers, light cruisers and destroyers. With the exception of aircraft carriers, these were differentiated by their displacement and the size of their largest-caliber gun, as shown in Table 2–3.

The treaty was a dead letter by 1936. The British brought back the terms "corvette" and "frigate," this time referring to "dedicated anti-submarine vessels designed for convoy escort." The Americans instead called these vessels "destroyer escorts." After World War II, the U.S. Navy brought back the term "frigate" for ships with missile batteries that were larger than destroyers but too small to be called cruisers. Note that in other navies a "frigate" continued to denote a warship smaller than a destroyer (McGrath 2018).

Table 2–3

	Displacement	*Gun Caliber*
Capital Ship	>10,000 tons AND	>8 inches
Cruiser	>1,850 tons OR	>5.1 inches
Heavy		>6.1 inches
Light		<=6.1 inches
Destroyer	<=1,850 tons AND	<=5.1 inches

(McGrath 2018)

Warship Battery Composition

In June 1574, "there were 45 demi cannon, 37 cannon periers [stone throwers], 89 culverins, 142 demi culverins, 183 sakers, 56 minions, and 66 falcons on board 24 vessels" of Queen Elizabeth's navy (Oppenheim 1896, 155).

The first ship-by-ship breakdown for the Royal Navy dated to 1585 and covered twenty-one ships, as seen in Table 2–4.

Table 2–4: Royal Navy Armament (1585)

Ship	Demi-cannon	Cannon Perriers	Culverins	Demi-culverins	Sakers	Minions	Falcons	Falconets	Port-Pieces	Fowlers	Bases
Elizabeth	9	4	14	7	6	2	8		4	10	12
Triumph	9	4	14	7	6	2			4	10	12
White Bear	11	6	17	10	10	4	4		4	10	12
Victory	6	4	14	8	2		4		6	10	12
Hope	4	2	6	10	4	2	1		4	6	4
Mary Rose	4	2	8	6	8				2	6	12
Nonpareil	4	2	4	6	12	1	1		4	6	12
Lion	4	4	6	8	6		2		4	6	6
Revenge	2	4	10	6	10		2		2	4	12
Bonaventure	4	2	6	8	6	2	2		4	6	8
Dreadnought		2	4	10	6		2		2	8	8
Swiftsure		2	4	8	8		4		2	6	10
Antelope		2	2	6	6	2	2		4	4	10
Swallow		2		4	8	2	6		4	4	8
Foresight			4	8	8	4			2	2	8
Aid				2	8	2	6	1	4	6	4
Bull				6	8	2	1		4	4	
Tiger				6	10	2	2		4	6	
Scout					8	2	6	2	2	4	
Achates					2	4	10		2	2	
Merlin							6	2	2		

(Oppenheim 1896, 158)

For the British navy, there was no systematic distribution of the different gun sizes among ships of different classes, and among the different decks of a given ship, until 1677, when it adopted a "solemn, universal, and unalterable adjustment of the gunning and manning of the whole fleet" (Tanner 1903, 233ff).

An overview of the Royal Navy of 1677 is available that provides, for every rate and class of warship, the number of ships in the class, the years built, the complement, and the number and type of gun on each deck (James 1837, Volume 1, Appendix 1). For example, the most powerful warship (the *Sovereign of the Seas*, built in 1637, but renamed *Royal Sovereign*, rebuilt and rearmed in 1660) had twenty-six cannon-of-seven on the first deck, twenty-eight 24-pdrs on the second, twenty-eight demi-culverins on the third, ten light sakers on the quarter deck and four on the forecastle, and four 3-pdrs on the poop deck. The most numerous class (twenty ships) was a third rate with seventy guns: twenty-six demi-cannons on the first deck, twenty-six 12-pdrs on the second, and ten light sakers on the quarter deck. The oldest ship still in service was a second-rate vessel built in 1617, but it had no doubt gone through several rebuilds.

The 1677 establishment was succeeded by those of 1691, 1706, 1719, and 1745. After that time, warship design became somewhat more idiosyncratic again.

Theophilus Beauchant (1828, 105–6) provides the proportions of the various long guns and carronades for all rates of ships in his Royal Navy, which are listed in Tables 2–5A and 2–5B.

Table 2–5A: Armament Mix for Ships of the Line, Royal Navy, circa 1828

	Long Guns				Carronades			
	32	24	18	12	32	24	18	12
First Rate, First Class	32	34	34	8	12		1	
First Rate, Second Class	30	32	30	8	10		1	
First Rate, Third Class	30	30	32	18			1	
Second Rate, First Class	28		30	36	10		1	
Second Rate, Second Class	28		30	32	16		1	
Second Rate, Third Class	28		34	30	10		1	
Third Rate, First Class	28		28	6			7	
Third Rate, Second Class	30	32		8	12	12		
Third Rate, Third Class		26	26	2	12	7	5	

Table 2–5B: Armament Mix for Lesser Ships, Royal Navy, circa 1828

	Long Guns				Carronades			
	18	12	9	6	32	24	18	12
Fourth Rate	24	24	2			6	1	
Fifth Rate, First Class	30		8		12	1		
Fifth Rate, Second Class	26		2		14			1
Fifth Rate, Third Class		26		2	12			1
Sixth Rate, First Class				2	16		8	1
Sixth Rate, Second Class				2	16			1
Sixth Rate, Third Class				2		14		
Gun Brigs, First Class				2			10	
Gun Brigs, Second Class				2			8	
Cutter								10
Bomb Vessel*				2		8		1

(*also, one 13-inch and one 10-inch mortar)

It can be seen from the tables that it was not unusual for a battleship to carry guns of three or even four different calibers. The choice of guns for a particular warship was driven by three competing considerations: firepower, seaworthiness, and logistic simplicity.

The reason a captain might want the heaviest possible guns in every possible location is obvious, but that would increase the draft, bringing the lower gunports close to the water, and heavy guns mounted on the forecastle or quarterdeck would reduce the ship's roll stability.

A compromise was to put large-caliber guns on the decks below, and smaller-caliber guns higher up, but that approach led to the logistical headache of providing each ship with several different calibers of shot.

In the United States, after the War of 1812, there was a movement to simplify naval ammunition logistics by, for example, having all guns on a particular ship of the line use 32-pound shot but varying gun barrel length, so that there were "heavy 32s" on the lower deck, "medium 32s" on the gun deck, and "light 32s" on the spar deck (Glete 1993, 30; Chapelle 1949, 318). But in 1820, fighting ability was boosted by arming frigates "with the long 32-pdr below, and the 42-pdr carronade above," in addition to giving battleships "a tier of 42-pdrs in the lowest battery" (Dahlgren 1856, 276).

Similarly, in 1829, the French navy adopted the 30-pdr, albeit in different weights, for all batteries (Dahlgren 1856, 260). But by 1848, a French third rate carried 22 cm shell guns as well as long, short and carronade 30s (261); a year later, 50-pdrs were added (263).

In 1825, Colonel Munro proposed to the Admiralty the use of just 32-pound shot (Dahlgren 1856, 267). But in 1848, a British third class was expected to carry twelve 8-inch shell guns and twenty heavy and forty-eight light 32-pdrs (268).

A twentieth-century battleship would typically have main and secondary batteries for targeting enemy craft, as well as one or more calibers of anti-aircraft guns. The USS *Iowa* (BB-61) carried nine 16-inch and twenty 5-inch guns, as well as 40- and 20-mm AA guns (Dramiński 2020, 18–22). A twentieth-century warship might also have torpedo tubes and, after World War II, missile batteries. The 1980s reincarnation of the *Iowa* could fire Tomahawk cruise and Harpoon anti-ship missiles (22).

Armed Merchantmen

Premodern merchant ships carried armament only when necessary. In the southern Baltic, where piracy was rare, they typically were unarmed. In dangerous waters such as the Caribbean, the Mediterranean, and certain Asian regions, they either had guns or were accompanied by armed escorts.

The cheapness of cast iron guns made it possible to increase the armament of the merchant ship (Glete 1993, 52). While specialized warships existed even in the sixteenth century, most powers at that time didn't maintain permanent navies of significant size. Hence, they had to hire armed merchantmen. And to make sure that the civilian shipyards built ships that would be of value in wartime, the state provided economic incentives, such as reduced custom duties (53).

Nonetheless, the specialized warship of the seventeenth century carried not only more guns but often heavier ones. An armed merchantman might carry 12-pounders, but, according to Glete, 24-pounders and heavier guns were "exclusively warship armament" (1993, 28).

Because of the flimsiness of their hulls, the armed merchantmen couldn't slug it out for very long. Moreover, their crews were too small to maintain sustained fire. If the guns were already loaded, then, with one man per gun, they could get off one broadside quickly. If both sides had preloaded, and the ship turned, it could get off a second broadside the same way. After that, sustained fire was limited to a few guns (Glete 1993, 53). They were slow, too.

Nonetheless, in the 1630s, an armed trader could be loaned, voluntarily or otherwise, to the Crown for emergency use in the fleet. But by the mid-seventeenth century, their military use was usually as convoy escorts, not fleet units (Glete 1993, 170). The Swedes were the last European power to abandon the use of hired armed merchantmen in the main battle fleet (Glete 1993, 193; Glete 2010, 441). However, the concept reappeared in the form of the early twentieth-century Imperial Russian Volunteer Fleet, government-subsidized merchant ships built to an enhanced standard with a view toward wartime conversion (Ireland and Grove 1997, 28).

The East Indiamen had an unusually large number of guns for merchantmen, along with large crews, but the guns were still usually of relatively light caliber. The *Hollandia* (1742) and *Amsterdam* (1748) had eight 12-pdrs, sixteen 8-pdrs, eight 4-pdrs, and 10 swivel guns (ageofsail.net).

The *Duc de Duras* (1765) of the French East India Company was unusual; its heaviest ordnance were 18-pounders, but it was intended to be used as a warship in wartime as well as a merchant ship in peacetime. The ship was sold in 1779 and, with a new armament plan, became the *Bonhomme Richard* captained by John Paul Jones during the American Revolution (Boudriot 1987, 12).

Privateers

Privateers were fast, and had large crews, but they, too, were lightly built, intended to prey on the defenseless. The privateer was essentially a privately owned frigate or smaller vessel intended for commerce raiding. They could be fairly formidable; the *Red Dragon* (1595), for example, had thirty-eight guns (two demi-cannons, sixteen culverins, twelve demi-culverins, and eight sakers) (Grey and MacMunn 1932, 36–37).

Horizontal Distribution of Guns

We may recognize three basic gun arrangements: predominantly frontal, predominantly broadside, and turreted. The sixteenth-century Mediterranean galleys are in the first category. One of the more powerful Venetian galleys at Lepanto (1571) might have had a 52–55-pound full cannon, flanked by an inner pair of 12-pounders and an outer pair of 6-pounders. And it could have had a second deck, carrying swivel guns, as was certainly the case for the larger Spanish galleys (Guilmartin 2003, 322–23). In the eighteenth and nineteenth centuries, one could also find heavy frontal armament in certain specialized warships, bomb ketches and rocket ships. In the twentieth century, a similar arrangement could be observed on some torpedo boats and missile boats. In addition, attack submarines may be said to have a spinal armament, firing torpedoes from bow or stern.

Most warships of the late sixteenth through mid-nineteenth centuries were designed to deliver powerful broadsides, but they had rather weak bow and stern armament. Once the "line ahead" formation and related tactics (which lent themselves to delivering broadsides) were developed in the mid-seventeenth century, this arrangement was particularly true of capital ships. A frigate or lesser vessel was more likely to have chase guns.

Despite the importance of the broadside, seventeenth-century French warships tended to have relatively powerful bow and stern armament, because they were used in the Mediterranean against galleys. This approach required some adjustment in the hull to provide a good firing arc (Langstrom 1961, 167). In general, since the number of bow and stern guns was limited by space, those tended to be the ones with the best range and accuracy (Chapelle 1949, 12).

Some warship designers of the second half of the nineteenth century were persuaded by the successful ramming of enemy ships at the battles of Hampton Roads (1862) and Lissa (1866) that warships should be designed for ramming; this development led to an undue emphasis on frontal firepower for steam-powered ironclads (Hill 2006, 60).

For a ship with broadside armament, the length determines how many guns it can carry per deck. Length was limited by structural concerns; local inequalities of weight and buoyancy would cause the deck to droop in the center (hogging) or sometimes at the ends (sagging). These issues in turn imposed strains on the hull; they were (as a first approximation) proportional to the square of the length. Wooden-hulled warships consequently weren't much longer than 200 feet; a British first rate of the 1745 establishment was 179 feet at the gun deck (Ireland 2000, 41).

Of course, the number of guns carried on a deck of particular length depended on the spacing between the gunports, and how close they came to the bow or stern. On the *Dauphin Royal* (1735), with 74 guns, there were 13 ports to a side, the foremost about 18 feet from the stem and the aftmost about 10 feet from the stern. The port width was 2 feet, 10 inches and the distance between ports (edge to edge) was 7 feet, 7 inches (du Monceau 1764, 4).

Gunport spacing was limited by the area and crew needed to work the guns; the more powerful the gun, the greater these were. Gunport breadth, for example, was 3 feet for a 48-pdr and 1.5 for at 4-pdr (du Monceau 1764). The spacing was also affected by the framing; you didn't want to cut through a frame and weaken the hull. A mid-seventeenth-century Dutch admiralty had the following rules of thumb: gunport spacing (center to center) would be 20 shot diameters; height, six diameters; width, five (Hoving and Wildeman 2012, 104). A mid-eighteenth-century rule allows for 25-shot-diameter spacing and 6.5-diameter width, with the sill 3.5 diameters above the deck (Davis 1984, 110).

In the British 1745 establishment, no warship had more than 28 guns on a single full deck. However, there were post-establishment warships, such as the first-rate *Victory* (1765) and the "Large" class 74s, with 30 guns on the lowest gun deck (Lavery 1987, 121ff). And in 1764, du Monceau said that a 112-gun French warship had 32 guns (24-pdrs) on its second deck.

If you wanted more guns than could fit on the main deck, you put them on the quarterdeck or forecastle, or, if that still wasn't enough (or the guns were too heavy for that disposition), you added a second (or, if need be, a third) full deck.

The mid-nineteenth-century introduction of iron and steel construction allowed warships to be lengthened, and thus history has some examples of long "broadside ironclads." The longest of these was the HMS *Minotaur* (1863), 407 feet long, a sail/steam hybrid. There were also two-decker broadside ironclads, such as the French *Magenta* (1862), which was 282 feet long (Konstam 2019, 19).

Ordinarily, broadside armament was disposed symmetrically on either side of the centerline. However, on ships with extremely narrow beams, it might not then be possible to fire the port and starboard armament simultaneously, as they would recoil into each other. In 1787, Samuel Bentham armed some Russian barges of 22.5-foot beam with "eight long guns, 36-pounders, four on each side, to recoil; the four on one side placed not opposite to the four on the other, but opposite to the middle of the intermediate spaces" (Bentham 1828, 54–55). This staggered arrangement was highly unusual.

Premodern broadside carriage guns had a limited firing arc. This arc was determined by geometry and physics: the curve of the bulwark; the width and beveling of the gunport; the dimensions of the gun and its carriage; the width of the deck; the place to which the carriage had to be run out in order to have adequate room for recoil. It was not until the late eighteenth century that the arc was 45 degrees fore and aft (Robertson 1921, 152).

In some early steam ironclads like HMS *Warrior* (1860), the gunports were narrowed, thereby reducing the arc of fire. The theory was that with steam propulsion, they weren't subject to the vagaries of the wind and, therefore, could maneuver as needed to bring the guns to bear. Moreover, firing at extreme angles reduced the rate of fire. The narrower gunports also meant that the guns were less vulnerable to counterfire (Lambert 1987, 89, 95). On the *Audacious* class (built 1867–1870), the main guns could train only 30 degrees each way (Robertson 1921, 274).

However, on USS *Kearsarge* (BB-5, launched 1898), each of the fourteen 5-inch rapid-fire guns fired through an arc of 90 degrees (Raines 1903, 140). The broadside guns of the Japanese cruiser *Yoshino* (1892) had a 120-degree arc (Jane 1904, 99).

Vertical Arrangement of Guns

Positioning the gun on a higher deck has the advantage that the gunports are less likely to be forced to close as a result of rough sea conditions. Sir Walter Raleigh urged that the ship be designed and laden so that the lowest tier of ordnance was four feet above the water (Creuze 1846, 17). An upper deck gun will also have increased range (see chapter 10) and can take advantage of plunging fire (shooting at the flimsy enemy deck, not the relatively stout side; see chapter 14). However, if the enemy is close at hand, the gun might not be able to depress enough to fire on it, and the higher the guns are, the higher the ship's center of gravity must be, reducing its lateral stability.

In the fifteenth century, ships had guns mounted high up, in the aptly named forecastles and sterncastles. The size and number of these guns was limited by their effect on stability. In the early sixteenth century, gundecks and gunports were introduced. Since the armament was lower, it could be made heavier (Sicking 2004, 382). As broadsides became more effective, the superstructures became less useful and were reduced in size. The early seventeenth century was a transitional period in which the capital ships mounted heavy broadside armaments but still had significant superstructures.

The depth (and draft!) of the ship limits the number of gun decks. Over the course of the sixteenth century, a second and then a third gundeck (~1591) was introduced (Creuze 1846, 14–15). The Dutch didn't use three-deck vessels, but the English and French did (Anderson and Anderson 1963, 158). British designers of the late eighteenth century found that three-deck 80-gun ships were top heavy; two-deck 80s were too long for their height and hogged (drooped amidships); the two-deck 74s were ideal. Even though they were considered of the "third rate," they became the most common "battleships" in "foreign service" (Millar 1986, 9).

A first rate, of 110 guns, sailing by the wind on the larboard (port) tack. Note the three closed gun decks (illustration is from Miles 1841, 40).

On a Georgian frigate, the lower deck was called the gun deck but had no guns (Millar 1986, 10). But this arrangement did help ensure that the guns on the upper deck were safely above the water.

Turrets

For this discussion, "turreted" may mean a true turret (rotating armor) or a barbette (stationary armor).

Ericsson's ironclad USS *Monitor* (commissioned in February 1862) was the first turret ship built, as well as the first to engage in battle. (While there were turrets on the French and British floating batteries used in the Crimean War, they don't qualify as ships. And the *Royal Sovereign* [1857], sometimes touted as the first turret ship, wasn't converted into a turret ship until 1864.)

The advantage of the turret was that by rotation it could bring its gun(s) to bear in any direction, save for those obstructed by the ship's superstructure (including funnels, masts, and other turrets). Thus, a turret replaced at least two broadside guns (port and starboard).

Because of the size and expense of the turret, the tendency was for turreted warships to be fitted with a small number of very powerful guns. Some deplored this trend. Sir Edward James Reed, for example, complained that a vessel with all its armament in two turrets could fire "at any moment in two directions only," whereas "in a broadside ship ... all of the guns ... may be directed upon separate points." Moreover, the enemy would aim at the turrets, and if one was disabled, it would deprive the two-turret ship of half its firepower. But Reed had to admit that the turret ship could more easily concentrate firepower on a single target and that the turret ports were small targets (Reed 1869, 233–237).

With muzzleloaders, the turrets had to be of large diameter, but the guns short barreled, so they could be run back and reloaded inside (Ireland and Grove 1997, 38).

A turret could carry one to four guns, but a two-gun installation was the most common. (Note that the terms "twin," "triple" and "quadruple" imply that the guns are elevated together, so a twin turret is not quite the same as a two-gun turret. The advantage of independent elevation is that if the range to the target is uncertain, the turret guns can bracket the estimated location.)

All of the guns in a turret could be fired simultaneously (at the same target), and indeed the 1880 British gunnery manual preferred this option to them firing independently, as the turret could be turned away from the enemy while all of its guns reloaded (Admiralty 1880, 230).

The USS *Monitor* had nearly a 360-degree firing arc, made possible by being a single turret, low freeboard, steam-powered vessel with just one funnel.

Sails, masts, spars and stays would, of course, restrict the firing arc. Nonetheless, many early turreted warships were hybrids (sail/steam) because of doubts as to the reliability of the engine or the availability of coal.

This uncertainty led to a variety of curious expedients. On the ill-fated HMS *Captain* (1869; sank in 1970), the two turrets were on the lower (main) deck, and the masts were stayed to the upper (hurricane) deck. Captain Cowper Phipps Coles, its designer, therefore proposed using iron shrouds and stays, to reduce the ship's damage to its own rigging. The hurricane deck was dispensed with on the double-turreted HMS *Wivern* and HMS *Scorpion* (1864), on which the turrets flanked the main mast.

HMS *Inflexible* (1876) had two screws driven by compound steam engines, as well as two masts that could carry 18,500 square feet of sail (Ross 2015). The latter was removed in 1885 (Breyer 1970, 34). While I am not aware of later turreted warships with sails, the broadside-armed HMS *Calypso* (1883) was ship-rigged (Ireland and Grove 1997, 36), and the Russian cruiser *Rurik* (1892), barque-rigged.

Early turreted warships included those with one (USS *Monitor*), two (USS *Onondaga*) and even three (USS *Roanoke*) turrets. With multiple turret designs, one

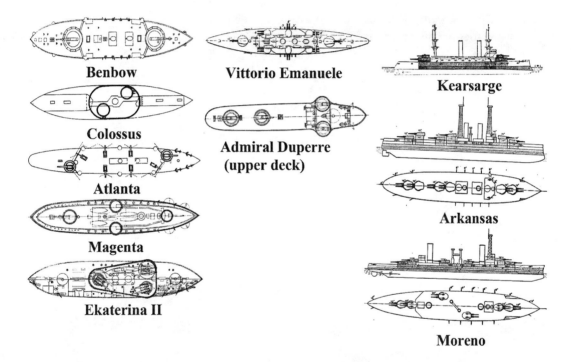

Potpourri of turret arrangements. No attempt was made to locate the first exemplar of a given arrangement. *Benbow* (UK, launched 1885, completed 1888), fore-and-aft centerline turrets (Brassey 1886); *Colossus* (UK, launched 1882, commissioned 1886), two wing turrets mounted en echelon (*ibid.*); *Atlanta* (U.S., protected cruiser, commissioned 1886), fore-and-aft turrets en echelon (Brassey 1889); *Magenta* (France, laid down 1883, commissioned 1892), two fore-and-aft centerline and two symmetrical wing turrets (*ibid.*); *Ekaterina II* (Russia, launched 1886, completed 1889), three turrets in a triangular central citadel, two fore and one aft (*ibid.*); *Vittorio Emanuele* (Italy, laid down 1901, completed 1908), fore-and-aft centerline turrets and six symmetric wing turrets (Brassey 1903); *Admiral Duperré* (France, commissioned 1883), upper deck, two forward turrets in sponsons and two centerline aft (Brassey 1889); *Kearsarge* (BB-5, launched 1898), fore-and-aft centerline stacked turrets (ibid.); *Arkansas* (U.S., commissioned 1912), three centerline superfiring turret pairs (Brassey 1916); *Moreno* (Argentina, commissioned 1915), fore-and-aft centerline superfiring turret pairs and two en echelon wing turrets (Id). Dates from Wikipedia, plans from Thomas Brassey's *Naval Annual* as noted.

has the concern of where to place the turrets. The most obvious arrangement was to place them single file on the centerline. But then a bow turret couldn't fire directly astern, and a central turret (as on the HMS *Monarch* [1868]) couldn't safely shoot directly fore or aft.

One alternative was to mount the extra turrets on the side (wings), as may be seen on HMS *Dreadnought* (1906). This approach increased the frontal fire at the expense of broadside fire. On the *Dreadnought*, the fore and aft turrets had a 270-degree firing arc, and the wing turrets 180 degrees. Since they flanked the super-structure, they could not fire across the deck (Roden 1911, 202).

The turrets could be mounted over the hull proper or on semicircular projections (sponsons). Wing turrets could be disposed symmetrically on either side of the centerline, or they might be staggered (*en echelon*). On the Argentine *Moreno*-class battleships, the centerline turrets had a 300-degree firing arc, and the wing turrets had a 180-degree normal broadside arc and a 100-degree cross-deck arc (Roden 1911, 205).

The centerline design was structurally sounder than the wing turret design, and so other options were explored. One was to stack the turrets, like the tiers on a wedding cake. This was done on USS *Kearsarge* (BB-5, 1898). While the superposition of turrets was economical of space, and gave both turrets a large firing arc, "the blast effects of the upper guns on the gun crews in the lower turrets was considered by most authorities to make this arrangement impractical" (Hough 2003, 38).

An in-between strategy kept the turrets on the centerline, but with the "inner" turrets higher than the "outer" ones. This "superfiring pairs" arrangement may be seen on pre–World War I dreadnoughts of the *South Carolina* class.

The USS *Iowa* (BB-61) had a superfiring pair of turrets, three 16-inch guns apiece, in the bow section and a single such turret in the stern section. These had a 300-degree firing arc (Dramiński 2020, 18–19). Its ten 5-inch twin turrets were on the superstructure deck and had a 180-degree firing arc (20).

CHAPTER 3

Gunfounding

Gunfounding technically refers to the casting of guns in a foundry, but we will use the term to cover all methods of gun barrel manufacture, whether they involve casting or not. Up through the nineteenth century, it was more art than science.

Available Metals

Wrought iron, steel and cast iron are distinguished by their carbon content. Wrought iron is iron essentially free of carbon—less than, say, 0.05–0.08 percent (Brady et al. 1996, 154, 984). Steel has a carbon content of up to about 2–2.5 percent, but less than 1 percent is common (154, 166, 859). Steels are further classified as carbon steels (just iron and carbon) or alloy steels (with substantial additional alloying elements). The carbon steels themselves may be characterized as low/mild (up to 0.3 percent), medium (0.31–0.55 percent), high (0.56–1 percent) or ultra-high (1–2 percent) carbon. Different authorities will define these metals slightly differently. In the twentieth century, the commercially available alloy steels included nickel, nickel-chromium, molybdenum, chromium, chromium-vanadium, tungsten-chromium and silicon-manganese steels.

Cast iron is an iron alloy with a carbon content greater than steel. Depending on how the carbon is combined, it may be called white (hard but brittle) or grey (softer but tougher, preferred for cannons) (Brady et al. 1996, 166).

The term "bronze" originally identified a copper alloy whose principal alloying element was tin. Later it came to mean any copper alloy whose principal alloying element was one other than zinc (the brasses) or nickel (Brady et al. 1996, 125). "Gunmetal" is a bronze composed of 88 percent copper, 10 percent tin, and 2 percent zinc (424).

While in theory aluminum or titanium could be used in naval gun construction, their use in practice has been insignificant.

History of Metal Usage in Gun Construction

Wrought iron. Until the sixteenth century, cannons were forged; the tubes were built up from longitudinal metal strips, which were held together by metal

37

hoops. The hoops were added while red-hot and thus would contract when cooled (López-Martín 2007, 176).

The hooped bombard of the fourteenth century was made of wrought iron. But by the mid-sixteenth century, the large wrought iron pieces were found only on small merchant ships and in peripheral fortifications.

Wrought iron reappeared as a reinforcing element in the mid-nineteenth century. It was used, for example, on the Parrott rifled cannon of the American Civil War (Kinard 2007, 190).

Bronze first appeared in hooped bombards in the early fifteenth century. By the beginning of the sixteenth century, it was the dominant gun metal. (The British navy has the incredibly annoying habit of identifying bronze guns as "brass." Brass is a copper-zinc alloy.) Bronze is a copper-tin alloy; in the sixteenth century, the preferred ratio was 90–10 (Guilmartin 2003, 307).

While tough, bronze is soft and thus subject to abrasion, especially if the barrel is hot from repeated firing. Bronze also suffered from a lack of homogeneity. When cooling, the tin tends to separate from the copper, causing white blotches called "tin spots," which are eaten away by the powder gas (U.S. Navy 1880, 76ff).

Cast iron bombards are referred to in Taccola's *De ingeneis* (1433) (López-Martín 2007, 186). Over the course of the seventeenth century, cast iron gradually supplanted bronze as cannon material.

The change occurred despite bronze's advantages: it didn't rust; it was easier to cast ("iron had a tendency to harden before all of it could be poured into the mould" [Lavery 1987, 84]); it could be recast without loss of strength; and bronze cannons could always be made lighter than cast iron guns of equal strength. For example, in 1742, a British navy "32–9.5" weighed 6,048 pounds in bronze and 6,384 in cast iron, and a "42–10" was 7,392 pounds in bronze and a walloping 8,400 in iron (Meide 2002).

Unfortunately, bronze cannons were much more expensive—initially three- or four-fold (Gardiner and Unger 1994, 149), and almost sixteen-fold for 3- to 8-pounders in Sweden around 1671 (Glete 2010, 557). This difference was the result of a decrease in the price of cast iron; bronze prices were stable. Consequently, bronze guns sometimes remained in service for more than a century (Rodger 1997, 215).

In 1639, a Spanish fleet carried 270 bronze and 265 cast iron guns. In 1677, two-thirds of the Spanish navy's artillery pieces were cast iron. And in 1793, the Spanish navy had only "25 bronze guns out of ... 10,000 pieces" (López-Martín 2007, 385). In the second half of the seventeenth century, cast iron was also the majority gun metal in the navies of England, France and Sweden (66, 385).

First the lighter guns were made from cast iron, and then all guns—save those on "prestige" ships (flagships and royal yachts)—went ferrous (Glete 1993, 24ff). The 42-pounder was first cast in iron in 1657, but 30 percent of culverins were still bronze in 1660 (Nelson 2001).

Even on first-class warships, bronze was pretty much no longer on deck by the 1770s. (However, the British navy still had some bronze mortars in the 1860s.) Bronze continued to be used as a gun metal for field artillery in the nineteenth century, as late as the Crimean War and American Civil War, no doubt because of its weight advantage.

Nineteenth-century cast iron had a lower yield and breaking strength than bronze (Ord1800, 189), so additional metal was used, preferably at the breech (Hazlett et al. 1988, 82). While a more uniform cast iron could be made in the early nineteenth century, thanks to improvements in iron making (coke replacing charcoal, steam replacing water power) (Morriss 2010, 188–89), it remained unpredictably brittle (light field pieces were especially prone to bursting [Hazlett et al. 1988, 220]), presumably thanks to variations in the minor nonferrous constituents (phosphorus, sulfur, etc.). In the Civil War era, Thomas Rodman wrote, "We are at present far from possessing a practical knowledge of the properties of cast iron in its application to gunfounding" (Wertime 1961, 164), and Augustus Cooke (1875, 53) made a similar complaint.

Unfortunately, bronze wasn't suitable for rifled weapons. Since bronze is softer than iron, and the rifling exposed more tin spots, "repeated firings rapidly wore down the lands, thus making the pieces increasingly inaccurate" (Kinard 2007, 193; Hazlett et al. 1988, 52). Even for smoothbores, the softness and the tin spots were problematic when challenged by the heavier projectiles and more powerful charges of the nineteenth century.

In the 1870s, the Italians and French found that guns cast from phosphor bronze (a stronger, more homogeneous metal) were superior to those made using ordinary bronze, but they concluded that the advantage was too small to be practical; the phosphorus had to be added in exact proportions and was "unstable." So-called "bronze steel" (an ordinary bronze cast under pressure while chilling the interior and subsequently forged cold) was also considered, but this option was eclipsed by steel (U.S. Navy 1880, 77, 187).

Cast steel. Steel is potentially superior to cast iron, and to wrought iron and bronze, but it is quite difficult to cast without hidden defects (Kinard 2007, 230). Alfred Krupp cast his first steel cannon in 1847 (Krause 1995, 59). There was only limited use of cast steel rifled cannons (3-inch Sawyer) in the American Civil War. In 1910, cast steel was used for American naval gun mounts but not for the guns themselves (Officers 1910, 5).

Forged steel. This term refers to steel worked by hammering or pressing. The tubes, jackets and hoops of naval guns were made of steel that was forged and then tempered and annealed (*ibid.*, 28).

Nickel steel. When alloyed with steel in moderate quantities, nickel increases the metal's hardness, toughness, ductility, and tensile strength (U.S. Navy 1913, 9). Nickel steel guns were introduced in the 1890s (Krooth 2004, 89), in part because of the development of the more powerful "smokeless powders" (see chapter 4) (Sondhaus 2012, 166).

In one experiment, 3.5-inch field guns, "one made of ordinary Krupp steel and the other of nickel steel," were "loaded with shell containing 170 grammes of picric acid, the center of the shell in each case being 300 millimetres from the muzzle. When the shells were exploded [inside the bore] the crucible steel gun burst into many pieces, while the nickel steel gun remained entire, showing an increase of the bore of 7.4 millimetres at the site of the projectile, but no cracks anywhere" (OboM 1893, 140).

By 1910, in the U.S. Navy, the main forgings and the breech plug of "all naval guns of 3-inch caliber or above" were made from nickel steel (Officers 1910, 4).

Cannon Manufacture (Gunfounding)

Hollow Casting

Until the eighteenth century, muzzleloading cannons were cast as single hollow blocks. Making the mold was tricky. The earliest detailed description of the process is in Vannoccio Biringuccio's *De la Pirotechnia* (1540), Book VI, chapters 5–11 (1990, 234–60, 452) and Book VII, chapter 8 (307–18). According to him, "every gun mould needs three pieces."

The construction of the first piece began with a wood pattern (spindle; model), preferably a single piece of fir, a bit longer than the intended length of the barrel and of a thickness corresponding to the intended outer dimension of the gun barrel. The extra length was needed so that it could be supported on "bearing trestles" at either end and turned on a lathe.

The pattern was "well smoothed from head to foot" and "well covered with fine wash ashes or with tallow or some other fat." (This was a release material, so the mold material wouldn't stick to it.) Several coats of clay were applied, each one being allowed to dry before the next was added. After the penultimate coat, a wire mesh was added, and then the final coat, so the wire was held in place. The mold was reinforced with an armature of iron rods and bands, which also received a clay coat. The assemblage was heated, to loosen the wax or tallow, and then lifted, at which point one end was struck against a wall, freeing the spindle. This piece was removed, leaving a hollow behind that would make "the outside of the finished gun." Clay could be used to repair "any small breaks that may appear on the inside or outside." This piece was provided with a "feeding head."

Regarding the nature of the clay, Biringuccio's first chapter in Book VI speaks of "the requisite quality of clay for making moulds for casting in bronze." He cautions readers to avoid both clays that have "unctuous viscosity," as they "shrink and break," and clays that are "lean" and "hold together poorly by themselves when dry." Pure clay is too "unctuous" and must be "tempered," preferably with wool-cloth clippings, but other options include dry dung, cane flowers, straw, and so forth.

The second piece, the core, "makes the empty hole in the middle of the gun." An iron spindle was required to support the weight of the clay without wobbling. It was covered with ashes or other release material and loosely wrapped with a layer of rope. This was covered with a clay including "a small amount of cloth clippings and much sifted horse dung and some … ashes." (The clay, so formulated, could resist the heat of the molten metal during casting, but it was "crumbly," so it could be removed after casting.) The core was enlarged with additional alternating layers of rope (or hemp tow) and clay, drying after each clay layer was applied.

Next, the crude core was placed on a board with a cutting edge and turned, the edge removing excess material so the core was left smooth and cylindrical. The dried core was then covered with "damp wash ashes."

The third piece made the breech, "the part which forms the bottom and closes the whole mold. It is also the one that sustains the entire burden of the bronze," so one had to take "care to make it strong with clay and with iron bands." The pattern was covered with "a clay made with good cloth clippings," bound with iron wire, and reinforced "with a cage of iron rings and plates." The pattern was removed, leaving the breech cavity. Obviously, care had to be taken to ensure that this cavity matched that of the first piece.

The reasoning underlying the creation of a separate breech piece is probably that keeping it separate "would make the insertion of the core easier as the founder would have access to both ends of the mold, and thus a greater ability to align the core in the collar correctly" (Hoskins 2003, 41).

All three pieces had to be properly baked and then cooled, and any cracks repaired. The main piece had guides ("wheels") for the introduction of the core and breech pieces.

When the three pieces were assembled to form the mold, the core had to be held centrally. This was done near the top of the core by means of a disc, which preferably was made as part of the core, though it could be added afterward. Near the bottom, it was held by a metal structure, placed in the breech. Biringuccio preferred an "iron ring which has four arms in a cross, or sometimes three," but an alternative was a four-legged candelabra-like "castle." Together, the disc and the metalwork provided two constraints on the position of the core, and the disc additionally served to keep out debris (Hoskins 2003, 38–40).

These various pieces were assembled to form the gun mold. The armatures of the breech mold and the first mold had hooks that were joined together. The mold was placed in a pit with the muzzle end up. A spike at the bottom of the pit engaged a hole in the end of the core iron, and other metalwork engaged the top of the mold. The pit was filled with earth that was tamped down.

The bronze (Biringuccio didn't discuss casting an iron cannon) was melted in the furnace and then allowed to enter the mold through the feeding head. The bronze had to have the right fluidity to properly fill the mold. After one was sure the mold had filled completely, the fill was allowed to cool and solidify. Then the mold was broken so the casting could be removed. This process meant that no two cannons could be identical (Hall 1952, 10).

The feeding head was sawn off, the core spindle was removed, the remaining clay (outside and inside) scraped away, and the bronze smoothed by hammering on the outside and reaming on the inside. Finally, a touch-hole was drilled into the barrel.

Later descriptions of essentially the same process were published by Diego Prado y Tovar (1603) and Surirey de Saint-Remy (1697). However, it is worth noting that Prado "draws a picture of an efficient vertical boring machine driven by power" (Hall 1952, 10). Baker et al. (1841, 292–301) provide a detailed description of clay molding practice in 1840 Europe.

Note that the interior (core) mold had to be held centered inside the larger mold by a metal spacer that would become part of the gun. In general, this method didn't work out perfectly; the core would shift, so the bore wouldn't be quite centered (Weir

2006, 132). Sara Hoskins reports that in a Spanish demi-culverin recovered from the 1588 *El Gran Grifon* wreck, the bore was "extremely off-center" (2003, 38).

Another problem was intrinsic to the vertical casting method: since the bottom (breech) was under greater pressure than the top, and also better insulated, it would have been the last to solidify, and therefore tin would have migrated downward. The muzzles (of bronze cannon) were thus only 3–5 percent tin, resulting in brittleness, which was compensated for by flaring the muzzle (Guilmartin 2003, 312). Biringuccio also refers to adding tin late in the pouring process.

Solid Casting

Over the period 1715–1745, Johann Maritz developed a new fabrication method. The cannon was cast solid, breech down, and then the bore was drilled out horizontally. The mold construction and the casting were carried out much as in prior times, except that the core mold was no longer required. "It took 6 to 10 days, depending on the hardness of the metal, to bore a 24-pounder" (Tucker 2008).

One curious aspect of the process is that it was the cannon that was rotated, the bore remaining stationary (Alder 2010, 42). That way, if the boring bar were off-axis, it would describe a "conical motion," readily detected. But if the cannon were stationary and the bore rotated, there was no such telltale indication (1824 Supplement,

In 1917, at the U.S. Navy Yard, workers bore out the breech of a 14-inch gun. Photograph by Harris & Ewing. Gifted to the Library of Congress in 1955. Reproduction Number: LC-DIG-hec-10073. Call Number: LC-H261-9953 [P&P]. Library of Congress Prints and Photographs Division.

Encyclopædia Britannica, "Cannon," 2:608; U.S. Army 1922, 87). In 1776, the British Ordnance Office required that all guns be solid cast (Lavery 1987, 84).

There were other modest improvements over the eighteenth century. In Britain, these changes included providing full-size drawings to the gun founders (1716) and using copper rather than wood cores.

We may deduce the improvement in tolerances by examining the weight variation of the pieces. "In 1665, guns from a single batch of 9ft demi-cannon varied from 44 to 62cwt, those of 8.5 feet from 43 to 47, and culverins of 10ft varied from 40 to 46 cwt" (Lavery 1987, 83). In contrast, the 32-pounders surveyed in 1803–1806 were 55–57 cwt (84).

Sand Molds

An alternative to the tempered clay ("loam") mold was a sand mold. Biringuccio (Book VIII, Chapter 4, 327) describes casting "every kind of metal in green sand." According to the translator, this term then meant a "burned sand bonded with flour and moisture." Biringuccio's preference was for a mixture of baked "fine river gravel," ashes, fine-sifted old flour, and urine or wine. He said that sand molds could be used to "make large and small bells, mortars, and other works."

It appears that in Britain, by 1750, it was "normal" to use sand molds to cast cannons (Lavery 1987, 84). It is likely that this statement should be qualified as referring to iron ordnance.

In 1840, the Woolwich arsenal was one of the bronze foundries still using clay molds (Baker et al. 1841, 305).

The 1815 *Encyclopædia Britannica* ("Cannon," 605) states, "The most approved method of constructing the mould of a gun is in dry sand, and this is the method now practiced in Britain. Guns cast in loam do not come from the mould with a surface so correctly resembling that of the model as those cast in dry sand." Thus, sand molding permitted founders to dispense with the "process of turning" to smooth out the defects.

Nonetheless, in 1841, American ordnance officers who had visited Europe the preceding year reported that both sand and clay molds were used in making bronze cannons (which were still in demand for field cannons, because of their reduced weight) and that "clay moulds" were "still most generally used" for that purpose. "Opinions are much divided as to the advantages of either method; but experiments made lately do not show that there is any material differences in the quality of guns made by either process" (Baker et al. 1841, 292). They also opined, "Sand moulding has over other methods the advantage of considerable economy in time, labor, and fuel; but there are different opinions as to the quality of its products, particularly for the larger calibers."

Despite the name, the "dry sand" was "made by mixing a quantity of sharp refractory sand with water in which clay has been diluted." The mixture was such that "if a handful is grasped … on opening the hand the sand retains the form given it" (1815 Encyclopedia; cp. Baker et al. 1841, 300-303).

Sand molds were used for casting both iron and bronze guns. The gun model was made of cast iron or "brass" (bronze), "divided into conical sections, by planes perpendicular to its axis, and these different sections are united together very accurately by rabbets." The model was "rubbed with black lead, to lessen the adherence of the sand to its surface" (Baker et al. 1841, 265, 272, 302–3).

The mold for the barrel was formed in cast iron flasks, each corresponding with a section of the pattern. "All the flasks, except that of the breech, were divided longitudinally into two equal parts." Beginning at the breech end, the space between the model and the flask was filled with sand, rammed down to harden it. The flasks were then inverted by a crane, as needed, so both parts were filled with sand. Wedges were placed between adjacent flasks, to "occupy the space which is calculated equal to the shrinkage of the moulds, so that, after they are dried, they will join exactly" (Baker et al. 1841, 303–4).

Because of the longitudinal division of the mold, the pattern section in a given flask could be removed once that flask was no longer required for the molding operation (Baker et al. 1841, 304). Thus, patterns could be reused, with a consequent greater uniformity in fabricating a series of guns.

The different parts of the mold were oven dried, united together, and lowered into the casting pit.

Dahlgren Guns

These were solid cast smoothbore muzzleloading shell guns, but from a gunfounding perspective, they are noteworthy for their "soda bottle" shape, which is explained in chapter 9. Dahlgren guns were used extensively in the Union navy.

Rodman Guns

These guns were hollow cast, with a trick: the core was itself hollow; in fact, it consisted of two concentric tubes and was cooled with water pumped through the inner tube while the molten iron was poured in through the annulus. The heating of the outside was slowly diminished, too. The metal would thus cool inside out, pre-stressing it into a uniform state of compression (Tucker 2020, 218). In one experiment, two guns with 8-inch bores were cast in pairs: one solid cast, the other by Rodman's method. "The solid gun burst at the seventy-third discharge." The hollow cast one stood fifteen hundred and did not fail (Kettell 1864, 336).

While primarily used in seacoast fortifications, in 1864 General Smith mounted "two thirteen-inch Rodman guns upon the hurricane deck of the *Emerald*" during a Union campaign in Louisiana (Lossing 2010, 263).

The ironclads *Monadnock*, *Canonicus*, *Mahopac*, *Saugus*, and so on carried XV-inch shell guns (Ammen 1883, 230), which had the Dahlgren shape but were cast by Rodman's method (Marriott and Forty 2017, 79).

Parrott Rifles

Wrought iron's advantage was that it was four times stronger than cast iron and thus able to help resist the higher internal stresses of a rifled gun. Saving

300-pounder Parrott rifle on Morris Island outside Charleston Harbor. Photographed by Haas & Peale in summer 1863, after its muzzle burst. While this rifle was heavier than any in naval service, it illustrates the problematic character of this weapon. Civil War Photographs, 1861–1865, Library of Congress Prints and Photographs Division. Reproduction Number: LC-DIG-cwpb-04726.

manufacturing cost and time, Robert Parrott shrunk a wrought iron reinforcing hoop onto the breech of a rifled barrel cast in the usual way. However, "large Parrott rifles had the worst record of any Union cannon for premature bursting…. Of 110 large caliber Union cannon that cracked or burst in action during the war, 83 were Parrotts." After the first 1864 assault on Wilmington, Admiral David Dixon Porter declared that the guns were "calculated to kill more of our men than those of the enemy" (Bell 2003, 8).

As of January 1, 1865, there were 703 Parrott guns in Union naval service, ranging in size from 20- to 150-pounders. Of these, twenty-one had failed (nine by cracking or bursting at the muzzle). The 100- and 150-pounders accounted for sixteen of the failures (Welles 1865, 123).

Built-Up Construction

A built-up gun is essentially a gun whose barrel is reinforced by spiral or multiple circumferential elements. The Parrott rifle may be considered a transitional form in the evolution of the built-up gun, as it featured only a single hoop (ANJ 1863, 37).

Since rifled guns have minimal windage, the internal pressures are higher, and the gun must be strong enough to withstand those pressures. Hence, William Armstrong adopted a built-up construction for his rifled breechloader (U.S. Army 1922, 51–52). It went through several permutations. In one, wrought iron bars were twisted into spirals and welded on their edges to form the barrel (Tennent 1864, 106). In some cases, the twisted coils were themselves shrunk onto an inner "A" tube of mild steel (or, originally, wrought iron) (Morgan 1884, 4; Holley 1865, 25).

For naval service, Armstrong designed (under protest) a 110-pounder, 7-inch rifled breechloader of 81 cwt. In 1859, the Royal Navy ordered one hundred of these guns (Tennent 1864, 143, 211; Holley 1865, 14). They were used in the 1863 bombardment of Kagoshima and the 1864 battle of Shimonoseki Strait (Wikipedia). The breechloader design was abandoned (see chapter 1), but built-up construction methods were applied to the subsequent rifled muzzleloaders (Holley 1865, 15).

Around the end of the nineteenth century, the British and Japanese made use of wire-wound construction, essentially a "poor man's" built-up gun. The "A" tube was wrapped multiple times with a high-tensile-strength wire, and then the "B" tube was shrunk over this base (DiGiulian 2023). As of 1910, "no wire-wound guns [were] in use in [the U.S.] Navy," although "the English use them extensively." They were relatively cheap, but their "great disadvantage" was "insufficient longitudinal strength" (Officers 1910, 27).

By the early twentieth century, heavy naval guns were built up in hoop-over-tube fashion. The inner tube was placed breech end down in a cold pit, supported by a short mandrel. Heated hoops were placed one by one over the tube and cooled with a water spray, shrinking them onto the tube (NAVORD 1937, 136). These "hoops" were not narrow like the reinforcing rings of premodern guns.

We turn next to two processes that could be used to cast stronger monobloc guns, although the 1957 navy ordnance manual noted that "built-up" guns were "still made in sizes over 8-inch" (NAVORD 1957, 5B2).

Armstrong 100-pdr breechloader. Note the shunting tracks. National Archives. Courtesy of the Naval History and Heritage Command, Catalog USN 900042.

A heated "hoop" has been raised out of a furnace and is ready to be dropped vertically over the gun barrel. As it cools, it will shrink (Figure 18 from EB 1911, "Ordnance," page 195).

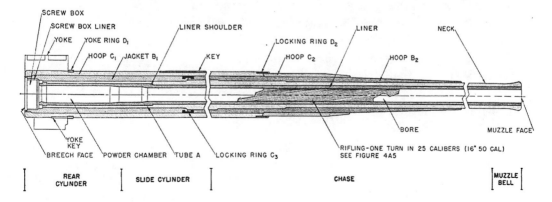

This is a schematic of a complete built-up gun (a 16-inch/50). Moving radially outward, note Tube A, Jacket B1 and Hoop B2, and Hoop C1 and C2. The locking rings prevent longitudinal movement of the hoops (Figure 4A2 from NAVORD 1944).

Centrifugal Casting

This process involves pouring molten metal into a revolving mold. Centrifugal force hurls the metal out to the periphery, creating a single tube (monobloc). Centrifugal casting was first applied to cannon barrels in 1925 (Thomson and Mayo 1955).

Autofrettage (Radial Expansion)

In the nineteenth century, rough-bored solid cast rifle barrels were tested for defects by firing a larger-than-normal charge, thus subjecting the barrel to high internal pressure. It was discovered that this procedure "imparted greater elastic strength to the rifle barrel." In the early twentieth century, gun designers sought to achieve this increased strength in artillery barrels by applying "controlled hydraulic pressure up to 150,000 pounds per square inch." If the pressure was sufficient to "permanently enlarge the bore," the barrel was also strengthened, apparently by "imprisoning internal compressions at the bore comparable to those created in a built-up gun when a heated jacket or hoop was slipped on the barrel ... and allowed to cool, shrinking to a very tight fit." The hydraulic process was called "autofrettage" (self-hooping) because it achieved an effect similar to that of hooping (Thomson and Mayo 1955).

The smaller (under 8-inch) guns of the 1950s American navy were monobloc guns subjected to autofrettage (NAVORD 1957, 5B2).

The two processes could be combined. The tube was first formed by centrifugal casting; then this piece was assembled together with a breech ring and a liner by means of autofrettage (DiGiulian 2023).

Manufacturing Tolerances; Windage

In the sixteenth century, windage wasn't standardized, but it was typically 0.25 inches (Sephton 2011, 82). The British later adopted the rule that the bore diameter should be $2\frac{1}{20}$th the shot diameter. In 1787, this rule was changed to $2\frac{5}{24}$th for the Blomefield pattern guns. The short-barreled carronades could be bored more accurately; bore diameter was $3\frac{5}{34}$th shot diameter (Collins, "British Cannonball Sizes"). The French, in contrast, allowed just 0.133 inches (1.6 "lines"; $\frac{1}{45}$th caliber for a 24-pounder) for heavy (18+) guns and 0.088 inches (1 line) for field guns (Douglas 1829, 74).

It should perhaps be noted that even if shot and bore were a perfect fit initially, they wouldn't necessarily stay that way. The shot would rust; the bore would be fouled. Both were subject to expansion when heated, which I would think would especially be a problem for the gun if it had been fired repeatedly. Douglas suggested that at white heat, 24-pound shot expanded by $\frac{1}{70}$th diameter, and smaller shots by less.

Quality Control

Inspection

Before a gun was accepted (and paid for) by the military, it was examined and tested. First, there was an examination for the correctness of the bore diameter and the accuracy of the bore. Initially, this evaluation was visual, with the aid of a candle or a mirror. But in late eighteenth-century France, the Gribeauvalist inspectors used a caliper gauge to measure the diameter to within 0.025 mm (Alder 2010, 150). In mid-nineteenth-century America, inspectors measured "the exact diameter of the bore at points not more than a caliber apart throughout its whole length" (Ward 1845, 46).

Cooke (1880) describes several bore inspection tools, including a searcher, a cylinder gauge, a chamber gauge, a star gauge, and a measuring staff. The "searcher" consisted of "a long staff of wood, fitted with a head of eight steel points," each with an L shape (200); these had "a tendency to spring out" that was restrained by a hoop. This tool was used "for detecting the presence of small cracks and flaws" by inserting it deep into the bore and then pulling back the hoop (with a cord?). The points sprang out, and the searcher was "slowly withdrawn, turning it at the same time." The location of any cavity found was marked on the exterior of the gun, and it was further evaluated by taking a wax impression.

The cylinder gauge was a hollow cylinder, one caliber long, turned to "the least allowed diameter of the bore," and mountable on a staff. For the gun to pass, "it must pass freely to the bottom of the bore" (Cooke 1880, 201). The chamber gauge was for similarly checking the powder chamber. The star gauge was similar to the searcher, but it had a head of four adjustable points (204), and it was used "to obtain the exact diameter of the bore" (207). The measuring staff was used to determine "the length of the bore of the gun" (202). There were additional tools for inspecting the vent (207–9), the outer profile of the gun (209–10), and the trunnions (211–13).

By the early twentieth century, there were borescopes. A rigid borescope would be something like a periscope with a magnifier and a light attachment. A flexible borescope (fiberscope) used optical fibers. These were inspired by medical and industrial endoscopes (IT 1924).

Proofing

The British proofed guns by loading them with a double charge and setting them off. The gun was then examined for cracks; this process included filling it with water to see whether it leaked (Lavery 1987, 84).

The review process was sometimes long and drawn out, as it was partially weather dependent, and it was not unheard of for gunfounders to make secret repairs rather than recast (Verbeek 2013; Brown 2001).

Barrel Wear

The fast-moving, high-pressure, hot-powder gases and the accelerating projectiles cause various forms of damage to the gun when it's fired. Erosion (by abrasion) can be uniform or irregular, resulting in furrows and cavities. The compression-relaxation cycles can fatigue the metal, resulting in micro-cracking, and cracks may widen and lengthen with time. There may be permanent bore expansion as a result of exceeding the "elastic limit." These phenomena all can, in turn, result in gas leakage and consequent loss of muzzle velocity. The worst-case scenario, of course, is catastrophic rupture.

Barrels can be inspected for deterioration in a number of ways in much the way they were inspected initially.

Rapid fire could also cause the touchhole to enlarge, as a result of corrosion by escaping gases (which included sulfuric acid). This process would reduce muzzle velocity until the touchhole was repaired (Hoskins 2003, 27).

For rifled cannons, it was reported that the erosion (increase in the diameter of the lands per round) was proportional to the ratio of the weight of the charge to the diameter of the bore, multiplied by the square of the maximum pressure. The loss in muzzle velocity, in turn, was proportional to the erosion (Manning 1919, 494ff).

The barrel wear limits the service life of the gun. Baker et al. (1841, 171) "estimated that an iron cannon will not safely bear more than one thousand two hundred discharges with the service charge, after which it should be broken up." In the 1860s, it was customary for the Union army to have a sample gun from a lot fired continuously for one thousand rounds, to prove that endurance was adequate (Benton 1862, 146, 208ff). For the World War II *Iowa*, the barrel life estimates were 290–350 (16-inch gun), 4,600 (5-inch), 9,500 (Bofors 40 mm), and 9,000 rounds (Oerlikon 20 mm) (Dramiński 2020, 19–21).

In the Union navy, "impressions of the vent and bore" were to be "taken after every ten shotted rounds in practice, and at the close of an action," with respect to "XI and IX inch guns, and all iron rifles" (U.S. Navy 1866, 75, 16).

Guns tend to wear out at the breech end first, and they may be rechambered. This process "consists of machining out the forward end of the powder chamber until the eroded metal is removed and a new forcing cone formed." It may add 40 percent to the life of the gun, but the powder charge must be increased (Miller 1921, 671).

Guns may be rebored or relined, essentially restoring their original life expectancy. "Reboring consists of turning out the entire interior of the bore to a larger diameter and rerifling." In relining, after the bore is enlarged, a liner is inserted, "in which the rifling of the original caliber is cut." The gun barrel may be shrunk over the liner, or the liner may be expanded "into the gun by hydraulic pressure." The advantage of relining is that the original caliber is retained, and thus there is no change in ammunition or range. Its disadvantage is that it requires more equipment and work ("nearly 900 hours on the … 12-inch gun") (Miller 1921, 672). Nonetheless, Hayes reported that one 14-inch gun had "been successfully relined fourteen times" (1938, 82).

Retubing is a step beyond reboring; it "consists of disassembling and building it up again around a new tube" (Miller 1921).

The choice of propellant may affect barrel wear. In the 1950s, NACO—a "cooler-burning propellant"—was shown to extend "the life of 3-inch gun barrels by a factor of eight" (Muir 1996, 106). This "Navy Cool" was a "single-base" (nitrocellulose) propellant with reduced nitration (DiGiulian 2022).

In the 1960s, it was discovered that bore erosion could be reduced by coating the inside of the bore with "Swedish additive," which contained titanium dioxide and wax (Muir 1996, 168; DiGiulian 2023b). When the *Iowa*-class battleships were reactivated during the Vietnam War, they made use of "Swedish additive," and it was "credited with at least quadrupling the liner life" (DiGiulian 2023b).

CHAPTER 4

Gunpowder
and Other Propellants

A gun accelerates a projectile in the bore by the rapid expansion of a gas. Conventionally, the gas is produced by the combustion of a fuel (gunpowder). However, there have been experimental guns using steam or compressed air.

Black powder was the original gunpowder, and even after it was eclipsed by smokeless powders as the propulsive charge, it remained in use as an ingredient of a primer or ignition charge for the main charge (see chapter 6 for its use in fuses). The hot solids produced by its combustion are more efficient than hot gases in igniting other materials (von Maltitz 2001, 27).

Black Powder Combustion (Deflagration)

In 1635, John Bate poetically described the roles of the ingredients of black powder: "The Saltpeter is the Soule, the Sulfur the Life, and Coales the Body" (Rose 1980, 545).

When black powder is ignited, the carbon in the charcoal is oxidized, producing gaseous carbon dioxide. The reaction also releases heat. Since the heated gas is confined by the gun, that results in an increase in pressure, which is what pushes the projectile out. It also stresses the barrel, so you can't use too much powder, and how much can be used depends on its burn rate.

It's time to look more closely at the chemistry and physics of the black powder combustion.

A chemical reaction may result in the release of heat (exothermic reaction) or the absorption of heat (endothermic reaction). The internal energy level of a chemical compound is called its enthalpy. The "enthalpy of reaction" (ΔH) is the summed internal energies of the products, minus the summed internal energies of the reactants for a reaction at constant pressure, and it is negative for an exothermic reaction. It is measured in a bomb calorimeter.

Combustion—the oxidation of carbon—is an exothermic reaction and yields about 418 kilojoules of heat energy per "mole" of oxygen (Schmidt-Rohr 2015). (A kilowatt-hour of electricity is 3,600 kilojoules of electrical energy. A "mole" of a chemical is the number of grams equal to the chemical's mass in grams, so for molecular oxygen, one mole is 32 grams.)

The combustion of black powder releases a lot of energy rapidly. A flame front expands from the ignition site, and the heated gaseous combustion products behind the flame front attempt to expand. Since they are largely confined (by the barrel and the projectile seated in the bore), there is an increase in pressure. In fact, what we have is a slow explosion: a deflagration. Scientists distinguish between a deflagration (an explosion in which the flame front moves more slowly than the speed of sound) and a detonation (in which it travels more quickly). High explosives (which we'll discuss when we get to shells in the next chapter) detonate rather than deflagrate, and they create higher pressures.

Combustion requires oxygen, and the bore or powder chamber of a gun doesn't contain much. Hence, gunpowder contains an internal source of oxygen: potassium nitrate. Potassium nitrate is considered an oxidizer (an oxygen source) because (1) it contains oxygen and (2) it is readily decomposable to release that oxygen. Potassium nitrate (KNO_3) has molecular weight of about 101 grams/mol and oxygen molecules (O_2) of 32, so every 101 grams of potassium nitrate can potentially provide 32 grams of molecular oxygen.

In 1825, Michel Chevreul proposed (Noble and Abel 1875, 53) that in the gun, the net chemical reaction was as follows:

$$2KNO_3 + S + 3C \rightarrow K_2S + N_2 + 3CO_2$$

Put in English, two molecules of potassium nitrate (KNO_3) react with one molecule of sulfur (S) and three of carbon I to form one molecule of potassium sulfide (K_2S), one molecule of nitrogen (N_2) and three molecules of carbon dioxide (CO_2). (If we assume that the charcoal is pure carbon [it isn't], then the reactants on the left side of the equation have the weight proportions of 74.8 percent, 11.9 percent, and 13.3 percent, respectively [von Maltitz 2001, 29].) At room temperature and pressure, potassium sulfide is a solid, while nitrogen and carbon dioxide are gases.

It is important to recognize that this does not really explain the chemical mechanism. Rather, we would expect that Chevreul's net reaction (and the more complex ones postulated by later writers) was the result of the combination of a series of reactions, sequential or simultaneous.

The result of the decomposition of one gram of black powder was "about 43 per cent by weight of permanent gases, occupying, at 0°C and [normal atmospheric] pressure, a volume of about 280 cubic centimeters," and "about 57 per cent by weight of liquid product, occupying, when in the solid form and at 0°C, a volume of about 0.3 cubic centimeters" (Noble and Abel 1875, 102).

Andrew Noble and Frederick Abel collected and analyzed the gases produced by combustion of gunpowder and found that they included (in decreasing order of volume) carbon dioxide, nitrogen, carbon monoxide, hydrogen sulfide, hydrogen, oxygen and methane (1875, 66). Carbon monoxide is the result of incomplete combustion of carbon. The final four products are explainable in that charcoal isn't just carbon; it is a complex mixture of organic compounds that also contain hydrogen and oxygen. In the pebble powder used by Noble and Abel, the charcoal constituted 14.22 percent of the gunpowder, and its breakdown was 12.12 percent carbon, 0.42 percent hydrogen, 1.45 percent oxygen, and 0.23 percent "ash" (inorganic material) (72).

In addition, there are liquid products that, once cooled by mixing with ambient air, solidify. These solid residuals were also complex, and potassium sulfide was not even the most common component—that was potassium carbonate. The solid residues also included potassium sulfate, potassium hyposulfite, and small amounts of potassium sulfocyanate, potassium nitrate, and sometimes potassium oxide (Noble and Abel 1875, Table III). If carried away by the combustion gases, they create the smoke that black powder is known for.

In 1876, Berthelot attempted to account for the complex makeup of the combustion products by postulating that more than a dozen different chemical reactions were taking place simultaneously. However, there was substantial variation in the composition of the products of combustion even when the same powder was used. Consequently, in 1880 Noble and Abel concluded that "no value whatever can be attached to any attempt to give a general chemical expression to the metamorphosis of a gunpowder of normal composition" (Noble 1906, 234).

Potassium nitrate reacts with carbon to generate potassium nitrite (KNO_2) and carbon dioxide, and the nitrite reacts with additional carbon to yield potassium carbonate, carbon dioxide and nitrogen. The total heat production is 359 kilocalories/mole (Seel 1984, 63).

What, then, is the role of sulfur? The melting point of sulfur is just 115°C, whereas that of potassium nitrate is 334°C. Thus, the heat generated by the ignition source will melt the sulfur first. At 150–180°C, sulfur reacts with hydrogen impurities in the charcoal to form hydrogen sulfide. Hydrogen sulfide, in turn, reacts with potassium nitrate at 285–290°C to produce potassium thiosulfate and nitrogen oxide, producing 66.45 kilocalories/mole (Seel 1984, 65; von Maltitz 2001, 35; Blackwood and Bowden 1952, 296). The nature of the hydrogen impurities is not entirely clear; they could be occluded hydrogen gas in the charcoal pores or perhaps oxyhydrocarbons such as aldehydes, ketones and alcohols (Ball 1964, 36; Blackwood and Bowden 1952, 297), but we know hydrogen sulfide is produced. And charcoal releases its volatile constituents at temperatures exceeding 100°C (Russell 2015, 32).

As the temperature increases further, to 350°C, a reaction becomes possible between sulfur and potassium nitrate (Seel 1984, 62). Sulfur may also react with potassium nitrite, an intermediate in the reaction of potassium nitrate and carbon, yielding potassium thiosulfate and nitrogen oxide (64).

This list hardly exhausts the reactions that take place during black powder combustion. Nitrogen dioxide may react with hydrogen sulfide, regenerating the sulfur and producing a dinitrogen oxide. It may also react with sulfur, yielding sulfur dioxide and nitrogen. And sulfur dioxide may react with potassium nitrate to yield potassium sulfate and nitrogen dioxide. The first two reactions are endothermic, but the third is strongly exothermic (Blackwood and Bowden 1952, 305–6).

Black Powder Ingredients

The discussion of the ingredients of black powder in books on naval warfare is usually perfunctory. This lack of information is unfortunate, for two reasons. First, the difficulties in sourcing two of the ingredients affected national preparedness. Second, those difficulties (combined with those involved in processing) meant that the final product was variable in its properties, thus making it more difficult to hit and damage the enemy.

Sulfur

Sulfur (brimstone) could be obtained either as elemental sulfur or from sulfide ores. In 1637, Song Yingxing, in his encyclopedia *Tiangong kaiwu*, described how sulfur was refined by making a pile of pyrites mixed with coal, surrounding the pile with packed earth to form a furnace with a hole at the top, covering the hole with an inverted earthenware bowl, heating the pile, and condensing the sulfur vapor on the inside of the bowl. His illustration even shows a pipe leading the sulfur condensate from a hole in the rim of the bowl to a receptacle (Schafer 2011, 208–10; Golas 1999, 177–81).

But that wasn't the only method known to the Chinese. In 1696, after the imperial gunpowder store in Fuzhou exploded, local officials were desperate to replace the lost five hundred thousand pounds. Knowing that sulfur was found on nearby Taiwan, they sent Yu Yonghe, a scholar of adventurous disposition, to lead an expedition to buy sulfur-rich material from the aborigines and then refine it. There were sulfur hot springs of volcanic origin in northern Taiwan, and Yonghe extracted the sulfur from the nearby dirt by heating it in a wok containing oil. The temperature had to be controlled so the sulfur melted but didn't boil away (Golas 1999, 177–81; Keliher 2003, 5–6, 155, 166). Elemental sulfur melts at 115.21°C and boils at 444.6°C.

The principal sources of sulfur for European powdermakers were Iceland and Italy (Sicily and Romagna).

The Icelandic sulfur trade was originally in the hands of German (Bremen, Hamburg and Lübeck) and English merchants, and it is believed to have begun in the thirteenth century (Mehler 2015, 201–2). In 1561, the trade was declared a Danish royal monopoly, but there was "intensive smuggling" (205). Sulfur mining continued into the nineteenth century (194).

"The richest sulphur deposits in Iceland lie along the Mid-Atlantic Ridge where active volcanoes are concentrated" (Mehler 2015, 195). Hydrogen sulfide gas is emitted from *solfatares* and reacts with the oxygen in the air to form elemental sulfur and sulfur dioxide gas (193).

The principal mining area was in northeastern Iceland. The most productive mine was near Reykjahlíðnámur. The sulfur was refined at Húsavík and also exported from that port. A secondary mining area was Krýsuvík on the Reykjanes Peninsula in southwestern Iceland; its export port was Straumur (Mehler 2015, 195). A "map of northern Europe created by the Swedish ... cartographer Olaus Magnus ... printed in 1539" depicts Iceland; "a barrel labelled SULVUR [*sic*] is drawn on the southern coast, roughly in the area of Krýsuvík" (197).

The sulfur was heated in pans, and when it "started to melt, train or fish oil was added." The impurities adhered to the oil and were skimmed off the top of the pan. The sulfur was poured into cold molds and then removed as solid blocks. Sulfur was refined in Iceland until 1562, when a sulfur house was built near the royal castle in Copenhagen, Denmark (Mehler 2015, 200).

Sulfur was first mined in Sicily in Roman times. (Obviously, it wasn't used to make gunpowder back then.) The Sicilian sulfur is mostly "disseminated in cellular limestone" but also occurs in "bands of pure sulphur up to one inch in thickness." The limestone is "interstratified with bituminous shale and gypsum." The "sulphur content [of the limestone] ranges from 12 to 50 percent and averages 26 percent" (Bateman 1950, 176; Hunt 1915, 577).

Italian sulfur mining technology evolved over the centuries. Initially, surface deposits were mined by melting the sulfur in an open stack (*calcarelle*). Since wood was scarce, some of the sulfur was burned to provide the heat to melt the remainder. This method wasted two-thirds of the sulfur. In the nineteenth century, the Sicilians employed "melting furnaces called *calcarelli* and *calcaroni*," the latter being the larger of the two. These furnaces were lined with firebrick. Their main advantage was that they could process more sulfur ore, but there may have been somewhat less waste, too (because of the insulating effect of the firebrick) (FHTD 2016; Kutney 2007, 47–48).

In 1880, Robert Gill invented a multichambered furnace. This device was more efficient than its predecessors, as the heat from one chamber was used to preheat and ignite the sulfur in the succeeding one. This process reduced wastage to 7–10 percent (FHTD 2016).

It is likely that Spain obtained some of its sulfur from the pyrite and chalcopyrite (copper iron sulfide) deposits of the Rio Tinto in Huelva (southern Spain). These deposits have been "mined for 3,000 years" (Bateman 1950, 523). Smith (2021) suggests another domestic source: Las Minas in Albacete (southeastern Spain). However, Sicily was under Spanish control from the fourteenth century until its absorption into the Kingdom of Italy in 1861. Hence, Sicilian sulphur would have also been available.

Beginning in 1561, gunpowder was manufactured in England at a factory known as "Waltham Abbey." At least in the nineteenth century, it imported sulfur from Sicily. "As imported, the sulfur contains from 3 to 4 per cent of earthy impurities." It was further purified at Waltham Abbey by distillation (FHTD 2016; Simpson 1873, 140).

When the price of Sicilian sulphur was excessive, or it was otherwise unavailable, powdermakers turned to other sources, such as Iceland, or to domestic pyrites. The Confederacy, for example, treated pyrite with nitric acid (Johnston and Johnston 1990, 128).

In 1883, Carl Friedrich Claus patented a process for oxidizing hydrogen sulfide gas, yielding elemental sulfur; four years later, Alexander and C.F. Chance combined the Claus process with the LeBlanc soda ash synthesis by converting calcium sulfide waste to hydrogen sulfide. (The LeBlanc process used sulfuric acid as a reagent.) Hydrogen sulfide is also sometimes found in natural gas (FHTD 2016a).

The geology of the Gulf Coast, including Louisiana, is characterized by the presence of numerous salt domes. These form when salt deposits are uplifted by some geological mechanism. The caprock above the salt domes may contain sulfur deposits (as of 1950, there were 12 proven sulfur deposits out of 300 known Gulf Coast salt domes [Bateman 1950, 793]), and the pierced sediments are bent, possibly forming oil and gas traps. The first such deposit discovered in Louisiana couldn't be mined by normal means, as it was "beneath quicksand" (*ibid.*), but in 1894 Herman Frasch realized that one could drill into the sulfur deposit and use a triple concentric pipe to pump superheated water and hot air down and bring molten sulfur up. If there was oil in the vicinity, it could be burned to heat the water. Commercial production began at Sulphur Mines, Louisiana, in 1903.

In 1923, the U.S. Navy ammunition manual declared, "Up to a few years ago sulphur was obtained from the Sicilian sulphur mines.... More recently it has been obtained to some extent from coal gas, but by far the best and most abundant source is the sulphur fields of Louisiana.... Due to the cheapness of the product obtained in Louisiana, Sicilian sulphur could not compete with it, and the mines would have been abandoned except for the action of the Italian Government in supporting the industry" (U.S. Navy 1923, 25–26).

Charcoal

If wood is heated to a high temperature, while minimizing its exposure to air, it is pyrolyzed (decomposed), forming charcoal. Charcoal is not pure carbon; 70 percent carbon is usually considered optimal (Howard 2006, 24; Rose 1980, 553; but see Sasse 1981, 11).

Charcoal itself is an extremely variable component, depending on the species of tree and individual variations. The latter exist "due to such factors as weather, soil conditions, the age of the tree and the part of the tree from which the wood is taken" (von Maltitz 2001, 33). The charring (carbonization) temperature affects the ignition temperature. While charcoal carbonized at a lower temperature will also ignite and burn at a lower temperature, it more readily absorbs moisture (*ibid.*). The navy ammunition manual recommended a carbonization temperature of 280°C (U.S. Navy 1923, 26).

Henry Manwayring's *Seaman's Dictionary* (1644) said that the best charcoal was "made of the lightest wood." Norton's *The Gunner* (1628, 144) advocated use of "Willow, or Alder coales wel burned." At the nineteenth-century Waltham Abbey operation, the charcoal was made from "willow, alder, and dogwood." The wood was "cut in the spring of the year when the sap is rising, as then the bark is readily removed" (Simpson 1873, 140). The 1923 U.S. Navy ammunition manual generally advised the use of soft wood, "such as the alder, dogwood, yew and willow," with willow being favored in the United States. The most complete list of woods used for gunpowder charcoal is that of Geoff Smith (2021a).

Smith notes, "The defining physical characteristic of charcoal is that it retains, to a large extent, the cellular structure of the wood from which it originated resulting in a very large surface area, up to 4000 sq metres per gram." Robert Howard adds, "The softer, less dense woods give a more complex and larger maze than the denser hardwoods." They are also "not as difficult to pulverize" (2006, 24).

In 1783, "cylinder powder" was invented (or reinvented), although it didn't come into common use until 1803 (Rodger 1997, 421; Rose 1980, 550). It incorporated a better grade of charcoal. The wood was placed in cast iron cylinders and heated over a stove, rather than charred in a kiln or pit (*ibid.*; Douglas 1829, 201). This method permitted reducing the standard charge to one-third the weight of the ball for ordinary guns, and a mere one-twelfth for carronades (Lavery 1987, 84). Gunners were also instructed to use the cylinder ("Red") powder for distance shooting, reserving "Blue" (old) or "White" (an old-new mixture) for a "close fight" (Morris 2010, 220).

Smith has argued that as early as the sixteenth century, gunpowder charcoal was already produced in a sealed container, quoting Peter Whitehorne (1573) to the effect that the wood, cut into little pieces, was placed "in a greate earthern pot, or other vessell of yron or brasse." Smith speculates that as the demand for gunpowder grew, manufacturers chose to use "stack" (pit, heap) charcoal, which could be produced more quickly and cheaply. The wood was either placed in a pit or heaped up on the ground (Rose 1980, 550), after which it was set on fire and then covered up to limit oxygen intake.

When charcoal was once again manufactured in heated cylinders, it was with some refinements, such as more uniform preparation of the wood and heating at a more controlled temperature (Smith 2021a).

Saltpeter

Another ingredient of gunpowder is potassium nitrate (niter). The term "saltpeter" is sometimes used to refer collectively to several nitrates, but here we will use it as a synonym for potassium nitrate.

"Natural" saltpeter is ultimately a product of the nitrogen cycle. The atmosphere is about 78 percent nitrogen. Certain bacteria (including the free-living *Azotobacter* and the plant symbiote *Rhizobia*) take up nitrogen and combine it with hydrogen to produce ammonia ("nitrogen fixation"). Other bacteria (including *Nitrosomonas*, *Nitrosospira*, and *Nitrosococcus*) oxidize ammonia to the nitrite ion (NO_2^-). Still another group (*Nitrospira*, *Nitrobacter*, *Nitrococcus*, and *Nitrospina*) oxidize nitrite ions to nitrate ions (NO_3^-). The overall conversion of ammonia to nitrate is called nitrification (Bernhard 2010). Nitrates are formed in soil when organic material containing ammonia (or a precursor) is deposited on soil that contains the appropriate nitrifying organisms, under conditions favorable to their growth and metabolism. (The organic material in question may be decomposing animal or plant matter, or perhaps human or animal waste.)

All nitrate salts are soluble, and in general they are more soluble than, say, phosphate salts. So if the nitrate-containing soil is in a region where there is no dry season, the nitrates will tend to be leached out and end up in the ocean. However, if that soil is in a region with a long dry season for part of the year, during that period, water will evaporate from the soil. If the soil has suitable permeability, water carrying the nitrate (and other) salts is wicked up by capillary action. The less soluble salts precipitate out first, below the surface. The nitrate salts precipitate last and remain as a crust on the top of the soil (Smith 2020). This is in fact what happens in the Bihar region of India, and in the nineteenth century the salt-peter was mined where the superficial soil contained at least 3–5 percent nitrate (Hutchinson 1917, 2).

It is debatable whether any saltpeter (other than that found in bat guano) can be termed "natural." The organic waste from which it develops is ultimately the result of human activity.

However, we can distinguish between saltpeter that is biogenic and that syn-thesized by the reaction of pure industrial chemicals. And we may also distinguish between the mere harvesting of biogenic saltpeter and deliberate efforts to foster its formation.

Saltpeter was traded by India for centuries. "The Portuguese entered the inter-Asian saltpeter trade, in a limited way, in the sixteenth century" (Frey 2009, 508). "Indian saltpeter was first shipped to Europe by the VOC [*Verenigde Oostin-dische Compagnie*, the Dutch East India Company] in 1618" (512). Soon thereaf-ter, it faced competition from the "Company of London Merchants, precursor to the English East India Company" (508). The Dutch remained the main European importer until the mid-eighteenth century, when the East India Company achieved military and political control of Bihar (509).

Europeans also sought to obtain saltpeter domestically, both before and after the trade with India began. As gunpowder weapons became more important, on both land and sea, saltpeter became a vital strategic material. In 1600, Robert Cecil wrote that "there is infinite security to her majesty and the state, that the land hath means in itself to defend itself" (Cressy 2013, 72).

There were two basic approaches: scour the places where it might form natu-rally, or construct artificial "nitraries."

Biringuccio said that he saw saltpeter "extracted in Tuscany from a natural soil" (1990, Book II, Chapter 8, 111). If you were lucky, crude saltpeter was found as an efflorescence on walls in cellars or in caves. Such blooms could be "surpris-ingly pure, often greater than 95% KNO_3" (Kaiho 2014, 198). But more likely the saltpeter-containing matter was dug from old dunghills or "out of floors in cellars, vaults, stables, ox-stalls, goat or sheep cotes, pigeon houses, or … the lowermost rooms in other houses" (Cressy 2013, 16, 20).

From the early sixteenth until the mid-seventeenth century, England's strat-egy toward securing a domestic saltpeter supply was primarily hunt-and-gather. In 1515, Hans Wolf was authorized "to go from shire to shire to find a place where there is stuff to make saltpeter of" (Cressy 2013, 43). The commissioned saltpetermen were allowed to enter private property, break ground, and take wood for use as fuel and carts for transporting the product (44).

"The Armada crisis accelerated the English saltpeter enterprise" (Cressy 2013, 62). In 1625, "owners of dovecotes and stables were forbidden to lay down flooring of stone, brick, plank or gravel" (98). Sometimes the digging was so deep that it "endan-gered the foundations" of the building (99). Nonetheless, in 1627, only one-third of the British saltpeter requirement was met domestically (90). Public resistance to the encroachments was probably a factor; it was not until 1630 that the saltpeter-men promised "not to dig where people lay in bed" (107), and only in 1642 were they forbidden to enter "dwelling houses" (128). And there was reluctance on the government's part to push too hard, given the "social costs" (67).

In early seventeenth-century Sweden, there was a somewhat different approach: "Each homestead (*hemman*) in the vicinity of saltpetre works had to deliver four barrels of soil, one barrel of sheep's dung, half a barrel of ashes, three loads of wood, and two sheaves of straw" (Kaiserfeld 2006, 144).

Around 1400, Conrad Kyeser described a saltpeter plantation, which consisted of a pit or a big clay pot containing a mixture of soil and burnt-out grass. This blend was

Saltpeter plantation as depicted by Lazarus Ercker in *Beschreibung, Allerfurnemisten Mineralischen Ertzt vnnd Bergkwercks arten* (1598), page 133.

covered with alternating layers of a "salty liquid, urine or wine" and "crushed lime" (Gruntman 2004, 17). In 1574, the Bohemian minemaster Lazarus Ercker published a treatise that depicted artificial saltpeter beds, laid out in rows of heaped earth (Cressy 2013, 22). The "semi-artificial" production of saltpeter came to be practiced in "Switzerland, France, Germany, Sweden," and other countries (Aikman 1894, 164).

In the mid-eighteenth century, Sweden introduced "saltpeter barns": "wooden sheds where soil—mixed with manure, stale urine, composted wastes or even carcasses—was stored in oblong pyramidal heaps." The soil "was turned every fortnight" (Kaiserfeld 2009, 7). This approach proved more productive than the traditional system. The soil from the barns could be productively processed every two to four years, whereas saltpeter from "natural" soil was harvested, at best, every four years in southern Sweden and every six in the north (*ibid.*).

In the late eighteenth century, France faced the fact that its access to Indian saltpeter was controlled by Great Britain. In response, it established a commission for reviewing proposals for improving saltpeter manufacture. In 1775, the commission classified the "arrangements for induced putrefaction … into vaults, walls, trenches and beds…. The conventional form … consisted of a bed, or heap, of triangular cross section, placed under a protecting roof but otherwise open to the air" (Multhauf 1971, 169).

According to Antoine Lavoisier, a member of the commission, a nitrary at Villers-Cotterets had been operating for 140 years. "Beds of unspecified size were formed of earth from which saltpeter had already been extracted." (Note that this previous extraction would guarantee the presence of the nitrifying bacteria.) "After being allowed to stand three years, the earth was recomposed to a thickness of 8 feet with alternate layers of cow manure, and every eight months the mass was mixed and the layers reestablished" (Multhauf 1971, 172). The mixing would have helped keep the bacteria oxygenated. Lavoisier published instructions for the artificial fabrication of saltpeter in 1777, but it appears that most of France's domestic production still came from scraping building walls and scouring stables (*ibid.*).

The French mode of artificial saltpeter production was considered capable of yielding, after two years' cultivation, five pounds of saltpeter from 1,000 pounds of earth (Aikman 1894, 165; cp. Hager 2009, 16).

While they were aware of the association of saltpeter with decomposing organic matter, powdermakers did not know until 1877 that this was the work of microorganisms (Aikman 1894). The bacteria are active only when wet, but, as noted above, nitrate can be leached away. Hence "nitrate beds are commonly roofed over to protect them in rainy climates but are regularly moistened, commonly with urine" (Smith 2020).

The urine is valuable because it contains urea. Urease-producing bacteria convert urea into ammonia, and the nitrification bacteria will convert some of the ammonia to nitrate. Since there will be a mixture of cations (potassium, calcium, ammonium, sodium, etc.) in the "earth," a mixture of nitrates will form. (When dissolved in water, the nitrate salts almost completely dissociate into their component ions, and the different salts are no longer discernible. However, the different nitrate salts will appear when the water evaporates [Addiscott 2005, 15].)

The nitrification bacteria are aerobic (require oxygen), and therefore the bed has to be porous (you need the right kind of soil) and turned over periodically. They also have particular pH and temperature requirements.

Because of the dependence on decomposition of human and animal waste, nitraries had to be "close to populated areas." The process was also "slow and labor-intensive" (Lappalainen 2021). One could not ignore the need for saltpeter during peacetime and quickly ramp up saltpeter production if war broke out.

Biringuccio's *Pirotechnia* (1540) described how to refine the saltpeter. He mixed manurial earth with quicklime and "cerris or oak ashes." Quicklime (calcium oxide) tends to react with water to form calcium carbonate, and it may have been added to neutralize excess acidity. The wood ashes contain potash (potassium carbonate). This substance undergoes a double displacement reaction with calcium nitrate, forming potassium nitrate and calcium carbonate. Other sources of potassium (e.g., alum or cream of tartar) may also be used. In 1561, Gerard Honricke warned English entrepreneurs that without adding wood ash (with oak preferred), "the saltpetre cannot be made at all" (Buchanan 2014, 65).

Biringuccio placed his mixture in tubs with a hole in the bottom and allowed water to percolate through it. This water, he said, "carries with it all of the substance and virtue of the saltpeter that was in the earth." This is a leaching step and takes advantage of the great solubility of nitrates relative to, for example, calcium carbonate, sulfate and phosphate.

This filtrate was placed in a copper kettle "bricked in at the top" and "boiled very slowly." It was allowed to cool and settle, and an "earthy thick sediment" was removed. This substance was put to the boil again. After several iterations, the sediment was allowed to drain and dry (Biringuccio 1990, Book X, Chapter 1, 404ff). Biringuccio also speaks of adding more wood ashes, as well as rock alum.

The timing of removal of the "sediment" is actually important. The closest Biringuccio comes to pointing this fact out is to say that the water is "reduced to the point where it congeals" (1990, Book X, Chapter 1, 407).

If a mixture of nitrates is brought to a boil and then allowed to cool, potassium nitrate will be the first to crystallize out as the temperature declines. This process is called separation by fractional crystallization.

Table 4–1: Nitrate Solubility in Water

Salt	$g/100g\ H_2O$ at 20°C	$g/100g\ H_2O$ at 40°C	$g/100g\ H_2O$ at 100°C
Potassium nitrate	31.66	63.9	245.2
Magnesium nitrate (hexahydrate)	70.07	81.8	?
Sodium nitrate	88.3	104.9	176
Calcium nitrate (tetrahydrate)	129.39	196	†363
Ammonium nitrate	187.7	283	1000

(MilliporeSigma 2023; †Wikipedia)

Note that the solubility of potassium nitrate is very strongly temperature dependent, even when compared to other nitrates. This quality is even more evident when it is compared to other salts, such as sodium chloride (35.9 at 20°C; 39 at 100°C) (MGRG 2014).

Attempts have been made to replicate early methods of saltpeter production (MGRG 2004; MGRG 2013; MGRG 2014).

During the runup to the American Revolution, Benjamin Franklin, Benjamin Rush, John Adams, Thomas Paine and other patriots searched for information on saltpeter manufacturing, disseminated their findings, and even experimented with the process. Massachusetts produced forty-five tons of saltpeter by midsummer 1776. However, the domestic production remained small and unimportant. By 1777, the rebels were receiving saltpeter from the French, Spanish and Dutch, and, in a few cases, they even brought it in from Bengal themselves (Cressy 2013, 155–65).

In the American Civil War, the South's access to foreign saltpeter was cut off by the Union blockade, so it set up nitraries and also harvested cave saltpeter (Whisonant 2001).

Biringuccio wrote, "Saltpeter is also generated in moist caves" (1990, Book II, Chapter 8, 111). In 1861, Major George Rains of the Confederate Corps of Artillery and Ordnance published "Notes on Making Saltpetre from the Earth of the Caves." Numerous caves were worked for saltpeter during the Civil War (Whisonant 2001).

It was once thought that cave saltpeter necessarily originated from bat guano. Most bats feed on insects. Insects, being animals, have a high protein content, and proteins are composed of amino acids, which all contain nitrogen. Bat guano from Missouri caves is reported to have had a nitrogen content ranging as high as 10.44 percent (Albrecht 1981, 6), and modern commercial bat guano (sold as a fertilizer) is 3–8.5 percent nitrogen (Schnug et al. 2018). In fresh guano, the nitrogen is in organic form (e.g., urea), and decomposition converts the organic nitrogen (in urea and insectile chitin and arthropodin) to ammonia and nitrate. The level of nitrate in cave guano is relatively low, which is probably attributable to nitrate being carried away by water as the guano aged (5). Hill (1981, 256–57) attributes cave saltpeter primarily to the transfer of surface soil ammonia through seeping groundwater to the cave, where it is acted on by nitrifying bacteria to produce nitrate. Nonetheless, in Arkansas, the Confederates specifically collected bat guano and refined saltpeter from it (Johnston and Johnston 1990, 127), and there is evidence for in situ transformation of organic matter to nitrate in Upper Mississippi Valley cave deposits (Brick 2013, 97).

In the twentieth century, potassium nitrate was usually produced through the reaction of a potassium source (chloride, sulfate, hydroxide, carbonate, or bicarbonate) with a nitrate source (nitric acid or sodium, magnesium, calcium, ammonium or aluminum nitrate). The reaction of potassium chloride (from salt or brine deposits) with sodium nitrate (from the Chilean beds) was known in the 1850s and was the dominant approach in the 1930s (Whittaker and Lundstrom 1934, 2, 15).

Black Powder Manufacture

Ingredient Processing

Braddock (1832, 40–63) compares the practices in Madras, India, with those at Waltham Abbey. He sets forth the following steps: pulverizing, weighing and mixing the ingredients, "incorporation" (compaction), granulation, pressing, glazing, drying and barreling.

Biringuccio refers to several different approaches to compounding gunpowder. You could grind the three ingredients together. Or you could grind each ingredient separately and then combine them. The powder needed to be ground while moist enough "so that it sticks together when squeezed in the hand," lest one run the risk of igniting it accidentally (1990, 413–15).

But ultimately the powder needed to be dried. "Powder should be about only 1 percent water." It could be sun dried or dried in a house "heated by a stove fired from the exterior." Howard comments, "Sometimes the powder was ground dry and drying was not needed. This economy in steps was offset by the loss of powder makers" (Howard 1975, 17, 19).

In later practice, there was some reduction in risk by mixing and grinding the sulfur and charcoal first, using a ball mill. It was only when the saltpeter was added that there was an explosion risk (Howard 1975, 14).

Powder was first corned (formed into grains) by forcing it through "a punched parchment sieve." Later, powder was compressed with a hand press (late eighteenth century) or a hydraulic press (mid-nineteenth century), and the resulting slabs were broken up with a hammer (later a chipping machine) and fed into a corning (graining) mill, which ground down the pieces by passing them between pairs of rollers (Howard 1975, 17, 21).

Powdermakers experimented with a variety of grain sizes and shapes, seeking the best burning characteristics.

With the relatively large grains used by artillery, sharp corners resulted in "irregular ignition." Hence, the powder was rotated in a barrel ("dusting") to make the grains more spherical. The grains could also be glazed by rotating them with a glazing agent such as powdered graphite. This process made the grains more resistant to moisture (Crawford 2021, 71–72).

The resulting grains were sorted, based on grain size, using sieves. For example, in 1845, the United States Ordnance Department wanted grains of 0.085–0.10 inches for "large bore artillery" and 0.07–0.085 inches for "small bore artillery." The smallest-size powder was used "for pistols and filler for shells" or recycled (Crawford 2021, 71).

The risk of explosion strongly affected the design of powder mills. The steps of the operation were performed in different buildings, widely separated, to reduce the potential loss. The building might be designed with three heavy walls (thus directing the explosion in the fourth direction) (Howard 1975) or with four heavy walls and a light roof. Within the building, precautions were taken to avoid sparks.

Ingredient Proportions

In H. Beam Piper's classic "multiple universe" novel, *Lord Kalvan of Otherwhen*, Calvin Morrison is accidentally "transposed" to an alternate timeline dominated by a theocracy whose power depends on its possession of the "fireseed" secret. But Morrison is a military history buff and remembers "saltpeter was seventy-five percent,

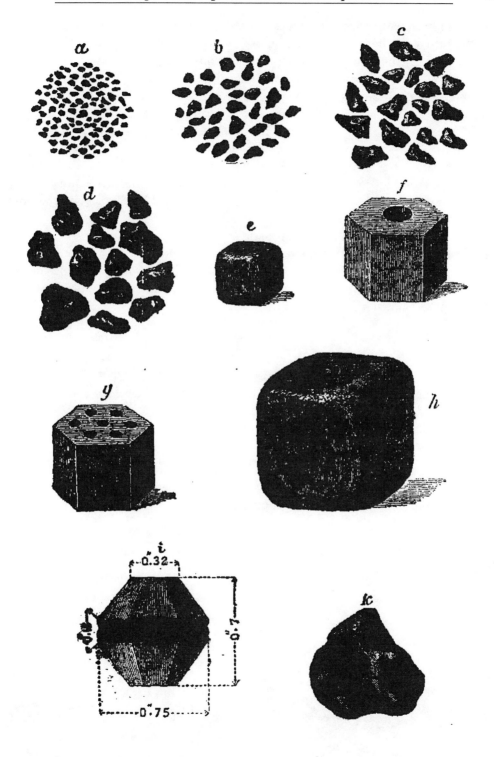

The figure shows "the relative size and shapes of [black powder grains], except" e–h "are half-size to save space." Powder a "is for small arms, all the others are for cannon of various sizes." (Figure 1 from EB 1911, "Gunpowder," page 726).

charcoal fifteen, sulfur ten." That was, indeed, a popular formula in the late eighteenth century, but hardly the only one.

In the early modern period, there was no consensus as to the proper formula for gunpowder (black powder). Just one master gunner, Peter Whitehorne (1560), presented twenty different recipes, with saltpeter content of 16–84 percent, charcoal 8–64 percent, and sulfur 8–28 percent (Walton 1999, 123). In 1647, the formula of 66.6 percent saltpeter, 16.6 percent charcoal, and 16.6 percent sulfur was used in Britain. By 1781, the proportions were 75–15–10. Other formulae included 52.2–26.1–21.7 (Germany 1596), 68.3–23.2–8.5 (Denmark 1608), 75.6–13.6–10.8 (France 1650), and 73–17–10 (Sweden 1697) (EB 1911, "Gunpowder"). Even in the nineteenth century, different countries had different preferences, with saltpeter 70–80 percent, charcoal 11–18.5 percent, and sulfur 9.5–13 percent (Beauchant 1828, 149).

Data on the efficacy of different proportions are scarce. The Medieval Gunpowder Research Group (2002) studied the effect of variations in saltpeter content in simple gunpowder mixtures on the muzzle velocity obtained with a replica of the fourteenth-century Loshult gun (firing a 184-gram ball with a charge of 50 grams). The results are shown in Table 4–2.

Table 4–2: Muzzle Velocity versus Powder Composition, Loshult Gun

Powder	Potassium Nitrate	Sulfur	Charcoal	Muzzle Velocity (m/s)
Rouen	50%	25%	25%	110
Lilly	55.6%	22.2%	22.2%	126
Marcus Graecus	66.7%	11.1%	22.2%	133
Rothenberg	75%	12.5%	12.5%	142

In the early nineteenth century, the Military Board at Madras compared the ranges achieved by a variety of mortars (two shown below), each charged with eight different gunpowder formulations (four shown below), with the results listed in Table 4–3.

Table 4–3: Range versus Powder Composition, Mortars

				Powder			
				1	2	7	8
			KNO_3	66.67	80	75	75
			Charcoal	20	15	15	15
			Sulfur	13.33	5	10	10
Gun (elev 45 degrees)	Shell (lbs)	Powder (lbs)		"Medium" (average?) Range (yards)			
13-inch iron mortar	200	9		2,246	2,395	2,449	2,386
8-inch iron mortar	64	1		589	662	671	738

(Braddock 1832, 35–36)

The powder formulation 7 was "His Majesty's cannon powder" (1813) and 8 the corresponding musket powder—hence a different grain size despite having the same proportions. Formulations 1 and 2 were the most extreme variations tested. Note that 7 and 8 outperformed 1 and 2 (as well as 3–6, not shown), but 7 was best in the 13-inch mortar and 8 in the 8-inch mortar.

Benton (1862, 42) sets forth the effect of varying the proportions of sulfur and charcoal—each between 0 and 60 parts, while holding the saltpeter (nitre) at 60 parts—on the velocity of combustion in inches per second. This is the rate of movement of the surface of combustion, measured in the direction perpendicular to that surface. The rate reached a maximum (0.51) with 11 parts charcoal and 8 parts sulfur (data for 12 parts charcoal and 8 parts sulfur, corresponding to the 75–15–10 formula, were not reported).

Ulrich Bretscher provided a three-dimensional graph showing the variation in muzzle energy (in joules), as calculated from measurement of the velocity of a patched 17.3-gram lead ball, roughly one yard from the muzzle of .58 caliber (14.7-mm) Enfield rifle given a 2-gram charge. Note that in his graph, the saltpeter is fixed at 100 parts, and the other ingredients were varied (coal 0–30; sulfur 0–24), and all parts are by weight. A broad peak of 400–450 joules/gram, centered (judged by eye) on 20 parts charcoal and 8 parts sulfur, was observed—this result corresponds to a 78.125–15.625–6.250 formula.

Brown and Rugunanan (1989) tested mixtures resulting from adding sulfur to a 12.5 percent charcoal/87.5 percent potassium nitrate composition. Sulfur was added in sufficient amounts to bring it to as high as 30 percent of the final mixture, in 5 percent increments. The most heat was produced and the maximum temperature (1350°C) reached at 10 percent sulfur; the maximum burning rate was at 20 percent sulfur. In the absence of sulfur, the maximum temperature was only 900°C and the burning rate was about one-fifth of that achieved with 20 percent sulfur.

Gunpowder Geometry

Grain Size

Two principal types of powder were available to Henry VIII's navy, "serpentine" and "corned." They were distinguished primarily by grain size. The serpentine was the weaker (and cheaper) of the two.

We have no exact measurements for serpentine, but William Bourne, in *The Art of Shooting in Great Ordnaunce*, said that it should be "as fine as sand and as soft as flour," and Henry Manwayring's *Seaman's Dictionary* compared it to "dust" (Robins 1742, xxxvi).

The "corned" powder was formed into larger particles. It should be noted that while in the United States the term "corn" refers specifically to maize (a New World plant that was part of the "Columbian Exchange"), in Europe it is a generic term for a cereal grain. Hence one cannot assume that the size of the grains of corned powder was similar to that of a kernel of maize (which, I must add, was smaller in the fifteenth century than a modern kernel). The size of the grains could be controlled by sieving.

Moving forward in time to the Elizabethan navy, referring to a 1562 offer to

sell powder to the Crown, Oppenheim comments that "corn, or large grain, powder was used for small arms; serpentine for the heavy guns, but the latter was going
out of use at sea" (1896, 159n5). Nonetheless, in 1577 the *Triumph* carried 750 pounds
of corned powder and 4,470 of serpentine, while the *Victory* had 600 of corned and
4,347 of serpentine (155).

By 1625, "corned" powder was common (Lavery 1987, 135). In 1644, Sir Henry
Manwayring (*Seaman's Dictionary*, "Powder") said that serpentine powder was
"never taken to sea ... both because it is of a small force, and also for that it will, with
the air of the sea, quickly drie and lose its force" (Hime 1904, 180). Likewise, Sir William Monson's *Naval Tracts* (written in 1635–1643) declares that it is "weak, and will
not keep at sea" (Churchill et al. 1704, 344). Robert Norton commented, "Often times
in forts, but usually at Sea, powder cannot be kept so farre from humid vapors, but
that it decayeth the same, and maketh it of little, and sometimes of no use without
renewing it" (1628, 146).

Corned powder was stronger than serpentine; how much stronger depends on
the source consulted, but Henry Hime cites Conrad von Schongau's 1429 *Firebook*
to the effect that "2 lbs of corned did the same work as 3 lbs of serpentine powder"
(1904, 182). The same rule of thumb is given by William Bourne (Robins 1742, xxxvi)
and by Thomas Smith (1628, 38). Norton (1628, 53) presented a table showing English
ordnance and indicating the appropriate charges of serpentine or corned powder.
For the 30-pdr demi-cannon, it was 20 of serpentine or 14 of corned, and for the
15-pdr whole culverin, 14 of serpentine or 10 of corned.

It was also hard to ram serpentine powder down to the right degree of compression. According to Bourne (1587), "The powder rammed in too hard ... it will be long
before the peece goeth off ... the powder too loose ... will make the shotte to come
short of the mark" (Hime 1904, 181).

The "small force" of serpentine powder was an advantage until cannons were
cast strongly enough to withstand the pressures generated by burning corned
powder. In 1560, Whitehorne said that if corned powder—then used in handguns—"should be used in pieces of ordnance, without great discretion, it would
quickly break or marre them" (Hime 1904, 183; Baldwin 2014).

The "air of the sea" that Manwayring referred to contains moisture. While
potassium nitrate itself is only slightly hygroscopic (i.e., tending to absorb water
from the surroundings), calcium nitrate is highly hygroscopic and is a possible con-
taminant of period saltpeter.

Deliquescence is the "process by which a substance absorbs moisture from the
atmosphere until it dissolves in the absorbed water and forms a solution" (*Britannica Online*). "Relative humidity" is the ratio of the current water vapor content of
the air to its maximum water vapor content (which increases with air temperature).
The "deliquescent relative humidity" (DRH) at 298°K is 92–94 percent for potassium nitrate, but only 49–56 percent for $Ca(NO_3)2 \cdot 4H_2O$ ("nitrocalcite") (Peng et al.
2022), the "stable" tetrahydrate form of calcium nitrate. The other forms of calcium
nitrate have even lower DRH values: anhydrous (9 percent), dihydrate (13 percent)
and trihydrate (22 percent) (Stahlbuhk 2015).

Charcoal is also hygroscopic, but its ability to absorb moisture is heavily dependent on carbonization temperature (Dias et al. 2016), and the pulverization process would also have reduced its hygroscopicity.

The chemist Geoff Smith has challenged the assertion that water absorption was more of a problem with serpentine powder than with corned powder. He acknowledged that a "finely divided powder has more surface area than the same mass" in the form of larger grains, but he argued that "contained in a barrel, the exposed surface is tiny compared with corned powder where air can circulate freely between the grains" (2019, n.p.).

It is certainly reasonable to hypothesize that air would circulate less freely in a fine-grained powder than a coarse-grained one, thus reducing the rate of water absorption per unit surface area, but whether this effect would balance out the increased surface area of the fine-grained powder is a question that can be settled only by experiment.

There is evidence that corned powder in barrels can likewise absorb deleterious amounts of moisture. Volo and Volo (2003, 155) assert that in 1778, the British army suffered "a severe shortage" of powder due to it "being stored aboard ship in the damp hold too long." That was, given the date, corned powder, although if it were musket powder, it would have been a relatively fine version.

Smith contends that there is an "absence of contemporary evidence" of water absorption ruining serpentine powder, but I think that claim is contradicted by Manwayring, Monson and Norton, all of whom agreed that it spoiled more quickly at sea. (Although why Manwayring said that the sea air would "drie" the powder is a mystery to me.)

Admittedly, Smith is right to question some of the other published criticisms of serpentine powder. For example, Hime states that "being merely a loose mechanical mixture of three substances with different specific gravities, serpentine powder had a tendency, when shaken in transport, to resolve itself into three strata, the heaviest substance (the sulphur) settling down to the bottom, and the lightest (the charcoal) remaining on top" (1904, 181). Cathal Nolan (2006, 180) asserts that saltpeter was the heaviest component but agrees that charcoal was the lightest. Whatever the order, it supposedly "was a common practice to periodically invert the barrels of serpentine powder stored in armories" (Kosanke et al. 2012, 996) and even to remix the powder after transport (Hime 1904).

This problem (or perceived problem) was also believed to occur in corned powder. John Seller's *The Sea-Gunner* (1691) says that "to preserve good Powder, gunner ought to … keep their Store in as dry a place that can be had in the Ship, and every Fortnight or three Weeks to turn all the Barrels and Cartridges upside down, so that the Petre may be dispersed to every part alike; for if it stands long, the Petre will always descend downwards" (190). Similar advice was given by John Roberts in *The Compleat Canonier* (1672, 51).

For separation by vibration to occur, there must be a substantial difference in either the density or the size of the particles. Geoff Smith (2019, n.p.) points out that the densities of the gunpowder components are as follows: saltpeter, 2.11 g/cc; sulfur, "c. 2 g/cc depending on the allotrope"; and for powdered charcoal, somewhere between c. 2 g/cc (the density of pure carbon) and 0.2 g/cc (the effective density of charcoal "due to the air trapped in the pores"). He hypothesizes that the pulverization "reduces the entrained air tending to a limiting case density nearer to that of pure carbon. The difference in densities is evidently trivial and cannot account for any segregation."

If the saltpeter was heavily contaminated with calcium nitrate, which has a somewhat higher density (2.5 g/cc), there conceivably could be separation of sulfur and saltpeter as suggested by Nolan. But the differences would still be small enough so that the vibrations would have to be severe and prolonged to achieve a significant separation. A separation of charcoal from the other ingredients is more plausible.

Smith acknowledges that particles of similar densities but different sizes may also segregate as a result of the "Brazil nut effect." When a can of mixed nuts is shaken, some of the oblong, initially horizontal Brazil nuts tilt toward the vertical, opening up voids that the smaller nuts may pass down through (Temming 2021). Several mechanisms have been proposed for the Brazil nut effect, but there is no need to examine the phenomenon further, as I agree with Smith that "in a finely ground serpentine where particles are of very similar size," it is unlikely to play a significant role.

Ironically, the Brazil nut effect could occur in barrels of *corned* powder. Smith quotes Lieutenant Colonel Kevlay (1855) to the effect that "when gunpowder is transported by land carriage in barrels" over rough terrain, some of it is "ground down to fine dust, which falls to the bottom of the barrel." Smith speculates that this problem of corned powder was falsely attributed to serpentine powder.

Smith concedes that a good reason for abandoning serpentine powder was that, as a fine dust, "it is easily blown about and presents a major fire/explosion hazard wherever it settles" (2019, n.p.)

Just prior to the outbreak of the Civil War, Thomas Rodman concluded that the conventional cannon powder, with a one-tenth-inch grain, was "too quick for guns of large caliber." He and Lammot du Pont (owner of the du Pont powder mills) agreed that increasing the grain diameter should reduce the pressure developed, and it remained to be determined what the effect on muzzle velocity might be. Rodman found that with a 42-pounder and an 8-pound charge, increasing the diameter from 0.1 to 0.4 inches decreased the bottom of the bore pressure from 48,200 psi to 31,900 psi, and the muzzle velocity only from 1,261 to 1,187 (Rodman 1861, 203). And with an 11-inch gun firing 186.3-pound shot via a 12.67-pound charge, increasing the grain diameter from 0.3 to 0.6 inches decreased the bottom of the bore pressure from 35,330 psi to 21,370, but the muzzle velocity actually increased from 890 feet per second to 933 (274).

Rodman's "mammoth" powder, with a grain size greater than 0.6 inches, was used extensively by the Union army and navy, perhaps notably by the USS *Monitor* when it engaged the CSS *Virginia* (built on the hull of the USS *Merrimack*) in 1862 (Ezell 1962, 25).

Grain Shape

The shape of the grains is also significant. Some changes in shape were relatively minor; for example, in 1866, England experimented with powders having cylindrical (pellet powder) or cubical (pebble powder) grains (Officer 1884). Du Pont determined that "angular grains produced higher pressures, with less initial velocity, than rounded grains, but the effect was small" (Ezell 1962, 35).

Normally, as deflagration continues, the particles are consumed inward, reducing the total burning surface and thus reducing the burn (regressive burn). This effect is experienced with all solid grains, whether they be spheres, cylinders or plates.

In "shaped powders," the grains had one or more perforations, so they were consumed both inward and outward, resulting in a constant burn rate (neutral burn) with a one perforation grain, or even an increasing burn rate (progressive burn) with a multiperforated grain. The "perforated cake" powder was apparently invented by Captain Rodman. In 1860, in a trial of the 15-inch gun, he compared a perforated cake charge to a powder of solid 0.6-inch grain (see Table 4–4).

Table 4–4: Range and Gas Pressure versus Grain Type

	Charge Wt (lbs)	Shell + Sabot Wt (lbs)	Gas Pressure (psi)	Elevation	Range (yds)
0.6-inch	35	330	13,133	28°35'	5,070
0.6-inch	40	330	18,833	28°35'	5,088
perforated	40	330	3,289		
perforated	50	345	8,000	28°35'	5,208

(Rodman 1861, 284)

It can be seen that it was possible to achieve a greater range, while subjecting the barrel to a lesser pressure, with the perforated cake charge, albeit using a greater amount of the latter. (Rodman noted that the cake walls in the test charge were too thick, and if the thickness were reduced, "the same velocities might have been obtained with a less weight of charge" [1861, 295].)

Rodman formed the perforated cakes "by placing either mealed or grained powder, moistened with … water, in a mould of the proper form, and subjecting it to a pressure such as to render it impermeable to gas, under the pressure to which it will be subjected in the gun." "For the 15-inch gun trial, he started with Hazard's cannon powder of 1857." The mold was placed on top of a bed piece with holes covered with a sheet of paper. A piston with projecting teeth, matching the holes in the bed sheet, was driven down by a hydraulic press into the mold, creating

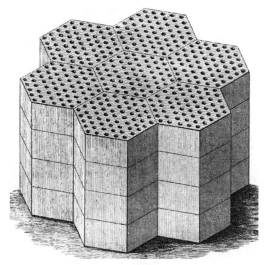

A four-tiered cartridge, with seven cakes per tier, for the 15-inch gun. Each cake contains numerous perforations (Rodman 1861, Plate II).

the perforations. For "guns of ordinary caliber," the cakes could be cylindrical in form, with the same diameter as the bore, and "piled one on another." But for the 15-inch gun, because of the difficulty of retracting the teeth from a full-bore cake of that size, Rodman used smaller hexagonal cakes, "of such diameter that seven cakes would form one tier in the cartridge" (Rodman 1861, 294–95).

Rodman's "hexagonal cakes" also qualify as a "prismatic powder." In geometry, a prismatic shape is one with a constant polygonal cross-section—a faceted cylinder.

Black Powder Charge

The powder charge used was in proportion to the shot weight. However, the ratio depended on the quality of the powder. According to Norton and Eldred, a whole cannon (47-pdr) needed 18 pounds of corned or 34 serpentine; a demi-cannon (27-pdr), 16 or 25; a whole culverin (15-pdr), 12 or 18; and a demi-culverin (9-pdr), 6 or 9 (Hime 1870, 285).

Improvements were also made in the preparation of the gunpowder components. In 1750, the maximum service charges ranged from 40 percent for a 42-pounder to 66 percent for a 9-pounder (Lavery 1989, 22).

Gunners could use less than the maximum service charge if they were trying to conserve powder or were hoping to produce more splinters if the shot didn't hole the target. A one-sixth charge is sufficient to "drive a ball from any large gun through the side of a ship at 1100 yards," but a 24-pounder would require twice the elevation as a one-third charge, thus reducing accuracy (Douglas 1829, 54).

Black Powder Quality Control

With black powder manufacture, the principal considerations were strength, freedom from fouling, and proneness to deterioration. These were affected by composition, density, moisture content, and grain size, shape, hardness and "glazing."

Until 1868, powder density was measured by "cubing"—that is, weighing it in a box of standardized volume (Mauskopf 2006, 334n36). This process was improved on by the mercury densimeter (Farrow 1885, 2:313).

Powder strength varied from manufacturer to manufacturer, from lot to lot, and even from barrel to barrel—in the latter case, in 1854, the muzzle velocities achieved in the test cannon ranged from 1,531 to 1,573 (Dahlgren 1865, 180). Even at the end of the black powder era, powder manufacture was an art, not a science. In 1881, 150,000 pounds of Westphalian Company prismatic powder was rejected because it didn't meet the standards; the representative blamed it on manufacturing "during very cold weather" (Buchanan 2006, 325).

Powder strength was originally tested by setting a small amount afire in the open air and observing the results. Eprouvettes ("provers"), which ignited the powder in a confined space simulating a cannon barrel, provided more useful data (von Maltitz 2003, 163ff).

An early eprouvette was described by William Bourne in 1578. This device was essentially a box with a hinged and ratcheted lid and a small fuse hole. A set quantity of powder was placed inside and set off. The force of the combustion gases would drive the lid open, and the lid would be kept from dropping back into place by the ratchet. The angle reached by the lid was a measure of the strength of the powder. In 1627, Furtenbach used a lid that was simply laid on the box but had two vertical guide wires. Thus, it was the linear rather than angular movement of the lid that was measured. As on the Bourne device, a retaining mechanism kept the lid from falling back down (Hime 1904, 193).

In Bourne's and Furtenbach's eprouvettes, the propulsive force was resisted by the weight of the lid, but some later devices used a spring mechanism, and Du Me's eprouvette (1702) employed water resistance (von Maltitz 2003, 172). In addition, instead of measuring the movement of the propelled object, one could measure the eprouvette's recoil, as proposed by du Pont (*ibid.*).

Most of the eprouvettes just worked on an indicator object like Bourne's lid, but the mortar eprouvette, invented by Natheniel Nye in 1647, actually fired a projectile at a fixed angle, usually 45 degrees, so the power was inferred from the range achieved (Hime 1904).

The Trauzl test (circa 1903) "involved measuring the deformation caused by the detonation of 10 grams of an explosive in a hole within a cylindrical block of lead" under controlled conditions (Brown 2011).

A set amount of the powder could also be used to fire a standard projectile and the muzzle velocity measured using the ballistic pendulum (see chapter 9).

Brown (Cocoa) Prismatic Powder

The slower-burning "brown" powder was developed in Germany in 1882. The grains were hexagonal prisms with a central cylindrical hole. Its initial composition was 79 percent saltpeter, 3 percent sulfur, and 18 percent "a very lightly-baked brown charcoal." In 1884, Heidemann patented the use of "very slightly carbonized straw for the brown charcoal" (Deering 1889, 1).

A prismatic brown powder was used for the 12-inch rifled breechloaders of HMS *Colossus* (Brassington 2008a).

Smokeless Powder Chemistry

In the late nineteenth century, gunpowder was largely replaced for military (especially artillery) use by nitrocellulose-based propellants (the so-called "smokeless powders"). These produced less smoke and flash, burned progressively, and caused less damage to the barrels. Nitrocellulose (guncotton, nitrocotton, cellulose nitrate) is a self-oxidizing fuel; it doesn't need a separate oxidant like saltpeter. It was first synthesized in 1845. It is the product of the action of a mixture of nitric and sulfuric acids on cellulose, such as that of cotton (EB 1911, "Guncotton"). Mono-, di-, or trinitrocellulose may be formed.

It's not necessary to use cotton as the source of cellulose, but "a given fiber requires an adaptation of the nitrating method" to accord with the fiber's cellular structure. "Flax is more difficult of nitration" because of the thickness of the fiber walls (Worden 1911, 1:40).Around 1930, the British Admiralty adopted wood paper in place of cotton as the source of cellulose (Mellor 1958, 348); the questionable availability of overseas cotton was surely a driving factor in this decision. Wood paper had been experimented with earlier, but its problems were the low content of cellulose (40–60 percent) and the difficulty of obtaining a uniform product (the cells of the spring and autumn growths have different structures) (Worden 1921, 320).

Smokeless powders are classified as being single base (nitrocellulose), double base (adds nitroglycerin), or triple base (also adds nitroguanidine). Nitroglycerin was first synthesized in 1847 and is obtained by nitration of glycerin (EB 1911, "Nitroglycerin"), which itself was obtained by the saponification of fats (EB 1911, "Glycerin"). Nitroguanidine was synthesized in 1892 by reacting guanidine with nitric acid in the presence of sulfuric acid.

The decomposition products of black powder are 43 percent gaseous and 57 percent solid, the latter being responsible for the smoke of the proverbial "smoking gun." In contrast, the combustion product of modern smokeless powder is more than 99 percent gaseous. Gases can be accelerated to higher velocities than solids for a given internal pressure. Consequently, black powder has a low "specific impulse" (pounds thrust produced per pound propellant burned per second) of around 50–70 seconds, whereas the specific impulse from double-base powders is around 180–210 seconds (Guilmartin 2003, 300).

Smokeless Powder Development

"Nitrocellulose in its natural fibrous form … has too high a rate of combustion to be suitable as a propellant" (Bebie 1943, 134). Paul Vielle's poudre B, adopted by the French navy in 1884, was "the first smokeless powder which was satisfactory for use in rifled guns…. It was made by treating a mixture of soluble and insoluble nitrocotton with ether-alcohol" (Davis 1943, 292; Rice 2006, 357). The solvent gelatinized the nitrocellulose, which stabilized it and permitted it to be formed into grains of the desired size and shape (Bebie 1943, 134; Bobic et al. 2017, 31).

Ballistite was patented by Alfred Nobel. Nobel mixed two high explosives—nitroglycerine and nitrocellulose—in equal proportions, stabilizing the mixture with roughly 6 percent camphor. In addition, his patent taught, "the less of the insoluble nitrocellulose there is mixed up with or contained in the nitrocellulose used … the more sluggish will be the combustion of the explosive material contained," and he favored use of "soluble nitrated cotton." The greater the degree of nitration, the less soluble the nitrocellulose would be in the conventional solvent (ether and alcohol) (Rowlinson 2016). One problem with ballistite, however, was that the camphor gradually evaporated away, reducing the propellant's stability.

In Britain, Frederick Abel and James Dewar corresponded with Nobel and persuaded him to provide samples of ballistite. Subsequently, they developed a modified ballistite, without camphor. Cordite Mark I (1889) was 37 percent nitrocellulose, 58 percent nitroglycerin, and 5 percent vaseline. It was so called because it was extruded through holes (Rowlinson 2016) and thus "shaped into cords" (Amiable 2006, 346).

The development of cordite by the British provoked Nobel to sue for infringement of his ballistite patent. However, cordite used insoluble (trinitrated) nitrocellulose, and he lost (Romer 1894).

Cordite had its own problem: it corroded gun barrels. This result was probably attributable to formation of nitrogen oxides (which provide the characteristic whiff). In 1900, the British reduced the nitroglycerin content from 58 percent to 30 percent to ameliorate this problem (U.S. Army, Military Explosives 1989, 2–8). Thus, the less powerful but less corrosive Cordite MD (1902) had the proportions 65–30–5 (EB 1911, "Cordite"; Rinker 1999, 34).

Unless nitrocellulose was correctly made (e.g., sufficient nitrating time) from pure raw material ("clean carded cotton sliver" was better than "cotton waste"), "devastating explosions [of cordite] could occur spontaneously," like those that destroyed the warships *Iena* (1907), *Liberté* (1911), *Bulwark* (1914), *Natal* (1915), and *Vanguard* (1917) (Campbell 1978, 139; Head 1989).

"Solventless" Cordite SC (41.5 percent nitroglycerin, 49.5 percent nitrocellulose, and 9 percent the stabilizer diethyl diphenyl urea, "centralite" or "carbamite") was introduced in 1927 and used in World War II. It was safer than the older cordites (DiGiulian 2022a; Campbell and Campbell 1985, 5).

In America, the first smokeless powder used was fulminate of mercury. However, in "larger guns … it was entirely too violent" (Henderson 1904).

The single-base "Navy Smokeless" powder (SP), first manufactured by the U.S. Navy in 1900 (Earle 1914), was "a solution of three parts by weight of soluble nitro-cellulose in two parts of ethyl either and one part of ethyl alcohol," and the degree of nitration of the nitrocellulose was 12.45–12.80 percent (Strauss 1901). In a 6-pounder, with 610 grams powder, it was expected to achieve a muzzle velocity of 2,250 feet per second, with a peak internal pressure not exceeding 13.5 tons (Henderson 1904).

SPD (essentially SP with diphenylamine as a stabilizer) became standard in 1912 and was used through World War II (DiGiulian 2022a).

Gunpowder Performance

"A charge of 45.5 pounds of brown-prismatic [gave, in the 6-inch 40-caliber gun] a velocity of 2000 fs [feet per second] with 15 tons pressure; twenty tons of smokeless gives the same velocity with 10.8 tons pressure" (Strauss 1901). Joseph Strauss pointed out that with brown prismatic, only "about 35 percent of the weight of the powder becomes gas useful in propelling the projectile." Moreover, that gas must propel not only the projectile (itself 100 pounds) but also "about 23 pounds of inert products of combustion in the shape of smoke."

Table 4–5 compares the strength of brown prismatic, Navy Smokeless and cordite powders.

Table 4–5: Powder Performance Comparison

Gun	Gun	Charge Wt (lbs)	Projectile Wt (lbs)	Muzzle Vel (ft/sec)
Cordite	6"-45	29.9	100	2,821
Navy Smokeless	6"-40	27.8	100	2,367
Brown Prismatic	6"-40	41.5	100	1,932
Navy Smokeless	12"-35	286	1,200	2,340
Brown Prismatic	12"-35	406	850	1,955

(Van Duzer 1901, 627)

Alternative Propellants

Combustible Liquid Propellants

These propellants became popular in rocketry, but for artillery, despite a half-century of effort, their time hasn't yet come (McCoy 1992).

Compressed Air

The blowgun is the earliest compressed-air weapon, limited in propulsive force by the ratio of the volume of air one can huff (about 60 cubic inches) to the bore volume of the blowgun (14 cubic inches for a six-footer with a half-inch caliber) (Gurstelle 2007, 142). A "pneumatic rifle was built at the beginning of the seventeenth century," and some Austrian jaegers carried the model 1780 rifle (300 m/s muzzle velocity), which was a great weapon for covert operations against French occupation forces (Rossi et al. 2009, 232).

The USS *Vesuvius* (1888) carried three 15-inch pneumatic "dynamite" guns. Compressed air from a 1,000-psi reservoir was fed into the barrels, which were 55 feet long (!), partially below deck, and mounted at a fixed elevation of 16 degrees. Range was changed by adjusting the pressure. The guns couldn't be traversed; you aimed the ship to aim the gun. The barrel was unrifled, but the shells had spiral fins (navweaps.com 2008; navsource.org 2023; Zalinski 1888, 11, 30).

The term "dynamite gun" is somewhat misleading. The bursting charge inside the projectile was "uncamphorated explosive gelatin, having a core of dynamite." The latter, being more sensitive, ignited first, but the gelatin was about 42 percent more explosive per unit weight and 89 percent per unit volume (Zalinski 1888, 12). "The full caliber shell will carry 600 pounds explosive gelatine…. Shell containing smaller charges can also be thrown by the system of sub-caliber recently developed" (30). The full caliber shell could be thrown about one mile (26).

Because of the low pressure, a 20-inch gun could have a steel or aluminum bronze barrel that was half an inch thick (Zalinski 1888, 10). In trials, the gun had good accuracy and could fire about one round a minute (17).

The secret to understanding the dynamite gun is to think of it not as a gun but as a torpedo launch system. Ship armor had reached the point at which ordinary

Forward deck of the dynamite gun vessel *Vesuvius* showing the muzzles of the three fixed-inclination guns. Courtesy of the Naval History and Heritage Command, Catalog NH 556.

shells weren't reliably penetrating it. The projectiles fired by the dynamite gun were conceptualized as "aerial torpedoes," traveling faster and farther than any underwater torpedo and exploding underwater against the unarmored bilge of the enemy craft (Parkerson 1898, 83).

At a U.S. Naval Institute proceeding, the commentators conceded that the gun would be useful for countermining—that is, using explosives to set off enemy mines (stationary targets). They were less sanguine that it could be used effectively against a rapidly closing foe, as the elevation limited the zone of danger for the target and ranges are difficult to estimate. If the pressure were reduced because the enemy was close, the projectile would have a lower velocity and be more vulnerable to deflection by the wind. The naysayers doubted that the countermining advantage was sufficient to justify building a ship with the dynamite gun as the main armament.

In practice, USS *Vesuvius* proved reasonably useful for shore bombardment—the quietness of the pneumatic action meant that the enemy didn't hear the guns fire—but the system was quite obviously impractical for use against another warship. USS *Vesuvius* would have been outranged by conventional guns, and the inability to traverse the gun other than by turning the ship meant that a fast attacker could evade its fire (McSherry 2023).

Compressed-air projection reappeared in an anti-aircraft gun format in World War II. The Mark I Holman projector had a 4.5-foot smoothbore barrel and used compressed-air bottles to fire fragmentation grenades up to 30 rounds/minute to perhaps 600 feet. Since the barrel was not rifled, it could fire improvised projectiles. Its advantages were that the low barrel pressures meant that it could use cast iron and mild steel, its recoil was small, and of course it didn't need any cordite (Pawle 1957, 97). Its disadvantage was that it was quite inaccurate. Nonetheless, "in its first year the Projector claimed at least a dozen enemy aircraft destroyed" (100). The Holman projector was primarily used to defend civilian vessels from air attack, but it was also used by Coastal Force motor-gunboats to fire flares at German motor tor-pedo boats (101).

Steam

In World War II, Holman projectors were adapted to steam trawlers and to use steam rather than compressed air as the propellant (Pawle 1957, 99).

The concept of using steam to throw a projectile wasn't new; Leonardo da Vinci had speculated that Archimedes had used a steam cannon at the siege of Syracuse, even drawing one. In 1828, Jacob Perkins built a 1,500-psi steam gun, with a barrel six feet long and three inches caliber, firing 4-pound balls, for the French. It worked, but it had range and weight problems, and the Union navy declined to adopt a later version (BPHS n.d.; Bruce 2017). In 2006, an MIT team built a steam cannon running at 3,500–4,000 psi and fired a one-pound projectile with a muzzle velocity over 300 mps. They were able to fire one round every two minutes (MIT 2011).

Electromagnetic Propulsion (Railguns)

In 2005–2021, the United States Navy toyed with the notion of using the electromagnetic fields generated by a railgun to launch a projectile at hypersonic speed. The rail gun consisted of a smoothbore barrel, two parallel conductive rails, a moving armature that carried the projectile, and an electric power source (capacitors or pulsed alternators). The projectile had a conductive element that completed the circuit. The combination of the electric and magnetic fields generated by this circuit created a Lorentz force acting on the projectile in a direction parallel to the rails. The projectile itself could be non-explosive, doing damage solely by virtue of its kinetic energy (proportional to the square of its speed). In a 2008 test firing, "the railgun was fired at 10.64 [megajoules energy] and the 7 lbs (3.2 kg) test slug projectile attained a muzzle velocity of 8,268 fps (2,520 mps)" (navweaps.com 2021; Exmundo 2022).

The advantage of the railgun is that it doesn't require an explosive propellant, and thus there is no such propellant to be set on fire by enemy action. And if it uses kinetic energy weapons, then there are no shells, either. But it has several serious problems. First, an enormous amount of electrical power is needed, limiting which warships can carry it, as well as its rate of fire and range. Second, the wear on the gun is severe. The rail gun generates a large amount of heat (as a result of the electrical resistance of the rails and armature, along with the friction between the armature and the barrel), and there are also Lorentz forces on the rails, attempting to push them apart. Third, the ship's electronic equipment needs to be shielded (navweaps. com 2021; Exmundo 2022). The U.S. Navy abandoned the program, but there are rumors that the Chinese navy is still developing rail guns.

CHAPTER 5

Gun-Fired Projectiles

Projectile Material

All else being equal, the greater the density of the material, the lower the muzzle velocity, but the less the retardation in flight and the greater the penetration.

Simple artillery projectiles were initially made of stone, later of cast iron, and some, in modern times, of tungsten or depleted uranium.

Compound projectiles—those that fragmented or exploded during flight or on impact to release sub-projectiles—were more varied in composition. They were intended for anti-personnel use.

Stone varies in density, typically in the range of 2.2–2.8 grams per cubic centimeter (g/cc). It had the advantage of being compatible with lighter artillery. The problem was that the stone shot had to be hand carved, which was expensive, whereas iron could be cast. Hence, economic considerations led to the abandonment of stone throwers in Europe in the mid-seventeenth century. The practice lasted longer in the Ottoman Empire and in Portuguese India, where labor costs were lower (Guilmartin 2003, 286). Stone cannonballs were still in production in the Dardanelles region in 1822, although the Turks sometimes cut them from the column sections and statues of antiquity (Greenhalgh 2019, 146).

Pure iron has a density of about 7.87 g/cc, whereas cast iron is typically 6.85–7.75 (Engineers Edge 2023). It was the dominant artillery projectile material for centuries, until it was supplanted by various forms of steel. Methods of making iron projectiles are discussed later in this chapter.

While lead is denser (11.3), as George Ripley said (*New American Cyclopaedia* 1870), lead "is too dear and too scarce for cannonballs." While that was normally the case, at the beginning of the fifteenth century, forty "large" French vessels (galleys?) were to be armed with four culverins apiece, each firing lead projectiles (Guilmartin 2007, 662). And at the siege of Cadiz in 1812, the French filled shells with lead, thereby increasing range (Douglas 1829, 61).

Copper (8.96) is also usually too expensive. But when Captain David Porter's frigate *Essex* captured the fifteen-gun Peruvian privateer *Nereyda* in 1813, Porter was surprised to discover that all of its shot was made of copper (Porter 1823, 29–30). Porter later discovered that in Peru and Chile, copper was much cheaper than iron.

Tungsten (19.3) was first isolated in 1783. The first experimental tungsten bullets were made in 1882; tungsten powder was compressed into a nickel jacket. Armor penetration range was increased about two-thirds.

Depleted uranium (19.1) is defined as uranium that contains less than 0.711 wt percent of the fissile isotope U-235. In practice, the depleted uranium used by the American military is about 0.2 percent U-235. Thus, it is primarily U-238 (density of 19.1 g/cc).

The U.S. Navy's Phalanx Close-in Weapons System (CIWS) uses a 20-mm six-barrel Gatling autocannon. The first production unit was deployed in 1980 on the USS *Coral Sea* (CVA-43). One version or another has been deployed on most major U.S. warships since 1980. Originally, it fired a depleted-uranium sub-caliber penetrator. The navy switched to tungsten penetrators in 1988 (navweaps.com 2022a).

Projectile Diameter

We have already referred to windage in smoothbore guns. Windage is small; if the projectile diameter is substantially smaller than the caliber, it is called a sub-caliber projectile. These projectiles will typically be used in conjunction with sabots (see chapter 6) to prevent the escape of the propulsive combustion cases and to keep the projectile centered in the bore.

Common (Solid, Spherical) Shot

A common shot is a solid, spherical projectile and thus is characterized just by its diameter and density. Because of voids, the density of a cast iron projectile is less than that of bulk cast iron.

Table 5–1 compares seventeenth- and early nineteenth-century British guns and the shot they fired.

Specialty Shot

Case Shot

"Case shot" is a generic term for several different kinds of anti-personnel munitions. Smaller projectiles are packed inside a bag (hailshot, grapeshot) or a cylindrical metal (tin) canister; the interstices of the canister were usually filled with sawdust. If the shot was equipped with explosive for spreading the goodies farther, it was called a shrapnel shell (see "Anti-Personnel Shells" later in this chapter). The projectiles could be lead or iron balls (hence "grape"), cubes ("dice shot") or scrap metal (langrage). Canister shot was used by the British navy at least as early as 1625 (Lavery 1987, 137). Langrage was found inside a one-pounder on the *Queen Anne's Revenge* wreck (Carroll 2020).

Typically, the mini-projectiles of grape shot were larger than those of canister; during the American Civil War, grape shot might deliver nine lead "golf balls" to the enemy, whereas the canister might hold hundreds of lead "marbles" (McNeese 2003, 74).

Table 5–1: British Guns and Their Cannonballs

17c Gun	Shot Weight (lbs)	Shot Diameter (in)	Equivalent 19c Gun (nominal shot wt)	Nominal Shot Diameter (in)
Minion	3.25–3.75	2.875–3	3	2.775
Saker	4.75–7.5	3.25–3.75	6	3.498
demi-culverin	9–12.75	4–4.5	9	4
"			12	4.403
Culverin	15–20	4.75–5.25	18	5.043 5.040***
"			24	5.475† 5.547***
demi-cannon	30–36	6–6.375	32	6.105
cannon of 7			42*	6.684
cannon royal			68**	8†

(17c data per Collins, A.R. "British Cannonball Sizes" http://arc.id.au/Cannonballs.html [n.d.], citing c. 1590 Gunner's Rule; 19c data per Beauchant 1828, 40.)

* first major use at sea in 1637; rare until 1650, even then mostly on first rates.
** mid-19th century.
*** from EB 1824, "Cannon," 609.
† inconsistent implied density. Griffiths (1868, 374) suggests that the diameter (inches) of iron shot is 1.923 times the cube root of the shot's weight (pounds), implying 68-pdr is 7.849 inches. Collins suggests a cast iron ball density of 0.2682 lb/in³, in which case the multiplier is 1.937.

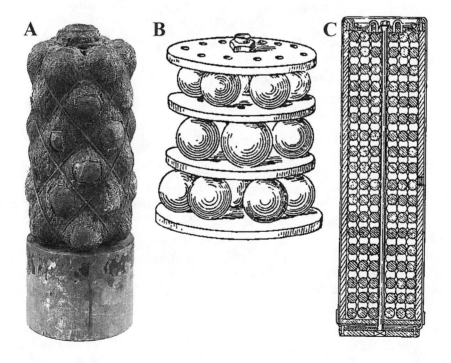

Anti-personnel shot. (A) Seventeenth-century grape shot, made in Austria; 19 cm tall. Note the sabot (see chapter 6) on the bottom. George F. Harding Collection. Courtesy of the Art Institute of Chicago, Reference 1982.2990. (B) Caffin grape shot, nineteenth century (Garbett 1897, 232). (C) Case shot, for the Armstrong 12-pounder rifled breechloader. It was "filled with lead and antimony bullets packed in clay and sand, or coal dust" (244).

Heated Shot

Heated common shot was used by shore batteries up until the mid-nineteenth century, when iron came into use for warship construction. The logic behind heated shot is impeccable: wooden sailing warships are very flammable (wood, cotton, tar, hemp); start a fire, and the ship's own substance will do the rest of the work for you. However, that same logic tended to work against the heated shot being fired from a wooden ship. For this reason, the British navy prohibited the practice.

Still, warships were occasionally given this capability. For example, Captain Charles Stewart of USS *Constitution* decided to equip his new command with a portable sheet iron furnace for heating shot. He intended to use it only in an emergency (Berube and Rodgaard 2005, 73).

The first documented use of heated shot by a warship was actually earlier, by the French at the 1794 Battle of the Glorious (to the English!) First of June. It should be noted that even if there is no misadventure in handling the heated shot, there are risks in having a shot furnace on board. In that battle, the *Scipion*'s furnaces "were knocked down, and the hot shot in them scattered about the deck" (James 1826, 1:168).

The first truly successful use of shipborne heated shot appears to have been by Captain Frank Hastings' steamship *Karteria* in the Greek War for Independence. She reportedly fired 18,000 hot shells(!), "mainly against shore batteries," in her first year of service (Dakin 2022, 172). Other sources suggest that it was 18,000 shots total, but it was still remarkable that she did this without any injury to the gun crew (Roberts 2010, 76). And Hastings certainly made effective use of both heated shot and carcass (see below) at the Battle of Salona (Blackwood's 58:510).

Carcass

This was an incendiary munition that was used both on land and at sea. On land, of course, its utility depended on the flammability of the target.

Incendiary projectiles were used in Renaissance warfare. For example, there was the incendiary that set fire to Ronda during the 1486 siege. There is some dispute as to whether this material was thrown by a trebuchet (Turnbull 2018, 58) or fired by a cannon (Partington 1999, 123). Hand-thrown bombs containing "wildfire" ("Spanish pitch, black pitch, saltpetre, sulphur, camphor, turpentine, rock oil and ardent spirit") were employed by the defenders of Famagusta in 1571 (135). Fire pots (clay pots presumed to have contained incendiaries) have been recovered from various sixteenth- and seventeenth-century wrecks (Hamilton 1997).

In one embodiment, the cannonball was covered with a flammable concoction and wrapped in a bag. A fancier version was a hollow metal sphere filled with the material and having holes for both igniting the stuff and having it "jet out" against the target. A "spike shot" added spikes to the standard carcass; the theory was that these would stick into the target (Kinard 2007, 125). In the 1796 British carcasses, the incendiary was a little less than 10 percent of the weight of the projectile and burned for 3–12 minutes (Beauchant 1828, 66).

Double or Triple Shot

You may load two or even three shots into the cannon and fire them simultaneously. However, the muzzle velocity is reduced unless you increase the charge to compensate (Douglas 1829, 65). Accuracy is less than with single shot, as the balls will push each other in opposite directions, vertically or horizontally, when leaving the barrel (67). The shots can easily land more than a hundred yards apart (285).

Disabling Shot

Two balls or half-balls could be joined together by a chain or bar, forming "double-headed shot." The theory behind their use in naval warfare was that they would be more effective against sails, masts and rigging than common shot. They were used prior to the seventeenth century, as evidenced by a display at the Stockholm Medieval Museum. All dismantling shots were more likely to be effective with a fresh wind than in light breezes, as the force of the wind would tend to open up a small hole (Douglas 1829, 253). Both rigid and sliding ("expanding") bar shot were found on Blackbeard's *Queen Anne's Revenge* (Atkinson 2019), and jointed bar was used by the Americans in the War of 1812.

Cross-barred shot was also intended for cutting rigging, but it was a ball with two opposed spikes, loaded (presumably) with the spikes facing up and down bore. It was in "common use" in Henry VIII's navy (Oppenheim 1896, 97), and I have a photo of one from the *Vasa*.

Chain (angel) shot was reportedly used by Martin Frobisher's ships against the vanguard of the Spanish Armada (McDermott 2005, 252). Chain shot had a greater spread than bar shot, perhaps 5–6 calibers of the gun firing it (Silverstone 2006, xix). An eighteenth-century chain shot sold on December 9, 2021 (Lot 1628), by Alexander Historical Auctions had two 3-inch diameter balls connected by a 26-inch chain (AHA 2021). In the "Old Tower Collection," there is another eighteenth-century specimen "consisting of two roughly forged weights connected by four links of heavy chain." The total weight was 11.3125 pounds, and the length was 33 inches (Royal Armouries, "Chain Shot").

Hemispherical ("split") chain shot was found on the shipwreck (1622) of the *Nuestra Senora de Atocha*. It is believed that the hemispheres were joined to form a ball, and the connecting chain was doubled over, splinted, and tied with twine (which would have been burned away by the fired powder) (MFMM 1986).

Manwayring's *Seaman's Dictionary* (1644, "Shot") says that "chaine-shot … is good to plye amongst men." Hence, it also had an anti-personnel function, at least at close range.

The Dutch warships in the 1666 Four Days' Battle carried "large proportions of bar and chain shot for guns of all sizes," and their gunners "deliberately fired on the 'up roll'" to disable the English warships' rigging (Fox 2009). (The Dutch are sometimes erroneously credited [such as in Marx 1987, 104] with having invented chain shot in 1666.)

Variations included star (spider) shot, in which several "heads" were linked by chain to an iron ring (Fox 2009). William Falconer comments, "Their flight and execution are precarious at any tolerable distance" (1769, "Shot"). Nonetheless, Stephen Decatur, commanding USS *President* in 1814, disabled the *Endymion* with star-shot (Hickey 2012, 225), although he had to surrender anyway, as there were four more British ships present.

In 1811, the Royal Navy stopped issuing disabling shot. However, in the War of 1812, "the Americans deployed large numbers of dismantling shot as the key to their tactical system." In the *Shannon–Chesapeake* engagement, the *Shannon* suffered fourteen hits by bar shot (although they did minimal damage), and the *Chesapeake* also carried star shot (Lambert 2012).

In practice, there were numerous problems with the use of chain shot. For example, the balls could break loose from the chain. And even if they didn't, the aerodynamic behavior of the projectile was peculiar, causing both accuracy and range to suffer.

Of course, once steam power fully replaced wind power for warships, there was no rigging to target. In 1846, HMS *Excellent* compared the effects of solid and bar shot on the funnel of the sort used by steamships. The bar shot (42 pounds) made "far more serious holes" than those made by 32-pound and 8-inch round shot. But neither proved capable of knocking down the funnel (*Experiments* 1854, 56).

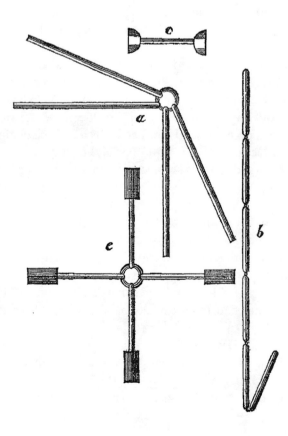

William James (1816, 76) describes several forms of American dismantling shot used in the War of 1812. My copy of his book was rather poor in reproduction quality, so his figure is taken from the book review appearing in the *Colonial Journal*, 2 (1816): 427. Per James, the projectiles are as follows: (a) star shot ("Each arm is about two feet in length. Some of these shot had five, others three arms"); (b) chain shot (his term; I would call it jointed bar shot: "Its extended length is six feet"); (c) double-headed shot (hemispheric bar shot); (d) [omitted, not dismantling shot]; (e) another form of star shot (with four arms). James' (f) and (g), presenting additional views of (e), have been omitted. But the arms of (e) were laid parallel for insertion into the bore, with the connecting ring breech first.

Choice of Round Shot versus Specialty Shot

The tactical situation affected whether round shot or a specialty shot was used. In general, round shot had a greater effective range than the specialty shot.

The positions of the ships relative to the wind could also affect the choice of projectile. If ship A is upwind of ship B, then ship B is heeled away from A, exposing more of its lower strakes but hiding its deck. It's better, then, to try for hull damage using common shot. B, by contrast, should note the greater exposure of A's deck and perhaps essay a double charge of case shot, to devastate A's crew (Douglas 1829, 240ff).

Economic considerations also affected the proportions of common and specialty shot with which a ship was supplied. In 1603, the English Ordnance Office paid 8 pounds a ton for cast iron round shot, sixpence to two shillings apiece for stone shot, and two shillings, sixpence to eight shillings each for jointed shot and cross-bar shot (Oppenheim 1896, 160). In 1627, the price of round shot was 11 pounds a ton, whereas powder was 5 pounds/barrel (301).

Some inkling of the relative importance of the ordinary round shot and the various specialty shots to the British armed forces in the early modern period may be gleaned from a 1592 inventory of the British Ordnance Office Stores (which would have been for both land and sea forces), shown in Table 5–2.

Table 5–2: Shot Inventory (Britain, 1592)

spherical	73,944
hail shot	38,166
stone shot	16,784
cross-barred shot	5,714
dice shot	2,886
jointed shot	82
chain shot	51
"hollow shot armed with fireworks"	38
lead-covered falcon shot	34
Total	137,699

(Walton 1999, 228)

In 1632, a second-rate warship carried "three lasts of powder, Six cwt. of match, 970 round, 100 cross-bar, 70 double cross-bar shot" (Oppenheim 1896, 289).

Table 5–3A lists the projectiles in the 74-gun *Milford*'s ordnance stores in 1809.

Table 5–3A Ammunition Loadout (1809)

Projectile	for 30 × 18 pdrs	for 28 × 32 pdrs
round shot	2,730	2,940
double-headed shot	96	84
grape shot	224	84
tin case shot	222	124
	for 18-pdr carronades	for 32-pdr carronades
tin case	88	132
grape	48	124

(Blake and Lawrence 2005, 220–21)

In contrast, in 1828, a third-rate, first-class British warship in "Channel service" would have carried the ammunition outline in Table 5–3B.

Table 5–3B: Ammunition Loadout (1828)

	32	24	12
round shot	2,640	2,730	
grape shot	90	224	56
case shot	224		56
shot, tin case	84	49	
grape, tin case	84	49	

If in "foreign service," its round shot allotment would increase by 1,260 for 32-pdrs, 1,170 for 24-pdrs, and 240 for 12-pdrs (Beauchant 1828, 111–12). Note the absence of any allotment of bar, chain or star shot.

Elongated Shot

The original elongated shot was oblong shot, a cylindrical bar with hemispherical ends (thus somewhat similar to bar shot). Douglas recommended firing it from 9- or 12-pounders at close range, to carry away a mast (1829, 61). Range was reduced, of course, given the increased shot weight relative to charge, but Douglas preferred it to bar shot (63, 304).

Elongated shot has higher sectional density (mass per unit cross-sectional area) than spherical shot of the same diameter and material. While increased density is disadvantageous from the point of view of interior ballistics (the muzzle velocity will be lower for the same charge), it's advantageous from an exterior or terminal ballistics standpoint. The greater mass means less deceleration as a result of air resistance during flight, which can be improved on by giving the shot a more aerodynamic shape. And less deceleration means higher impact velocity, which, together with the higher sectional density, means more momentum and kinetic energy—hence more damage.

Simple elongated shot "tumbled as soon as they left the cannon," and the normal solution was to impart spin by "rifling" (engineering the projectile to engage spiral grooves in the bore) (U.S. Army 1922, 44).

Armor-Piercing (AP) Shot

Palliser shot (1864) had chill-hardened, cast iron ogive ends (Barlow 1874, 157) to penetrate the wrought iron armor of early ironclads. When defenders adopted steel armor, the points had to be made of forged steel (initially carbon steel, later nickel-chrome or tungsten steel).

Palliser shot was generally cast with a hollow in the center, "as it is very difficult to cast such a dense metal well when quite solid" (Barlow 1874, 166). Palliser shot was thought to "penetrate better [than the corresponding shells] when firing at oblique angles," but it isn't clear why that would be the case, as the external and internal differences between them were small, other than the explosive in the shell (168).

Sub-Caliber Penetrators

Elongated shot is sometimes sub-caliber—that is, of a diameter substantially less than the diameter of the bore. A properly fitted sabot (see chapter 6) keeps the propulsive gases from escaping.

A sub-caliber projectile will have a greater muzzle velocity than its same-length, full-bore homologue, fired from the same gun with the same charge, because the sabot keeps the force the same even though the projectile's weight is reduced. The higher muzzle velocity results in a shorter time of flight, which can be advantageous for anti-aircraft use.

If a projectile is non-explosive, it does damage by virtue of its kinetic energy, which is proportional to the square of the impact velocity. This in turn depends on the range, projectile drag characteristics and muzzle velocity. The same weight reduction does mean a faster retardation in velocity with distance, but, up to a critical range, the penetration will be increased. The larger the diameter of the projectile, the greater that critical range will be.

Shells

Shells are hollow shot, round or elongated, filled with explosive substances (or something equally nasty). If elongated, they should be spin or fin stabilized (see chapter 10). The explosives are set off by a fuse (see chapter 6).

In the seventeenth century, shells were mainly used in land warfare, and they were fired on high-angle trajectories from mortars.

In 1682, the French navy used its new *galiote à bombes* (bomb ketch) to bombard Algiers (quite successfully, I might add). The first bomb ketches had forward-pointing side-by-side mortars, and you essentially aimed the ship to aim the mortars. Later British bomb vessels had mortars on rotating platforms. In the eighteenth century, bomb vessels were the only ships making regular use of explosive shells.

The first significant use of low-trajectory shell guns was at the 1853 Battle of Sinope, where the Russians used them against the Ottomans' wooden ships (Martin 2015).

Common Shells

A "common" shell was filled with black powder (EB 1911, "Ammunition"). In 1853, the established bursting charge for a British 32-pound shell was just one pound of black powder, and a 10-inch shell would hold 5.5 pounds (*Experiments* 1854, 9).

High Explosives

Explosives vary in both explosive power and sensitivity, which are often compared to that of trinitrotoluene (TNT). Black powder had about 33–50 percent the explosive power of TNT (DiGiulian 2023a) and is considered a "low explosive."

The first high explosives, such as TNT, were too sensitive for main charge artillery use, absent an expedient such as compressed-air propulsion. While TNT could be desensitized with beeswax (as in some German shells), by 1911, a high-explosive shell typically used picric acid (trinitrophenol) in some form (dunnite, emmensite, lyddite, melinite, picrine) (DiGiulian 2023a).

"Picric acid is slightly more powerful than TNT.... Ammonium picrate is somewhat less powerful." But unlike picric acid, ammonium picrate does not react with metals (MacDougall and Newmark 1946, 48). In World War II, the U.S. Navy favored "explosive D" (ammonium picrate with dinitrobenzol and vaseline desensitizers) as the main charge for armor-piercing shells "because of its great insensitivity" (thus avoiding premature detonation) (Budge 2014; DiGiulian 2023a). You wanted an AP shell to explode after it penetrated all the armor.

Other explosives were used in torpedo warheads, depth charges and mines.

High-Explosive (HE) Shell Design

The effect of the burst is roughly proportional to the square root of the weight of the bursting charge (DiGiulian 2023a). A typical bursting charge was at least 6.5 percent (Okun 1998a) and not more than 25 percent of the projectile weight (Hempstead and Worthington 2005, 893).

To prevent premature detonation of even the more stable high explosives, the walls of the HE shell had to be thicker than those of a common shell, and a strong material had to be used.

In World War II, the rule of thumb was that shells made of steel with a 23-ton yield strength could have a 15 percent HE fill, whereas those made of a lesser steel (19-ton yield strength) had to be thicker, leaving room for only a 7 percent fill (Evans 2014).

The USS *Iowa* (BB-61) was equipped with a 1,900-pound Mark 13 high-capacity shell (Dramiński 2020, 18).

Anti-Personnel Shells

Anti-personnel shells are intended to spray out smaller projectiles (sub-munitions).

Shrapnel shell (1784) was a common shell in which lead bullets were mixed with gunpowder.

The original version (common shrapnel) was improved on by separating "the bullets from the bursting charge." Edward Boxer initially did this by "placing the powder in a cylinder in a continuation of the fuse hole" (Garbett 1897, 232).

Shrapnel shells were introduced into the U.S. Navy in 1849, as ammunition for the guns carried by ships' boats (Dahlgren 1856a, 84). John Dahlgren and Alfred Mordecai devised their own improvement on common shrapnel. The interstices between the balls were filled with sulfur rather than powder, but a cylindrical cavity, coincident with the long axis of the shell, was filled with powder (86). The sulfur (or a resin) was used "to prevent them from rattling around and perhaps cracking the shell prematurely" (Peterson 1969, 80). However, it caused the balls to stick together, hindering their separation (Bruff 1896, 289).

In 1852, Boxer proposed further improvements: separating the charge from the sub-projectiles with a "wrought-iron … diaphragm"; reducing the charge so they wouldn't spread as widely; weakening the shell with internal grooving to compensate; and using coal dust instead of sulfur to keep the balls in place during flight. This design was approved in Britain in 1864 (Garbett 1897, 232–33).

The great advantage of the shrapnel shell was that it meant an anti-personnel load could be delivered at long range. The disadvantage was that, to be effective, the fuses (chapter 6) had to be properly timed.

World War I and Spanish Civil War experience showed that high-explosive shells were just as effective against soldiers as shrapnel shells and, of course, more effective against other targets (Weir 2019, 92). Consequently, by World War II, HE shells had replaced shrapnel for anti-personnel use.

The effect depends on the number of shell fragments, the mass of the fragments, the initial fragment velocity (typically 3,000+ fps in World War II), and the directionality of the blast. There's a tradeoff, of course, between lots of small fragments and a few big ones, as well as between fragment velocity and fragment size. For a given initial fragment velocity, large fragments travel farther.

British World War II studies showed that the optimum anti-personnel fragmentation was achieved with quite small fragments, generated by a bursting charge of 25 percent, but the metallurgy wasn't then equal to the task of firing such a shell from artillery (Evans 2014).

The Korean and Vietnam War beehive round was the modern equivalent of a shrapnel shell; when it burst, it spewed out thousands of flechettes, essentially small metal darts. The U.S. Navy and Coast Guard 81 mm, used on assault support patrol boats, could fire such rounds. That version contained 1,200 steel flechettes (Gutzman 2010, 471).

Armor-Piercing Shells

Armor-piercing shells and armor (see chapter 14) co-evolved, like predators and prey in nature. Early armor-piercing shells were made of forged steel (essentially second-generation Palliser shot with an explosive fill) and "would usually shatter on impact with face-hardened armor" (battleshipbean 2019).

In 1878, Captain English proposed placing a soft cap of wrought iron over the steel nose (Tucker 2015, 122). It was successful when first tried, but the British Ordnance Department rejected it in 1879 (Staunton 1901). The concept was rediscovered, and by 1897 the U.S. Navy adopted the Johnson cap. The cap spreads the force of impact so it is not concentrated at the point (Tucker 2105).

The best shape for penetration was rather blunt, and by 1914 AP shells were also given a "ballistic cap" ("windscreen") of light steel, for better aerodynamics (U.S. War Department 1914, 187).

AP shells carry only a small bursting charge (under 5 percent [Hempstead and Worthington 2005]; 2–3 percent [EB 1911, "Ammunition"]; 1.4–3.5 percent [Okun 1998a]). Initially, this charge was black powder, out of concern for premature detonation (Alger 1900), but that was replaced with high explosive. These shells carry base

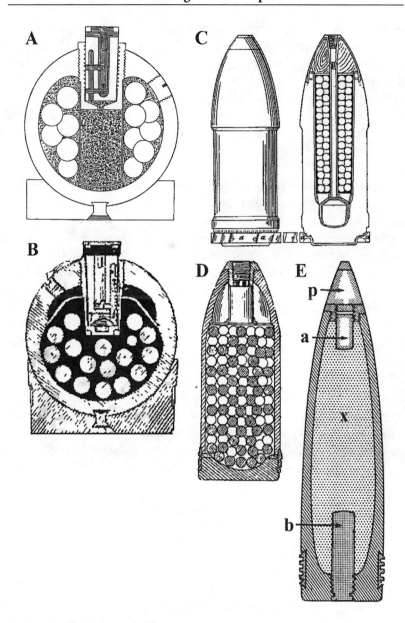

Anti-personnel shells. (A) Boxer improved shrapnel, spherical (Garbett 1897, 236). (B) Boxer diaphragm shrapnel, spherical (237). (C) Shrapnel shell, rifled muzzleloader. The body is thick cast iron, but the head is thin. Note the gas pipe running from the nose fuse to the bursting charge at the base. "The bullets are packed in melted resin" with "a brown paper lining" between them and the shell (250). (D) Shrapnel shell, rifled breechloader, with a nose fuse and the bursting charge immediately below it (255). (E) High-capacity shell for 6-inch/47 gun (NAVORD 1957, 28), with point-detonating fuse (p), auxiliary-detonating fuse (a), and base-detonating fuse (b); most of shell is filled with high-explosive Composition "B" (x), about 60 percent RDX and 40 percent TNT (17). The high-capacity shell is primarily intended for attacking lightly armored ship superstructures, or ground targets, but does have a secondary anti-personnel function.

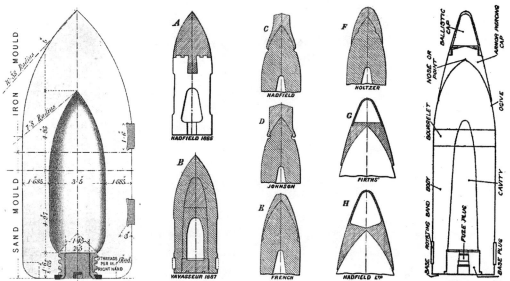

1.Palliser Shell (1874)   2.Capped Shells (1880s-1890s)   3.Shell w/Windscreen

(1) Palliser shell for 7-inch rifled muzzleloader—112.5 pounds cast iron and 2.5 pounds loose powder. Ogive radius of 10.38 inches, body diameter 6.925 inches (6.87 inches?), over studs 7.31 inches. This projectile had two rings of three studs each to engage the rifling. The shell was formed partly in iron mold and partly in sand mold, as indicated (Barlow 1874, 335). There were later, studless versions, and eventually Palliser shells were converted back to shot and filled instead with sand of the same weight as the former bursting charge (War Office 1902, 252). (2) Various forms of capped shells (Brassey 1921, 175; cp. Staunton 1901). (3) Shell with "ballistic cap" and "armour piercing cap" (U.S. War Department 1914, 187).

fuses, rather than nose fuses, to protect the fuse from damage by the armor. These would be delay fuses so the explosion would occur only after penetration. In the twentieth century, a typical setting would be 0.03–0.07 seconds after impact (DiGiulian 2023a).

Some literature also refers to a rather ill-defined intermediate class called "semi-armor-piercing shells." These appear to be common shells made of forged steel (thus having greater penetration) and with an intermediate nose thickness and bursting charge (3.5–6.5 percent [Okun 1998a]; 7.5–9 percent [battleshipbean 2019]). An AP shell was "expected to penetrate a full caliber of armor" and an SAP shell "about half that" (battleshipbean 2019).

The USS *Iowa* (BB-61) was equipped with 2,700-pound Mark 8 armor-piercing shells (Dramiński 2020, 18).

Diving Shells

The Zalinski pneumatic "torpedo" was essentially a diving shell, with a fuse designed "to cause the explosion to take place an interval of time after striking the water" (Zalinski 1888, 14). It had a conical nose, "made strong enough to resist crushing from impact with water" (12).

The British introduced a 7.5-inch anti-submarine howitzer in 1917. There were both rifled and smoothbored versions. Its projectiles carried TNT and "used a special fuse that delayed detonation for two seconds after impact, which would allow them to sink about 20 feet (6 m). The round was designed to penetrate the outer casing of a U-boat and then detonate on contact with the pressure hull." The 1918 version had "a flat nose disk that caused the rounds to dive at a steeper angle" (navweaps. com 2023).

The Squid (1943) was a three-barrel, 12-inch mortar; all barrels fired simultaneously. Its projectiles had a clockwork time fuse, so you chose a depth by estimating the sinking time (the sinking speed was 43.5 feet per second, and the maximum depth was 900 feet). HMS *Loch Killin* used a Squid to sink *U-333* (navweaps.com 2023).

The Japanese type 91 diving shells were intended for use against surface ships, not submarines. They had caps that broke away on water impact to reveal an inner blunt head suitable for a stable underwater trajectory, along with extra-long fuses to give them time to reach the unarmored underwater hull. Well, that was the theory. While in 1942 this devise damed the USS *Boise*, it could be used only at moderate ranges (so that the velocity on water impact was high enough), and there was a risk that the shell would pass under or even through the target without exploding (Evans and Peattie 2012, 263ff).

Incendiary and Kindred Shells

A shell could be filled with an incendiary concoction instead of explosive. The compositions used were quite similar to those of carcasses. One variation on the incendiary shell was the illuminating shell (star shell). Another was the smoke shell; the French had one in 1852, and it produced smoke "of a dense and distressing nature," but not dangerous to life (*Experiments* 1854, 14).

Red-hot shot was replaced around 1860 by Martin's Molten Iron Shell (hollow spheres filled with molten iron). For a ship to use this shot, it would need a furnace (HMS *Warrior* had one). You had to wait until at least four minutes after pouring before firing the shot, but the shot stayed hot for an hour (Lambert 1987, 7, 87; EB 1911, "Ammunition").

According to experiments conducted in 1859, their effectiveness increased greatly with the size of the shot, the 32-pound shell (holding 16 pounds of molten iron) being "of comparatively little use." The 8- and 10-inch shells held 26 and 45 pounds, respectively. "They can be loaded more easily than red hot shot and have a greater incendiary effect" (Experiments 1866, 28–30).

Shells with Shaped Charges

The use of a hollow charge, in order to focus the explosive force, was proposed by F.X. Von Baader in 1792. It was used in mining, though not very effectively, since gunpowder is a "low" explosive. There was further work with hollow charges in the late nineteenth century, notably by Charles Munroe, who used both a high explosive (dynamite) and a tin can liner (1894), although he did not recognize the value of the latter (Kennedy 1990, 3, 6).

The focused blast will turn any material it encounters into a high-speed projectile. The principle found practical application in the anti-tank weapons (bazooka, panzerfaust) of World War II (hence the name "HEAT" charge, for "High-Explosive Anti-Tank"). A biconical head, typically copper, fits into the conical hole in the charge. The charge detonates when the head comes into contact with the target, which puts the charge at just the right distance away for the explosion to convert the copper into a high speed (8–9 kilometers per second at leading edge) stream (Denny 2011, 153ff). The jet has high kinetic energy, and its force of impact is concentrated on a small area—hence its effectiveness in penetrating armor. The best modern "precision shaped charges can penetrate 10 or more charge diameters" of steel (Newhouse 2022).

Time is needed for the formation of the high-speed jet, so a relatively low striking velocity is desirable. If fired from a gun, that would mean low muzzle velocity and thus low range.

There were several demonstrations of the potential effectiveness of shaped charges (in aerial bombs) against battleship armor. In 1944, the Germans placed "a shaped charge of the SH1–400 type … against a forward gun turret" of an "upgraded 1911 French battleship." It penetrated the turret "and exploded shells that had been placed inside" (Johnsen 2018, 13–14). And in 1945, the National Defense Research Committee showed that the jet from a shaped charge could penetrate five armor plates (11, 4, and 3.75 inches), each pair separated by eight feet of air, and detonate some unfused 100-pound bombs placed between the second and third plates (Spencer 1946, 47). This result showed the potential vulnerability of a battleship magazine. Nonetheless, shaped charges were not used in naval munitions in World War II.

Armor on modern warships is less substantial, and warships in coastal waters may be attacked by high-speed boats at close range. Therefore, shaped charges may now be of greater concern. In 1978, Lieutenant Commander Charles Jones wrote, "Shaped charge warheads constitute one of the biggest challenges to the ship designer since it is nearly impossible to defend even the most vital areas from them due to the tremendous mass of armor plate required to stop shaped charge fragments. Moreover, penetration of armor plate or even standard bulkheads by these high-speed particles causes secondary particles to be torn off, producing extensive damage to equipment and injury to personnel."

Spherical Projectile (Shot and Shell) Manufacture

Inadequacy of Shot Towers

The shot towers used in the nineteenth century to cast lead musket balls aren't practical for making cannonballs. The shot was heated to a particular temperature above its melting point at the top of the shot tower. The shot tower operation achieves sphericity because the molten droplet falling through air is in free fall—zero gravity—and thus assumes spherical shape. The fall must be long enough for it to solidify without losing that shape.

The "heat content" to be lost will be the latent heat of fusion (over ten times as high for iron as for lead) multiplied by volume (thus proportional to diameter cubed). The heat transfer will be proportional to surface area (and thus to squared diameter). Thus, the required time of fall for solidification will be proportional to the diameter. The average velocity will be roughly half the terminal velocity, which in turn is proportional to the square root of the diameter, and the necessary height is approximately the fall time multiplied by the average velocity—that is, proportional to the 1.5th power of the diameter.

Lipscombe and Mungan (2012) suggest that the fall had to allow additional time for the balls to cool below the boiling point of water, so when they landed in water for final cooling, they wouldn't create steam. That, of course, would make significant the difference between the melting point of the shot and the boiling point of water, which would be greater for iron. Lipscombe and Mungan say that "it takes about one-third of the height of the tower for it to solidify and the remaining two-thirds for it to cool down."

The shot tower drops were substantial, typically over 150 feet for making lead musket balls. In 1801 (shot towers were invented in 1782), British lead musket balls had a diameter of 0.68 inches for muskets and 0.89 for wall pieces (Egerton 1801, 30). Consider now how much more of a drop would be needed for an iron cannonball with a diameter of 3.49–6.68 inches (for 6–42-pound balls) (Collins, "British Cannonball Sizes").

Casting

Biringuccio's *Pirotechnia* (1540) presented the first written description of the casting of cannonballs. The founder must first make molds. It appears that the earliest molds were made of clay, which could be used only once. These were replaced by metal molds; Biringuccio preferred iron to bronze, but the latter were sometimes used even in the 18c.

The molds are hemispheric half-shells that fit together, one on top of the other. Biringuccio (1990, 319ff) says that the molds have "little openings for the gates and vents and likewise four holes for pegging the parts together" and "that each pair of molds is filled until the iron overflows." The early nineteenth-century artillerist Louis de Tousard (1809, 2:349) says that the molten iron is poured into a hole in the superior half-shell, and once the halfway mark is reached, the flow rate should be reduced to give air time to escape. Despite the pegs, there is leakage at the seam; this results in an "excrescence called *the beard*, which is broken off to render the ball completely round."

By 1809, hammering mills were used to render the projectile more spherical (de Tousard 1809, 2:355). By the 1830s, it was recognized that it was beneficial to roll the shot before hammering it (Culmann 1836, 88). "Rolling polishes the surface of the shot and exposes slight flaws…. Shots which have been first rolled may be hammered more quickly and at a lower heat, and receive a much finer surface" (90).

In the American Civil War, solid shot was cast by filling the joined molds through a "slanted-L" channel that communicated with the seam between the mold, and the excess metal vented from the top (Poche and George n.d.).

Casting spherical shells (hollow shot) was a little more complicated. One method mentioned by Biringuccio required the use of a core in the middle of the molds, held in place by iron projections. The molten metal filled the space between the molds and the core. The other method was a bit unclear, but I think it was a variant on the "lost wax" process used in bell making. In any event, the metal alloy was deliberately brittle, such a "copper strongly corrupted with tin, or cast iron." The shell naturally had a hole for filling it with powder; the fuse was then inserted into the hole.

Round shot cast in sand molds was superior in smoothness, sphericity and homogeneity to that cast in iron molds, possibly because the pores of the sand allowed air to escape (Jeffers 1850, 119; Hebert 1849, 2:595). Iron molds came first, and Culman (1836, 88) states that sand molds (for projectiles) weren't introduced until around 1824. In 1880 America, grape and canister shot were cast in iron molds, whereas other spherical projectiles were cast in sand (U.S. Navy 1880, 201). The sand molds were also used to make the cores for hollow shot.

First-generation Palliser shot was cast point down using an iron mold for the nose and a sand mold for the body. Because of the high thermal conductivity of the iron, the nose could be chilled rapidly and thereby hardened. The body would cool slowly and be toughened (EB 1911, "Ammunition").

Quality Control

Just because a cannonball is supposed to be a homogeneous sphere of a particular diameter doesn't mean it actually is. It can be over- or undersized, it can be lopsided, and it can have cavities. It may also be under- or overweight.

"If a ball were a bit too large, the gunner might try, unsuccessfully, to ram it all the way down," and "the cannon is rendered useless until the charge can be fired off. This operation is long, difficult, and occasions much injury to the metal." If it were too small, it "cannot have all of the range of which it is capable, because a great part of the inflammation of the powder will escape through the excess of windage" (de Tousard 1809, 1:351–52).

"Solid" shot is usually not entirely solid; the outside cools first and contracts, leaving a shrinkage cavity inside. As a result of the shrinkage cavity, the apparent density of seventeenth-century cannonballs was less than would be expected, given the density of cast iron. For example, a study of an English Civil War cannonball found that it weighed 14.25 pounds and was 4.92 inches diameter, for an average density of just 6.13 g/cc (Walton 1999, 143). And if the cavity was off-center, that would affect how the shot flew.

There were other imperfections too. Air bubbles in the molten iron could form additional cavities. Williams and Johnson (2000) cast a cannonball in the laboratory and, slicing it in half, found three large defects clustered together; these would have shifted the center of mass away from the center of pressure, thus altering the ball's aerodynamics.

There would be a seam where the halves of the mold met, along with a disturbance at the vent sprue where the excess metal escaped. Other problems were created by impurities in the melt. It might have been possible to remove some imperfections by rolling or hammering the shot while it was heated. In the early nineteenth century, the balls were heated beyond cherry red and hammered on all sides until they were perfectly smooth; this process typically took 100–130 strokes of a water-powered hammer of 30–120 pounds (de Tousard 1809, 1:350). Later, a revolving iron cylinder holding several balls was used to polish the shot by friction (Simpson 1862, 211).

Consequently, the cannonball was cast slightly larger than the size corresponding to the nominal weight and then compressed by the hammering; therefore, it would end up a bit heavier. For example, a 24-pound shot might weigh 24.5 pounds (de Tousard 1809, 1:355). But shot was rejected if its weight departed too far from expectations (Simpson 1862).

Cannonball quality control was primitive. The simplest scheme was to pass the ball through a circular "go" gauge (*lunette*); balls that were too large to fit were rejected, as they presumably wouldn't fit into the bore.

In France, Jean Baptiste Vaquette de Gribeauval's innovation was to insist that the balls also not pass through a "no-go" gauge. (That doesn't mean that the artillerists of the past uncritically accepted undersized cannonballs—just that they judged whether they were large enough by eye.) The French artillery service wanted to set a spread of six points (one point = 7.4 mils) between the two gauges but was forced (by political pressure) to settle for nine. Of course, all this supposes that the gauges were identical. And so each arsenal had a master gauge, and the working gauges couldn't diverge from it by more than two points (Alder 2010, 150–51). In early nineteenth-century American practice, the "go" and "no-go" gauges differed in diameter by 0.07 inches (de Tousard 1809, 1:353).

What about lopsidedness? The "go" lunette was replaced by a tube 5 calibers long, fastened obliquely to a support in such a manner that the ball would have to be rolled through the tube (Alder 2010, 152).

Precautions had to be taken "to prevent the manufacturers from inserting such as have been discarded, among such as are received and weighed. These last are kept under locks and keys, until they are shipped, and the inspector keeps a good look-out at the moment they are put on board, or loaded on carts, to prevent any others being substituted in their place" (de Tousard 1809, 1:355).

Elongated Projectile Manufacture

Casting

You might expect that elongated projectiles would also be cast using two symmetric half-molds, but that was not the case. Rather, one sand mold shaped the fore- and midbody, and the other the aftbody (U.S. Navy 1880, Appendix 9A, Plate XII). But note that for forming an armor-piercing shell, a Palliser projectile was cast point downward, forming the head initially in an iron mold that was suddenly chilled (rendering the head hard, although brittle) and then transferring the casting, still warm, to a sand mold (Hamilton 1916, 9).

Forging

By the early twentieth century, there was a new manufacturing method, involving processing a heated solid cast steel blank by forging—punching, perhaps with a steam hammer (a depression into the blank held by an indexed die), and then, if need be, drawing up the lip to lengthen the cavity that received the explosive fill. At least the outside of the rough shell was machined to give it a proper aerodynamic shape; the inside of the cavity could be machined or left rough (Hamilton 1916, 42ff; Alford 1917, 243; Marzetta 1946).

CHAPTER 6

Ammunition

Explosive Trains

An explosive train is a series of two or more explosives disposed so that one component ignites the next one in sequence. The explosive train may be used for propulsion or for damaging the target.

Propulsive Explosive Train

In modern guns, propulsion begins with ignition of a primer charge, usually by heat or friction. Its flame sets off an ignition charge. And the ignition charge ignites the propulsive charge, a smokeless powder (NAVORD 1957, 2B7). Fine-grain black powder may serve as a primer charge, and granular black powder as an ignition charge (2C7). For primer use, the black powder may be mixed with a more sensitive explosive, such as lead azide (2B8).

High-Explosive Train

The purpose of a high-explosive train is to burst the shell. In twentieth-century shells, it typically consists of the detonator, the booster charge, and the main charge. The detonator is ignited by a fuse (see later in this chapter). It in turn ignites the booster charge, which sets off the main charge. The detonator is of high sensitivity but low explosive power, the main charge is the opposite, and the booster charge is of intermediate character (NAVORD 1957, 2B7). This arrangement exists because it is critical that the main charge not be set off by the shock of firing the gun.

The first detonator was fulminate of mercury; later, potassium chlorate was also used.

In the 1930s, the U.S. Navy used fulminate of mercury, or mixtures of it with TNT, tetryl (trinitrophenylmethylnitramine) or trinitrobenzene, as a detonator (NAVORD 1937, s106, s228). Granular TNT (s223) and tetryl (s227) were used for booster charges. In the 1950s, the typical detonator was "lead azide or lead styphnate, either alone with granular TNT or tetryl" (NAVORD 1957, 2B8).

The earliest booster charges were essentially just smaller amounts of the same explosive used as the main charge but compressed. The booster series then worked as a delay element.

Later, it was thought safer to use a small amount of a sensitive explosive to set off a larger amount of a less sensitive one. That approach worked fine in a common or high-explosive shell. However, in an armor-piercing shell, the booster had to be small, and there were a lot of duds because the TNT or Dunnite wasn't sensitive enough. This mismatch of booster to main charge was overcome by introducing a new, much more sensitive booster: tetryl (2,4,6-trinitrophenylmethylnitramine) (Okun 2004). Tetryl, in turn, was replaced by RDX.

Ammunition Rounds

A complete round of ammunition is everything you need to fire a weapon once. For a cannon, that would be the projectile, the propellant charge, and the primer (and the intermediate ignition charge, if need be). If the projectile was a shell, this combination would also include a fuse.

There are three modern types of ammunition: bag, semifixed and fixed. "In bag ammunition, the primer, propelling charge, and projectile are separate units. In semifixed ammunition, the primer and propelling charge are contained in one unit, while the projectile is separate. In fixed ammunition, all 3 components are assembled in 1 unit" (NAVORD 1957, 3A3). For fixed or semifixed ammunition, the common container is called a case or cartridge (3B5).

In modern bag ammunition, there is an ignition charge in the base of the bag containing the actual propulsive charge. The advantage is that the same primer may be used "for bag guns of all sizes," while the ignition charge is made proportionate to the propulsive charge in the same bag (NAVORD 1957, 3C1).

Fixed ammunition lends itself to automatic loading. Semifixed ammunition must be manually loaded, but it can be handled more rapidly than bag ammunition. "The factor that determines whether ammunition for a certain gun will be fixed or semifixed is the size and weight of a unit which can be handled by one man" (NAVORD 1957, 3B5).

In the early modern period, the charge and primer were usually loose powder that had to be ladled out to measure, and all the components were separate. However, even in the late sixteenth century, occasionally the powder was in bags (Peterson 1969, 27); multiple bags would be used if you needed more oomph.

Bags offered a greater rate of fire but less flexibility in adjusting the charge. In France, loose powder was abandoned only after it was shown that there was a "maximum" (critical) charge beyond which range couldn't be increased (Nosworthy 1996, 367). (This result would correspond to when burn-out occurred at the muzzle; see chapter 9.)

A cannonball could be strapped together with a powder bag to a wooden sabot (see "Sabot" later in this chapter) (Peterson 1969, 63). That would, presumably, have sped up handling further.

Cartridges first appeared for small arms. Paper cartridges were "known as early

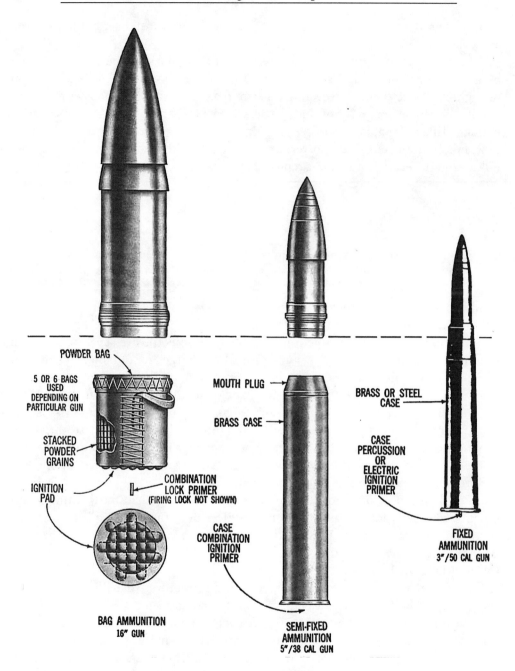

Modern naval ordnance ammunition types: bag; semifixed; and fixed (BNW 1963).

as the 16th century" (Guthrie 2003, 36), but Thomas Hayes says that they weren't true cartridges, but rather paper wrapping for powder. He credits Gustavus Adolphus with introducing the true paper cartridge, including the bullet, to the Swedish army in 1625 (Hayes 1938, 656). Unfortunately, they are easily damaged, so cloth (especially flannel) cartridges came to be preferred in the eighteenth century. (The British admiralty ordered the switch in 1755 [Pope 1987, 206].)

Metal cartridges appeared in the nineteenth century. Lead cartridges were used by the American navy in the War of 1812 (James 1826, 6:103). The first brass cartridge (for the Enfield rifle) was invented by Colonel Edward Boxer in 1865 (Hamilton 1916a, 2).

In the late nineteenth-century British navy, fixed ammunition was used for the rapid-fire guns and bag ammunition for the larger guns.

At the Battle of Jutland, the British lost three battle cruisers because enemy shell fire caused a secondary explosion of the ship's magazine. The powder in the British silk bags was immediately ignited and exploded. In contrast, the Germans used brass cartridge boxes and cases. These protected the powder from explosion for a time, providing an opportunity for the sprinkler systems to kick in (Ott 2010, 7).

Even in 1955, the U.S. Navy used bag charges "in some 8-inch guns and all guns larger than 8-inch. As recently as the beginning of World War II, bag-type 5- and 6-inch guns were still in use." The bags were "nylon or silk, because only such fabric will completely burn away when combustion of the charge takes place, leaving no smoldering residue to cause the premature explosion of the next charge loaded" (NAVORD 1957, 3B2).

Gas-Checks and Cartridge Extraction

If a breechloader uses bag ammunition, a sealing mechanism is needed to prevent gas blowing back through the breech closure. The U.S. military used the DeBange gas-check (obturator) system, whose principal element was a mushroom-like structure with a stem that fitted into the breech plug and a head that was seated inside the powder chamber. "In a 16-inch gun, it weighs 220 pounds" (NAVORD 1957, 58).

With case ammunition, a gas check isn't needed, as the cartridge prevents the rearward escape of the combustion gases. However, the cartridge must be extracted before the gun can fire again (NAVORD 1957, 59–60).

Ammunition Storage

Shot

The weight of the shot for an early modern warship was great enough that it was typically stowed before the waterline, which, given the leakiness of wooden ships, pretty much guaranteed that the shot would get corroded by seawater.

The "shot locker" (garland) was an apartment "built up in the hold to contain the shot." There were also shot racks (ranges): "pieces of oak plank, fixed against the head ledges and coamings of the hatch and ladderways, or against the side between the ports, to contain the shot." These pieces were "hollowed out to near one third of [the shot's] diameter, so that the balls lie in them about one inch asunder" (Steel 1812, 62, 54; Folio XXVII).

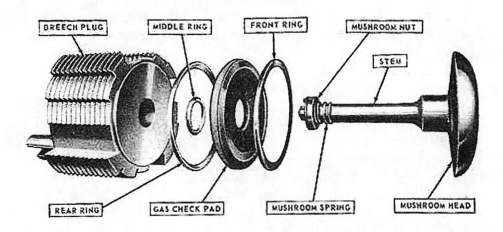

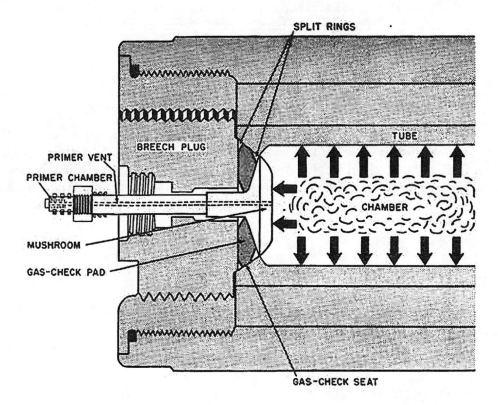

Top: Exploded view showing how the DeBange "mushroom" fits on to the Welin-type breech plug. Bottom: View showing the mushroom installed inside the powder chamber (NAVORD 1957, 58).

Douglas (1829, 97ff) proposed that fifteen double-shotted rounds be kept on deck, in some kind of container that would keep it out of the water sloshing across the deck.

Powder

In the Georgian navy, gunpowder was delivered to warships in wooden barrels, "copper- or hazel-hooped," and holding 100 pounds (Blake and Lawrence 2005, 104). In 1809, the ordnance stores on the 74-gun *Milford* included 295 gunpowder barrels (totaling 29,488 pounds) and another four half-barrels of powder for priming (221).

After the adoption of the cartridge, those were delivered separately to the gunner, and the cartridges would be filled aboard the ship. The *Milford* received several thousand paper cartridges with flannel bottoms for long guns, as well as flannel cartridges for carronades (221–22). Admiralty instructions stated that "no more than three rounds of parchment-cartridges are to be filled at a time" (Steel 1801, 32).

David Steel describes the "magazine" as "the apartment used to lodge powder in; which, in large ships, is situated forward, and in small ships abaft" (1812, 44). The "powder room," in contrast, was used "for holding cartridges filled with powder," and it was disposed at the opposite end of the ship from the magazine (52).

There were two basic concerns: fire and water. The former was the greater concern, as a powder explosion could destroy the ship. For better protection against enemy fire, the magazine was "always be situated as low down as possible" (Steel 1812, 44). It had bulkheads (13), and the deck above was more thickly planked (281). The powder room has "racks for stowing the filled cartridges" (285).

Magazines (and powder rooms) "have their passages lined with lead, 5 lbs. to the foot square, and turned up five inches at the sides and ends," so "as to hold water when required." The lower sills of the doors are "not to be less than seven inches deep," presumably to keep powder from shifting out. "The doors are plastered with mortar inside and out, with slit deal over it," and the bulkheads were covered "with plaster of mortar and hair." The door hardware was of brass and copper (Steel 1812, Folio XVII; 30, 57). The "insides and outsides" of the room "joints" were "sheathed with thin copper," so "should fire happen in any part of the ship, the repositories for powder may be readily filled with water."

They were lit with a lantern whose candle was behind tin and glass (41) and set in a "light-room," "a small place parted off [from] the magazine" (Steel 1812, 43; Folio XVII). The light was reflected (probably rather dimly) off obliquely set "spla-board" (65).

Steel indicates that the system of pumps and wells used to keep the ship dry could also be used to instantly drown the magazine (Steel 1812, 168), although it isn't clear how widely implemented this method was at the time. He also refers to "hanging magazines," meaning the floors of the magazines being displaced several feet below the deck on which they were nominally situated. This arrangement can be seen in a drawing of HMS *Victory* (Pope 1987, xiv); the magazines are keyed 33 and 35. That made them easier to flood.

The sailors entering the powder room "wore only linen and leather goods and they even wore wicker shoes or leather slippers" (Glover 2021, 59).

In storage, powder could become damp, and once its moisture content rose above 1 percent, it began losing explosive power (Kelly 2004, 59) and became more difficult to ignite (Brown and Rugunanan 1989, 73). Hence, the barrels sat on a pallet, "a slight platform … to keep the powder from moisture" (Steel 1812, 50). And "by the mid-19th century aboard ships it was stored in watertight sealed containers" (Tucker 2015, 34).

Keeping powder away from seawater isn't enough because it can actually absorb water vapor (Douglas 1829, 199). It follows that what's needed is airtight storage or, if that isn't possible, storage together with some desiccant or protective coating.

Powder was examined for dampness and, if damp, was dried. This was a ticklish operation, as the drying process could melt the sulfur or even explode the grains (Douglas 1829, 200). If the powder were past redemption, one could at least attempt to recover the saltpeter, which was a rare and valuable commodity in Europe (201).

Modern Practice

In the mid-twentieth-century U.S. Navy, (smokeless) powder bags were stored in tanks, since the bags themselves were neither airtight nor watertight. The bags were separated by "wooden spacers to prevent building of a static charge which might ignite the powder by a spark" (NAVORD 1957, 3B4). Projectiles were stored in a stowage compartment under a turret, standing in rings on their bases, lashed to the bulkhead (7D1).

Sabots

Sabots are single or multipart full-caliber devices placed behind or around the projectile for various purposes.

Sabots were first used for convenience, associating the propellant charge with the shot and in connection with fused projectiles to keep the fuse facing forward (Kinard 2007, 124). For round shot or early modern shells, the sabot was likely to be a wooden (usually elm) disc with a hollow on one side to receive the rear of the shot, and it was strapped to the shot, typically with strips of tin.

In the American Civil War, "sabots" were introduced that were attached to the rear of a projectile, and which expanded to engage the rifling, like a "driving band" (McCaul 2005, 319). These were made of wrought iron, lead, copper, brass or *papier-mâché* (Bell 2003, 41, 506; Kinard 2007, 187). Shapes included ring, cup, band and disk sabots (Bell 2003, 507). John Brooke's "copper ratchet disk sabot" was the "core of the Confederate Navy artillery sabot program" (510). The Type 2 Parrott brass ring sabot was "found on Union Navy projectiles, from 3-inch to 12-inch calibers" (518). The Dahlgren lead cup sabot was used by both sides (512).

In modern use, a sabot holds a sub-caliber projectile centered in the bore (if the projectile has full bore fins, those help, too). It also seals the bore and transfers the pressure from the propellant gases to the projectile. Under the late 1960s "Gunfighter" program, the U.S. Navy developed a "long range bombardment" projectile. This device was an "arrow" (finned) shell with a body diameter of 4.125 inches and a fin diameter of 5 inches, to be used with a sabot in an 8-inch gun. The USS *Saint Paul*, in 1970 the only active 8-inch gun cruiser in the navy, was able to hit enemy targets at a range of 70,000 yards (Gutzman 2010, 158; navweaps.com 2022).

There was also a plan for the reactivated battleships with 16-inch guns, such as USS *Iowa*, to fire sub-caliber shells with a sabot. Thus, in 1967, it was proposed that the USS *New Jersey* would use some leftover 11-inch army shells, but *New Jersey* was decommissioned in 1969. And there were experiments in the 1980s with firing a 13.65-inch shell with a sabot, but development was cancelled in 1991 (navweaps. com 2023a).

Discarding Sabots

Generally speaking, you want the sabot to be as light as possible, because accelerating the sabot is a waste of propulsive force—the heavier the sabot, the less the muzzle velocity. But the sabot must be strong enough to center the projectile and efficiently transfer the gas pressure to it. If the sabot remains attached to the projectile after it leaves the muzzle, it will impair the projectile's aerodynamic characteristics. So a modern sabot is designed to discard reliably without interfering with the projectile trajectory (Carlucci and Jacobsen 2018, 152). These aren't trivial engineering considerations.

The U.S. Navy's PHALANX close-in weapons system uses a plastic, four-petal discarding sabot (Wilds 1986, 7–14).

Fusing

Design Issues

Shells (as well as rockets, missiles, and torpedoes) are equipped with fuses, whose purpose is to cause an explosion when it will do the most damage to the target. With a shell, you don't want it to explode when it is accidentally dropped, or in the gun barrel, or on a mere ricochet, but only when it strikes the actual target. If you are attacking an armored target, results will be better if the explosion is delayed until the projectile penetrates the armor. For an anti-personnel munition, an overhead burst might be desirable.

Fuses can be characterized according to how they are armed (preferably not until the shell leaves the muzzle and attains a safe distance) and how they sense when to initiate the explosive train (preferably in the presence of the enemy).

In modern warfare, fuses are manufactured in enormous quantities. If a fuse design requires tolerances that are high by the current standards, the defect rate may be high. Even in the early 1900s, it was desirable that tolerances not be stricter than 0.01 inches (Young 1920, 506ff). In addition, one must consider the number and size of elements and how they are to be fabricated—for example, a complex shape might need to be machined rather than cast. If the fuse is drastically different from those made in the past, then you might need to make many new gauges, tools and machines in order to make the device in volume. If the fuse is replacing an older version, will it fit the old fuse hole? If not, the projectile must also be reworked or replaced (Young 1920).

The smaller the projectile, the smaller the fuse it can accommodate, and thus the more difficult it is to provide a long enough powder track to achieve the desired time-to-burst. Moreover, in borderline cases, the fuse spoils the aerodynamic shape of the projectile (McCaul 2005, 107). For armor-piercing shells, the larger the fuse, the more the shell is weakened, reducing penetration (Smith 1998, 41).

Safety is critical. Can a part be left out, misplaced or reversed, and, if so, what is the effect? How much handling (especially of a sensitive material like fulminate) is necessary? Is the charge subject to deterioration with age? Safety in manufacturing is even more important than safety in use—think about the quantity of explosive stored in a munitions factory (Young 1920).

Fuse designs were often kept secret. The Union navy's instructions stated, "It is strictly forbidden to show or explain to foreigners or others the construction of any fuses, except so far as may be necessary for the service of the guns" (U.S. Navy 1866, 89).

Scores of different fuse designs have been invented, so only a few can be discussed here.

Time Fuses

Until the mid-nineteenth century, only time fuses were used, and the original time fuse was a slow match or port fire placed in the fuse hole of the shell. It was cut to burn for 14–20 seconds (Marshall 1915, 19).

One method of igniting the fuse is described in a 1561 text. The shell was placed in a sack containing a priming compound, with the fuse hole facing the muzzle. When the mortar was fired, the burning charge would ignite the compound, which in turn would ignite the fuse. At any rate, that was the theory, but it didn't always work. Another approach was to put the shell in with the fuse hole facing the breech. No problem lighting the fuse, but the fuse might be driven into the shell and explode right in the barrel, which was not good for artillery crew morale (Peterson 1969, 27).

In the technique known as "firing at two strokes" or "double firing," the fuse faced the muzzle, and the gunner first lit the shell fuse and then set off the cannon (64). If the cannon misfired, the crew would need to put out the bomb fuse very quickly if they didn't want to earn a Darwin Award. Harold Peterson says that this method didn't come into general use until 1650, while Paul Lacombe and Charles Boutell (1870, 231) and Edwin Tunis (1954, 90) maintain that it was the dominant method until then.

In the eighteenth century, someone discovered (perhaps by accident) that the flash could ignite the fuse even with the fuse facing the muzzle end. That, in turn, meant that it was possible to fire a shell from a long-muzzled smoothbore.

Improvement in fuses became a matter of urgency due to the development of the rifled musket, as the infantry could hit artillery outside the range of canister fire. Thus, survival of field artillery depended on the development of a time fuse accurate at long range so the shrapnel burst would be at the right position (50–130 yards in front, 15–20 feet above) relative to advancing infantry (McCaul 2005, 46, 78).

The American Civil War wooden fuse had a hollow, fine-grained hardwood (beech, ash) fuse body filled with a hand or screw press–compacted fuse composition, with uncompacted gunpowder as a primer. The setback forces exerted by firing a heavy gun could throw out the fuse or cause the filler to break the wood; hence the wooden fuse was used only in mortar projectiles. The advantage of the wooden fuse was that it could be cut on the spot to just the right length to achieve a desired flight time-to-burst. The paper fuse was also used with mortars; the paper case was a truncated cone and was filled with the burning composition.

The Royal Navy favored the Boxer wood time fuse (c. 1855). Like prior fuses, it had a truncated cone shape, with a longitudinal channel containing fuse composition (or mealed powder). But rather than being cut to length, it had radial holes stopped with clay at intervals along the length of the cone. These holes communicated with side channels containing pistol powder. To set the time, the gunner bored through the clay, connecting the side channel with the main channel. When ignited, the flame burned down the fuse composition in the main channel until it reached the connected side channel and then flashed through the latter to ignite the shell. With rifled guns, which lacked windage, a detonator was added. They were still in use, although not in production, at the end of the nineteenth century (Garbett 1897, 268–71).

In naval use, wood fuses swelled, so they no longer fit in the fuse hole, and paper fuses deteriorated once they got wet (McCaul 2005, 64). This situation led to the adoption of the Navy (Alger) Water Cap (Seacoast) Fuse (70ff) in time for the Mexican War. A cylindrical paper fuse was placed inside a brass fuse case just before loading the piece. The opening was closed with a threaded metal "water cap" that had three or four holes; these holes communicated, through a zigzag mealed powder train in the cap, with the paper fuse. This arrangement effectively waterproofed the fuse. Before Alger's death (1856), he added a lead safety knob; this piece was broken off by setback forces. The top of the water cap had a recess that was filled with primer, which was covered with a lead disc until the fuse was ready for use. The fuse was precut for five, ten or fifteen seconds, and the disc was marked to indicate which. The Alger fuse was used by both the navy and the army and was still in use in 1880 (McCaul 2005, 76). In the Union navy, it was used with most shells (U.S. Navy 1866, 89).

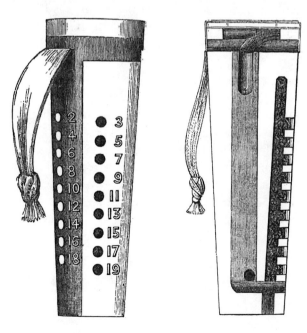

Boxer time fuse, exterior (left) and interior (right) (Owen 1873, Figures 65–66, p. 130).

In the Bormann fuse, the fuse composition was completely sealed in a soft metal case. To prepare the fuse for use, holes were punched into the tin sheet at the base to allow communication with the bursting charge. The fuse was screwed into the projectile and a hole was punched into the top of the fuse at a location that determined the fuse time. This hole communicated with a horizontal, curved channel filled with powder. When the gun was fired, the flame would enter the hole and the powder would burn in both directions (McCaul 2005, 82ff; Kinard 2007, 186). While the Bormann fuse was safe and reliable, the maximum burn time was typically five seconds, limiting its range to 1,300 yards with a 12-pound field gun (McCaul 2005, 85). In the Union navy, the Bormann fuse was used with 12- and 24-pdr boat howitzers, and all shrapnel (U.S. Navy 1866, 90).

Unfortunately, flame ignition didn't adapt well to rifled artillery. The reduced windage made it more difficult to ignite the fuse (Hess 2022, 33). This situation led to the development of concussion-time fuses; the "concussion" (force of firing) ignited an otherwise conventional time fuse. I have found no reference to their use by the U.S. Navy (cp. Cooke 1875, 542).

Time fuses didn't always burn consistently; consequently, there was interest in achieving greater precision using a clockwork timing mechanism. Clockwork fuses worked well enough for "enhanced" fireships carrying explosives; Federico Gianibelli's "hellburner," a ship-size shrapnel device, was successfully deployed against the Spanish siege troops at Antwerp in 1585 (Gurstelle 2007, 104ff). However, fancier engineering was necessary for clockwork to keep ticking as it flew along a ballistic trajectory.

The first successful clockwork shell fuses appeared just before World War I. The source of power for mechanical timers is likely to be either the spinning projectile's rotational kinetic energy or the potential elastic energy stored in a spring. The mid-twentieth-century U.S. Navy used mechanical time fuses "to obtain timed air bursts" (NAVORD 1957, 3E6).

The first electric time fuse (1937) was for a German bomb; when dropped, a circuit closed and a storage condenser charged a firing condenser (WRG 2017). But in 1957, "a highly accurate electric time fuse that can be set very quickly" was still "under development" (NAVORD 1957, 3E6).

If you don't have proximity fuses (see later in this chapter), and you are firing at a small fast target (torpedo boat, aircraft), the chance of a direct hit is not good, and you must either lay down a heavy volume of fire or use time fuses (or both) (Smith 1998, 53). If the fuse detonated at a fixed time from when it was set, as opposed to when the gun was fired, you would need to maintain a uniform rate of anti-aircraft fire, or the shells would explode at the wrong range or altitude (Okun).

Percussion Fuses

These fuses are triggered, directly or indirectly, by the impact of the shell with a solid object (ideally the target). The 1799 discovery of mercury fulminate (a very sensitive explosive) made it possible, but it took a half-century more to develop the percussion fuse.

A fuse could detonate the charge by virtue of impact, friction, or heat. Impact could throw a non-explosive "hammer" against an "anvil" bearing a sensitive explosive, or vice versa. Setting off an armed fuse by impact may seem trivial, but sometimes projectiles failed to strike point-first. If the fuse were designed so a glancing blow would result in detonation, then it might also be triggered by a ricochet.

The Zalinski "pneumatic torpedo" had two fuses, one of which was a percussion fuse. This fuse used a wet silver chloride battery to generate a red heat when the outer shell was crushed down on a copper cone that was part of the circuit (Zalinski 1888, 14).

Percussion fuses may be located in the base or the nose of the shell. Both common and high-explosive shells are usually equipped with nose fuses.

Base fuses were necessary for armor-piercing projectiles; a fuse hole in front would unduly weaken the shell (Smith 1998, 34). However, as Major C.G. Young notes, base fuses must be protected from the powder gases by a plate and therefore cannot be changed or set (if they have variable functions) easily.

We may classify percussion fuses depending on how they are armed: (1) by impact with the target (always a nose fuse); (2) by the shock (setback force) of discharge (nose or base); (3) by the rotation of the shell in flight (ditto); and (4) by the gas pressure of discharge (always a base fuse).

The *direct impact* type minimizes the time interval from impact to detonation. Typically, a protruding plunger would be forced back. (Obviously, you would not want to use this kind of fuse with a muzzleloader. Yet Rollins, USP 34,268 [1862], proposed that this approach would be fine if a "hollow or concave rammer" were used.)

Many early percussion fuses relied on the setback forces created by the linear acceleration of the projectile in the bore to arm the fuse.

The Royal Navy used the Moorsom fuse (1850) until 1865. It had a metal body containing three hammers, which were freed to act by the shearing of retaining wires on discharge. On impact, a hammer was thrown against a patch of detonating composition (Garbett 1897, 275–76).

The 1911 *Encyclopedia Britannica* article "Ammunition" characterized the original Pettman fuse as the first practical percussion fuse. W.R. Barlow (1874, 37–43) describes it in detail: A roughened ball is covered with a detonating composition (including potassium chlorate, antimony sulfide, sulfur and mealed powder). When the gun is discharged, a lead cup is crushed, and the ball is forced back, with various plugs preventing it from rebounding or touching the sides. It is disengaged by the motion of the shell, and when the target is struck, the ball hits the wall of the housing and explodes. To prevent detonation on graze, the ball can be covered with two thin copper hemispheres.

The Pettman fuse was tested in 1860, with excellent results: 0/20 premature bursts; 1/20 duds (*Experiments* 1854, 41). The British adopted it for land (1861) and sea (1862) service.

The Pettman fuse was originally developed for use in spherical shells, which of course had the particular problem that you had no control over what part of the shell hit the target.

A modified version was also found to work with rifled shells (Experiments 1878, 46) and adopted. However, American tests in 1878 in rifled guns reported frequent failures to explode, and this option was deemed inferior to, among others, the Schenkl and Hotchkiss percussion fuses (Ordnance 1866, 405–6, 421).

In the American Civil War, the leading nose percussion fuse was probably Schenkl's. This was a double action device: firing the cannon created setback forces that broke a side-mounted safety screw and freed a slider; impact created forces that caused the percussion cap-bearing slider to strike the opposing surface (anvil) and cause a flash. The anvil was flat on one side, concave on the other. In storage and transport, the anvil was screwed concave side-in and thus avoided accidental explosion even if the screw broke prematurely. The main problem was training related; the men would occasionally forget to reverse the anvil (McCaul 2005, 173ff).

Pettman GS (General Service) fuse (Owen 1873, Figure 74, p. 152). Parts are Body (A); Top Plug (B); Plain Ball (C); Steady Plug (D); Detonating Ball (E); Cone Plug (F); Lead Cup (G); Suspending Wire (H).

The 1880 U.S. Navy ordnance instructions state, "The Schenkl percussion fuse is now exclusively used in the Navy for great guns" (U.S. Navy 1880, 207). It was compatible with "rifle shell" (149).

In World War II, the German navy made use of base percussion fuses, armed by setback (Okun 2004).

The fuse may be armed by virtue of a rifled shell's rotation rather than setback on firing. For example, Augustus Cooke (1880, 634) describes a German percussion fuse in which the plunger is initially retained by a transverse pin. The "centrifugal force … throws out the pin…; the plunger by its inertia is retained…; at the moment of impact the plunger impinges against the fulminate."

In the "Semple centrifugal plunger," the firing pin was pivotably mounted and, in the disarmed position, was shielded from the detonation charge. It was held in that position by a spring. Centrifugal force, if great enough, would overcome the spring force and bring the pin to the firing position. But because of inertia, this didn't happen until after the projectile left the bore. A "creep spring" kept the plunger from creeping forward as a result of it not experiencing air resistance as did the projectile, but the spring was too weak to prevent it from flying forward on impact (Tschappat 1917, 553–56). I have not been able to formally document this device's naval use, but it is mentioned in the 1944 USN ordnance manual (NAVORD 1944, 38).

Centrifugal arming definitely results, if implemented properly, in a safer fuse. Dropping a shell could conceivably result in a sufficient setback force to arm the older kind of percussion fuse, but "under no circumstances could a shell be accidentally rotated over 2000 rpm" (Smith 1998, 37).

The Union navy disliked percussion fuses because they didn't allow the shell time to penetrate the enemy hull and therefore used them only for shore bombardment (McCaul 2005, 64).

With German Naval World War II percussion fuses, there was a slight time interval between impact and detonation, as it took perhaps 0.003 seconds (Okun 2004) for inertial forces to slam the slider into the primer. If that wasn't enough delay to permit the projectile to penetrate an armored target, then you need delayed action.

In general, in a *delayed action percussion fuse*, the impact ignites a primer that in turn sets off a relatively slow-burning train of pressed black powder or some other delay composition. When the train is burned through, it ignites a larger, faster-acting detonator charge. The length of the train and the characteristic burn rate of the composition determine the maximum delay. As with an ordinary time fuse, the delayed action percussion fuse may have several settings, each determining a different ignition starting point within the train.

Various additives can speed up (high-energy density fuels, oxidizers) or slow down (inert materials like chalk) the burn of a powder train, and small particles tend to burn faster.

While I have found reports of late nineteenth-century experiments with delayed action nose fuses (Baylay 1888, 9), I believe that in World War II the naval delay fuses were base fuses. The base position gave the fuse more protection, so the delay mechanism had time to do its job (Garzke and Dulin 1985, 501).

In the early 1900s, the goal for armor-piercing shell fuses was to reliably achieve 40–50-foot penetration (obviously that's not just armor); it took more than a decade to arrive at a practical design: Harry James Nichols' 1928 VD7F variable delay fuse (Carlisle 2002, 74). Details are difficult to ascertain, but Rodney Carlisle says he was ultimately allowed to patent the fuse, and the only good match is Nichols (issued 1948; filed 1932). The patent says that the fuse, after being centrifugally armed, is triggered based on the magnitude and duration of the deceleration after a major impact sufficient to overcome a retaining spring, and the delay is thus variable since those are greater for heavy armor than light armor.

The World War II USN Mark 23 base detonating fuse, used in 6–16-inch AP shells, had a 0.035-second delay (U.S. Navy, Bureau of Ordnance 1947, 133). German navy World War II fuses could be set for 0.015- or 0.035-second delay (Okun 2004). Since the Japanese type 91 "diving shell" was intended to travel underwater, it had a base fuse with a delay of 0.4 seconds (Lundgren and Okun 2022, 10, 14).

Proximity Fuses

These fuses weren't developed until World War II. There were five types: radar, photoelectric, magnetic, acoustic and hydrostatic.

Radar proximity fuses for AA shells, requiring several vacuum tubes, had to fit into a rather small package—they were half the size of a pint milk bottle (NAVORD 1957, 3E8)—and survive the acceleration in the barrel (20,000 Gs) (microworks.net).

The most common sort is based on putting a transmitter into the projectile and using the shell as an antenna. If the enemy had a metal hull, it would reflect the radio waves, creating a detectable and distance-dependent interference pattern. This pattern was filtered and amplified, and when the signal was strong enough (at 75–100-foot range), it triggered a thyratron that fired off a primer by passing a current through a resistance wire. The nose cone had to be non-metallic, so radio waves could pass through it. Of course, the electronics needed a source of power. For example, setback forces broke a vial of electrolyte, which filled and activated a battery (U.S. Navy, Bureau of Ordnance 1946).

With the old time-fused anti-aircraft shells, it took an average of 2,000 rounds to bring down a plane; with the VT (variable time, a deliberately misleading name) proximity fuse, it took 500 (Microworks.net n.d.).

It took seven months to progress from the first working shell (June 1941) to the first batch with over 50 percent reliability (January 1942). And it was still not until January 1943 that this shell was first used in combat (Microworks.net n.d.). Still, that's lightning speed for introduction of new military technology.

It's also amusing to note that the Germans captured 20,000 proximity fuse shells at the Battle of the Bulge but didn't appreciate their significance because their engineers told them that proximity fusing was impossible—the acceleration of the projectile would destroy, they thought, the necessary vacuum tubes (Salisbury 2007).

Radio-mediated proximity fuses may be jammed with a variable frequency transmitter tuned to the beat frequency (between the emitted and reflected waves) sensed by the proximity fuse (Salisbury 2007).

Photoelectric. In World War II, there were Anglo-American efforts to develop an aerial proximity fuse (for anti-aircraft rockets) that detected the reduction in light as a result of the sensor being shaded by the target. If dependent on sunlight, it wouldn't work at night and it could trigger if the sun moved in and out of the field of view, but it wasn't vulnerable to jamming. The project was shelved in favor of the radio proximity fuse (Ellet 1946). The Germans also experimented with photoelectric systems, including *Pistole*, in which the missile carried its own light source (Hogg 2016).

Magnetic. In World War II, there were torpedoes with magnetic proximity fuses that sensed the magnetic field around a vessel with a metal hull. Unfortunately, the torpedo's speed made it difficult for magnetic fuses to respond quickly enough, and countermeasures (degaussing, towed magnetic decoys) led to their withdrawal by 1942 (Zabecki 1999, 1123).

Acoustic. Yet another option was detecting sounds made by the enemy's engines (taking precautions so that the fuse wasn't triggered by the sound of the firing ship's engines, or by internal noise of the torpedo, or by swimming fish or sea mammals). To detect an enemy whose engines were off, the fuse would have needed active sonar.

Hydrostatic. These fuses may detect the slowly fluctuating pressure wave from a ship and distinguish it from ordinary water waves. They are "commonly associated with bottom mines" (FAS 2023, chapter 14). Or they may detect "steady state" pressure, as in depth-charge fuses.

Moisture-Sensitive Fuse

Zalinski's "dynamite" shell had backup nose and base fuses, both triggered "upon the shell entering the water." This would cause salt water to contact a pole of a battery, and the latter would pass a current "through a primer which ignites a time train" and, thereby, the detonator. "The time train is adjustable so that a variable submersion before explosion can be obtained" (Zalinski 1888, 14–15). The water apparently entered through holes covered with flaps (Hamilton 1888, 893).

CHAPTER 7

Gun Mounting, Traversal and Elevation

Gun Mounts

The purpose of the gun mount is to facilitate loading and aiming the gun. There are two basic gun mounts. First, the cannon can be mounted on a mobile carriage that recoils by rolling or sliding. Second, it can be mounted in a fixed position; the recoil force must then be absorbed by the ship structure.

Recoil

When a gun fires, the Law of Conservation of Momentum applies: in an isolated system, momentum is neither created nor destroyed—it may only be transferred. Momentum is mass times velocity; the backward momentum of the cannon (including its carriage) must equal the sum of the total forward momenta of the projectile and of the gases that escape out the muzzle. The cannon being a lot heavier than the projectile and the gases, the effect on it is less dramatic, though still quite visible: the cannon recoils backward.

On the battlefield, the distance of recoil is of minor importance. "On board of a ship, the limited space ... in the rear of the battery renders it necessary to restrain the recoil within certain limits" (Simpson 1862, 118–19).

On premodern gun carriages, the recoil was arrested as a result of the forces of friction (rolling or sliding), gravity (the deck was cambered so the backward movement was slightly uphill), and elastic tension (breeching rope).

The distance of recoil would depend on the weight of the cannon and shot, the powder charge, the elevation of the gun, and the particulars of the restraint. A 24–6.5 fired with a 6-pound charge at point-blank elevation had a recoil of 9.4 feet (Beauchant 1828, 21). On narrow-beamed ships, port guns could be staggered relative to those on starboard to allow more recoil room (Ireland 2000, 47).

A force, by definition, changes the momentum of the object it is acting on. The larger the mass of the gun, the smaller the deceleration (change in velocity) achieved by a given force. So increasing the mass of the gun reduces the initial speed of recoil, but it also makes the gun harder to slow down to a stop.

It's worth noting that if the gun is elevated, the force of recoil is partially

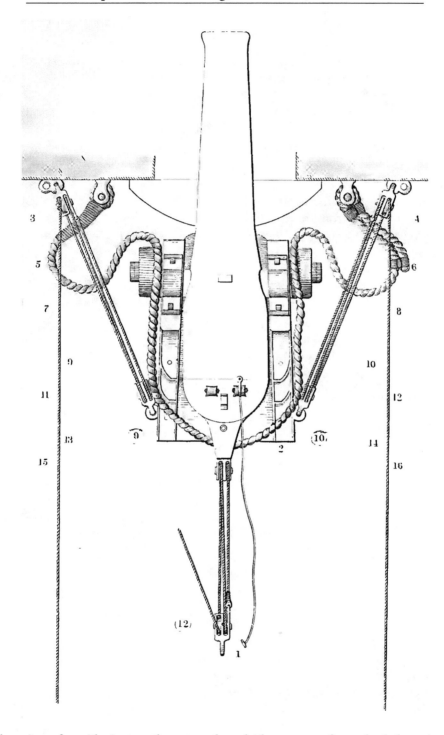

A plan view of a mid-nineteenth-century broadside gun on a four-wheeled carriage, in "Prime-Point" position. Note the location of the side tackles and the train-tackle (U.S. Navy 1866, Diagram 4, facing 51). The numbers 1–16 refer to the positions of those members of the gun crew, and the number and title of each crew member of a gun crew composed of 16 men and a powderman are defined on page 22 of the reference.

horizontal and partially vertical. While the gun carriage rolls backward as a result of the horizontal force, the deck must absorb the shock of the vertical component. That's one of the reasons that bomb ketches, whose principal armament was a large mortar, had a strongly reinforced mortar bed to absorb the shock.

Another problem caused by recoil is "jump." The trunnions (the horizontal axis on which the barrel turns when it is elevated or depressed) are several feet above the deck. Hence, as pointed out by Sir William Congreve, the reaction force exerted by the projectile and escaping gases on the gun acts along a horizontal or oblique line above the plane of the deck. The result is that a torque is exerted, "raising the fore trucks" (*London Encyclopaedia* 1829, Traversing Platform 22:186). The jump begins as the projectile is moving down-bore and therefore can perturb the line of departure of the projectile from the muzzle.

However, this torque is not entirely disadvantageous. Edward Simpson observes that "the higher the trunnions are raised above the axle trees, the longer is the arm of the lever which presses the inner trucks against the deck, and the more will the recoil be diminished" (1862, 121).

Frederick Robertson has alluded to "the lashing of guns fast to the ship, especially in chase, for the purpose of making them carry farther" (1921, 136). It's true that if recoil can be prevented, the muzzle speed (relative to the ground) increases. But the increase is small. Ignoring the effect of the escaped gas, it's by a factor equal to the square root of $(1 + m/M)$, where m is the mass of the projectile and M the mass of the gun (Denny 2011, 192).

Mobile Carriage

The sixteenth century was a period of transition when it came to mounting naval cannons. The ships of the Spanish Armada used field carriages like those of the Spanish army (Konstam 2017, 43). These had two large, spoked wheels and a rearward extension, the "trail" or "trace," which acted as a counterbalance and could also be used to hitch the carriage to a team of horses or oxen. In contrast, the Elizabethan navy used carriages with four small, solid wheels ("trucks").

Simpson explains, "The friction of a wheel is proportional to the ratio between the radii of the wheel and axle. The recoil of the carriage may be diminished by decreasing the diameter of its wheels…. For this reason gun carriages for sea service are mounted upon trucks, a species of solid wheel of small diameter" (1862, 120). On a 24-pdr, the fore-trucks were 18 inches in diameter, and the rear-trucks, 16—this arrangement compensated for the camber of the deck (Manucy 1985, 50).

The earliest known examples of these truck carriages to be recovered are from the 1545 wreck of the *Mary Rose* (Bunyard 2019, 54). The wrought iron guns of the *Mary Rose* were mounted on "wooden beds," said to resemble "hollowed tree trunks," and were equipped with one pair of wheels. In contrast, her bronze guns were mounted on four-wheeled truck carriages (Konstam 2017, 40; Bunyard 2019, 54). The gun carriages of the *Vasa* (1628) were of the latter type. This came to be the dominant design, until the second half of the nineteenth century, for mounting big guns. (There were small guns, mounted on swivels, for anti-personnel fire.)

A modern experiment has shown that a crew could load, fire, clean and reload a period gun on a four-wheeled truck carriage twice as fast as the same crew could achieve when the gun was mounted on a field carriage (Delgado 2019, 125).

Most of the time, guns on mobile carriages were secured. Chocks were placed against the rear part of the front trucks. The falls of the side tackles were passed "around the breech of the gun, through the jaws of the cascabel," and secured to "eyebolts on each side of the port." Likewise, the train-tackle was round about the breech and stopped. If the gun were housed, there were additional lashings, and either chocks were placed against the rear trucks or the latter were removed altogether (U.S. Navy 1866, 53–54).

If action was expected, the mobile carriages would be "cast loose" (47). But that doesn't mean that they were completely free; rather, the side tackles and train-tackle were arranged as discussed later in this chapter.

The mobile carriage was fastened to the hull with ropes ("breeching") that stretched taut when the gun moved backward enough. "The breeching is rove through an opening in the cascable, through the breeching shackles on the brackets, and the ends shackled to the starts … in the bulwarks on each side of the port" (Simpson 1862, 119). If the ropes broke, you had the proverbial "loose cannon on deck." Simpson warns that "when the gun is fired obliquely," the "strain upon the two legs … is not equalized."

In 1787, Sir Samuel Bentham, preparing a Russian flotilla for action against the Turks, in two vessels mounted "two 36-pounders as bow-chasers, so as to slide in grooves, one on each side of the middle line of the vessel, and attached one of these 36-pounders at each end of a single breeching, passed over a shieve fastened to the stem of the vessel, so that the recoil of one of these guns, drew out the other." While this arrangement meant that they fired alternately, "no labour or time was lost in replacing the guns after recoil" (Bentham 1828, 55).

One oddity was the three-wheeled carriage. This device had a single rear wheel, typically smaller than the front wheels and rolling in the same direction. One is depicted in a 1623 painting by Hendrik Cornelisz Vroom (Puype 2000, 115). A preserved example was recovered from the Texel Roads wreck designated *Scheurnak SO1* (built circa 1580) (107). Jan Piet Puype speculates that the reduced friction of three wheels relative to four was both an advantage (easier to change the direction the gun was pointing) and a disadvantage (increased recoil distance).

Pointing would be even easier if the rear wheel could roll in the direction perpendicular to the gun barrel. The only naval example I am aware of was a 1783 Dutch experimental design that used a 36-pound shot suspended in a ring as a caster (Puype 2000, 114).

In the nineteenth century, the French navy used the two-truck Marsilly carriage "for heavy cannon mounted in broadside" (Simpson 1862, 131), and it also was used by the Union navy (U.S. Navy 1866, s202, s238).

Unlike the field carriage, it did not have a long trace in the rear. The rear transom touched the deck, but it had an offset in back, providing a space for inserting a "roller handspike." This handspike was L-shaped, with the roller position at the vertex. The short arm of the "L" fit under the offset, and the long arm served as the lever for lifting the rear transom (with the roller as the fulcrum). Thus, recoil was dissipated by the friction between the bottom of the rear transom and the deck, but the carriage could be run out easily by means of the roller handspike. In addition, with this carriage, a 9-inch gun, weighing 9,000 pounds, could be transported from one side of the (ill-fated) USS *Merrimack* to the other in one minute, 45 seconds (Simpson 1862, 131).

Late eighteenth-century gunboats, because of space limitations on recoil, sometimes used "skid" carriages—that is, carriages without wheels (Chapelle 1949, 94).

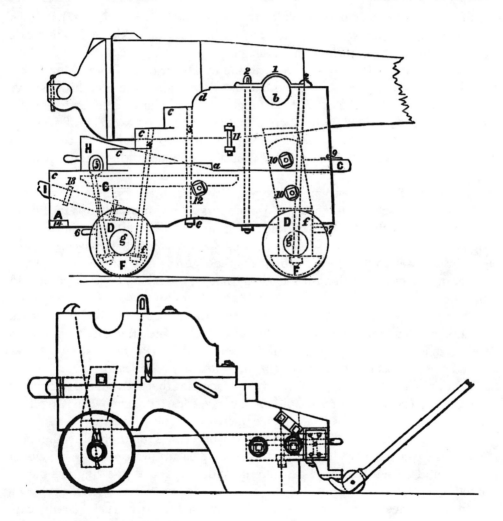

Top: Conventional four-wheel truck carriage (Simpson 1862, 124). Bottom: Marsilly carriage (Simpson 1862, 131). Edward Simpson reported that it had "superseded all others, in the French navy, for heavy cannon mounted in broadside." The commander of the USS *Merrimack* reported it took just 105 seconds for the 9,000-pound, 9-inch gun on a Marsilly carriage to be "loaded, run out, fired, sponged, loaded, transported to the opposite port and fired." The detailed specifications for the roller handspike are given by U.S. Navy 1866 (75).

Fixed Mounts

One method of avoiding recoil is to fix the gun securely and sturdily to the ship structure. This is not a Third Law violation; the force and momentum are transmitted to the entire ship, and that is so massive that the firing of a single gun is not going to have a discernible effect. (A full broadside would probably roll the ship substantially and could strain the hull, which is why broadsides were actually rippled, not simultaneous, even though broadside guns were mounted on recoiling carriages.)

The catch is the word "sturdily." The part of the ship structure to which the gun is attached must be sturdy enough to withstand the force and transmit it to the rest of the ship. It would not be very good for continued employment as a ship designer if the bulwark broke off.

Some late fifteenth-century galleys were equipped with rigidly mounted bow guns (Guilmartin 2003, 323), as shown in a 1486 woodcut (Guilmartin 2007, 666–67). But galleys had to be lightly built (because they were propelled by muscle power), and John Guilmartin presumes that as the Christian-Muslim arms race in the Mediterranean heated up, galleys were equipped with slide mounts (see "Non-Pivoting Slide Mount" later in this chapter).

The traditional mortar mounting was a "bed"—"a pair of wooden cheeks held together by transoms." The bed did not have any inherent ability to traverse, and some early mortar mounts were fixed elevation, too (Manucy 1985, 58–59).

The bomb vessels of the late seventeenth to early nineteenth centuries were armed with mortars. These were mounted initially on a rigid bed (McLaughlan 2014, 112). The bed was "a solid carriage of timber … whose different parts are strongly bolted together. By means of this it is firmly secured" (Steel 1812, 398). The mortar bed in turn was supported by a heavily reinforced deck, as can be seen in a 1797 sectional view of HMS *Vesuvius* (1776) (Royal Museum Greenwich n.d.). Working from bottom to top, the reinforcements take the form of "transverse floor riders," "support pillars," "longitudinal timbers," and finally the "deck beams" (Goodwin 2019). The most detailed description of the supporting structure comes from David Steel (1812, Folio XVIII).

In the late eighteenth and early nineteenth centuries, Samuel Bentham advocated mounting "a single gun, or a few guns only … on a small vessel either at the head or the sterns, resting as usual on the trunnions, and so fixed as to be easily elevated or depressed, while the horizontal pointing may be effected by directing the vessel itself." This arrangement, he argued, would require fewer hands and could be fired more rapidly than if the gun had to be traversed with handspikes, allowed to recoil after firing, and then run out by tackle (Bentham 1828, 75–76).

In Russia (1787), Bentham was driven by necessity: when mounting large guns on small vessels, even "the half-breadth of the vessels would not be sufficient for the recoil of any of the guns, since they could scarcely even be housed clear of the hatchways." So he mounted them "without any distinct carriage, by bedding the trunnions of the piece in two fore and aft bulkheads" (Bentham 1828, 55). Bentham's small, shallow-drafted vessels, heavily armed for their size, were able to engage a large Ottoman naval force in shoal water and decisively defeat it. His "principle of non-recoil" is discussed in greater detail later in this chapter.

The mortars on the American World War II LCI(M) amphibious gunboats were "fixed and fired over the bow." The mortar was mounted on a "reinforced box … filled with a mixture of sand and sawdust," which presumably would act as a viscous damper. The deck was also reinforced, "but it was not unusual for the support rods and mounts to break" (Rielly 2013, 26).

Non-Pivoting Slide Mount

Some early sixteenth-century galleys were armed with a centerline bow gun firing heavy (30–50-pound) balls, and Guilmartin asserts that "the recoil of these large and powerful pieces required the development of sliding gun carriages" (2003, 320–23; cp. Rodger 2004, xlvii). I am presently unaware of archaeological or contemporary documentary evidence for these sliding carriages on sixteenth-century galleys. However, Guilmartin bases his assertion on "the inescapable logic of structural and hydrodynamic considerations" (Guilmartin 2007, 557n68).

Fixed Pivot Mount

The first pivot-mounted guns were light weapons ("swivel guns"). On swivel guns, typically mounted on a ship's rail, the pivot point was near the center of mass of the barrel, thus minimizing the bending stress on the pivot post. The recoil had to be absorbed by the ship structure, but the shot mass was small. A good example of this type is the early sixteenth-century wrought iron breechloader (3-inch bore, 172 pounds) in the Tower of London collection (Royal Armouries, "Gun," XIX.3).

In the late seventeenth century, Colonel Jacob Richards (1660–1701) designed a traversing mount for mortars, which meant that the bomb vessels could adjust more easily to the local current and wind conditions (McLaughlan 2014, 113). Of course, the recoil still had to be absorbed by the ship structure.

In the late eighteenth century, Sir Samuel Bentham armed several Russian and British ships on what he called the "principle of non-recoil": "The mounting a piece of ordnance in such manner as that it shall have no other recoil than that which takes place in consequence of the elasticity of the materials employed to hold it" (Bentham 1862, 165). He refers here to the elasticity of the carriage, the bulwark and the "whole vessel." Bridges Adam later expressed the opinion that "elasticity of the supporting matter is an indispensable quality" (Bentham 1855, 193). "The small size of gun boats meant that 'the whole vessel may be considered as a sort of floating carriage'" (Morriss 2020).

The advantages claimed for non-recoil mounts included the ability to arm small vessels with large ordnance, to use smaller gun crews ("a single man" suffices for the working of the largest piece of ordnance, provided he has strength enough to lift the shot), to be constantly ready for action (the guns didn't have to be lashed to the sides), and to fire more rapidly (by two- or three-fold) (Bentham 1854, 691; Bentham 1862, 165–66).

As discussed earlier, Bentham had successfully applied the "non-recoil" principle to small vessels in Russia in 1787. He persuaded the British Admiralty to allow him to build seven experimental vessels in 1795. These were two sloops of war (*Arrow* and *Dart*), four war schooners (*Nelly, Eling, Redbridge,* and *Millbrook*), and a water tender (Bentham 1862, 106). Each of the sloops were equipped with twenty-eight 32-pdr carronades (120). The exact particulars of the mountings are not disclosed, but I assume that they omitted the recoil slide of the standard carronade mount (see next section) but were still able to pivot, given the number of guns per ship. The schooners were also armed with carronades.

The sloops initially went to war in 1796, with "half the ordnance on recoil carriages, the other half on the principle of non-recoil." Their commanders subsequently requested permission "to have all their guns mounted non-recoil." The schooner *Millbrook,* "armed solely with 16 carronades non-recoil," and with a crew one-seventh the size of its opponent, defeated the 36-gun frigate *Bellone.* The *Millbrook* delivered eleven broadsides in the time it took for the French warship to fire three (Bentham 1855, 193; Bentham 1862, 167). At the 1799 siege of Acre, pieces of ordnance were mounted by the non-recoil principle on a floating battery and were worked by "eleven men only" (Bentham 1828, 85). Robertson says that "their carriages [were attached] to vertical fir posts, built into the hull structure to serve as front pivots" (1921, 136).

Ultimately, "the system was found to be impracticable. The pivots successfully withstood the stresses of carronades fired with normal charges of powder; no permanent injury resulted to the elastic hull structures over which the blows were spread. But the factor of safety allowed by this arrangement was insufficient to cover the wild use of ordnance in emergencies. The regulation of charges and the prevention of double-shotting was difficult in action, and pieces were liable to be over-charged in the excitement of battle in a way which Sir Samuel Bentham had failed to realize. Pivots were broken, ships' structures strained, and the whole system found ill-adapted for warship requirements" (Robertson 1921, 136–37).

Nonetheless, as late as the 1840s, the "non-recoil" principle still had its proponents. An anonymous essayist challenged the assertion that the firing damaged the upper works to which the guns were attached. Several counter-examples were given, including the following: "The *Dart*, in 1779 [1799?], 'fired 80 rounds without the ship being least affected by it,'" and at the siege of Acre, the crew of the *Tigre* kept up an "incessant fire" for sixty days with two 68-pdr carronades, a 32-pdr carronade, a 42-pdr howitzer and a 24-pdr long gun, all mounted "non-recoil" on a floating battery made of old timber, without the latter being "materially affected by the shock" (MM 1848, 635–36). Indeed, in the 1850s, Mary Bentham (1854, 1855) was still promoting this method.

In modern usage, the term "pivot gun" is usually reserved for heavy guns (often heavier than the typical broadside guns), and these had slides to absorb recoil, as discussed in the next two sections.

Carronade (Slide-Pivot) Carriage

Carronades were first manufactured in 1778 (Tucker 1997, 15). They were mounted on a "carronade carriage" rather than the common four-wheeled truck carriage. The barrel was held by a ring (rather than supported by trunnions) attached to a horizontal axle (for elevation) (Inman 1828, 8). (If a short-barreled gun were equipped with trunnions and mounted on a truck carriage, it was called a "gunnade" [Tucker 1997, 19].)

The carriage was mounted on a slide. The slide featured a longitudinal groove about three or four inches wide, and a cylindrical iron pintle was attached to the underside of the carriage, engaging the groove of the slide. When the gun was fired, the carriage moved back on the slide, guided by the engagement of the pintle with the groove (Inman 1828, 8). If this sliding action and the gun's breechings were unable to absorb the full force of recoil, the remainder would be transmitted by the slide to the ship proper.

The slide also served as the pivot arm, as one end was pivotably attached to the side of the ship. The far end of the pivot arm carried wheels oriented with their axes parallel to the pivot arm. Thus, the carronade could be quite freely traversed (Inman 1828, 9).

We know that this carriage was in use at least by 1779, as John Smeaton disclosed "two methods of raising the slide carriages in a carronade" in a report dated January 20, 1779 (Smeaton 1797, 402–3).

In general, the coefficient of sliding friction for this mechanism is higher than that of rolling friction, and so, for a given recoil momentum, the recoil distance should be less. Nonetheless, recoil was considered more of a problem for carronades than for a long gun firing the same weight of shot. The reason was that they were light relative to their projectile's momentum. William Roberts (1996, 234) estimated that a 32-pounder long gun would have a muzzle velocity of 1,600 feet per second but would weigh 7,500 pounds (58 cwt—6,496 pounds—for the piece itself and another 1,000 pounds for the carriage); hence they would have a recoil speed of about 6.8 feet per second. In contrast, a 32-pounder carronade would have a muzzle velocity of 1,100 feet per second but would weigh about 2,100 pounds (about 1,900 pounds for the piece and another 200 pounds for the slide assembly), yielding a recoil speed of about 16.7 feet per second.

Roberts' calculation neglects the momentum of the escaping gas. If we apply the Lagrangian approximation (the powder charge is completely converted to gas, and that gas occupies a cylindrical volume behind the projectile of uniform density [Carlucci and Jacobsen 2018, 69–71]), then the momentum contribution of the gas is half

Opposite: (A) Crop of Plan 6184310, "War of 1812–era 32-Pound Carronade, 1985," "Gun Carriages for 32-pound Carronades–Spar Deck," showing elevation view 19-D and plan view 19-A. Said to be based on "a Shipcheck of the USS Constitution." Muzzle faces right. Note permissible elevation of ±20 degrees, effectuated by elevating screw.

(B) Crop of Plan 22364, "Gun Carriages for 32-Pound Carronades–Spar Deck," showing the "general arrangement" in an elevation view. Muzzle faces left. Note that unlike A, this illustration includes a third wheel, by the pivot pin. And it appears that the barrel has trunnions resting on the bed assembly and the apparent use of a quoin for elevation.

(C) Artist's representation of 32-pdr carronade of USS *Constitution* (Spears 1897, 1). This appears to have a three-wheeled skid, like B, but the bed assembly differs from both A and B.

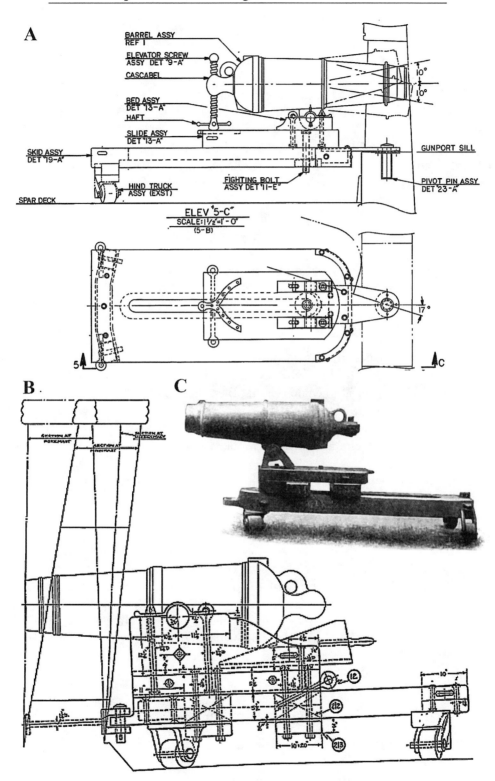

A

BARREL ASSY
REF 1

ELEVATOR SCREW
ASSY DET "9-A"

CASCABEL

BED ASSY
DET "13-A"

HAFT

SLIDE ASSY
DET "13-A"

SKID ASSY
DET "19-A"

HIND TRUCK
ASSY (EXST)

SPAR DECK

FIGHTING BOLT
ASSY DET "11-E"

GUNPORT SILL

PIVOT PIN ASSY
DET "23-A"

10°
10°

ELEV "5-C"
SCALE: 1½"=1'-0"
(5-B)

17°

5

C

B

C

its mass times the muzzle velocity (Carlucci and Jacobsen 2018, equation 3.28). The powder charge for a conventional 32-pounder was one-third the shot weight, so the total momentum is one-sixth greater than the projectile momentum alone. For the carronade, the powder charge is one-twelfth the shot weight, so the total momentum is one-twenty-fourth greater than the projectile momentum alone. But even with that correction, the recoil speed of the carronade remains greater than that of the conventional gun.

That said, the comparison is not an entirely fair one, as a 32-pounder carronade would probably be replacing the 6- to 12-pounders on the forecastle and upper decks (Tucker 1997, 18), which had masses more comparable to the 32-pounder carronade.

Long Gun (Pivot or Slide-Pivot) Mounts

Long guns were also pivot mounted. Early nineteenth-century pivot mounts varied. The gun was usually held by a standard broadside carriage without trucks (wheels), secured to skids. The skids were parallel timbers, joined by chocks. At the pivot point there was a pivot bolt that passed through a heavily bushed chock in the skid and engaged a socket in the deck timber. The "strains of recoil were largely concentrated on this structure," but recoil was also controlled by breechings. The pivot point could be in the middle of the center chock of the "skids" (in which case the ends traced a circle) or at one end, so that the other end traced an arc. There were rollers on the underside of the free end(s) of the skid, and these engaged an arcuate or circular U-shaped metal track in the deck (Chapelle 1949, 238–39).

In 1776, Major General Phillips proposed that gunboats be constructed for use on "the Lake" (Lake Champlain?). These gunboats were to "carry heavy twelve pounders, light twenty-four pounders, [or] eight inch howitzers in the bow, upon sliding carriages, on moveable platforms" (Parliament 1778, 200). The combination of a recoil slide and a pivot mount was also proposed by Richard Friend in an 1807 patent (Universal Magazine 1807, 529).

An explicit reference to a long gun having a slide-pivot mount appeared in 1832, with reference to the HMS steamship Dee. This was fitted with a 32-pounder before the foremast and an 84-cwt gun with a 10-inch bore abaft the mizzen mast. "Each gun is mounted on a slide, which moves on a pivot, so that the gun may be pointed in any direction all around. The velocity of the recoil is restrained by two powerful screws, which press the carriage on the slide with so much force that although there is a strong breeching, it is rarely, even in the case of the great gun, brought to its full stretch" (MM 1832, 32).

Modern Gun Mounts

By 1905, guns were constructed so that the barrel recoiled in a hollow support (the slide). The slide had trunnions, supported by the carriage, around which it rotated for elevation (Fullam and Hart 1905, 59).

The barrel may be fitted in a housing that "moves in recoil inside the slide." The portion of the barrel (or housing) that recoils into the slide is called the slide cylinder (U.S. Navy 1992, 5-1, 5-2). The slide itself doesn't recoil.

In imparting a spin to the projectile, the barrel experiences a counter-torque. A "key" (a long protuberance) on the outside of the slide cylinder engages a matching slot on the inside of the slide, to prevent rotation of the barrel during recoil (DiGiulian 2023).

On the USS *Iowa*, the recoil distance was 47 inches (relative to a gun length of 816 inches) for the 16-inch guns and 15 inches (relative to a gun length of 224 inches) for the 5-inch guns (Dramiński 2020, 19–20).

Recoil Reduction

Conventional Mechanisms

With a muzzleloader, recoil had the advantage of running the gun into a reloading position. With a breechloader, recoil was simply annoying.

To reduce the recoil distance, you need to supply some countervailing force. A simple system for recoil and counter-recoil was a slide inclined so it rose in the direction of recoil. Gravity would slow the recoil and then help run the gun back out.

On the Gover carriage, the upper carriage, carrying the gun, slid up the jack-adjustable incline provided by the lower carriage. However, given a trial on the *Narcissus* in 1803, "many of them broke" (Nelson 1845, 265). Nonetheless, it was patented in 1805 and had its proponents decades later.

The slide was more successful in the Armstrong breechloaders used by the Royal Navy in the 1860s (Tennent 1864, 116). One can be seen in the Armstrong gun in Fort No 1, Lévis, Québec, Canada (Gagnon 2015).

Most early brakes appear to be of the friction type. In 1779, Charles Douglas had wedges placed behind each truck of HMS *Duke*'s gun carriages, and the bottoms of the wedges, "to augment their friction against the deck, are pinked, tarred and rubbed with very rough sand or with coarse coal dust" (Laughton 1907, 269–70).

The "Hardy" carriage (invented by General William Millar), which enjoyed a brief vogue (1830–1850), featured a "compressor" (Antonicelli 2013). The "carriage … is so constructed as to admit of its being squeezed or compressed down on the slide … which produces a friction" (Peake 1897, 285). No details are given, but a typical compressor design was a pair of cheeks connected by an adjustable screw, which would press against both the carriage and the slide on which the carriage was mounted (Garbett 1897, 68). James Ward lamented that it was easy to set the degree of compression incorrectly ("the lee and weather-guns require different degrees of compression, differing according to the degree of heel") or even "forget to put it down" (1862, 160).

Likewise, the Erestham carriage possessed "friction clamps, designed to moderate the recoil" (Simpson 1862, 136). Edward Simpson complained that the crew "may, in the heat of action, forget to compress the carriage on the slide, thereby greatly endangering themselves" (119).

In 1833, the Society for the Encouragement of Arts, Manufactures and Commerce awarded Commander J. Pole a "Large Silver Medal" for his "Recoil Carriage for Pivot Guns" (Society 1836, 73). This was a "double carriage" with the lower carriage attached by a pivot and the upper carriage sliding on the lower, with the recoil "stopped by a geometrically increasing resistance." According to James Holman, it was "a self-acting compressor" (1834, 108; cp. USJ 1832, 516–17), but the method of operation is murky.

The Van Brunt carriage, like the Pole carriage, had a self-acting compressor. The movement of the carriage on its slide, releasing a "spring catch," caused levers to "press two compressor blocks down on the upper surface of the slide, pressure on the under side of the slide being at the same time produced by clamps" (Simpson 1862, 141).

Springs were apparently used by Charles Douglas as a recoil check on HMS *Duke* in 1781. They were made of "well-tempered steel," and those for a 24- or 18-pounder were nine inches in diameter (Laughton 1907, 271–74). The writer doesn't describe exactly how they were placed, but presumably they ran between the side of the port and the front of the carriage.

Douglas also experimented with a counterweight. A rope ran from the "breast-bolt of the carriage" to "a cleat overhead," and from there to a weight ("two half-pigs of iron ballast and two 33-lb shot") to the rear of the gun (Laughton 1907, 274). Presumably the cleat was also to the rear of the gun, so the weight was lifted as a gun recoiled.

The Powlett carriage, patented in 1886 (USP 339,466), used compressed air to absorb the recoil. The carriage was connected to a piston, so the recoiling carriage would move the piston within a compressed-air cylinder. The compressed air would, of course, resist the movement of the piston. A second cylinder was used to provide

Opposite: **Some recoil systems. (A) Figure 2 from Perley patent. Boldfaced elements not shown in this figure. The gun (g) is on carriage (f), supported by bed (e), which rests on the below-deck pintle (d). Water is pumped into cylinder (c), and cock (2) is opened, forcing out plunger (i) and moving the gun (and carriage—this includes the elevating mechanism) forward until stop (3) is reached. The gun is elevated or depressed by operating valves 5 or 6 so water flows into or out of cylinder (k), thereby acting on plunger (l) attached to the cascabel. Cock (2) is then closed and cock (4) opened. The gun is fired, and the recoil drives the plunger (i) back into chamber (h), forcing water out through cock (4). I have added a more legible label for element (i).**

(B) Recoil mount for a World War I medium-caliber broadside gun (Ramsey 1918, 28). Note that the breech end (8) is on the right. The plunger (piston rod, 10) recoils with the gun, as in the Perley patent, but here it is attached by the yoke (12) to the breech end. The recoil cylinders (9) and trunnions (4) are part of the slide (not numbered), which does not recoil. Neither does the carriage (14), which supports the trunnions. Thus, here the elevation mechanism (trunnions and support) does not recoil.

(C) Simplified schematic of the recoil system for a mid-twentieth-century 5-inch gun (BNW 1963, 249), such as the 5-inch/38. The key point is that here the cylinders are attached to the gun and recoil with it, whereas the pistons are attached to the slide and do not recoil. The same is true of the counter-recoil system (see below), but the differential cylinder is not included in the schematic.

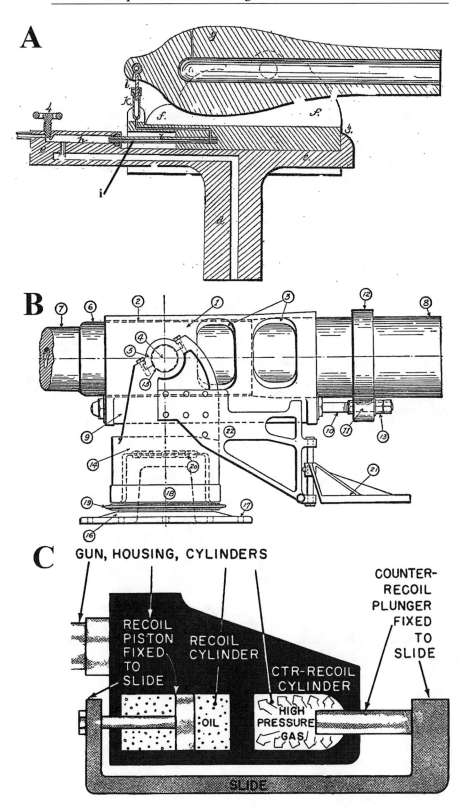

A

B

C GUN, HOUSING, CYLINDERS

COUNTER-
RECOIL
PLUNGER
FIXED
TO
SLIDE

RECOIL
PISTON
FIXED
TO
SLIDE

RECOIL
CYLINDER

CTR-RECOIL
CYLINDER

OIL

HIGH
PRESSURE
GAS

SLIDE

compressed air to run the gun out (counter-recoil). Further compressed-air cylinders were used to control the traversal and elevation of the carriage. While easy to work, there was the danger of it "being disabled by the pipes and cylinders being cut" by enemy fire; John Meigs and R.R. Ingersoll suggested leading "the supply pipes through armored conduits" (1887, 93–94).

The most successful recoil brakes were of a hydraulic nature. In 1865, Charles Perley received a patent (U.S. 51,475) on a "hydraulic recoil check, consisting of a plunger acting against liquid in a chamber, from which chamber there is an opening." The distance of the recoil would depend in part on the cross-sectional area of the piston relative to the size of the opening. The liquid could be "water, oil, or other practically non-compressible liquid." Perley also contemplated using hydraulic power to raise a gun into a firing position or to lower it to a loading position.

HMS *Thunderer* (1872) had two turrets. In 1874, the forward turret, carrying two 12.5-inch rifled muzzleloaders, was converted to hydraulic operation. "To run the carriage in or out, it is only necessary to admit to one side or other of the piston the water delivered from the steam pumps. When the gun recoils, the water is driven out of the press through a loaded and partly balanced valve, the resistance of which to its passage arrests the recoil" (Cooke 1880, 2:419).

Hydraulic recoil underwent a number of refinements. It is desirable that the hydraulic liquid be non-freezing, leading to adoption of a "mixture of glycerine and water." It is also desirable that the hydraulic pressure, and thus the resistance, remain constant. Since the resistance is proportional to the velocity of the piston, which is greatest at the beginning, and inversely proportional to the exposed escape opening, the system is engineered so the latter decreases in size as the recoil progresses (U.S. Navy, Bureau of Naval Weapons 1963, 250). With a suitable pressure, the recoil could be limited to two to four calibers of the gun (Alger 1905, 681).

In the monitor USS *Terror* (commissioned 1896), "compressed air is employed … in taking up the recoil on firing" (Morris 1898, 166). The recoil cylinders were charged to 500 psi, and of course the pressure within the cylinders increased as the gun recoiled. Charles Morris observed that "the elasticity of the air prevents all shock" (167)—that is, the deceleration was smooth. He criticized the hydraulic system as being subject to frequent leakage (166). But that criticism has also been levied against pneumatic systems.

Modern guns rely on hydraulics for recoil absorption. During World War II, there were two basic types: grooved wall and throttling rod. The grooved-wall type was older and had "orifices formed by grooves cut in the cylinder walls." Changes in the width or depth of the grooves changed the rate of fluid escape as the solid piston head moved past them (NAVORD 1944, 65). In the second type, tapered throttling rods, secured at both ends of the cylinder, passed through orifices in the piston head. The escape of fluid was regulated by the difference in diameter between the orifice and the rod at a given position of the piston head (64).

While, in Perley's scheme, the plunger moved with the gun, the brake could be designed so that the chamber moved instead (Fullam and Hart 1905, 164). This effect is seen, for example, in the U.S. Navy's World War II mainstay, the 5-inch, 38-caliber gun (NAVORD 1944, 66).

Counterblasts

The recoilless guns of land warfare use a different cheat: they eject a counterblast of equal momentum (mass × velocity) in the opposite direction at the time of firing. This counterblast may be propellant gas or a liquid or solid material that is forced out by the gas. The problem, of course, is that it is dangerous to stand behind the breech end of the cannon in the path of the counterblast. (Not that standing behind a recoiling cannon was smart.)

This phenomenon was demonstrated in the mid-nineteenth century by W. Bridges Adams, who showed that "when the charge of gunpowder is inserted in the middle of a hollow tube, the explosion of the powder would act with equal force upon both ends of the tube" (Bentham 1855, 193).

The Davis gun—essentially two guns, mounted breech-to-breech, in which the rear gun fired simultaneously a load of equal mass (typically pellets)—was "mounted on World War I–era sub chasers; at least 25 boats were so equipped." It was also mounted experimentally on a few USN seaplanes in 1918. The guns were produced in calibers ranging from 1.57 to 3 inches (Caiella 2018).

A recoilless rifle, a 305-mm "dynamo-reactive" Kurchevsky gun, was pivot mounted on the Russian destroyer *Engels* in the 1930s (Eger 2021). Based on Christopher Eger's photos, I estimate its overall length at 38.25 calibers. For obvious reasons, it could fire only to port and starboard, and the counterblast "arm" limited its elevation. It was not a successful design, and Leonid Kurchevsky was executed in 1937.

Muzzle Brakes

An intermediate solution is a muzzle brake. This is a baffle attached to the muzzle end;

the gases escaping with the projectile are deflected sideways and upward, so that they don't create a backward reaction force on the gun carriage (Carlucci and Jacobsen 2018, 63).

However, while muzzle brakes are found on howitzers and tank guns, they are rare on naval guns. Bear in mind that a ship is much more massive than a land vehicle and therefore much more capable of absorbing recoil.

The pre–World War II Waffenfabrik Solothurn ST-5 naval anti-aircraft gun's "recoil energy was more than what was needed for the next [reload and fire] cycle," so it "had a muzzle brake" (Friedman 2014, 350n29). However, the Kriegsmarine did not adopt it. More recently, the Royal Navy 4.5-inch, 55-caliber Mark-8 gun, which entered service in the 1970s (on corvettes, frigates and destroyers), has a muzzle brake (Jordan 2015, 149; Seaforces 2023).

Running Out the Gun

After the gun's recoil has completed, it must be loaded and run out (returned to the firing position).

With the four-wheeled truck carriage, running out was done with side tack-les. According to the U.S. Navy's 1866 ordnance instructions, there are two side tackles, one on either side of the carriage. The outer block of the side tackle is attached to the side tackle eye bolt, on the side of the carriage, near the rear axle. The inner block is attached to an eye bolt on the bulwark, to one side of the gun-port. So, the crew pulls on the fall (rope) from behind and to the side of the gun. If this is done evenly on both side tackles, the carriage moves in the outboard direction. More or less effort might be needed if the ship is heeled away or toward that side of the ship.

If the heel is severe, it might be necessary to restrain the carriage from smash-ing into the ship's side. This may be done with the train-tackle. Its outer block is attached to an eye bolt by the center of the rear axle tree, and its inner block to an eye bolt in the deck, to the rear of the gun. Thus, pulling on its fall causes the carriage to move inboard. The train-tackle may also be used to run in the gun if the recoil was too short (perhaps because of heel).

In 1905, most USN guns had hydraulic recoil and spring return (counter-recoil, recuperation). The spring might be inside the hydraulic cylinder and compressed as the gun recoiled. On the *New York*, the 8-inch turret mounts had hydraulic recoil and a gravity return (thanks to inclined rails). Hydraulic return was also possible, and it could use the same cylinder as for recoil (with reversed flow), as on the 13-inch guns of the *Indiana*, or independent cylinders, as on the 12-inch guns of the *Texas* (Fullam and Hart 1905, 164–65).

With barrel-only recoil, the gun would still be in an elevated position when the return sought to return it to "battery." Hence, it would be fighting gravity as well as friction, which must be considered in designing a counter-recoil system (NAVORD 1944, 65).

A counter-recoil system must ensure a return to "battery" (full forward), lest the next recoil damage ship structure. It is therefore provided with "reserve force." But to avoid damaging the mount, the counter-recoil movement must be slowed down toward the end; this is done with a buffer (dashpot) (NAVORD 1944, 64).

In 1944, spring return was largely limited to guns smaller than five inches. The springs needed for larger guns were "likely to become permanently set or broken" (65). Instead, a hydropneumatic system was used. The main cylinders were charged with high-pressure air, but a hydraulic "differential cylinder" was used to "maintain an effective seal of the packings in the main cylinders" (NAVORD 1944, 65–67).

Gun Laying

A gun is elevated vertically, and traversed horizontally, so that with the chosen projectile and charge, discharged at the correct moment, it will strike the target. The greater the range, the more important it is that the gun be elevated to compensate for the fall of the projectile and traversed to lead the target. (Elevation is the angle between the gun bore axis and the horizontal, not the height of the gun above sea level.)

The maximum elevation (depression) and traversal of a gun set behind a gunport are limited by the geometry of the gun (barrel length and diameter, trunnion height) and the port (lower and upper sill height, width, distance between ports); formulae are given by the 1880 Admiralty *Manual of Gunnery* (214–16).

Elevation

Since targets were generally moving, it was important to be able to adjust the elevation of the muzzle, to account for changes in range.

Elevation Mechanism

Elevating a premodern gun was relatively straightforward. Since about 1450, cannons were cast with trunnions—short lugs extending on either side of the barrel to serve as an axle. These fitted onto the gun carriage, and the barrel pivoted up-and-down around them.

Changing barrel elevation was a little tricky. There was a quoin—a moveable wooden block with a right triangle profile—on the quoin plate of the carriage, under the breech end of the barrel. The barrel would be lifted off the quoin, and then the quoin would be moved forward or backward to adjust the elevation angle. A second quoin could be used if one wasn't enough (Manucy 1985, 51).

"Handspikemen … place the heels of their handspikes on the steps of the carriage and under the breech of the gun, and raise it so the quoins may be eased and the lower half port let down, or when housed, the bed and quoin adjusted" (U.S. Navy 1866, s214). Obviously, the handspike was acting as a lever, with the step as a fulcrum (Simpson 1862, 126).

That method was enough for varying the degree of positive (above horizontal) elevation, but depressing the barrel below the horizontal was trickier. A wad had to be rammed down the muzzle so the ball wouldn't roll out, and it might be necessary to insert an additional or thicker quoin under the breech so the barrel would point downward (Manucy 1985, 51).

Simpson warns that "the elasticity of the carriage usually causes the quoin to jump out of the bed at each fire, endangering the men at the gun, and requiring time to replace it" (1962, 143).

By 1866, many guns were equipped with elevating screws. The elevating screw *per se* had been invented centuries earlier, as is evident from drawings by both Leonardo da Vinci and Albrecht Durer (Kinard 2007, 70). John Deane (1858, 48) says that a Jesuit, in 1650, was the first to equip a gun with an elevating screw. As for naval guns, the British introduced elevating screws around 1790 for use on carronades (Lavery 1987, 132).

A screw provides mechanical advantage—it is the equivalent of an inclined plane that has been coiled up. The pitch of the screw determines how much the gun is elevated per turn; the smaller the pitch, the slower the elevation, but the finer the control. Modern tests on nineteenth-century 6-pdrs revealed that each turn elevated the piece by 30–60 arc-minutes and that the obtainable accuracy of elevation was around 2 arc-minutes (Hughes 1975, 18–19).

Several elevating screws were in use in the Union navy. John Dahlgren's was "a single screw working through the cascable … one complete turn is equal to a degree of elevation or depression" (Simpson 1862, 143).

Without the elevating screw, it took at least four men to change elevation: at least two with handspikes to lift the breech end; the "first Captain" to sight the gun and judge when it was at the right elevation ("Raise!" "Lower!" "Well!"); and the "second Captain" to adjust the quoins to hold the gun ("Down!") at that elevation. With the screw, one man could sight the gun while turning the screw to suit.

Nonetheless, to make a rapid (albeit crude) change in elevation, quoins were apparently faster (Simpson 1862, 143), which is why carronades were also given molding under their breeches (Lavery 1987, 132). Quoins were likewise needed if the elevation change was greater than that permitted by the screw (Douglas 1829, 163; Simpson 1862), and they might be used, in addition to the screw, if it was at its extreme elevation ("to relieve the screw from the shock of the discharge" [Cooke 1875, 604]).

Some improved quoins were developed in the nineteenth century, and Simpson (1862, 147) says that David Porter's "may be considered now as the established

Parrott gun (rifle) on the gunboat *Mendota*, July 10, 1864. Note that the elevating screw (vertical) is attached on the left side of the cascabel. Library of Congress Prints and Photographs Division. Digital ID: ppmsca 11714.

quoin of the United States Navy when quoins are used." The quoin bed was equipped with two rows of ratchets, flanking the intended path of the quoin. This quoin had side projections (from a metal bracket screwed into its base) that engaged a pair of the ratchets. Thus, the quoin was locked into place, and the elevation corresponding to each ratchet pair was known. A roller was at the tapered end, so it could be moved forward and back if just the large end was raised clear of the ratchets.

Simpson also comments favorably on James Ward's screw-quoin, associated with Ward's "Novelty Carriage." The quoin was mounted on a crank shaft with a "worm" screw, the latter engaging a toothed track on the quoin bed. Turning the crank advanced or retired the quoin, thereby changing the elevation. It thus had the uniformity of motion of the elevating screw (1862, 143–46).

Maximum Elevation

Maximum elevation depended on the geometry of the barrel, carriage, and gun port, as well as the choice of elevation mechanism, but probably was about 15 degrees—the highest value typically given in nineteenth-century gunnery tables. Volo and Volo (2001, 206) say the limit was about 7 degrees, but ships could achieve a higher effective elevation by firing on the up-roll. Douglas (1829, 252) proposed that ships be equipped with "dismantling guns" that could achieve at least 30 degrees of elevation.

In the Union navy, ports were three feet high, with the guns mounted so that the center of the trunnions was a half-caliber below the center of the port, thus permitting about 11 degrees of elevation and 7 degrees of depression (Simpson 1862, 147). Consistent with those numbers, an 1858 plan for a 32-pounder (46 cwt) on the USS *Constitution* (Plan 753A) states that it can elevate 11 degrees and depress 7.5 degrees.

Before World War I, "it did not occur to designers to mount a gun to shoot further than one could see," and hence a large maximum elevation wasn't needed. Increasing the maximum elevation would, it was thought, necessitate increasing the vertical extent of the gun port, thus increasing the gun's exposure to enemy fire. For American ships, the maximum elevation was then 15 degrees, and for the British battleships retained under the Washington Treaty, 20 degrees (range 23,800 yards). After the *Blücher* was sunk at a range of 18,000 yards by indirect fire (Battle of Dogger Bank, 1915), there was a change of heart, and by 1924 America had five ships whose guns had a maximum elevation of 30 degrees (range over 30,000 yards) (Ballou 1924, 1511–14). The 16-inch guns of the USS *Iowa* (BB-61) were capable of 45 degrees of elevation, at a rate of 12 degrees/second (Dramiński 2020, 19).

The development of air power had not only increased the practicality of long-range indirect fire but also exposed warships to aerial attack. Anti-aircraft guns, of course, had to be capable of extreme elevation (see "Air Defense" later in this chapter), but some designers thought it prudent to design at least secondary armament so it could be used to shoot down aircraft as well as against surface targets.

Thus the Japanese *Takao* (1930) and British *Kent*-class heavy cruisers had heavy (8-inch) guns that could be elevated to 70 degrees. Later, "the Japanese came to consider 55° a practical maximum" (Friedman 2014; Friedman 2013, 127). However, the ability of heavy guns of the period to actually track aerial targets was questionable.

In the early 1930s, a British naval committee considered, and decided against, "dual-purpose" guns, capable of elevation above 50 degrees, for destroyers. The committee wanted it to be possible for "a man standing on deck to feed the gun" without a power assist, and with the gun mounted on the deck, not in a pit. "The higher the elevation of the gun, the higher the trunnions," so it could "recoil" (at maximum elevation) without hitting the deck. "Higher-powered guns required more trunnion height because they recoiled further." Increasing maximum elevation or shell size also increased the force needed to load the gun. The committee ultimately recommended "that all destroyer guns be capable of 40° elevation," which would at least permit them to engage bombers at long range (Friedman and Baker 2008, 29).

The battleship *Queen Elizabeth* (1912) was modified just prior to World War II to give it a 4.5-inch secondary battery. These guns "fired a 55 lb shell at a maximum elevation of 80 degrees," which obviously was intended for air defense (Stille 2020, 40). The same is true of the 5-inch/38-caliber guns of the battleship USS *Iowa* (BB-61), and they were capable of 85 degrees elevation and 15 degrees depression, with an elevation rate of 25 degrees/second (Dramiński 2020, 20).

Elevation Rate

William Dawson (1872, 3–4) discusses the time needed to change guns from extreme elevation to extreme depression. Much depended on how much weight had to be moved. On the *Wivern* and *Scorpion* (1864), armed with two 12.5-ton guns in each turret, this change took one hour, even "in smooth water on an even keel," as gun, carriage and slide all had to be moved. In contrast, on the *Monarch* (1868), the "gun alone" was moved, and the change could be performed with its 25-ton guns in "less than four minutes."

Traversal

For a target that is not moving relative to your gun, you traverse (train) the gun so it points horizontally at the target. If the target is moving, you must "lead it" (point to the place it will be when the projectile arrives).

Non-Traversing Mounts

The bow-mounted heavy guns on sixteenth-century galleys did not traverse; they were aimed by pointing the ship toward the enemy (Guilmartin 2003, 322). This was also the case for the dynamite gun on the USS *Vesuvius*.

Traversal of Truck Carriages

The wheels of the standard naval carriage all rolled forward and backward; thus, they would not have made it any easier to turn the gun toward the bow or stern. The carriage had to be turned to and fro by brute force, using side tackles and handspikes. The role of the side tackles is obvious: pull the fall on one side; ease it out on the other. The handspikes, presumably, would be used as levers to lift the rear of the carriage and shove it in the right direction. Some handspikes had flattened (Jeffers 1850, 201) or clawed (Falconer 1769, "Handspec") ends to aid in gun wrangling.

The rear trucks were lifted, and the gun pivoted around the fore trucks, until the chase contacted the side of the port. If the gun needed to be trained further, then the fore trucks had to be "moved bodily" (Kennish 1837, 12).

In traversing a gun, there was a risk of breaking the breechings, as happened "aboard the *Namur* at the Battle of Toulon" and "aboard the *Devonshire* at the Second Battle of Finisterre" (Willis 2008, 142).

N.A.M. Rodger suggests that, at least prior to the development of line of battle tactics in the mid-seventeenth century, in the Royal Navy it was common to "bow" the guns in the "fore part of the ship … to fire as nearly forward as possible," while "those further aft might be 'quartered' to fire aft" (1996, 312). And they would be left that way, rather than turned to and fro during the battle. He visualizes the ships as charging the enemy, firing the chase and "bowed" guns, and firing the stern and "quartered" guns after they passed the enemy or turned away from it (307). Henry Manwayring indeed recommended that ships be designed "to shoot as many pieces right forward, and bowing, as may be" (314).

In 1779, Captain Charles Douglas of the 98-gun HMS *Duke* placed bolts in her sides, "right in the middle between every two guns," and by hooking the gun tackles to those bolts as needed, he was able "point all of them, without using a crow or handspike, where knees called standards do not interfere, full four points [45 degrees] before or abaft the beam" (Laughton 1907, 268).

Previously, the difficulty of traversing the guns had meant that guns were often left at "neutral" and fired only when the enemy ship was directly off the beam. The result of Douglas' innovation was that a British ship passing a French ship "would fire two or three broadsides both before and after the guns of a French ship could be brought to bear, and, while they were opposite, the British were able to fire a great deal more rapidly" (Valin 2010).

Traversal of Carronades

Carronades were pivot mounted, and the wheels were positioned to roll circumferentially, making the traversal much more efficient (Blake and Lawrence 2005, 140). William Smyth (1867, 166) comments that "as the slide is bolted to the ship's side, and is a radius from bolt or pivot, carronades were once the only guns which could be truly concentrated on a given object."

On some pivot mounts, the rollers were dispensed with, and the pivot point was raised above the deck and the gun balanced around it. The free end of the skid could be lifted for quickly traversing the gun and then let down for firing (Chapelle 1949, 239).

Traversal of Turrets

There were basically two ways of mounting a turret; it could rotate around a central shaft (Ericsson's USS *Monitor*) or on a circular track with ball bearings (Eads' USS *Winnebago*) (Deogracias 2003, 39).

Machine-Assisted Gun Working

Until well into the nineteenth century, a gun was worked manually. The weight of the element that had to be moved determined the necessary size of the gun crew.

In some instances, simple machines could ease the work. Physics defines "work" as the product of force and distance, and simple machines could provide a "mechanical advantage"—requiring less force to move an object, at the cost of having to move a machine element over a greater distance. The elevating screw is a machine of this type. Some guns were equipped with training and elevating hand cranks; their mechanical advantage was the ratio of the crank radius to the wheel radius. Mechanical advantage may be increased further by gearing or equivalent friction rollers (Ramsey 1918, 32–34).

For heavier guns, it was desirable to rely on something other than muscle power. Once another source of motive power (the steam engine) became available, it was logical to apply it to multiple functions.

In 1858, Robert Mallet proposed a "hydraulic mounting" for a seacoast gun. The gun was pivoted near the muzzle, and chains were attached to the rear of the carriage. These chains communicated with hydraulic cylinders on either side. Depending on whether water was admitted or withdrawn from each of these cylinders, the gun could be elevated or traversed (or both). The pressure in the cylinders was supplied by an accumulator, which in turn was fed by a pump operated either by hand or by "a small high-pressure engine" (Mallet 1862, 4, 16–20). Recoil, however, was controlled by friction, and loading and run-out were both manual.

In 1864, H.D. Cunningham declared, "Watching the rapid growth in the sizes and weight of ordnance during the past two years, it appears to me ... that the arms of flesh and bone must give was to the iron arms and sinews of the mighty-steam engine" (68).

While the earliest naval turrets were hand cranked (Kinard 2007, 237), the USS *Monitor* (1862) was equipped with a pair of auxiliary steam engines to turn its turret. Steam engines radiate heat, and on June 11, 1862, the observed berth deck temperature, with hatches open, was 120°F. Lieutenant Jeffers, its second-in-command, opined that when in action, with the hatches closed, "the temperature of that deck, and the turret cannot be less than 130° to 140°," which obviously would have challenged "human endurance" (Rawson and Woods 1898, 483). In addition, the steam mechanism made training the [*Monitor*'s] guns jerky and imprecise" (Hore 2019, 63).

Presumably, this result was attributable to difficulty in maintaining constant steam production.

In 1874, George Rendel argued that steam power was "best applied through the medium of water under pressure." It "may be transmitted by water through a very small pipe, for long distances and by intricate ways; so that a steam pumping engine may be placed … in such a position as to be absolutely secure, and supply power … for working many guns." Rendel went on to describe the use of hydraulic power for recoil reduction, counter-recoil, and loading.

In 1888, the famous gun designer William Armstrong stated that for guns of less than 9.2 inches in caliber, "hydraulic power is employed only for absorbing the force of recoil, and for controlling the running and out of the gun," whereas for larger guns, "loading, training, elevating, and all other operations connected with the gun, are carried out by hydraulic power" (11). The 43-ton, 12-inch Mark IV rifled breechloaders on HMS *Colossus* (1882) were an example of the latter (Brassington 2008b).

There was some experimentation in the late nineteenth century with compressed-air systems, but the necessarily high working pressures posed dangers of explosion. By the early twentieth century, turret power was either hydraulic (British) or electric (American) in character (Fullam and Hart 1905, 214ff). Steam or internal combustion engines could drive dynamos or alternators that in turn powered electric pumps.

Air Defense

For defense against airships and aircraft, a pre-missile-era ship needed guns that could be elevated to a high angle, whose bearing and elevation could be adjusted rapidly, and which had a high muzzle velocity and rate of fire.

In the World War II American navy, the four-barreled, 40-mm Bofors gun had an elevation range of -15 to +90 degrees and an elevation rate of 24 degrees/second. It could train at a rate of roughly 25 degrees/second. It had a practical rate of fire per barrel of 80–90 rounds/minute. Its ceiling was 22,300 feet (Dramiński 2020, 21).

While air resistance has a much greater influence on the movement of a projectile than does gravity, the vertical range of a gun is likely to be only two-thirds to three-quarters of its horizontal range (Rinker 1999, 282). Moreover, wind strength increases with height, so wind deflection is more of a problem.

Tracer rounds may be useful for judging whether the shots are going where they should. These have an incendiary filler in the base; this is ignited when the round is fired (Rinker 1999, 203).

Shells, of course, have an advantage over solid shot, in that you don't have to hit the aircraft directly as long as the burst is close enough so that fragments strike it. But then the problem, if you don't have a proximity fuse, is timing the burst. There was a period when anti-aircraft shells used mechanical time fuses and AA gunners sought to achieve a fixed rate of fire consistent with the preset for the delay from setting the fuse and firing the gun (Okun).

Gun Shifting

Particularly in ships with only a small number of guns, their location could be found to be ill suited to a particular engagement. The privateer's "long tom" was shifted to wherever it was needed—bow if in pursuit, stern if pursued (Chapelle 1988, 54).

Normally, a warship could fire only half of the broadside guns she carried at one time, with the guns on the side facing away from the enemy being silent. The armament of the British *Wolverine* (1798) was disposed according to a suggestion of Captain (later Admiral) John Schank. It had eight main deck guns (two long eighteens and six 24-pdr carronades), which could be switched from side to side by shifting them along athwartship "tracks or skids" running between opposite gunports. These guns also had pivot mounts (Chapelle 1949, 422). The NMM (2023) model, dating to 1798, shows that the tracks are actually grooves. However, rather than there being a pair of parallel grooves, there is just one per gun. This arrangement suggests that the carriage was of an unusual nature. Unfortunately, the model doesn't include the gun and its carriage. It seems likely that the guns were placed on a pivot so the carriage didn't need to be turned around when moved to the other side of the ship.

While the tracking arrangement seemingly doubled its broadside, doubters argued that "she could only fight from the lee side of an enemy, so that the weight of the wind on the sails would counteract the weight of her whole battery on one side" (Henderson 2011, chapter 11).

Henry P. Moore (photographer), forward pivot gun, 200-pound rifle, USS *Wabash*, 1865. Albumen silver print. Bequest of Fae Heath Batten, public domain, 1997.58.110. Portland Art Museum. File 1997_0058_0110_P.jpg (downloaded). Note the pivot tracks on the deck.

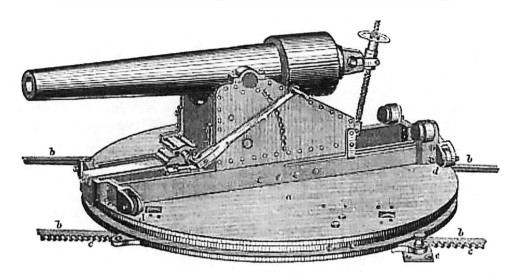

Ericcsson shiftable pivot gun from *Knight's American Mechanical Dictionary*, Volume 2, p. 1722 (Figure 3776) (1881).

The interest in shifting guns continued. The brigantine HMS *Dolphin* (1836) was equipped with a "long 32-pounder ... mounted midships as a pivot-gun, with five other shifting pivots, which enable the gun to fight a broadside, right a-head, or a-stern" (USJ 1836, 267).

With pivot guns, if there were holes in both ends of the pivotable frame, then it was possible to shift the pivot gun from one part of the deck to another by bolting down end A, swinging end B, bolting down end B and unbolting end B, swinging end A, and so on (Hall 2012). The U.S. Navy's 1866 ordnance instructions warned that for "heavy guns this is practicable in smooth water only" (s256).

John Ericsson invented a gun-shifting device that was installed on Spanish gunboats around 1870. A Parrott gun was mounted on a slide carriage on a turntable, and the base this turntable rested on was mounted on an athwartship track. Cogwheel gearing could be used to move it into firing position, and pins were then used to fasten the turntable to the deck (Knight, 2:1722).

Gun and Gun Crew Protection

Early pivot designs had to be combined with raised decks or cut-down bulwarks, which exposed the pivot gun crews to small-arms fire. This problem was corrected by a mount introduced during the War of 1812. Basically, the pivot point was placed on the aft end, and the pivot bolt and skid were raised sufficiently so that the gun could fire over the normal bulwark (Chapelle 1949, 319).

With a pivot mount, guns could be given a broad field of fire, but this change meant that to avoid obstruction, a ship had to carry fewer (but perhaps larger) guns. Larger ships nonetheless retained broadsides; it took time to abandon the notion that the rank and seniority required to command a large warship shouldn't be based on the number of guns, but rather on the weight thrown. Hence, pivot guns tended to be used mainly in smaller vessels until the 1840s (Chapelle 1949, 422). Eventually, design philosophy changed, and the big guns (say, 10 inches and up) were mounted on turntables and the smaller guns (9 inches, firing 72-pound shells, or smaller) broadside (Canfield 1968).

When pivoted guns became heavy enough to need to be mounted on a turntable, the designer had to decide whether to protect the crews from enemy fire and, if so, whether the armor would rotate with the gun (true turret) or be a fixed part of the hull, a semicircular parapet (hooded barbette) that the gun fired over. The "hood" could be a light hood, just to fend off splinters, or a heavy one, to resist shells directly. If there was no protection at all, just a turntable, that was an open barbette.

The problem with the hooded barbette was that it limited the gun's range of elevation, whereas the true turret was heavy (which led to the use of auxiliary engines to turn them).

Another option was the disappearing gun; after the gun fired, its turntable (or the gun itself) would sink more deeply down inside a barbette for reloading. This arrangement was particularly advantageous for big guns with a slow rate of fire. Disappearing gun mounts were first used on land.

In the original Moncrieff carriage (proposed 1858, introduced 1867), the gun was counterweighted around a horizontal axis. When the gun fired, the recoil moved the horizontal axis backward, and it also caused the gun to rotate around that axis, thus descending. This shift brought up the counterweight, which progressively retarded the recoil. The gun was also equipped with a "reflecting sight" (a periscope?), so it could be aimed while still in the protected position (Moncrieff 1868, 2–3; War Office 1879, 222–54; Kemmis 1876, 149–58).

In 1871, Alexander Moncrieff redesigned the carriage to take up part of the recoil through a combination of hydraulic and pneumatic resistance. The remainder of the recoil served to pivot the barrel down to the protected position (INMM 1885).

At sea, disappearing guns were used most extensively in some of the "flat-iron" ("Rendel") coastal gunboats. These carried a single large gun as spinal armament (that is, the gun was traversed by pointing the entire ship at the enemy) and were used for coastal bombardment. The first such vessel was HMS *Staunch* (1867), which carried a 9-inch (12-ton) rifled muzzleloader even though the ship was only 164 tons. Over forty were built for the Royal Navy in the period 1867–1894, and they were also built or purchased by the Australian, Argentinian, Chinese, Danish, German, Greek, Italian, Dutch, Norwegian, Russian and Swedish navies. It has been suggested that the ability to lower the gun was introduced to make the gunboats more seaworthy when en route to their theater of operations (Wikipedia, "Flat-Iron Gunboat").

The Royal Navy adopted a disappearing gun for the main armament of HMS *Temeraire* (1877). Each of its two barbettes mounted "one 11-inch RML [rifled muzzleloader] 25-ton gun" (Clarke 1890, 231). "The gun itself is raised and lowered by means of massive forged bell-crank levers, of which the heads are attached to the trunnions of the gun." The "outward or inward thrust" of hydraulic pistons "imparts the upward or downward motion to the piece." The recoil was absorbed, rather than used to drive the lowering of the gun. There was a nine-man crew: "one man to lay and fire electrically, two men to attend the elevating gear, one man to take charge of the levers for lifting the gun and rotating the platform, and five men to manage the rammer and shot hoist." The rate of fire was one shot every one and a half minutes (Bracebridge 1894, 780).

Despite *Temeraire*'s respectable performance during the 1882 bombardment of Alexandria, the Royal Navy declined to use disappearing guns in later capital ships. Nonetheless, disappearing guns were installed later on the Russian coastal defense ship *Vitse-Admiral Popov* (as modified 1872) and the battleship *Ekaterina II* (1886) (*ibid.*; *Scientific American* 1885).

Hobson (1895) argued that not only did the retraction of the disappearing gun increase its own protection, but it also potentially increased the arc of fire for other guns.

An obvious and unavoidable disadvantage of the disappearing gun is that the space into which the gun "disappears" cannot be used for any other purpose. That space is rather large, being equal in diameter to the length of the gun, plus clearances. Moreover, if the gun is to be fully protected when in the firing position, there must be a corresponding large and heavy barbette (Cramp 1894, 868). Charles

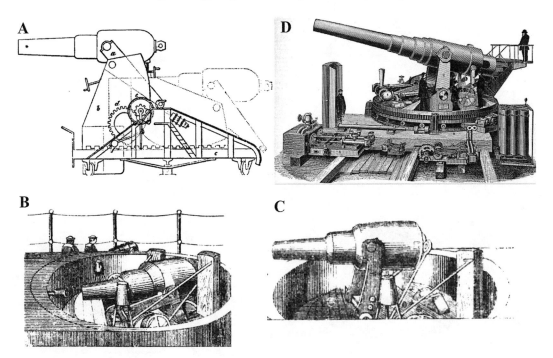

(A) The Moncrieff disappearing gun carriage, with the loading position shown in stippled lines (Owen 1873, 106). (B) The *Temeraire*'s disappearing gun in the loading position, and (C) in the firing position (Brassey 1886, Plate 15). (D) The disappearing gun for a Russian ironclad (*Scientific American* 1885). For the Russian dual-gun mount, photo source unknown; see https://i.gr-assets.com/images/S/compressed.photo.goodreads.com/hostedimages/1679659399i/34071026.jpg. For the profile of the Russian gun mount on the Popov, see http://www.modelshipgallery.com/gallery/misc/monitor/popov-700-vy/barbette-plan.jpg.

Cramp noted that the *Temeraire*'s muzzleloaders were "very short in comparison to modern breech-loaders of equal caliber, or even of equal weight."

In addition, it would be problematic if the mechanism failed when the gun was in the loading position (rendering it unable to fire). As Cramp stated, that mechanism must function "at any angle within [the ship's] arc of rolling."

CHAPTER 8

Load, Aim and Fire

Ammunition Transfer and Loading

Whether at the breech or the muzzle, manual loading was the norm for big guns until the nineteenth century. With muzzleloaders, in the sixteenth century it was not unusual to leave the cannon run out for the entire engagement and load it outboard. This process "required the loader to straddle the barrel of the gun outside the port and carry out all the clearing and charging operations from this exposed and difficult position" (Martin and Parker 1999, 193). "An Icelandic gunner in a Danish fleet … in 1622 reported, 'The ship rolled all the starboard guns under, and me on my gun with them. I swallowed much water and was nearly carried away'" (Andrade 2016, 205).

The transition to inboard loading was made in England in the 1620s and in Denmark in the 1640s (Bellamy 2006, 225, 245). It did require that the guns have room to recoil and a crew sufficient to run the gun back out again. Projectiles and powder also had to be brought up manually from below-deck storage.

When turrets were equipped with steam power for traversing the gun, thought was given to whether this same power could expedite the loading process. On James Eads' USS *Winnebago*, steam power was used to lower the gun platform to a (safe) loading position and raise it back for firing, and also to run out the guns, but it didn't actually load the projectiles (DANFS 1968, 783).

On the USS *Indiana* (BB-1, 1895), the 13-inch gun turrets were semi-automatically loaded. They were equipped with hydraulically powered ammunition hoists, the hoisted car having separate compartments for the powder and the projectile. However, in the magazine, these compartments were loaded by hand. A hydraulic rammer pushed the projectile into the gun breech (Fullam and Hart 1905, 185, 187).

A somewhat similar hatch loading system was used on the 16-inch rifled muzzleloaders of the HMS *Inflexible* (1876), but of course it communicated with the muzzle (Ellacott 1970, 58; King 1881, 112).

On the *Iowa*'s 16-inch guns, the chamber was long, to accommodate up to six powder bags and the projectile. Ramming those in hydraulically would require a prohibitively long hydraulic cylinder. Instead, a hydraulic motor was used to "drive a sprocket which engages the links in a rammer chain." The buffered chain head pushed in the projectile, retracted, and then pushed in the powder bags (NAVORD 1957, 71).

Turret designers experimented with both fixed (0–15 degrees) and "all-angle" elevation loading (Friedman 2011, 164, 253, 256). On the *Iowa*, the 16-inch guns were loaded at 5 degrees and the 5-inch guns at "any" angle (Dramiński 2020, 19–20).

Another design issue was whether the turret had to be rotated to a fixed position in order for the guns to be loaded, as on the British *Colossus* class (1886). The rotation brought "the breech of the gun over an ammunition hoist." Not only was this loading rotation time consuming, but it also "gave indication to the enemy when the guns were out of action and exposed a side view of them to the enemy's fire." In contrast, the French and American turrets of the same period permitted "all-around loading," because the hoist was on the vertical axis of the turret and rotated with it. The British didn't adopt a rotating hoist until the *Canopus* class (1897) (*Hearings* 1908, 612–14).

During World War I, the U.S. Navy trained crews using a "loading machine," which simulated the breech of a specific gun. The advantage of practicing loading and ramming on this simulator rather than on the actual gun was that it avoided "the possibility of marring the threads of the gun's screw box or of developing lost motion in the breech mechanism by too frequent operation" (Ramsey 1918, 228).

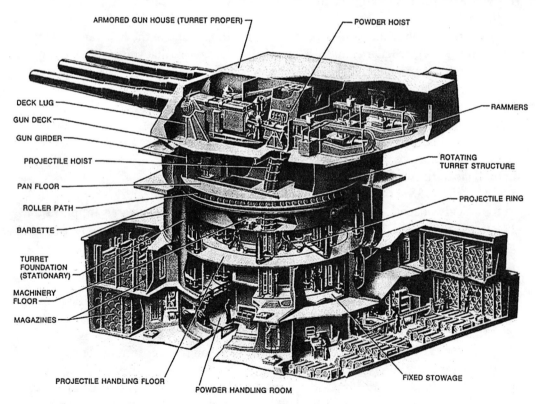

"Cutaway view of a modern turret (16-inch)" (NAVORD 1957, 98). It is a multilevel structure, with the armored gun house at the top. Note the separate projectile and powder hoists, which rotate with the turret.

During World War II, a would-be rammerman for the 5-inch, 38-caliber gun was expected to have practiced on the loading machine for "10 hours and more" (Fleet 1943, 26).

With smaller guns, ammunition may be "hand carried to the mounts." With larger guns, ammunition is hoisted, most often by an endless chain (with the ammunition carried on "flights") or an elevator car (NAVORD 1957, 73–75).

Gun Sights

Sighting could be physically difficult when large depressions or elevations were required.

With the muzzle depressed, "unless [the gun captain] be a very tall man he cannot look over the gun," and with the muzzle elevated, he might have to "bring his eye down almost to the level of the deck to sight along the gun" (Simpson 1862, 457–58).

Dispart Front Sights

The simplest method of sighting was to sight along the "line of metal" (the top of the cannon) directly at the target. However, the cannon was wider at the breech end than the muzzle end, so the line of metal was depressed below the line of fire, perhaps 1.5 degrees for long guns and 3–3.5 degrees for carronades (Douglas 1829, 293; Beauchant 1828, 16). This issue could be corrected for by adding a "dispart sight," a vertical front sight, with a height (the "dispart," or difference in the thickness of the

Checking and adjusting the sight on a 6-inch gun on the protected cruiser USS *Newark* (C-1). The ship was in commission 1891–1813 and carried twelve 6-inch/30 Mark 3 guns in sponsons on the sides (Wikipedia). Photograph (taken 1891–1901) by Edward H. Hart. Part of Detroit Publishing Company photograph collection (Catalog J [1901], no. 020657). Reproduction Number: LC-DIG-det-4a14472. Call Number: LC-D4-20657 [P&P]. Library of Congress Prints and Photographs Division. Cropped by author.

metal) equal to half the difference in diameters. If the bore wasn't quite centered, the gunner could customize the dispart for the peculiarities of that particular gun.

The dispart sight was known by the mid-seventeenth century, as evidenced by Nathaniel Nye's *The Art of Gunnery*, Volume 2 (1648). In chapter 38, he says to "set your dispart on the Muzzell ring, just over the center of the mouth of the piece," and "make some very small mark on the base ring," on its "highest part." He instructs the gunner to "hold your head about two foot from the base ring" and "observe, as the Peece is travissing [traversing], when you are in direct line with the Mark [and, of course, the dispart sight and the target]." In the next chapter, Nye discusses the correction of the dispart sight if the shot strikes over, under, to the left or to the right of the mark.

Sieur Guillet's *The Gentleman's Dictionary* (1705 "Dispart") likewise says that the dispart sight was "set on the Muzzle Ring." But later it was placed on the second reinforce ring (Douglas 1829, 217, 224), "in consequence of their liability to be knocked off or broken by the port" when the gun recoiled (Simpson 1862, 337).

Despite the teaching of the various gunnery treatises, Captain H. Garbett says that "disparts … like other sights, did not come into general use until the beginning of the [nineteenth] century." He notes that in 1801, Lord Nelson rejected a proposal to use sights, expecting that "our ships would be able, as usual, to get so close to our enemies that our shot cannot miss the object" (1897, 23).

Open Rear Sight

The open sight was created by replacing the base ring "mark" with a protruding rear sight, typically in the form of a V-shaped notch. "The chief defect in the open sight lies in the fact that the eye cannot simultaneously see the target and the two sight-points distinctly…. This sight is not only fatiguing to the eye but inaccurate … changes in the direction and intensity of the illumination of the front sight-point will make an apparent change in its position…. In addition … a considerable portion of [the target's] area is obscured by the sight points" (Curtin and Johnson 1915, 149–50).

A modest variation on the open sight was the peep sight. It reduced fatigue since the gunner didn't have to focus on the peep sight, just the front sight and target. However, if the radius of the hole were made small enough (to reduce parallax error from failing to center the eye), it would be smaller than the radius of the eye pupil at night, and hence night vision would be reduced (Curtin and Johnson 1915, 152).

Tangent (Breech) Sight (Scale, Hausse)

The tangent sight was a vertically adjustable rear sight. It was a vertical bar, graduated in degrees and ranges, and fitting into a socket at the center or on the side of the breech. The name is derived from a trigonometric relationship; the required height of this rear sight is the product of the distance from the rear sight to the front sight, by the tangent of the required angle of elevation. It doesn't appear to have been used on artillery until it was introduced by de Gribeauval in the late eighteenth century (Cummins 2009, 25). Bear in mind that this tool's use implies setting a specific angle of elevation, rather than just sighting on an aiming point (Ruffell 1996).

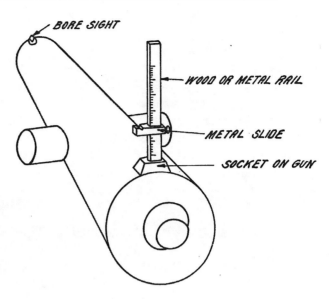

"Early American tangent sight" (U.S. Army 1922, 133). The gunner set the slide to the height corresponding to the desired elevation and sighted down the notch in the slide toward the "bore" (front) sight.

Properly speaking, a different scale would be needed for each gun, as the degree of elevation to which the height corresponded would vary depending on the length of the gun, and the range would also depend on the gun's caliber and charge (Ward 1861, 118). Augustus Cooke says that "every gun is furnished with two sight-bars, a long wooden and a short brass one; the longer is used for ranges over 1700 yards" (1875, 578).

Tangent sights were "in general use in America by 1812" but "not generally adopted in the British Navy … until about 1850" (U.S. Army 1922, 134). Union navy cannons were supplied with tangent sights (Simpson 1862, 329–30, 339–42, 350). However, to make effective use of them, the range had to be estimated and the sight set accordingly; the gunner then "lay the gun in such a manner that the coincidence of the three points [target, front sight, tangent sight] shall occur at that portion of the roll at which it is desired to fire" (459). According to Simpson, "the greatest distance at which we are accustomed to fire at sea [is] 1100 to 1300 yards" (337).

James Ward felt the advantage of the tangent sight was that it gave the commander on the quarterdeck more control. From his elevated (and ideally smoke-free) position, he could estimate the range and order the tangent sights of the entire broadside set for that distance (1861, 119).

Tangent sights were sometimes mounted so they could be inclined slightly to one side, forcing a change in the angle of train. The purpose was to correct for spin-drift (Curtin and Johnson 1915, 151) (see chapter 10).

Trunnion Sight

This device was not, strictly speaking, a "sight" at all—merely an elevation indicator placed at the trunnion axis (Cooke 1875, 587). It was probably used in the calibration of the tangent sight or with mortars (607) or with pivot guns at extreme elevations (809).

H-Speed Sight

This late nineteenth-century Royal Navy device combined a foresight in the form of a pole-mounted sphere with a rear sight consisting of "a fine aluminum wire stretched horizontally between two uprights [forming an 'H'] … on a sliding nut.… The nut is traversed by means of a screw," allowing it to be positioned with reference to "a deflection scale" graduated in both degrees and speed (knots). Thus, its purpose was to allow for the adjustment of the line of fire for the relative speeds of the ship and the enemy (or for wind). The scale was on a removable strip of aluminum in case the gun had to be recalibrated for a different weight projectile or charge (Garbett 1897, 201–3).

Ring-and-Post Sight

The front sight is a ring and the rear sight is a post, possibly with a ball on top. It can be advantageous for the "ring" part to have several concentric circles; these

"Leyte Operation, October 1944. The Australian heavy cruisers *Shropshire* (left) and *Australia* (right), with a U.S. heavy cruiser, photographed through a ring gun sight on board USS *Phoenix* (CL-46), off Leyte on 21 October 1944." Official U.S. Navy photograph, now in the collections of the National Archives. Courtesy of the Naval History and Heritage Command, Catalog No. 80-G-291377.

can be useful in "stadiametric ranging" (measuring the angular width of a target of known actual width).

The sight is hard to use if the target is far away; in addition, you have to hold your head just right to keep the ring and post aligned. Bear in mind that you are also trying to keep in focus the target, the rear sight and the front sight, all at different distances, while your ship is pitching and rolling.

Telescopic Sights

In 1640–1641, William Gascoigne mounted telescopic sights—essentially, Keplerian telescopes with crosshairs in the focal plane—on various scientific instruments, including a micrometer and a sextant. However, the first documented use of a telescopic sight on a firearm was in 1835, and that was for use with a percussion ignition sporting rifle (Pegler 2011, 50). The first use of a telescopic sight with artillery was in 1857 (Strauss 1896, 587). In the American navy, telescopes were first permanently mounted on (with) a gun by Bradley Fiske in 1892 (Curtin and Johnson 1915, 131). The eyepiece and objective lens of the telescope replaced the conventional rear and front sights.

By World War I, battle ranges were such that "it was necessary to have an apparent enlargement of the target in order to point the gun with sufficient accuracy." Since telescopes provided a magnified image, they necessarily had a narrowed field of view, but the magnification was variable (Curtin and Johnson 1915, 155).

In the 1918 U.S. Navy, "every modern broadside gun is fitted with two telescopes, one for the gun pointer … and the other for the gun trainer." The pointer's telescope was on the left side of the gun; the trainer's, on the right (Ramsey 1918, 173). Since they were on the sides, they were "zeroed" so their lines of sight intersected with the line of bore at the mean battle range of the gun (177). In double- and triple-gun turrets, there was just one gun (turret) trainer, but each gun had a pointer (175).

Dependent versus Independent Sight

A dependent sight is one whose line of sight is parallel to the line of bore. With an independent sight, the line of sight may be set at an angle, vertically and/or horizontally, with the line of bore.

A fire control system can calculate the vertical and horizontal offset from the line of sight that the gun's line of bore must be set to in order for the projectile to hit the target. If the sight is set to the complementary offsets (sight angle and sight deflection), then, assuming the gun crew keeps the target at the center of the sight up to the point when the projectile leaves the muzzle, the projectile should be on the right line of departure (NAVORD 1944, 253, 260).

But there is a catch. With the gun crew looking at the target, and not along the line of bore, there is the possibility that with a significant offset, the gun could be pointing at the ship's superstructure, not the enemy. To avoid self-inflicted wounds, a firing stop mechanism may be used. This may be a cam, customized for each gun, to sense whether the current elevation and train is dangerous and, if so, prevent firing (NAVORD 1957, 170–71).

Reflector Sights

If a half-silvered mirror is placed in the light path of a gunsight, it may be used to superimpose the virtual image of an illuminated crosshair over the gunsight's field of view. The virtual image is created either by a lens or by use of a curved mirror, in either case with the illuminated reticle at the focal point. The Grubb reflector sight (Grubb et al. 1902) obviated the need for the observer to view the distant target and the nearby rear sight simultaneously.

Gyroscopic Lead-Computing Sights

These sights were developed in World War II for use by anti-aircraft and dual-purpose guns (and aircraft).

Very simplistically, a spinning object resists a change in the spatial orientation of its axis and thus can be used to establish a reference line. A constant external torque will cause it to precess (its pole will describe a small circle). There are gyro sights, gyro compasses, and gyro stabilizers.

In a gyro sight, a reflector sight is linked to a spinning gyro, which makes it possible for the sight to compensate for motion by adjusting the reflector (Jarrett 2005, 190).

For anti-aircraft use, the target range was entered manually or received from radar. There were two reticles instead of one, both superimposed on the target image. One simply indicated the line of fire. The other was gyroscope-controlled so that, when the gun was laid to the correct lead and superelevation (the correction for the "drop"),

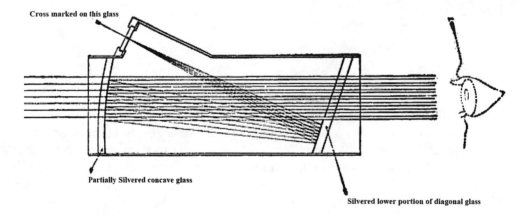

Cross marked on this glass

Partially Silvered concave glass

Silvered lower portion of diagonal glass

The original Grubb reflector sight. The curved surface of the front glass and the lower portion of the diagonal glass are partially silvered. The target is seen by the light passing horizontally through the two glasses. The glass diaphragm at the mouth of the diagonal hood is cut with a cross. Light shines through this diaphragm, which sits at the focal point of the curved mirror formed by the front glass, and thus is conveyed to the eye (MSIUS 1905).

the gyroscope reticle image would coincide with the bore reticle image. As the gunner tracked the target, the motion of the gun caused the gyroscope to precess, and its precession was constrained by springs or electromagnets whose strength was inversely proportional to the set range. The tilt therefore corresponded to the lead angle. A lever arm mechanism indicated the superelevation correction (BNP 1964, 169–72).

Selecting the Target

With a large target like a ship, especially at shorter ranges, one might aim for a particular part. In the Napoleonic Wars, the British tended to target the enemy hull, and the French, the rigging.

Targeting could be more specific than that: "Gunners could concentrate on the hull or below the waterline; on the gun ports or chain plates [used to attach the standing rigging to the hull]; or upperworks of the hull" (Willis 2008, 142).

Attempts were made to fire a cannonball to strike a target underwater, but these were generally ineffectual, the shot either rising and hitting the target above the waterline or only slightly indenting it below the waterline (*Experiments* 1854, 3). Of course, if a shot hit a sailing ship above but close to the waterline while the other vessel was heeled away from the firing ship, when the target came upright, the hole might lie below the waterline (Willis 2008, 142, 155).

Selecting the Elevation

At point-blank range, you could aim directly at the target, but at longer ranges you had to elevate the gun to allow for the fall of the projectile. The necessary elevation might be decided by the gun captain, by the officer in charge of a gun division, or by the captain. (And, once shells were in use, it would also be necessary to set the time of the fuse.)

In premodern naval warfare, one didn't estimate the range and then look up the proper elevation in a gunnery table. Rather, the appropriate elevation was determined by experience, as well as observing the fate of previous shots.

Rather than set a specific elevation, a rule of thumb might be used: for example, at point-blank range, aim at the hull, whereas at half a mile, aim at the fighting top, and at one mile, aim for the top of the main mast (NMRN 2012). (By aiming high, you allowed for the fall of the shot.)

In 1860, Howard Douglas published detailed guidelines for selecting aiming points at various ranges. For example, with an 8-inch gun, charged with ten pounds of powder, positioned 5 feet, 4 inches above the water, at a range of 1,225 yards, one should aim for "six feet above the truck of the mainmast"—this distance corresponded to a target height of 198 feet and an implied elevation of 3 degrees. But the practicality of such instructions remains in doubt.

In modern warfare, range tables would indicate what elevation to use, which would be "dialed in" directly.

Maximum Effective Range (MER)

The maximum effective range is the range at which, given the accuracy of the gun and its crew, there is an acceptable probability of hitting the target at a striking velocity and angle that would penetrate its armor and cause material damage.

Exterior ballistics (see chapter 10) can identify the range at which a particular projectile, fired at a particular muzzle velocity and elevation, can strike with a particular impact velocity. That calculation in turn may be compared with the empirical formulae of terminal ballistics (see chapter 14) to determine how many inches of wood or iron it will penetrate.

Statistics for a particular gun and gun crew can give a sense of the magnitude of the likely errors in shooting, along with their effect (chapters 11 and 12).

There is no golden rule regarding how high a probability is high enough. Is the projectile expensive and available only in small numbers (like a torpedo or missile), so you must make the shot count, or cheap and plentiful?

Given all the considerations, statements of "effective range" must be taken with a large grain of salt.

Modes of Fire

Fire may be classified as direct or indirect. Direct means that you can see the target, whereas indirect means that you can't (and are thus dependent on a spotter, as well as having a means for the spotter to communicate with the gunner). As a practical matter, once ranges exceed the distance to the horizon (which occurred in the early twentieth century), indirect fire is forced on you. Of course, a spotter may be helpful even in guiding direct fire.

Telescopes and binoculars have improved the effective range of direct fire by extending the distance at which the target is visible. However, the target may be obscured by atmospheric conditions, and an absolute limit on target visibility is set by the curvature of the Earth (i.e., the enemy may be below the horizon).

Indirect fire requires an observer in a forward or more elevated position. At sea, the observer could be on a kite balloon (possibly one tethered to the firing warship), on another vessel, or on an aircraft or airship. Telescopes and binoculars are, of course, useful to this observer, too, for spotting not only the target but also the location where a shot fell.

Concentration of Fire

In the early nineteenth century, Captain Philip Broke of HMS *Shannon* developed methods of concentrating his ship's fire on a single part of the enemy hull. Essentially, he had three preset aiming points. One, for example, was established by aiming the aftmost gun as far forward as possible at a buoy 300 yards away; once it could strike the buoy, the other guns were aimed to hit it too, and the gun carriage, deck and port-sill of each gun marked to show the necessary adjustment. In like manner, Broke established two other aiming points, one to the rear and another in the middle. He also leveled his guns by various means and marked the quoin and quoin bed so they could be realigned for the set range (Stevens 1834, 39; Voelcker 2013, 122).

A similar scheme was proposed by William Kennish, but he suggested a graduated quoin (for ranges exceeding point blank) and use of a "marine theodolite" by an officer directing the broadside (1837, 11, 13).

The British 1880 manual of gunnery adopted "600 yards as the distance at which to converge the broadside horizontally" (Admiralty 1880, 194).

The Union navy was skeptical of the merits of concentration, characterizing it as "of little efficacy" (U.S. Navy 1866, 87).

Gunlocks

A distinction is sometimes drawn between the "firing mechanism," which "directly explodes the primer," and the "firing attachments," such as lanyard, firing key, or electric firing battery and wiring, which "put the firing mechanism into operation" (Fullam and Hart 1905, 222). However, they are collectively known as the "gun lock."

The early modern gun had a vent (touch hole) that connected the powder chamber to the outside world. In preparing to fire the gun, the touch hole was filled with a "priming" powder, and some powder was deposited on the barrel just behind the touch hole. A linstock (forked staff) was used to bring a lit "slow match" (a slow-burning fuse, made by impregnating a rope with a saltpeter solution) over to the surface powder, igniting it. It in turn ignited the powder in the touch hole proper, which ignited the powder in the chamber (Little 2005, 145). Hence, the gun's firing mechanism was called a "matchlock."

Unfortunately, the slow match lived up to its name (Simpson 1862, 287). An alternative was to use the slow match just to light a "portfire"—a paper tube, closed at one end, filled with a mixture of gunpowder, sulfur and saltpeter in a linseed oil base; it burned rather like a motorist's emergency flare (Peterson 1969, 66). The portfire would be held ready (perhaps in a tub of water) and applied to the touch hole when the gunner deemed it appropriate. A typical portfire burned for 12–15 minutes and "should not go out even under water" (Falconer and Burney 1815, 350), which was an obvious advantage at sea.

Unfortunately, filling a vent with loose powder from a powder horn was a slow process (Simpson 1862, 288), and igniting loose powder tended to erode the vent. The solution was to provide the priming powder in a tin tube inserted into the vent. These were first used by the Royal Navy at the Battle of Quiberon Bay in 1759 (McLeod 2012, 60–61). However, Edward Hawke reported in 1760 that the tubes were "apt to fly out and wound the men" (Laughton 1907, 282n1). In 1779–1781, Charles Douglas made use of powder-filled goose quills instead (273–74, 282).

In 1755, the Admiralty ordered the fitting of flintlocks to all quarterdeck guns and intended that other guns would be so fitted in due course (Pope 1987, 206). In the flintlock, when the trigger was pulled, a piece of flint at the end of a hammer struck a steel plate, creating a spark, which ignited the priming powder in the flash pan.

However, it appears that this initiative fizzled out, as, in 1778, Charles Douglas fitted flintlocks to the guns of the *Duke* at his own expense, and his proselytization of this innovation led to him being regarded as the inventor of the naval flintlock (Hime 1915, 201). It appears that for a long time musket flintlocks were adapted to naval guns, and flintlocks weren't manufactured for naval use until 1790. A lanyard was used to pull the trigger (Dahlgren 1853, 11).

The next important development was the percussion lock. The basic concept was that the impact of a hammer on a cap containing mercury fulminate (a sensitive explosive) would detonate the cap, which in turn would initiate the propulsive train. The catch was that the "vent blast"—the combustion gases escaping through the vent—would destroy the hammer (Dahlgren 1853, 18). This problem was ultimately solved by the lock patented by E. Hidden and S. Sawyer in 1842, which was immediately accepted by the U.S. Navy (17). Essentially, the pull of the lanyard, which initially caused the hammer to pivot and strike the cap, led the hammer to move back along a slit, so it was no longer over the vent (39).

Mercury fulminate is dangerous to manufacture, and it was found (in 1897) that the mercury in the primer became amalgamated with the brass of nineteenth-century cartridge cases, embrittling them. These cases were a large part of the cost of a cartridge, and the authorities wanted to be able to reuse them.

Accordingly, mercury fulminate was replaced with potassium chlorate. It's not a panacea. When a gun using a potassium chlorate primer is fired, the priming reaction generates potassium chloride, which is deposited on the bore. This salt greedily absorbs water, causing rusting. In 1922, potassium chlorate was identified as the

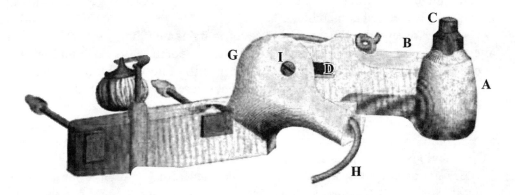

The "Hidden Navy Lock in use" (Simpson 1862, Figure 104). When the "lock string" (H) is pulled, because of how it is wrapped within G and attached to the hammer shank B, the "first effect … is to cause the hammer [A] to turn on its axial bolt [I], which it does until arrested by striking the primer" with the iron nipple (C). Continuing to pull on the lock string causes it to slide away from the primer about one inch, until the bolt is at the opposite end of slot D, thus moving the hammer out of the path of the vent gases. G are lock-lugs, the bearings for the axial bolt (295). Labels H and I added by author.

cause of the problem. In 1928, a non-corrosive primer (SINOXYDE) containing lead styphnate, barium nitrate and antimony sulfide was introduced (White 2010, 347).

An alternative to the percussion cap is the friction tube. This device took several different forms, but basically it was a vertical tube containing detonating composition, with a hole through which a roughened metal friction bar ran horizontally. When pulled out (typically by a lanyard), its friction with the composition heated and detonated the latter (Owen 1873, 163).

The final major development was electric ignition. Current flowing through a high-resistance bridge generated heat. In the British navy, the platinum/silver bridge was inside a quill containing priming composition (Very 1880, 213). This material was less sensitive than the fulminate used in percussion devices and hence permitted rougher handling (Fullam and Hart 222).

In 1880, the British navy fired guns by means of the friction tube or electricity (Very 1880, 212); the Germans, friction (267); and the French and Americans, friction or percussion (238, 304).

Electric firing made simultaneous "director" fire possible, but, initially, the reliability of the power source was a sticking point. While it would be possible to have the ship carry a generator and run lines from it to all the guns, that would mean a shot that took out the generator would render them useless. Hence, each gun had to have its own battery. And developing a working battery itself took some time. An 1894 article (Morgan) noted that while electrical ignition had until that time been in limited use, the Bureau of Ordnance had recently adopted a zinc/carbon dry battery as well as a new electric primer design. By World War I, electric ignition was the norm, with percussion systems as backup.

Firing Interval

The firing interval is the time elapsed between "the moment of willing to fire and the moment of exit of the projectile" (Alger 1908). Philip Alger broke this sequence down into four parts: (1) "the time from willing to fire until the firing device is actuated" (the "personal interval"); (2) the subsequent time "until the primer flame reaches the ignition charge" (the "primer interval"); (3) the subsequent time "until the projectile begins to move" (the "powder interval"); and (4) the subsequent time until the projectile reaches the muzzle (the "powder interval").

Alger's "personal interval" is really the sum of the gunner's reaction time and the time for the firing attachments to actuate the firing mechanism. He reported the results of an experiment comparing different firing attachments, as shown in Table 8–1.

These variously required movement of the teeth, cheeks, finger, hand, forearm, foot or lungs. Surprisingly (note bolded values), Alger pronounced the "present hand key" to be "the most efficient device." (There were later guns, such as the $5/38$, for which percussion firing was initiated by a foot pedal [NAVORD 1957, 52].)

There was not much to be done about the powder or travel interval, since in this area the concern was achieving a particular muzzle velocity without straining the gun. With a 7-inch gun, it was estimated as totaling .0572 seconds.

Table 8–1: Personal Interval

Actuator	Avg (s)	Range
Biting Mouthpiece	.198	.093
Mouthpiece Puff from Mouth	.214	.100
Service Hand Key	.274	.099
Self-Cocking Pistol Grip	.300	.159
Pistol Trigger Pull	.244	.093
Lanyard Pull on Hammer Lock	.354	.152
Lanyard Pull on Spring Lock	.268	.235
Foot	.288	.121
Mouthpiece Blow with Lungs	.276	.130

According to Alger, a 1908 experiment showed that the primer interval was shorter for percussion firing (.0143 seconds) than for electric firing (.0714). Other experiments reported averages of 0.031 and 0.044 seconds for electric firing and 0.004 for percussion (U.S. Navy 1918, 247–48).

In the case of percussion, this was the time for the fulminate to react to the shock of the hammer by igniting. For electric firing, it was the time for the resistance wire to heat up (as in a toaster) enough to ignite the primer. So it is conceivable that it could be slower. But the heat generated is proportional to the resistance of the wire and the square of the current, and the temperature change would depend on the wire's heat capacity, so this interval would be quite dependent on the choice of battery and wire.

Gun Crew

The assignment of the crew to the guns in the event of battle was specified in the quarter bill. The allocations varied depending on the size of the gun, as well as navy and period.

N.A.M. Rodger (1996, 312) asserts that up to the 1570s, there was only one gunner for each gun, and in the early seventeenth century, just two or three. If the gun were loaded outboard, and not traversed or elevated, this number may have been sufficient. Otherwise, they would have had to either assign soldiers or borrow topmen to assist the gunner.

For Samuel Pepys' navy, we have cannon of 7 (8 men), demi-cannon (7), culverin (5), 12-pounder (4), saker (3), and 3-pounder (2) (Tanner 1903, 240). For the late eighteenth and early nineteenth centuries, see Table 8–2A.

Lieutenant Colonel H.W. Miller (1921, 57) and R.L. Pope (1987, 206) provide the rule of thumb that one man was required for every 5 cwt (112 pounds) of gun weight. Miller observes that gun crews changed constantly; if only one side were engaged, the free crews would come over to help, but crewmen could also be pulled off to handle the ship or to form a boarding party.

Mid-nineteenth-century guns were heavier, and their crews reflected that change.

Table 8–2A: Gun Crews Relative to Weight of Shot*

Gun	Falconer 1769, 1780 "Quarters"	France (de Villehuet and de Sauseuil 1788, 196)	U.S./UK (de Tousard 1809, 364**)	France (Douglas 1829, 149, 163)
42	15			
36		15		14
32	13		18	
24	11		15	12
18	9	11		10
12	7		9	10
9	6		7	
8		7		8
6	5		5	6
4	4		4	6
3	3			
Carr				4

*The numbers do not include the boys who fetched powder.
**"Old Plan" with common carriage.

Table 8–2B: 1866 U.S. Navy Gun Crews

Pivot Guns	Broadside Guns	Crew
X, XI (16,000 lbs)		24
X (12,000 lbs), 64-pdr (100 cwt)		20
IX (9,000 lbs), 100-pdr rifle (9,700 lbs)	same	16
	VIII (60 cwt)	14
	VIII (6,500 lbs), VIII (56 cwt), 32-pdr (57 cwt)	12
60-pdr rifle (5,400 lbs)	Same, also 32-pdr (4,500 lbs), 32-pdr (42 cwt)	10
30-pdr rifle (3,550 lbs)	same, also 32-pdr (33 cwt)	8
20-pdr rifle (1,750 lbs)	same, also 32-pdr (27 cwt)	6

(U.S. Navy 1866, 16, 101)

In 1914, a USN 7-inch/45 rifled breechloader broadside gun had a crew of sixteen (including four powdermen) (U.S. Navy, Navy Department 1918, 70).

Rate of Fire

Several factors determine the rate of fire. At an absolute minimum, there is the time needed for the gun to recoil, be cleaned and reloaded, and run out. If the elevation of the gun has been disturbed (the quoin jumped out), or if the movements of the ships necessitate that the gun be relaid, then setting the proper elevation and train takes time. Shells cannot be fired as fast as shot because the fuses have to be prepared and adjusted; percussion fuses are less trouble than time fuses (Owen 1873, 338). The celerity with which these operations may be performed depends on the weight of the gun and carriage, the size and skill of the gun crew, and the availability of mechanical assistance.

Smoke, rain or sea spray may obscure the gun captain's view of the enemy (especially if he is looking through a gun port below deck), and the gun captain may need to wait for the roll to bring the gun into position. Hangfires and misfires could cause delays.

A modern crew of four handling a replica sixteenth-century wrought iron breechloader required 5–10 minutes per shot (Konstam 2008, 40). An experienced crew might well do better, but handling a large muzzleloader would be more time consuming. Elizabethan sea dogs might have just fired one broadside at point-blank range and then fought a boarding action (*ibid.*). "In 1646 Master gunner William Eldred stated, in *The Gunner's Glasse* that a maximum of ten rounds an hour could be fired from a gun" (Hughes 1975, 35).

On sixteenth- and early seventeenth-century English ships, the guns were typically undermanned. The actual rate of fire achieved can be judged from ammunition supply and consumption records. In 1588, the *Vanguard* fired "500 rounds of demi-cannon, culverin, and demi-culverin shot in nine hours," and since it carried "a total of 32 guns of these calibers, her rate of fire per gun was 1.75 rounds an hour" (Rodger 1996, 313).

If the guns were undermanned, then, after all the guns had fired, a team might move from gun to gun to reload. And if this step were necessary, then it was advantageous to move out of the enemy's range until the process was complete. In 1652, the *Sapphire* bore down on an enemy ship, fired its guns, and then "stood away." It appears to have taken close to "two glasses" (an hour) for it to reload and recover its attack position (Rodger 1996).

For eighteenth-century field artillery (3–12-pounders), a good rate of fire for an eight-man crew was considered two aimed shots per minute (Peterson 1969, 119), which could be doubled by eliminating steps (such as sponging the bore)—a dangerous tactic, but not as much as getting overrun by the enemy. Speed was affected by the weight of the piece; a 12-pounder might get off only one round a minute (Wise 1979, 31).

The rate of fire at sea was lower. In 1738, the 70-gun *Hampton Court* could "fire 400 rounds in twenty-five minutes which suggests that each gun fired about one round every two minutes" (Rodger 1997, 540). The USS *Constitution* could fire its 24-pounders, which had a twelve-man crew, one round every three minutes (Mehl 2002, 33).

Other published estimates include one round every three to five minutes for the early modern era (Volo and Volo 2001, 256); three broadsides in five minutes in 1805 (Hill 2000, 55); and, for best crews under perfect conditions, one round every four or five minutes in 1660 and one a minute in 1756 (Ireland 2000, 48).

Gunlocks improved the rate of fire; Collingwood's flagship *Dreadnought* "could fire her first three broadsides in three and a half minutes" (Rodger 2004, 540). Such a firing rate could not be sustained: the gunners would tire, there would be casualties, and smoke would slow down the aiming process.

The British and American crews of the Napoleonic period typically got off one and half to three times as many shots as a French or Spanish opponent (Toll 2008, 7). The 74-gun *Guerriere* at Minorca (1756) fired 659 rounds in 3.5 hours (5.5 rounds/ hour), and another French ship averaged 6 rounds/hour at the Saintes; either the crews were less handy or the French were deliberately taking their time (Rodger 2004, 540).

The heavy rifled breechloaders of HMS *Warrior* (1860) were a bit faster than the old smoothbore carriage guns, firing perhaps once a minute. However, the rifled muzzleloaders were very slow. To reload, the barrels had to be fully depressed, and sometimes they also had to be traversed to the fore or aft position. That gave them a rate of fire of just one shot every three minutes. When breechloaders were reintroduced, those with the full screw closure improved the situation only a little, increasing to once every two minutes (Hill 2006, 55).

The elevating screw increased accuracy but not necessarily speed. In tests at Shoeburyness, a 40-pdr rifled breechloader fired 10 rounds in 7.5 minutes using the screw and in just 6 minutes with the wedge (Owen 1873, 337).

In the American Civil War, the big guns were slow. With the 15-inch Dahlgren, the average time between shots was 6 minutes; depending on conditions, it might take three to ten minutes to fire again. By contrast, a long 32-pdr or 9-inch shell gun might be fired once every forty seconds (Canfield 1968).

Late nineteenth-century breechloading deck guns, with pivot mounts, appeared to have firing rates of 10 rounds/minute (Mehl 2002, 81, 85).

On the *Iowa*, the 16-inch guns could fire twice a minute, and the 5-inch, 16–22 rounds a minute (Dramiński 2020, 19–20).

Even with the same model of gun, rates of fire will differ from ship to ship. In 1902, with the Mark VII 6-inch quick-fire, nine British warships exhibited prize firing rates that ranged from 4.17 to 7.38 rounds/minute. With heavier guns, the range was 0.62–1.25 (Brassey 1904, 38).

The rate of fire can be limited by barrel overheating. William Eldred said "that after forty shots had been fired an interval of an hour must be allowed to cool the piece" (Hughes 1975). Heat is still an issue almost four centuries later. If the barrel becomes too hot, there are variety of potential problems, including increased erosion (thus loss of accuracy over the long term) and self-ignition of propellant. Barrel liquid-cooling systems have been used with some rapid-fire twentieth-century naval guns (Wu et al. 2008).

Rapid-Fire Designs

The fastest fixed guns on a premodern warship were the swivel guns. There were breechloaders with removable chambers, and by having several prepped chambers handy, one could get off several shots quickly—perhaps one a minute, at least until the preps were used up (Konstam 2008). They were short-range weapons, intended for anti-personnel use, so sustained rapid fire wasn't necessary; either the enemy boarding action was fended off or it wasn't.

In the 1820s and 1830s, the French experimented with *canon foudre* (drum cannon), "equipped with a carousel of multiple powder chambers that could be pre-loaded." It was not a success; the seal between the chamber and the barrel was inadequate (Mehl 2002, 36).

The logical solution was to use multiple barrels (i.e., a volley gun) rather than multiple chambers, as on the Swedish Nordenfelt 25-mm machine cannon (1877). It had a rate of fire of 120 rounds/minute and an effective range of 1,640 yards. This was a semi-automatic, gravity-fed weapon (Mehl 2002, 62).

On the Nordenfelt, the four barrels were fixed, horizontally parallel. Another approach was the Hotchkiss system revolving cannon; an 1896 Russian model fired 80 rounds/minute to 2,950 yards (Mehl 2002, 63). Another source claimed that 12 aimed shots/minute at 4,000 yards was possible (Ireland and Grove 1997, 42).

A high rate of fire was especially important for anti-aircraft guns, given the high speed and changing altitude of their targets. The *Iowa*'s Bofors 40 mm had a "practical" rate of 80–90 rounds per minute per barrel, and the Oerlikon 20 mm, 250–320 (Dramiński 2020, 20–21).

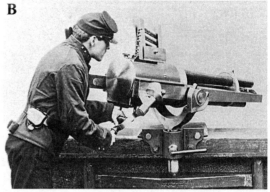

(A) "Breech-loading swivel gun with chamber on stand" (early sixteenth century). George F. Harding Collection. Courtesy of the Art Institute of Chicago, Reference Number 1982.3533a-b. Length overall of cannon: 33.5 inches (81.5 cm). Overall length of cannon in frame including handle: 58⅞ inches (149.6 cm). Diameter of breech opening of cannon: 2⅞ inches (7.3 cm). Diameter at flared muzzle: 2.25 inches (5.7 cm). Diameter of breech clock opening: 1⁵/₃₂ inches (3 cm). Diameter at base of breech block: 4.75 inches (11.2 cm). Overall length of breech block: 8¹¹/₃₂ inches (21.2 cm). Weight of breech block: 23 pounds, 7 ounces.

(B) Hotchkiss 37-mm light naval revolving cannon. From Alfred Koerner, *The Hotchkiss Revolving Cannon* (Paris, 1879). Courtesy of the Naval History and Heritage Command, Catalog No. 72798.

CHAPTER 9

Internal Ballistics
and Gun Design

The term "ballistics" was coined by Marin Mersenne in 1644. Ballistics may be divided into three broad categories: *interior (internal) ballistics*, explaining what happens inside the gun barrel; *exterior (external) ballistics*, describing the flight of the projectile through the air; and *terminal ballistics*, dealing with its penetration of (and damage to) the target.

How a Gun Works

The purpose of the propellant is to accelerate the projectile inside the bore of a gun to a useful muzzle speed without bursting the gun or causing excessive wear. The pressures, and thus the accelerations achieved, will depend on the amount of gunpowder and its burning characteristics, as well as on the diameter of the bore. The muzzle speed obtained will further depend on the length of the bore, the mass of the projectile, and the resistances it will encounter when traversing the bore.

A good propellant is one whose ingredients react very quickly ("deflagrate"), but not explosively, to form a gas. At normal temperature and pressure, this gas would occupy a much greater volume than the original ingredients, but initially the volume of the gas is limited by that of the propellant (powder) chamber and the position of the projectile, and so there is instead an increase in pressure. The deflagration reaction also generates heat, which further increases pressure.

As the reaction continues, the pressure reaches the point at which it's sufficient to overcome the friction holding the projectile in place ("shot-start force"), and it starts traveling down-bore.

The propulsive force on the projectile is the pressure times the area of the projectile base; the acceleration it feels is the force divided by the mass of the projectile. For spherical shot, the base area is proportional to the square of the diameter, and the mass to the cube, so acceleration is inversely proportional to the diameter.

When the net force on an object is greater than zero, it accelerates—that is, it changes its velocity. And when an object's velocity is greater than zero, its position in space changes. The net force on the projectile is not constant, and thus its acceleration is not constant. And since its acceleration isn't zero unless and until the net forces are zero, neither is its velocity.

As the projectile moves, the volume available to the gas increases, which tends to reduce the pressure. However, if the deflagration reaction is still going on, the newly produced gas and heat will tend to increase the pressure. One can thus draw a pressure-time or pressure-travel curve for the projectile, and the location of its peak will depend on the specific characteristics of the powder and projectile. Likewise, one can draw velocity-time or velocity-travel curves.

Once the powder is completely consumed, the propulsive force on the projectile can only decrease as it moves down-bore (unless, like a rocket, it carries its own fuel source), and once that propulsive force is less than the resisting forces, any farther travel in the bore will reduce the projectile's speed.

After the projectile exits the muzzle, the pressure on it drops precipitously, although it may experience a brief period of additional acceleration from the escaping gases (transitional ballistics).

The Gun as a Pressure Vessel

The combustion gas can expand in one of two ways: by moving the projectile down-bore or by bursting the gun barrel. Obviously, the former is preferred.

The gun is thus a pressure vessel, just like the boiler of a steam locomotive or a compressed gas tank. A nineteenth-century steam locomotive boiler typically had a maximum internal pressure of about 300 pounds psig, or about twenty-one times atmospheric pressure (14.7 psia). A modern compressed gas tank is typically pressurized to around 2,000 psig, although cylinders that can withstand 6,000 psig (about 400 "atmospheres") are commercially available.

The deepest part of the ocean, the Challenger Deep of the Mariana Trench, is almost seven miles deep, and the pressure of the water there is about 1,100 atmospheres. The spherical crew chamber of Jacques Piccard's bathyscape *Trieste*, which explored the deep, had 5-inch-thick walls to withstand the external pressure.

How does the pressure difference between the inside and the outside of a cannon compare to these values? The pressure in a cannon might, albeit for only a brief time, be tens of thousands of atmospheres (Rodman 1861, 176).

Pressure Measurement

Knowing the variation in internal gas pressure with the movement of the projectile within the bore is critical to designing the gun to withstand the stresses of firing while minimizing its weight.

Early work focused on determining the initial pressure, and the results were sometimes wildly different. This outcome is not entirely surprising. Indirect methods, working from an experimentally determined muzzle velocity, depended on the accuracy of the mathematical model devised to relate muzzle velocity to bore pressure. And direct methods had to cope with the extraordinary pressure and temperature generated by confined, ignited gunpowder.

The first attempt to estimate the internal pressure in a firearm was by Benjamin Robins (Chapter 1, Propositions II–IV). He dropped a known quantity of powder in a large, red-hot iron receiver connected to a "mercurial" gauge. The powder ignited, and he observed the change in the level of mercury as the expanding gas pushed against it. This result gave him a measurement of the volume of gas generated. Recognizing that the gas was at a temperature higher than room temperature, he calculated what the volume of the gas would have been at room temperature. He reported that one ounce of powder generated 460 cubic inches of gas. Knowing the density of the powder, he calculated that one cubic inch of powder generated 244 cubic inches of gas. Consequently, if the gas were confined to the original volume of the powder, and at room temperature, the pressure would be 244 times atmospheric pressure.

Robins then proceeded to determine how much pressure of air would be augmented by being heated to "the extreme heat of red-hot iron" (Proposition V). For this purpose, he used a modified musket barrel, closed at one end and drawn out conically at the other, with a narrow opening remaining. He heated it to red heat and immersed it with the open end down in water before allowing it to cool. Then he measured how much water entered the barrel (as the air inside contracted as it cooled). He found that the ratio of the heated volume to the cooled volume was 4.111:1.

Hence, assuming that the combustion gas would respond similarly to air, and that the temperature of the combustion gas in the gun would correspond to red-hot iron (just before it became white hot), the ratio of the internal pressure to atmospheric pressure would be 244 times 4.111, or about 1,000 "atmospheres."

In 1792, Count Rumford (Benjamin Thompson) made a direct measurement of the pressure generated by gunpowder burned in a confined space. A hammered iron barrel with a narrow bore, open at one end, was placed on a stone support with its opening facing upward.

After the powder was introduced into the bore, Rumford forced in a cylindrical leather stopper, and on top of the stopped opening he placed a solid hemisphere of hardened steel. At the bottom of the barrel was a narrow hollow projection (which served the same purpose as the vent on a cannon even though it was not open at both ends) that would be filled by the powder. This projection fitted into a hole in an iron ball. To fire the powder, the iron ball was heated red hot and attached to the projection. The heat was conducted to the powder in the "vent," and the powder was ignited (Rumford 1870, 115–19).

Rumford's idea was to find the smallest weight that could be placed on the hemisphere and thereby keep the opening closed when the powder was ignited. In practice, he sometimes used a set weight and found the largest charge that would "just move" the weight (141). Either way, knowing the size of the opening, the gas pressure exerted on the weight from below could be calculated.

The weight that Rumford used initially wasn't trivial; it was the barrel of a 24-pounder "brass" cannon, placed vertically on its cascabel. This barrel weighed 8,081 pounds (128). The largest charge for which he calculated a pressure was 70.2

percent (18 apothecary grains), which lifted the cannon barrel, with a deduced pressure of 10,977 atmospheres (141). In Rumford's second test of this charge, the vent tube burst, bringing this series of eighty-five experiments to an end.

In the early 1840s, U.S. Army Chief of Ordnance George Bomford drilled a hole into barrel of a cannon and screwed a pistol barrel into the hole. He loaded the pistol with a bullet and fired the cannon. The velocity of the bullet was recorded with a ballistic pendulum. By placing the hole at different locations along the cannon barrel, he could construct a relationship between the position and the velocity of the bullet, which would have been proportional (not necessarily linearly) to the gas pressure at that position. Some sources say that the holes were all placed at one time (Snow 2017, 64), and others that they were drilled in succession (Simpson 1862, 76). Bomford found that with the powder he used, the maximum pressure was where the shot was seated, and it declined by about half at four calibers down-bore (Simpson 1862, 77).

A somewhat less Rube Goldberg–esque sensor was the Rodman indenting gauge (1858). Its tube, like Bomford's pistol barrel, fitted into a drilled hole in the barrel wall, and the expanding gases moved a piston with a gas check, which in turn moved a knife that indented a copper disc. The depth of the indentation was compared to that achieved with a matching disc (from same copper bar) and knife using a standard testing machine (VNEM 1871). Thomas Rodman found a pressure of 13,333 atmospheres (closer to Rumford's results than to those of Robins or Hutton) (Benton 1862, 55).

In the Noble crusher gauge (1860), the Rodman disc was replaced with a cylinder of copper, resulting in the pressure being expressed as so many "copper units of pressure" (CUP). For guns developing lesser pressures, lead cylinders were used (EB 1911, "Ballistics"; Barnett 1919, 195ff; Buchanan 2006, 306).

Noble and Abel found that "the maximum pressure of fired gunpowder is but

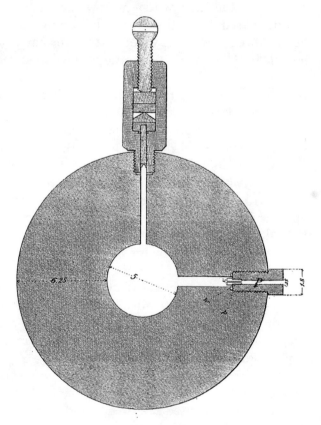

An instrumented gun barrel, ready for pressure measurement. The view is down-bore, and the indenting gauge is at the top of the barrel. The plug on the right side of the barrel is for holding a friction tube for igniting the charge (Rodman 1861, Plate II, after p. 204).

6,554 atmospheres, or 43 tons per square inch; and this result has been accepted by all writers on interior ballistics as being very near the truth" (Ingalls 1918, 6).

In the 1880s, interest shifted from black powder to the nitrocellulose-based smokeless powders, such as poudre B, ballistite and cordite. These had greater potency than black powder and consequently generated higher internal pressures.

The Physics of Combustion

Gunpowder, consisting of a multitude of grains of a controlled size range, is loaded into a powder chamber. There is air in the interstices between the grains, and there may be air above the bed of powder.

Combustion of black powder is believed to begin due to "the formation of a local hot spot." This hot spot may be formed directly by heat (e.g., from a burning fuse or the result of friction). Alternatively, shock may form one "by the adiabatic compression of entrapped air" (Blackwood and Bowden 1952, 302).

With typical grain sizes, the propagation of burning from grain to grain is much faster than the inward burning of an individual grain. For 12- to 25-mesh gunpowder at atmospheric pressure, the grain-grain propagation was 60 cm/s and the rate of grain burning (assuming the grains to be 2-mm diameter spheres) was 0.4 cm/s. At 30–50 atmospheres, the propagation rate was 2,000 cm/s and the grain burning rate 9 cm/s (Blackwood and Bowden 1952, 294).

"There is evidence that the propagation from grain to grain is due primarily to the emission of a fine host spray of molten particles (potassium salts).... Subsidiary experiments showed that it was difficult to ignite the powder by merely allowing hot gases to impinge on the grains" (Blackwood and Bowden 1952, 304).

With fine gunpowder (250 mesh), the behavior is quite different: "Propagation of this fine powder is much slower … in fact, the rate of propagation corresponds to the rate of burning … on the order of 1 cm/s.... If rapid propagation is to occur it is apparently necessary to have an open space between the grains so that the hot flying spray can be effective. In a densely compacted powder this cannot occur and the rate of propagation is governed by the rate of burning" (Blackwood and Bowden 1952, 296). Thus, we see why serpentine powder was weaker than corned powder.

In a recent study, the flame spread rate for grain black powder (41 percent 600–850 microns, 33 percent 860–1,000 microns) was "about 20–30 times as fast as that of the meal black powder" (under 150 microns). The authors attributed the rate difference to the larger spaces between larger grains (Ding and Yoshida 2012).

With corned powder, grain burning is obviously the rate-limiting step that determines the timing and magnitude of the changes in pressure and temperature that occur inside the gun.

This point brings us to Piobert's "Law" (1839): "Burning takes place by parallel layers where the surface of the grain regresses, layer by layer, normal to the surface at every point" (Russell 2015, 45).

This result has two implications. First, the burning (and thus the combustion gas production) at any given moment will be proportional to the exposed surface area of the grains. Second, in a given time interval, the same thickness of material will be consumed on all of the grains (Hunt and Wright 1922, 445). Piobert's Law has been found to apply to modern propellants (Russell 2015).

The grain burning rate, per unit surface area, depends on the pressure. The simplest formulation of that relationship is Paul Vielle's, in which it is proportional to the pressure raised to a particular exponent ("pressure index"). Both the constant of proportionality and the exponent depend on the propellant. Historically, there was considerable dispute as to the proper exponent, even for black powder. For Dayu Ding and Tadao Yoshida (2012)'s "grain black powder" in a closed tank, it was 0.2782. Émile Sarrau used 0.5, and some authors preferred 1.0, as it greatly simplifies interior ballistics calculations. For modern propellants, it is likely to be in the range 0.8–0.9 (Jones et al. 1965, 1–12).

The total exposed initial surface area is the number of grains multiplied by the exposed surface area of an individual grain. It can be shown that for spheres, this total surface area would be inversely proportional to the diameter, since packing density is independent of the diameter (cp. Song et al. 2008).

Since the initial burning rate is proportional to the initial exposed surface area, we would thus predict that small-grained propellant reacts (at least initially) faster than large-grained propellant. Indeed, it is found experimentally that not only is the initial increase in pressure faster, but the maximum pressure achieved is higher and occurs more quickly.

The grain geometry determines how the grains' surface area changes with time. If it increases, the grain is "progressive"; if it decreases, it is "regressive"; and if it's approximately constant, it's "neutral" (Kosanke et al. 2012, 889).

The advantage of using a progressive propellant over a neutral one (or a neutral one over a regressive one) was that it tended to delay the onset and reduce the magnitude of the maximum pressure.

The time to complete consumption of an individual grain is determined by its "least dimension" ("web thickness"), assuming the grain was completely exposed. Since "combustion takes place on all sides of a grain at once," a solid grain vanishes when the penetration from the original surface is half the web thickness (Ingalls 1912, 56).

Let us look at a single grain with some simple geometries, when the penetration is one-quarter of the critical dimension (web thickness).

Table 9-1: Effect of Grain Geometry

Geometry; Critical Dimension	Mass Rel Orig	Surf Area Rel Orig
Sphere or Cube; Diameter	12.5%	25% (regressive)
Long Cylinder (ignoring ends); Diameter	25%	50% (regressive)
Thin Plate (ignoring edges); Plate Thickness	50%	100% (neutral)

It is clear that if the critical dimension is of the same magnitude for each of these shapes, the surface area—and thus the burning rate—declines most rapidly for the sphere (or cube) and least for the thin plate, with the long cylinder falling in between. (Formulae were published that took the ends of cylinders and edges of plates into account [Ingalls 1912, 59ff].)

James Ingalls notes that "square flat grains" were "still used in certain rapid-firing guns," and if the grains were very thin, they would give a "constant emission of gas during the burning; … [But] the grain would be consumed in a very short interval of time" (1912, 61).

A neutral burning was achievable without the disadvantage of quick consumption by forming the grain as a cylinder with a single axial perforation. The web thickness would be the difference in radii. As the burning progressed, the outer surface area would decrease, but the inner surface area would increase, nearly balancing out the former (Ingalls 1912, 66).

There was a period in which the U.S. Navy used multiperforated grains for heavy artillery. These were cylindrical in form, pierced by "seven equal longitudinal perforations, one of which coincides with the axis of the grain, while the others are disposed symmetrically about the axis, their centers forming a regular hexagon."

As the burn progressed, the outer surface area decreased and the inner surface areas increased. When the perforations touched, the grain divided into "twelve slender, three-cornered pieces with curved slides" ("slivers") (Ingalls 1912, 68).

There are three geometric parameters: the radius of the grain (R), the radius of each perforation (r), and the length of the cylinder (m). There are actually two possible web thicknesses: the outer one between the outside of the cylinder and a perforation, and the inner one, between adjacent perforations. The latter equaled 0.5 × (R-3r) (Ingalls 1912, 67). Typically, R was 11 times r (69), so the inner web thickness controlled. The cylinder length was typically 13 times the inner web thickness and thus 4r (70). With those ratios, the surface area would increase during the entire burning of the web thickness (72). In the "sliver" stage, the surface area would decrease.

A progressive powder (burn rate increases with time) reduces the peak pressure and thus the required barrel strength. This method also reduces barrel wear, which tends to be more dependent on

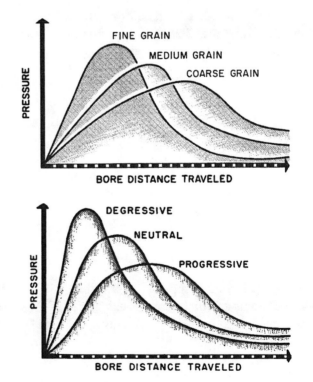

Schematics showing the effect of (A) grain size and (B) shape on the pressure-travel curve. Solid grains are regressive, singly perforated grains are neutral, and multiply perforated grains are progressive (BNW 1963, 93–94).

peak pressure than average pressure (Rinker 1999, 43). And it's likely to provide the highest exit velocity. However, if you have a short barrel, then use a degressive propellant, so you develop high projectile velocity quickly (ES310).

Fortifying the Gun

The cannon of the *Santissimo Sacramento* (sunk 1668) had a maximum barrel thickness about equal to the bore diameter (Guilmartin 1983). The reason for this considerable thickness of metal is the great pressure developed by the confined combustion gases. The greater the thickness of metal, the stronger the powder charge the gun could use and the greater the achievable range. But the greater the thickness of metal, the heavier the gun, which affected how it could be used.

So just as a late twentieth-century car dealer might offer subcompacts, compacts, intermediates and full-size cars, with a tradeoff between capacity and gas efficiency, the gunfounders offered light, medium and heavy guns in the same caliber. (The piquant sixteenth-century British terms for these categories were "bastard," "legitimate," and "double-fortified.")

Until the nineteenth century, the appropriate wall thickness was determined by trial and error. That is, if a cannon burst, either you reduced the powder charge when you received its replacement or you asked for a replacement with a thicker wall. Since a gunfounder was far more likely to be taken to task (and not paid) for guns that burst under a proof load than for guns that were excessively heavy, the tendency was probably to overdo wall thickness.

If a hollow cylinder, closed at both ends, contains a gas under pressure, the pressure will (1) push against the cylinder walls, compressing them (radial compressive stress) but also pushing them outward, which in turn creates a stretch tangential to the curve of the cylinder (circumferential) or "hoop" tensile stress; and (2) push against the ends of the cylinder, stretching the cylinder longitudinally (axial tensile stress).

The thick-walled tube hoop stress formula, if external pressure is ignored, is

$$p \times (Ri^2/r^2) \times ((Ro^2+r^2)/(Ro^2-Ri^2))$$

with Ri indicating the inner radius; Ro, the outer radius; p, internal pressure; r, the radius at which stress is calculated (Daly 2003; McEvily 2002, 53). The radial stress formula is similar, but change the "+" to "-" (Army 1964, 39).

The hoop stress reaches its maximum point at the inner wall and is greater than p. So the gun will crack first on the inside, and the crack will grow each time the gun is fired. The maximum radial stress is also at the inner wall and is equal to p. The axial stress is small, since the tube is not a closed cylinder (Army 1964).

Wall thickness, of course, is Ro-Ri, and bore diameter (caliber) is $2 \times Ri$. When increasing the barrel thickness, each additional layer decreases the hoop stress inflicted by a given internal pressure, but with diminishing returns (Table 9–2):

Table 9–2: Effect of Barrel Thickness on Hoop Stress

Barrel Thickness (rel Ri)	Ro (rel Ri)	Stress at Ri rel p	incremental relative stress reduction at Ri by increasing thickness	as %	Stress at Ro rel p
0.5	1.5	2.6			1.60
1.0	2	1.67	-0.93	35.8	0.67
1.5	2.5	1.38	-0.29	17.4	0.38
2.0	3	1.25	-0.13	9.4	0.25
2.5	3.5	1.18	-0.07	5.9	0.18

Chapter 3 mentioned pre-stressing in connection with cannon manufacture; its purpose is to "make the outer layers of metal in the barrel bear a greater proportion of the bursting load" (Payne 2006, 264). More complex stress formulae apply to pre-stressed or built-up guns.

In guns, the pressure varies according to the position of the projectile. Hence it is advantageous to match the thickness of the barrel wall to the pressures expected at that position along the bore. Excessive thickness wastes metal and increases weight unnecessarily; inadequate thickness risks loss of the gun and its crew.

It was known even to early modern gunfounders that the thickness had to be greater at the breech than at the muzzle, but they had to guess the proper proportions. For sixteenth-century Spanish bronze cannons and culverins, Albert Manucy (1985, 38) provides the tabulation seen in Table 9–3.

Table 9–3: Wall Thickness in Eighths of a Caliber at Stated Part of Gun

Piece	Vent	Trunnion	Chase
Light culverin	7	5	3
Medium culverin	8	5.5	3.5
Heavy culverin	9	6.5	4
Light cannon	6	4.5	2.5
Medium cannon	7	5	3.5
Heavy cannon	8	5.5	3.5

In table 9–4, I show selected dimensions for British "brass" (bronze) field pieces and iron ship and garrison pieces from 1766.

While the measurement points are different from those previously quoted, and the rings are raised slightly above the main surface of the gun barrel, this list does show how the wall thickness varied from breech to muzzle, as well as how it was greater for cast iron than for bronze with guns of the same caliber.

By the mid-nineteenth century, distance-pressure curves were available to designers.

For example, in 1861, the distance-pressure curve for a 42-pounder with the powder of that time might feature a maximum pressure of 45,000 psi, dropping to one-tenth that value by the time the shot exited the muzzle (Bruce 1989, 138).

These curves, in turn, permitted the design of guns to have metal exactly where it was needed. Rodman (1861, 217) set forth a complex formula for the bursting tendency (Z), and he argued that if an exterior shape is adopted for which Z is a constant throughout the length of the gun, "the gun would be equally strong in all of its parts." The shape of the Z function was powder dependent.

Table 9–4: Shape of Selected British Bronze
and Iron Guns (1766) and Weight of Iron Guns (1764)

	Brass 24	Iron 24	Brass 12	Iron 12	Brass 6	Iron 6
length (ft)*	5.5	9.5	5.0	9	4.5	6.5
base ring diameter (inches)*	12.2	20.8	10.2	17.9	9.4	15.3
muzzle ring diameter (inches)*	10.3	12.7	7.6	9.8	7.3	8.4
caliber (bore diameter) (inches)**	5.82		4.62		3.67	
weight of metal, pounds (cwt)***		5,488 (49)		3,640 (32.5)		2,016 (18)
weight/caliber cubed		27.84		36.91		40.78
weight/(length ft * caliber inches squared)		17.05		18.95		23.03

* McConnell 1988, Appendixes J and K.

** calculated by Collins based on shot weight and the Borgard specification of windage. It is consistent with the calibers given in McConnell's Appendix N, for the British 1764 establishment.

*** McConnell 1988, Appendix N.

In the 1850s, John Dahlgren designed a series of muzzleloading smoothbore guns with a soda bottle shape (Tucker 2013). In his 1861 patent, he claimed a cast iron gun in which "the quantities of metal disposed in the different parts of the gun are proportionate, or nearly so, to the relative degrees of strain exerted by the force of the exploded charge at those parts respectively." That is, of course, the same idea proposed by Rodman in the same year. In the patent, Dahlgren gave dimensions for a shell gun firing a spherical shell whose empty weight was seven times the weight of the powder charge.

Table 9–5: Dahlgren Shell Gun Proportions

section	length of section (in calibers)	diameter at forward end of section (in calibers)
breech (the metal behind the start of the bore)	1.511	3.022
fort (cylinder)	2.389	3.022
junction (truncated cone)	2.778	2.036
chase (nearly cylindrical)	6.883	1.4 (the muzzle)
bore	12	1 (by definition)
gun (end of breech to face of muzzle)	13.511	

The shape of the breech end could be hemispherical (strongest), hemi-spheroidal (by which I think Dahlgren meant the shape of a sphere cut off by a plane that doesn't pass through its center), or ellipsoidal (weakest). The ideal shape of the "fort" would have been curvilinear longitudinally, but it was made straight for ease of sighting in point-blank fire. Dahlgren also acknowledged that there could be a slight swell to the muzzle (beyond that indicated in Table 9–5) to protect it against fracture (if, say, the shell was banged against the edge).

A 9-inch Dahlgren smoothbore gun on a slide-pivot mount, carried by an unidentified gun-boat during the American Civil War. Photographed by Matthew Brady. Note the soda bottle shape, the breechings running from the bulwark to the cascabel, the anti-boarding netting, and the ramrod lying in the right foreground. The man standing behind the cascabel is hold-ing the lever arm of the elevating screw. It appears to have a twelve-man crew, and an officer is watching. Courtesy of the U.S. Naval History and Heritage Command, Catalog No. NH 61933.

Powder Chambers

Guns sometimes were designed with separate powder chambers; these were narrower than the bore (to reduce stress) but communicated with it. They could be cylindrical, spherical or conical in shape. Spherical chambers offered the greatest muzzle velocity but were difficult to construct, load and clean, and they strained the gun most. Conical offered the worst muzzle velocity, so cylindrical became the happy compromise (Jeffers 1850, 98).

The maximum quantity of powder that could be used in the gun was limited by the gun's bursting strength and the size of its powder chamber. One pound of 1820s powder occupied 30 cubic inches (Beauchant 1828, 104).

Overheating and Heat Dissipation

We've been focusing on pressure, but the deflagration also results in an increase in temperature. The temperature can reach 5,550°F, and "most barrel steel" melts at

2,500°F (Rinker 1999, 29). Fortunately, the projectile is in the barrel only for something like one ten-thousandth of a second. Still, gun barrels can definitely overheat. And such overheating can reduce the barrel's strength. It may be necessary to delay firing again until the barrel cools sufficiently, so overheating of cannons limited the rate of fire.

Thus, it is advantageous for gun barrels to have a high thermal conductivity so heat is dissipated quickly. That's another advantage of bronze (thermal conductivity: 189 watts/meter-degree Kelvin, at 20°C) over cast iron (48) (Neutrium 2013).

If a gun were fired too rapidly, the heat could cause the touchhole to fuse. Gunners would use powder to blow the touchhole open from the inside (Hoskins 2003, 27).

Windage

Bore windage had several internal ballistics effects. First, gas could escape around the ball, reducing the effective pressure driving the projectile. This result reduced muzzle velocity and wasted energy, but it also eased the stresses on the gun barrel. Second, as the ball progressed down-bore, it would glance off the walls of the bore. Each bounce drained some of the kinetic energy of the ball, further reducing muzzle velocity. All the bouncing around was also bad for the gun barrels (Douglas 1829, 81).

Charles Hutton (1812) assumed that the direct energy loss from escaped gas was proportional to the ratio of the annular area to the bore's cross-sectional area. Since windage is small, this ratio is roughly inversely proportional to the bore diameter. The indirect loss is difficult to calculate, as it depends on both the number of collisions with the wall and the elasticity of those collisions.

Howard Douglas (1829, 70) estimated that one-quarter to one-half of the force of the powder was lost in consequence of the early nineteenth-century standard windage. He urged that windage should be a fixed allowance, rather than one proportional to the gun's caliber. Only the degree of expansion due to heat, he reasoned, would be dependent on caliber (amounting to $\frac{1}{70}$th caliber at white heat); rusting of the shot and fouling of the bore wouldn't be. Douglas suggested reducing windage to 0.1–0.15 inches (74ff).

Edward Simpson (1862, 185) alludes to an experiment in which "four pounds of powder was found to give to a ball, without windage, nearly as great a velocity as is given by six pounds to a ball having the windage of .14 inch." In 1840, the U.S. Navy switched from a proportional windage of one-twentieth caliber to a fixed windage of 0.1–0.2 inches for all calibers (Simpson 1862, 225).

Rifled guns have virtually no windage. The maximum pressure usually obtained in the late nineteenth century was fifteen tons per square inch in rifled guns and three in smoothbores—this shows how much difference windage makes (Barnett 1919, 196)!

High-Low Pressure Guns

These guns represented an ambitious attempt to drastically alter the pressure-time and pressure-travel curves. They have a divided propellant chamber, with two compartments separated by a plate with holes. The powder is ignited in the first compartment, generating a high pressure. Because of the constricted communication with the second compartment, the pressure there is lower, resulting in a lower muzzle velocity but also a lower recoil. If you are wondering why one would not just use a conventional gun with a low powder charge, it's because the high pressure results in a better "burn" curve, and only the first chamber needs a thick wall. The concept was first implemented in the *Panzerabwehrwerfer* 600 (1945) and copied in the British Limbo depth-charge launcher (1955) and later the American M79 grenade launcher.

The U.S. Navy designed the Mark 19 grenade launcher for use as a deck gun on riverine patrol boats in Vietnam. It makes use of the high/low principle inside the cartridge, with a high chamber pressure of 35,000 psi and a low chamber pressure of 12,000 psi. The army placed it on a tripod mount (U.S. Army 1990), and it may also be mounted on vehicles.

Experimental Determination of Muzzle Velocity

The critical parameters for the calculation of the projectile's expected trajectory after it leaves the muzzle are the mass and geometry of the projectile, the angle of elevation, and the muzzle velocity. The mass and shape of the projectile are known when the gun is designed, and the elevation of the gun is under the control of the artillerist, within the limits set by the gun mount. The muzzle velocity that the gun will have is the great unknown.

The first measurements of muzzle velocity were made by Benjamin Robins in *New Principles of Gunnery* (1742), using the ballistic pendulum he invented. Immediately after leaving the muzzle, the projectile struck the "bob" of the pendulum and transferred its momentum to it, causing it to swing. The pendulum was constructed such that the bob (a "broad iron plate") was much more massive than the bullet, and thus the velocity it acquired was small. Robins measured the height of the pendulum swing and from that calculated the bullet's velocity (EB 1911, "Chronograph"; Collins, "Benjamin Robins on Ballistics").

Taking a correction he made in 1743 into account, Robins' measurements indicated that the muzzle velocity of a gun firing a 0.75-inch, one-twelfth-pound lead ball from a 45-inch barrel was 1,669 fps (Robins 1742, Proposition VIII, 87–88; cp. Collins, "Benjamin Robins on Ballistics").

Robins' Proposition IX describes his further experiments using three different lengths of barrels and several different charge sizes (1742, 93ff).

Later, Hutton built a much larger pendulum suitable for measuring the muzzle velocity of small cannons.

Dahlgren (1856, 178) provides the muzzle velocities listed in Table 9–6, which I assume were determined with the ballistic pendulum.

Table 9–6 Muzzle Velocities (mid-nineteenth century)

Shot Wt (lbs)	Charge (lbs)	Muzzle velocity (fps)	Gun
18	6	1,720	Long
24	8	1,720	Long
32	4.5	1,250	32 cwt
32	9	1,700	Long
42	10.5	1,620	
64	16	1,620	
Shell			
10-inch	10	1,160	86 cwt

Likewise, we are told by James Benton that "the mean of 11 fires with the 6-pdr gun pendulum … was 1436.5 feet [per second]" (1862, 387).

For earlier cannons, we must depend on modern test firings of replica cannons with replica powder. While enough sixteenth- and seventeenth-century cannons have survived to create reasonably accurate replicas, it is unlikely that the powder used in the replica cannons has the same characteristics, even when an attempt was made to be faithful to the original.

That said, one such test showed that the 3.5-inch bore cannon on the Alderney wreck (lost in 1592) had a muzzle velocity of 300 mps (984 fps) (BBC 2009, 55:00–56:00). The October 24, 2003, episode "Who Sank the Armada" in the Discovery Channel series *Battlefield Detectives* says that a replica "culverin extraordinary" achieved a muzzle velocity of 408 mps (1,339 fps); the speed of sound is about

Cannon Pendulum.

Partial cutaway view of cannon pendulum used by Alfred Mordecai (1845, Plate II). He experimented with a 32-pounder, similar to those used as sea-coast artillery, except it had shoulders for the suspension straps cast on it (42), as well as a 24-pounder. The weight of the 32-pounder barrel was 7,689 pounds, but the suspension frame added 2,811 pounds (21).

1,100 fps. A replica of the demi-cannon of the *Vasa* (1628), firing Swedish 24-pound (9.96 kg) shot, was test-fired with modern gunpowder, and charges of 2.2–3.3 kg produced muzzle velocities of 300–399 mps, respectively (Hocker 2017, 195). Stephen Bull (2008, 25) suggests that all of the English Civil War artillery had muzzle velocities in the 1,000–1,500 fps range, depending on the relative powder charge used.

Optimal Bore Length

For premodern guns, bore length was probably 92–94 percent of the barrel length (Douglas 1829, 293). In general, the longer the effective bore (from projectile starting position to muzzle), the greater the muzzle velocity for a given powder charge; the muzzle velocity in turn determines range and penetrating power. But that calculation assumes that the projectile is accelerating the entire time, which in turn requires that the charge is still burning and providing a sufficient expansive force to overcome any resistance. The sixteenth-century metallurgist Vannoccio Biringuccio indeed proposed that the charge and bore length be matched so that "all of the powder would have ignited just as the ball exited the gun" (Hoskins 2003, 20).

With diameter held constant, and bore length increased, muzzle velocity—and therefore range—will increase (provided the powder charge is adequate). Douglas (1829, 294) reports a point-blank range of 221 yards for a "24–6.5" and 248 for a "24–9.5," both with a 6-pound powder charge. The nineteenth-century British 24–6.5 given a 6-pound charge achieved 1,131 fps (Beauchant 1828, 46), whereas the 24–9.5 provided 1,306 fps (with 8-pound charge) or even 1,600 fps (12 pounds) (45).

But there are definitely diminishing returns. Experiments have been conducted in which a barrel is successively cut down and the new muzzle velocity determined. In 1862, Benton (130) reported that for a small change in length of a 12-pounder, the velocity was in fact proportional to the fourth root of the length. Douglas (1892, 101) says that it's proportional to between the square and cube root of the length of the bore. Rodger opines that there was no advantage to making a sixteenth-century gun longer than ten feet (1997, 215), and nineteenth-century British sea ordnance didn't exceed nine feet (Douglas 1829, 293).

Is there a limit beyond which increasing length has no effect or even reduces muzzle velocity? If the force propelling the projectile merely diminished as it traveled down-bore, then there would be no bore length at which muzzle velocity was maximized, merely diminishing returns from lengthening it. But there is such a length, because the projectile's movement faces opposition even as the propulsive forces decline.

Benton (1862, 128) suggested three opposing forces: (1) friction, (2) inelastic collision, and (3) the pressure of the air in front of the projectile. He urged that if the length is increased too much, keeping the charge constant, the muzzle velocity will decrease.

Strictly speaking, friction comes into play only for rifled barrels, in which the projectile engages the rifling. The frictional force is presumably constant throughout the length of the barrel, whereas the propulsive force declines as the projectile moves down-barrel. Since the length of the region of contact is kept small, the frictional force at any given moment should be proportional to the circumference of the bore and thus to the diameter.

Inelastic collision, by contrast, applies to smoothbores rather than rifled guns. The projectile can "ballot" (ping-pong) within the barrel, losing a little energy with each collision. It's difficult to quantify. Even if one presumes that the number of collisions would be proportional to the length divided by the windage (Denny 2011, 178), the energy loss per collision is highly debatable.

Like friction, outside atmospheric force is a constant resistive force, but it's proportional to the area and thus to the square of the diameter of the bore.

The barrel length may be increased for reasons other than achieving a higher muzzle velocity. With a greater length, one may use a slower-burning powder to yield the same muzzle velocity but with a reduced maximum pressure—permitting reduction of barrel thickness and weight, in addition to increasing barrel life (Sladen 1879, 34).

Longer guns also have the advantage of being heavier (if the barrel diameter and thickness are held constant) and therefore don't recoil as far if the charge is increased.

Optimal Powder Charge

The expectation was that up to a point, increasing the powder charge (relative to the shot weight) would increase muzzle velocity. Obviously, once the projectile left the muzzle, any unconsumed powder would fail to provide any further boost to its speed.

There was great controversy, however, as to whether a point could be reached at which any further increase in charge would actually reduce the muzzle velocity. Robins was insistent that this could not possibly be the case. However, Benton (1862, 130) reported on French experiments showing a progressive decrease in muzzle velocity, from 1,320 to 191 fps, for a 36-pounder firing charges ranging from 36 to 77 pounds.

Denny (2011, 49–50) argues that this decrease occurred because there was unburned powder when the projectile left the muzzle: "The unburned powder would have been expelled from the cannon…. So the powder that did burn caused both the cannonball and the unburned powder to accelerate. Accelerating unburned powder is a waste of energy of energy…. Also, a large charge would take up more space … thus decreasing the effective length of the barrel, from cannonball [rest position] to mouth."

Even if there weren't diminishing returns regarding muzzle velocity, the amount of powder used would be constrained by the size of the powder chamber, fear of bursting the gun, and the recoil.

It has also been reported that the maximum velocity charge increases with the length of the gun (Simpson 1862, 177). This result makes sense, as, for the same rate of acceleration, it gives more time for useful consumption of powder.

Experimental Determination of In-Bore Velocities

In 1862, Sir Andrew Noble invented a "chronoscope" for measuring the successive velocities of a projectile as it traveled down-bore (CSGB 1916). One version is described here: Discs, the edges of which are covered with lamp black, are mounted on a shaft rotating at a high, uniform speed. The gun barrel is "pierced to receive cutting plugs" in selected locations. Each plug is associated with an induction (spark) coil, as well as with one of the discs. The coil has primary and secondary windings. When the projectile encounters a plug, the latter pivots to be flush with the bore, cutting the current in the primary winding. That in turn causes a spark to be emitted across the gap separating the discharge terminals of the secondary winding, burning off the lamp black at a spot on the corresponding disc. Because the discs are rotating as the projectile moves down-bore, the "line of spots forms a spiral round the cylinder represented by the disks." Since the rotation rate of the shaft is known, the positions of the spots can be converted to times of arrival, and differences converted to velocities (*Encyclopedia Brittanica* 9, "Gunnery," 11:265–66). The changes in velocity reflect the accelerations, which in turn correspond to the pressures, so those may be determined indirectly.

Prediction of Muzzle Velocity and Gun Pressures

The Robins Model

Robins' mathematical model of internal ballistics (1742, Chapter II, Proposition VII) was the only physics-based model for over a century. My analysis follows that of A.R. Collins ("Benjamin Robins on Ballistics"; "Smooth Bore Cannon Ballistics").

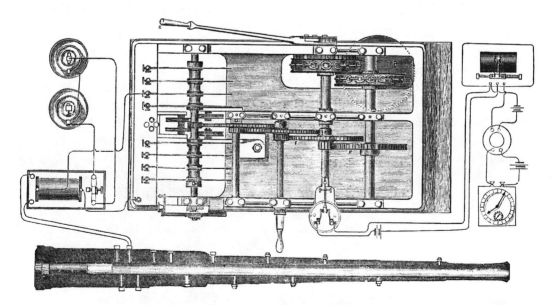

"Chronoscope Plan View" (Noble 1906, Figure VII, facing p. 430). Only a single induction coil and its corresponding sampling point on the gun are shown. A lead goes from the coil to one of the discs (only eight depicted).

Robins assumed that the powder was completely consumed before the projectile began to move and that this process generated a gas occupying the same volume as that occupied by the gunpowder before its ignition.

The force on the projectile would be the gas pressure times the cross-sectional area of the projectile. However, Robins actually used the cross-sectional area of the bore. In contemporary muzzleloaders, these weren't the same; the diameter of the bore (GE in his diagram) was about 5 percent larger than the diameter of the projectile. (Use of the bore area would be appropriate if a sabot was placed behind the projectile.)

As the projectile moved down the bore in response to this force, the volume available to the gas would increase. According to Boyle's Law (1662), which was based on observations of the effect of varying air volume at room temperature and is a corollary of the ideal gas law (stated 1834), the pressure of a gas is inversely linearly proportional to the volume it occupies. And so the force on the projectile is inversely proportional to its position ("x" from starting point) within the bore.

Indeed, the force at projectile position x, $F(x)$, is $P_0 \times A_{bore} \times (c/x)$, where P_0 is the gas pressure immediately after combustion and before projectile movement ($x = 0$), A_{bore} is the cross-sectional area of the bore (with the caveat mentioned above), and c is the initial position of the base of the projectile (and thus the length of the powder within the bore).

The work done by a force is the integral of the force over the distance (which simplifies to force times distance when the force is constant). Robins assumed that all of the work done by the expanding gas is converted into the kinetic energy of the projectile (i.e., there is no gas escape, friction, air resistance, etc.). Setting the integral equal to the kinetic energy ($0.5 \times m \times v^2$) and solving for v at $x = L$ (the muzzle), Robins obtained the following formula:

$$v = \text{square root} ((2 \times P_0 \times A_{bore} \times c\,/m) \times \ln(L/c))$$

(This formula also yielded a predicted velocity at any point within the bore, if the appropriate value of x is used instead of L.)

To calculate the muzzle velocity, Robins would need to know the pressure (P_0). Robins assumed this number to be 1,000 atmospheres (1742, 76). Robins (138) predicted that a cannon firing 24-pound shot with a two-thirds charge (i.e., two-thirds of the weight of the shot) would impart a muzzle velocity of 1,650 fps and, with a one-half charge, 1,490 fps.

Hutton (1812, Tract 37) criticized some aspects of Robins' analysis. He thought the maximum pressure was 1,500 atmospheres, not Robins' 1,000. He also replaced "m" in the denominator with "m + 0.5p," where p is the mass of the powder. Hutton's reasoning was that as the gas expanded down-bore, its center of mass moved forward at half the velocity of the projectile, and so some of the energy of the gas must have been invested in moving the center of mass of the gas.

Charles Owen and Thomas Danes (1861, 99) proposed a modified formula in which the constant factor of 2 was replaced with a variable factor dependent on windage (expressed as a diameter difference): 6.6 for 0 windage; 5 for 0.09 inches; 4.4 for 0.125; 3.6 for 0.175; 3.4 for 0.2 and 3.2 for 0.233. Thomas Simmons (1837, 50) provides a detailed relationship between muzzle velocity and windage.

Collins, taking the changes in the quality of gunpowder and the degree of windage into account, suggests formulae for eighteenth- and nineteenth-century smoothbores based on the Robins model:

$$v = K \times \text{square root} ((p/(m+\tfrac{1}{3}p)) \times \ln (L/c))$$

with K equaling 1,928 for the eighteenth century and 1,991 for the nineteenth (Collins, "Smooth Bore Cannon Ballistics"); note the use of one-third rather than Hutton's one-half, as well as p (mass of powder).

Benton (1862, 386) presented a similar formula, but ln (L/c) was replaced with the logarithm of the ratio of the weight of powder that would fill the bore to that actually used, and he reduced the speed by a second term that was proportional to ratio of the windage to the radius of the bore. For Dupont's powder, the constant for the first term was found to be 3,500, and the constant of proportionality for the windage reduction was 3,200. So, for a ⅟₂₀th windage, the muzzle speed would be reduced by 160 fps. For a 6.25-pound shot, 1.25-pound charge, 57.5-inch by 1.83-inch bore, .09-inch windage, Benton predicted a muzzle velocity of 1,444 fps (387).

Implications of the Robins Model

Robins' formula has some interesting implications. One is that increasing the total length of the bore (L) increases muzzle velocity, albeit with diminishing returns (as the muzzle velocity is proportional to the logarithm of the length).

The ratio of the length of the bore (L) to the length of the charge (c) within the bore that yields the maximum muzzle velocity is equal to the base (e) of the natural logarithm, which equals 2.71728. This result was first pointed out by Hutton (1812a, 2:395), who noted that in practice, the value of L/c for maximizing the muzzle velocity is a bit larger than e. Hutton suggested that this was because combustion was not instantaneously complete, as assumed by Robins.

Robins' model also predicts that the muzzle velocity is inversely proportional to the diameter of the ball. (The cross-sectional area of the bore is proportional to the square of the diameter of the bore. The diameter of the bore is linearly proportional to the diameter of the ball D_b. The mass [m] of the ball is proportional to the cube of the diameter of the ball. So, within the square root, we have a diameter divided by a cubed diameter.)

An important concern for gunners was matching the powder charge to the weight of the shot. In the Robins formula, the product $A_{bore} \times c$ (i.e., the cross-sectional area times the length, thus the cylindrical volume occupied by the powder charge) must equal the mass of the powder charge divided by the density of the charge. Therefore, $A_{bore} \times c / m$ equals the ratio of the powder mass to the projectile mass, divided by the density of the charge. So since the velocity is proportional to the square root of $A_{bore} \times c / m$, it seemingly follows that it is proportional to the square root of the ratio of the powder mass to the projectile mass. Early nineteenth-century artillerists agreed that this was the case (Beauchant 1828, 45; Douglas 1829, 53, 57; cp. Sladen 1879).

Hutton (1812a, 2:142) proposed this simple formula for muzzle velocity:

$$MV \text{ (feet/sec)} = 1{,}600 \times \text{sqrt} (2 \times \text{powder weight} / \text{shot weight})$$

The formula is duplicated, without acknowledgment, by Theophilus Beauchant (1828, 45, 133). (The "1600" is powder-specific.)

The Robins model also had implications for projectile design. The sectional density of a projectile is defined as its mass divided by its cross-sectional area. If we ignore windage, it is m/A_{bore}. So the muzzle velocity is inversely proportional to the square root of the sectional density.

There are two ways of changing sectional density. First, we can increase the length of the projectile while keeping the cross-sectional area constant. For example, we can replace a spherical projectile with an oblong one. This change increases the mass and thus the sectional density. If we want to maintain muzzle velocity, we will have to increase the powder charge accordingly.

Second, we can make the projectile out of a material with a higher or lower density (mass/volume). For a given caliber and shape, stone projectiles have a lower sectional density (mass/frontal area) than cast iron, which means that for a given barrel length, they require less force to accelerate them to a given muzzle velocity. Less force means less pressure, which means a smaller charge. Stone projectiles can therefore be fired from lighter cannons than metal ones of the same weight.

The Sarrau Semi-Empirical Model

In the late nineteenth century, the "gold standard" for predicting muzzle velocity was Émile Sarrau's monomial (for quick powders) or binomial (for slow powders) approximation.

Like Robins, Sarrau sought to determine the changes in pressure and volume within the bore based on thermodynamic principles. Also like Robins, Sarrau assumed that all of the chemical energy of the burned powder was converted into projectile kinetic energy.

An implicit assumption of the Robins model was that the product of pressure and volume was a constant. Since, in the ideal gas law, this product is proportional to the temperature, it implies that the temperature remains constant as the gas expands.

While Sarrau, like Robins, assumed that the combustion gases behaved as an ideal gas, he also assumed that those gases would expand adiabatically (neither taking heat from the unburned powder nor releasing it to the barrel wall). (In adiabatic expansion, the temperature of the gas drops, and if the gas is ideal, it is PV^{γ}, where γ is the ratio between the heat capacities [specific heats] of the gas at constant pressure and constant volume, that is constant.)

Had Sarrau kept Robins' assumption of instantaneous total combustion, he would have found that the muzzle velocity is then roughly proportional to the bore length raised to the power $0.5 \times (1-\gamma)$ (Carlucci and Jacobsen 2018, equation 2.23). If γ is 1.4, then this result evaluates to -0.2—that is, because of the sharp decline in pressure as the gas expands, the muzzle velocity *decreases* with the fifth root of the bore length. If, however, Sarrau assumed that there was a constant burn rate, with burn-out occurring just as the projectile exited the muzzle, the muzzle velocity would *increase* as the fifth root of the bore length (Denny 2011, 184).

Sarrau instead assumed that the burn rate would be proportional to the exposed area of the remaining powder and to the square root of the gas pressure. Both would change in the course of the combustion. This assumption resulted in very complex differential equations, which could not be solved analytically, only by numerical integration.

Sarrau made various simplifications and rearrangements, and he ended up with a binomial equation for the muzzle velocity of the form AαY × (1-BβZ), where A and B were general constants (to be determined experimentally, ideally once and for all) and α and β were constants related to characteristics of the powder (also to be determined experimentally, but unaffected by the choice of gun). Y and Z depended on the specific heat ratio, and Sarrau assumed that it had the value 1.375. If so, Y equaled the three-eighths' power of the product of the projectile mass and the projectile's travel distance from the ignition position to the muzzle, times the fourth root of the ratio of the density of loading of the powder to the product of the weight of the projectile times the caliber. And Z equaled the ratio of the square root of the product of the projectile mass and the travel distance to the caliber (Sarrau 1884, 167, formula [6]).

Rather than determine A, B, α and β separately, one may set A' = A × α and B' = B × β. And then, using the same powder under different firing conditions (so Y and Z are very different), one may compute A' and B'. Subsequently, Sarrau's formula may be used for that powder under any firing condition. And the process may be repeated for each powder of interest.

When B'Z was 0.273 or larger (implying a "quick powder"), Sarrau recommended use of an alternative, monomial formula that I will not delve into here.

The Le Duc Model

Unfortunately, the Sarrau formulae, developed for black and brown powder, did not give accurate predictions in the case of smokeless powder. Patterson (1911) tweaked Sarrau's velocity formula but kept its general form. Others, such as Captain A. Le Duc, made more drastic changes.

The 1937 USN ordnance manual commented that the Le Duc formulae (Alger 1911), as modified by G.W. Patterson (1912), had been adopted "as the standard for interior ballistic problems" and were "still in daily use at the Naval Proving Ground" (NAVORD 1937, s319). The manual admitted that an internal ballistics model ideally would be "sufficiently flexible to account accurately for the effects due to changes in any or all of the significant factors (e.g., properties of the powder, gun reaction, bore resistance, etc.) and the Le Due [Duc] system cannot quite do this."

The following discussion of Le Duc is based on Thomas Hayes (1938, 73–80). Le Duc hypothesized that the relationship between the velocity (v) of the projectile and its travel within the bore (u) was a hyperbolic curve of the form v = au / (b + u). (Note that here u is defined as zero at the rest position of the projectile.)

Implicitly, the pressure curve follows the acceleration curve of the projectile and is thus proportional to $a^2bu / (b + u)^3$. Given Le Duc's formula, the acceleration (and therefore the pressure) would be a maximum at when $u = b / 2$, so parameter b is "twice the travel of the projectile to the point of maximum pressure." The parameter "a" corresponds to the muzzle velocity for a bore of infinite length.

Based on both thermodynamic analysis and test firings, a formula for parameter a was proposed, relating it to the weight of the charge, the weight of the projectile, and the density of loading of the charge (charge weight relative to the weight of water required to fill the powder chamber). Likewise, a formula for parameter b was determined, based on the specific gravity of the powder, the volume of the powder chamber, the density of loading, the weight of the projectile, and a powder constant. The latter was "dependent upon the composition, form, and dimensions of the grains, and varies inversely with the burning rate" (Hayes 1938, 73).

If the powder constant was not known, a test firing was conducted and the muzzle velocity measured. The powder constant and the specific gravity of the powder applied to the powder alone, so once the powder constant was determined for one gun, it could be applied in calculations for any other gun using the same powder.

According to G.L. Schuyler (1915), "The commonest use of such formulae is to see how a new powder being proved suits the gun," by determining "how the factor of safety varies along the bore."

Anthony San Miguel (1971, 5) applied the Le Duc model to a U.S. Navy 5-inch, 54-caliber gun and found its predictions to be "within 10% of those made using a more complex theory." (Le Duc is also cited by U.S. Navy, Bureau of Naval Weapons 1963, 95; Muldoon 1977, 4. For comparisons with other models, see Rao and Sharma 1982.)

Modern Internal Ballistics Models

Modern internal ballistics models make more realistic assumptions (burning laws based on powder composition and geometry; non-ideal combustion gas behavior; non-uniform gas density; loss of energy to friction and convection, etc.), and they are solved by numerical integration, facilitated by high-speed computers. Space does not allow us to delve into details, but citations are provided (Miner 2013; Carlucci and Jacobsen 2018).

CHAPTER 10

Exterior Ballistics
and Projectile Design

The range achieved by a projectile is primarily determined by its muzzle velocity, the elevation angle at which it is fired, and the action on it of two forces: gravity and aerodynamic drag. The gravity acts vertically and the drag acts opposite the direction of motion of projectile (that direction varies along the trajectory). (Some other forces that act on a projectile in flight are considered in later chapters.)

The Early History of Exterior Ballistics

In the sixteenth century, the leading work on ballistics was Niccolò Tartaglia's *Nova Scientia* (1537). The "physics" underlying Tartaglia's propositions was Aristotelian: a projectile was thought to follow first a straight line in which "impetus" was dominant, and then a transitional curve, before finally falling straight down ("natural motion")—"Wile E. Coyote" physics. Nonetheless, Tartaglia predicted that maximum range would be obtained if the projectile were fired at an elevation angle of 45 degrees—true if the trajectory is in a vacuum.

Galileo Galilei also studied ballistics, and he published his *Discourses and Mathematical Demonstrations Relating to Two New Sciences* in 1638. He was the first to point out that gravity wouldn't affect the horizontal motion of the projectile, that a body without an initial upward motion would fall a distance proportional to the square of the time elapsed, and that the combination of these propositions indicated that the path of a projectile would be a parabola. This is all true—in a vacuum.

Galileo's disciple Evangelista Torricelli published additional ballistics theorems in *Opera Geometrica* (1644). When Giovanni Renieri complained that his experiments did not agree with Torricelli's formulae for the relationship of the point-blank range to the maximum range, Torricelli reminded him that the text was intended for philosophers, not gunners.

In 1668–1669, Christiaan Huygens demonstrated that water resistance was proportional to the square of the speed of the object moving through it, and he hypothesized that the same was true of air resistance. Isaac Newton later advanced a similar proposition in his *Principia*.

The air resistance (drag force) is

$$0.5 \times \rho \times C_D \times A \times V^2$$

with ρ indicating air density (which changes with altitude); C_D, dimensionless drag coefficient; A, reference area for which C_D is determined (typically the frontal area for a projectile); and V, air speed. The drag coefficient depends on projectile shape. In addition, to the extent that the air resistance on the projectile is non–Newtonian (that is, it is not strictly proportional to the square of the air speed), it will have some dependence on speed.

At typical muzzle velocities, the drag force is more than twenty times as strong as the gravitational force.

Now, a force equals the mass of the object times its acceleration (negative for drag). It is evident that the deceleration due to air resistance will be proportional to A divided by the mass. If A is cross-sectional area, that means the deceleration is inversely proportional to the sectional density (mass divided by frontal area).

All else being equal, the deceleration will be lowest for the projectile made of the densest material. Stone will slow down faster than cast iron, and cast iron faster than lead. Therefore, stone will have the least range and lead the most.

For a spherical projectile, mass is proportional to diameter cubed and frontal area to diameter squared, so deceleration is inversely proportional to the diameter. Thus, while a larger-caliber shot will start with a lower muzzle velocity than a smaller one (given the same charge), it will eventually overtake the latter and achieve a greater range (Beauchant 1828, 47).

Point-Blank Range

Standard practice for naval warfare, up through the early nineteenth century, was to fire broadsides at point-blank range (or less).

Point-blank range (PBR) is the farthest that the gun can be assumed to "shoot straight"—that is, the range at which the average gunner will use zero elevation. Strictly speaking, it is the range at which the "drop off" equals the height of the muzzle above the water surface, so the projectile will hit the target at the waterline. (Yes, that means that PBR should vary depending on which deck the gun is mounted on!) Nineteenth-century range data rarely give trunnion height, but, where mentioned, it ranged from 5 feet, 4 inches (Douglas 1860, Appendix B. VI, XXII) to 9 feet (Douglas 1829, Table XIII) above the water.

Theophilus Beauchant estimated that the 18-, 24- and 32-pounders, all 9.5 feet long, fired from the main deck of a frigate, had a point-blank range of 400 yards with a one-third charge, 300 with a one-quarter, and 250 with one-sixth (1828, 27). Benerson Little, writing about the golden age of piracy (1630–1730), estimates PBRs of 490 yards for a 3-pounder, 500 for a 6-pounder, 550–650 for an 8- or 9-pounder, 600 for a 12-pounder, 550 for an 18-pounder, and 535 for a 24-pounder (2005, 251–52).

The point-blank range given is usually to "first graze," but because of the shallowness of the trajectory, the extreme range (as a result of ricochet) may be much greater. For example, Beauchant states that a 24–6.5 with a 6-pound charge (one-quarter shot weight), firing point blank, has first graze at 248 yards but an extreme range of 1,990 yards (1828, 26).

Projectile Speed Measurement

The real breakthrough in exterior ballistics was the 1742 invention of the ballistic pendulum (see chapter 9) by Benjamin Robins, who used it to measure the speed of projectiles at the muzzle and at various ranges (the latter permitting the effect of air resistance to be quantified [Douglas 1829, 129]).

Robins not only confirmed that the normal drag was proportional to the square of the speed but also detected the sharp increase in resistance at, he reported, 1,100–1,200 fps, which later became known as the "sound barrier," or "Mach One."

The main concerns with ballistic pendulum measurements are projectile deformation and deflection, friction, gravity and calibration. With modern methods, the accuracy of the ballistic pendulum for testing of small arms is a respectable 2 percent (Rinker 1999, 148–49).

The catch is that cannonballs are heavier than bullets, and the ballistic pendulum must be scaled up to match. Charles Hutton used an 1,800-pound pendulum for studies on 6-pound balls, and in 1839–1840, to measure the speed of 50-pound projectiles, French ballisticians used a six-ton receiver (Bashforth 1873, 25).

The Reverend Francis Bashforth achieved even greater accuracy by timing when the projectile passed through wire screens separated by a known distance; the penetrations interrupted the electric current to a chronograph (Cantwell 2002, 46; EB 1911, "Chronograph").

The modern approach to measuring projectile speed is to use Doppler radar, which has the advantage that the position, speed and acceleration of the projectile may be visualized along the entire trajectory.

Range Tables

The range in a vacuum (with no change in air density or gravity, gun and target on same level, and ignoring the curvature of the Earth) is easily calculated:

$$R_{vac} = V^2 \sin (2\theta) / g$$

with V indicating muzzle velocity; g, gravitational acceleration, and θ, elevation angle.

In a vacuum, the maximum range would be at an angle of 45 degrees, and for any lesser range, there would be two equally acceptable elevation angles for achieving it.

Because of air resistance, the maximum range is lower than R_{vac} and is achieved at an elevation angle that's less than 45 degrees and may be as low as 30 degrees (Rinker 1999, 332; Douglas 1829, 43, 136). The lower the elevation angle (thus, the flatter and shorter the trajectory), the less the effect of air resistance. High-angle trajectories nonetheless had their uses, mostly in attacks on fortifications where one needed to put a shell over a wall to hit a higher-value target beyond.

A range table for a gun lists, for each projectile and charge (or muzzle velocity) the gun typically uses, a series of ranges, as well as the angle of departure or elevation needed to achieve each range, given standard conditions. Modern range tables may also provide the maximum ordinate (height), time of flight, drift, angle of fall, striking velocity, armor penetration, danger space for a target of standard height, and correction factors to use for non-standard projectile weight, air density, and muzzle velocity and for wind, gun and target motion (U.S. Navy, Bureau of Ordnance 1941).

Simple range tables are available from sixteenth- and seventeenth-century artillerist manuals, but they must be taken with great caution. It's quite doubtful that they were based on test firings; the more likely explanation is that they stemmed from imperfect recollection (and wishful thinking). Regarding the maximum ranges given by Luis Collado (1592) and all examined ranges given by Diego Prado y Tovar (1603), ballistics experts at Aberdeen Proving Ground determined that muzzle velocities of around 6,000 fps would have been required (Guilmartin 2003, 297).

The first reliable range tables were compiled based on experimental firings. But these went only so far. Bear in mind that because of all the factors that affect trajectories, it's not enough to fire one shot at each elevation of interest. You must fire multiple shots, and average the results, to get reliable data. Multiply all this by the number of different guns, projectiles, and standard charges for those projectiles, and you can see that the ammunition expenditure would be considerable. In 1919, Forest Ray Moulton wrote, "At present the performance of a gun at all ranges can only be determined by trial at the proving grounds. The range firing of a large gun costs tens of thousands of dollars besides wearing out the gun itself" (Gluchoff 2011, 515).

Nineteenth-Century Range Expectations

Ranges are provided in various nineteenth-century texts, but it is not always clear when the author is reporting experimental results and when he is just "guesstimating" from experience or predicting the range using a ballistics formula.

Muzzle Velocity

Range is definitely a function of muzzle velocity, as shown in Table 10–1.

**Table 10–1: Range, 32-Pounder (1843),
Average of Four Rounds (Boxer 1859, 136)**

Powder (lbs)	Muzzle Velocity* (fps)	Range, water level (ft)
4	1,218	1,212
8	1,570	1,627

*ballistic pendulum

Charge

In general, the larger the charge, the higher the muzzle velocity and the greater the range (see Table 10–2).

**Table 10–2: Range (Yards) of 24-Pounder
as Function of Charge and Elevation**

	1 lb	*2 lbs*	*3 lbs*
PB	157	223	360
5 degrees	548	966	1,397

(From 1813, "media" of three rounds, as noted in Beauchant 1828, 24; however, see Beauchant 1928, 20, which gives a 258-yard PBR with a 6-pound charge.)

Common Shot Size

Since the mass of the shot, by which it resists deceleration by air resistance, is proportional to the cube of the diameter, and the actual air resistance proportional only to the square, large shots are less retarded by air resistance than small ones. Hence, even if the initial muzzle velocity is less, they typically will range farther (Beauchant 1928, 47).

Specialty Shot

According to Beauchant (1928, 28–29), the range of grape shot and double-headed shot (chain shot) is two-thirds that of round shot, whereas double shot (two balls, unconnected) has half the range of single shot. Howard Douglas (1829, 65) says that if the absolute weight of the powder charge is unchanged, double shot will receive 71 percent of the muzzle velocity of the single shot and require double the elevation to achieve the same range.

Shells

In 1801, the 13-inch sea service mortar, given a 20-pound charge and a 45-degree elevation, had a maximum range of 4,200 yards, and its 10-inch counterpart, with a 10-pound charge, had a range of 4,000 yards (Landmann 1801, 39).

Ballistics Calculations

The equations of motion for a projectile subject to both gravity and air resistance are easy to write, given calculus, but difficult to solve. Some first-class mathematicians addressed this problem, including Daniel Bernoulli and Leonhard Euler. The Siacci-Ingalls approximation method was still in use for artillery in World War I (EB 1911, "Ballistics").

Once high-speed computers became available, the equations were "solved" by numerical integration (calculating position, velocity and acceleration in small time increments—say, a millisecond at a time), and indeed that is the only viable approach if the speeds are supersonic and the trajectories are high (so air density varies with altitude) (cp. Cline 2004).

Completing this task requires knowing the dependence of air density on air temperature and pressure, and of those on altitude, and determining the drag function (the speed dependence of the drag coefficient) for the projectile of interest, which was possible by quantifying, for each of a variety of charges, its muzzle and down-range velocity from a particular gun.

Drag Regimes

The drag coefficient (C_D) depends on the dimensionless Mach number, which is the speed as a fraction of the speed of sound (340.45 meters/second; 1,117 feet/second; sea level, 15°C, 59°F). The Mach number is used to determine how reasonable it is to treat a fluid flow as incompressible. Wave drag—the cause of the so-called "sound barrier"—is drag resulting from compression of the air flow; it is associated with flight near the speed of sound.

A projectile traveling at a speed close to the speed of sound (Mach 1.0) exhibits a mixture of subsonic (under speed of sound) and supersonic (over) air flows. The range of speeds at which this mixed flow occurs is called *transonic* and extends from 0.8 (or 0.7) to 1.2 (or 1.3). Authorities differ regarding how to define the terms "subsonic" and "supersonic." Some based them on whether the projectile is traveling at less than or greater than Mach 1 (El-Sayed 2016, 119), referring to under Mach 0.7–0.8 as "total subsonic" and over Mach 1.2–1.3 as "total supersonic" (Hirschel et al. 2012, 182). Others define them so as not to overlap with the transonic range (Vos and Farokhi 2015, 5; Fletcher 2012, 124). I prefer the second approach.

At under Mach 0.7–0.8 (the "critical Mach number"), drag is primarily frictional drag (air retarded as it passes over the surface) and pressure drag (air pushed out of the way). Mach 0.7–0.8 is roughly where wave drag (from compression of air) first appears.

The speed of sound, by the way, is proportional to the square root of the temperature and thus depends on altitude. Older ballistics literature attempted to relate drag to air speed rather than Mach number and thus overlooked temperature effects.

C_D is also dependent on the Reynolds number, as is well known from studies of aircraft and airships. The Reynolds number is proportional to both the length and the air speed of the projectile. The Reynolds number likewise depends on the properties of the fluid (air) through which the projectile is traveling, as it is proportional to the density of the air divided by the air's dynamic viscosity (both of which change with altitude). It is dimensionless and sometimes characterized as the ratio of inertial forces to viscous forces.

The air flow around the projectile is laminar (smooth streamlines) if the Reynolds number is low. As the Reynolds number increases past a critical value (10^5–10^6), a transition to turbulent flow (eddies, etc.) begins. The turbulence develops first at the tail, and as the Reynolds number continues to increase, the point of transition moves forward. At a high enough Reynolds number, the flow is fully turbulent.

So we have the interesting situation that an increase in the Reynolds number beyond a critical value results in a sharp decrease in drag, and that in the Mach number, a sharp increase, although both are proportional to velocity.

According to Donald Miller and Allan Bailey (1979, 462), "Reynolds number effects are very much less for ogive-cylinder or cone-cylinder projectiles" than for spherical projectiles. Hence, for modern small arms and artillery projectiles, "the dependence of the drag on Reynolds number is slight" (McCoy 2012, 55). Robert McCoy explains that "at transonic and supersonic speeds, boundary layer separation is dominated by the shock wave system rather than by Reynolds number." It occurs "regardless of whether the boundary layer is laminar or turbulent."

Consequently, "many modern approaches to computing trajectories for artillery ... treat drag coefficients as a function of Mach number and assume no dependence on Reynolds number" (Courtney et al. 2015, abstract). However, spherical projectiles present a "notable exception to this general rule" (McCoy 2012, 76).

Drag Functions for Elongated Projectiles

Historically, experimental firings of a small number of standard projectiles were used to construct drag functions relating retardation (deceleration) to velocity ($R = kV^m$), which in turn allowed approximate calculation of the trajectories for a wide variety of elevations and each service gun's expected muzzle velocities (for each of its standard loads), under "standard conditions." (It was more accurate overall to use the average muzzle velocity for the service life of the gun, rather than the "new gun" design velocity.) Note that "k" here does not equal the physicists' drag coefficient C_D, although the two are related.

Based on Krupp's experimental firings in 1881, Mayevski and Zaboudski formulated a seven-piece drag function (the "Gavre" function) for a "standard projectile," with, for example, m = 2 for speeds below 790 fps, m = 5 for 970–1,230 fps, and m = 1.55 for 2,600–3,600 fps (Ingalls 1918, iv). The British developed a somewhat different drag function in which m was as high as 6.45.

The ballisticians assumed that the drag functions could be applied to a non-standard projectile by adjusting a parameter known as the "uncorrected" ballistic coefficient (BC), which in turn considered projectile weight, diameter and "coefficient of form," the last essentially embracing not just form but all other projectile characteristics that would affect its trajectory. For the standard projectile, the BC was unity. The coefficient of form for each non-standard projectile was itself determined from a more limited set of test firings, and its BC would be its mass divided by the product of the coefficient of form and the square of its diameter.

The actual drag at a given velocity was assumed to be the standard drag divided by the ballistic coefficient, corrected for non-standard air density. There are actually two standard densities in the literature: "standard metro" and "ICAO" (Schaefer 2015).

The ballisticians erred in assuming that the coefficient of form was a constant—that is, projectile shape would have the same effect at all velocities. You could, of course, construct a separate drag function for every projectile and throw the ballistic coefficient "out the window."

In practice, the ballisticians developed a small number of drag functions—one for each "family" of projectile shapes—and accepted the residual imperfection of the coefficient of form (sometimes ridiculed as the "coefficient of ignorance"). These are known as G1 through G8 (the drag function for a spherical projectile is sometimes denoted G0).

The modern ballistics approach to defining drag functions for projectiles is to develop a table relating the aerodynamicists' drag coefficient (rather than retardation) to the Mach number (rather than velocity). And this calculation can be done, relatively easily, for any projectile, not just the standard projectiles, so the ballistic coefficient is usually not used in modern artillery projectile design.

McCoy (1981) developed a computer program ("McDrag") for estimating the drag coefficients of typical ordnance projectiles, based on their shape and Mach number.

Ballistics Tables

Ballistics tables were developed to reduce the work involved in calculating range tables (Hackborn). An early example is that of Bashforth (1873). The early twentieth-century tables pre-computed, for various velocities, the space, altitude, inclination and time functions used by Francesco Siacci's method for calculating

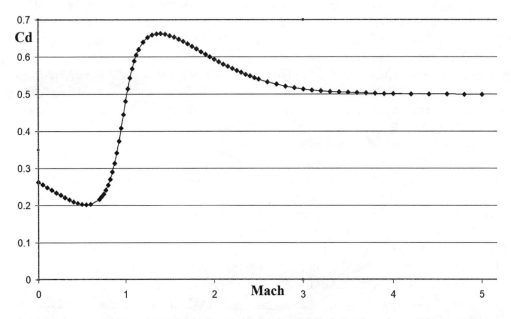

The drag function (CD versus Mach) for a standard G1 projectile, data from (JBMBallistics/G1) for Mach 0.05–5. Author's creation.

the trajectory. The horizontal and vertical coordinates of the trajectory depended on these functions and on the properly corrected ballistic coefficient.

Projectile Design

For elongated projectiles, projectile shape is affected by considerations of internal, exterior and terminal ballistics. The designer wants to efficiently transfer the pressure of the expanding gases to the projectile and minimize wobble, yaw, friction, and abrasion of the bore as the projectile moves down-bore. In flight, aerodynamic drag and trajectory deviation should be minimized. Finally, shape affects how deeply the target is penetrated and how large an explosive charge may be carried.

In discussing shape aerodynamics, it's helpful to imagine the projectile as composed of up to three sections: the forebody, in which its radius is increasing as you move rearward; the midbody, in which the radius is essentially constant (cylindrical form); and the aftbody, in which the radius is decreasing.

The surface of the midbody is called the "bearing surface"; it's responsible for holding the projectile in alignment. Too little midbody, and the projectile nose yaws; too much, and friction unnecessarily reduces muzzle velocity (Rinker 1999, 207). The midbody also adds to frictional drag.

We have to consider the effect of shape on drag in two or even three speed regimes. In subsonic flight, drag is dominated by frictional drag, which in turn is proportional to wetted area; the half-ellipsoid shape gives the best ratio of volume to surface area at a given length/diameter ratio.

The teardrop shape (preferably with length three times the diameter) gives the lowest subsonic drag for a given diameter (Benjamin and Wolf 1993, 19). Unfortunately, a projectile that tapers to a point in the rear is problematic; at the muzzle, it's likely to be deflected by the escaping gases (Rinker 1999, 211).

Shells generally have ogive forebodies. A tangent ogive is a surface of revolution obtained by rotating an arc of a circle, with the generated base being on the radius of that circle. A secant ogive is similarly obtained, but the base is not on the radius; rather, it is on a secant (and thus meets the midbody at an angle). A variety of forebody shapes are used for rockets and missiles.

In the supersonic regime, the best forebody is sharp; a conical shape is possible, but the tip may be rounded slightly (meplat). For high supersonic speeds, a projectile might even have a spike (Rinker 1999, 208).

According to wind tunnel experiments, we can conclude the following about drag: Above Mach 1.5, the best shape is the "¾ power" nose, followed by the cone, the parabola, and the ogive. At low supersonic (1.2–1.5), the best shape is the parabola (Perkins 1952). At transonic (0.8–1.2), the best shapes are the Von Karman ogive and the parabola (Stoney 1954).

There are a variety of reasons why a projectile might be given a blunt rather than pointed nose. This is done sometimes with armor-piercing projectiles, or so-called "diving shells," used to attack submarines close to the surface. If so, to improve the

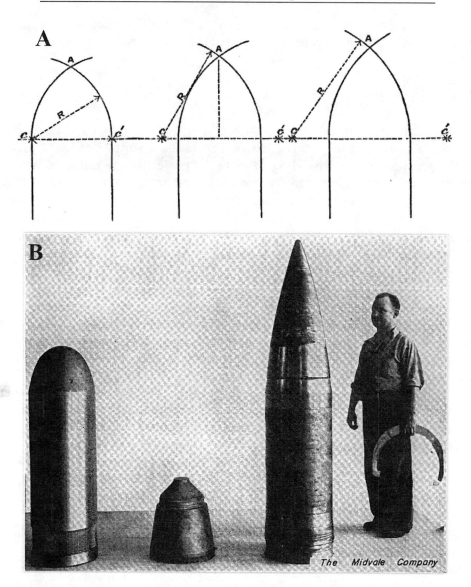

(A) The construction of tangent ogive noses with an ogive radius equal to 1, 1.25 or 1.5 projectile calibers (Browne 1870, 63). Lawrence Bruff (1903, 310) said that the heads of projectiles in his day had an ogive radius of 2–3 calibers, the lower limit being aerodynamic and the upper limit, structural. (B) "An assembled 16-inch projectile [right center] standing beside a body [left] and a cap [left center]. Addition of a windshield [the cone, not separately shown] made the 2700-pound projectile taller than the man with calipers" (Rowland and Boyd 1953, 54). According to range tables for the 16-inch/50 gun, the 2,700-pound projectile had an ogive radius of 9 calibers. This plainly refers to the windshield.

aerodynamics, the projectile may be given a "false ogive" (windscreen) that collapses on impact (Crain 1922, 253).

    The aftbody is usually either nonexistent (projectile has flat base) or what's called a boat-tail—a short, truncated cone that angles in slightly in the aftward direction. The flat base creates a vacuum behind the projectile, and thus a lot of drag. That's alleviated by the boat-tail. While it increases range, it reduces accuracy (Evans and Peattie 2012, 260). Its advantage was recognized by Joseph Whitworth in 1854 (Hazlett et al. 1988, 206).

The standard projectiles used in ballistics calculations in the late nineteenth to mid-twentieth centuries are defined in Table 10–3. The G3 and G4 projectiles are omitted, as they were rarely used.

Table 10–3: Standard Projectile Geometry (McCoy 2012, 10–16)

	Length (calibers)	Forebody Length (calibers)	Forebody Shape	Aftbody (length in calibers; boat-tail angle)
G1 Bashforth			tangent ogive radius 1.49R (R = caliber/2)	none
G1 Mayevski	3.28	1.32	tangent ogive radius 2R	none
G2 (3.3-inch Aberdeen Projectile J, 1922)	5.19	2.7	20° cone with short tangent ogive radius 2.34R transition to midbody	0.5, 6° boat-tail
G5 (75-mm high-explosive shell, Mark IV)	4.29	2.10	tangent ogive radius 6.19R with a "button"	0.49, 7°30' boat-tail
G6 (3-inch M1915 shell)	4.807	2.527	secant ogive radius 6.99R, slightly blunted nose	none
G7 (British Standard Streamline Projectile, 1940)	4.23	2.19	secant ogive radius 10R with a 0.67R tip	0.6, 7°30' boat-tail
G8 (ditto, with cylindrical base)	3.64	2.18	ditto	none

The 2,700-pound, 16-inch shells fired by the main guns of the *Iowa*-class battleship had a length of 4.5 calibers and an ogive radius of 9 calibers (U.S. Navy, Bureau of Ordnance 1941, 6) (but remember that the caliber is the diameter of the bore and thus twice the radius of the projectile).

Flight Stabilization

A projectile can experience two different kinds of motion: translational (changing its position) and rotational (changing its orientation). Rotation of a projectile in free flight is the result of a torque, a force applied along a line of action that does not intersect the center of mass (gravity). Just as a force creates a linear acceleration, a torque creates an angular acceleration. The magnitude of the torque (moment) equals the product of the moment arm (the minimum distance between the line of action of the off-center force and the center of mass) and the component of the force perpendicular to the moment arm.

Imagine a simple elongated projectile. If it is fired, and acted on only by gravity, then its pitch (the vertical angle between its longitudinal axis and the horizontal plane defined by the gravitational vector) will remain constant. It will not rotate, because gravity by definition acts vertically downward through the center of mass and thus does not create a torque.

Now add the effect of air resistance. Besides drag, which acts opposite the direction of motion, there may also be lift, which acts perpendicular to that direction. Lift depends on the angle of attack, which is the difference between the pitch angle of the projectile and the glidepath angle (the angle between the direction of motion—the tangent to the trajectory—and the horizontal plane).

Artillery projectiles, unlike airplane wings, have top-bottom symmetry. With such a shape, if the angle of attack is zero, there is no lift. If it is positive, there is positive (upward) lift; if it is negative, there is negative (downward) lift.

Now, because of gravity, the glidepath angle keeps decreasing as the projectile flies. If the pitch remains equal to the angle of elevation of the gun, the projectile (which we assume for now is unfinned and non-spinning) develops a positive angle of attack, and thus positive (nose-raising) lift.

What happens next depends on the line of action of the lift. The aerodynamic lift force passes through the center of pressure. If the center of pressure is forward of the center of mass, the lift-created torque creates a backward (overturning) pitching moment, increasing the angle of attack. Thus, the projectile will tumble.

By contrast, if the center of pressure is aft of the center of mass, the lift-created torque creates a forward (restoring) pitching moment, pushing the angle of attack back toward zero.

If the projectile yaws (points to the left or right of its direction of motion), the lift force acts sideways, and whether it yaws further, or corrects, depends once again on the location of the center of pressure relative to the center of mass.

So, where is the center of pressure for an elongated projectile? We start by noting that the center of pressure is "the average location of all of the pressure acting on a body moving through a fluid," and its position varies with the angle of attack (SKYbrary 2023).

The simplest form of elongated projectile is probably a cone-cylinder, and that shape is a reasonable approximation to a real projectile. It turns out that at small angles of attack, the pressures on the cylinder average out, so it does not contribute significantly to the position of the center of pressure. The center of pressure of the conical forebody is aft of the nose, at a distance two-thirds of the length of the cone.

The location of the center of mass of the cone-cylinder depends on the relative lengths of the cone and cylinder portions (and their homogeneity), but typically the conical portion is shorter than the cylindrical portion. Hence, it is rather likely that the center of mass will be to the rear of the center of pressure, which means that the cone-cylinder projectile is aerodynamically unstable. Indeed, many artillery shells have pointed noses (to reduce forebody drag) and a flat base (for protection from muzzle pressure) and therefore would be aerodynamically unstable if stabilizing means were not introduced (De Mestre 1990, 114). Elongated projectiles are typically stabilized by aerodynamic or gyroscopic forces.

Aerodynamic (Dart or Fin) Stabilization

Aerodynamic stabilization is achieved by adjusting either the center of gravity (CoG, the effective point of action of gravity) or the center of pressure (CoP, the effective point of action of aerodynamic forces) so the CoP is to the rear of the CoG. For the projectile to have "static stability," the distance between the two centers must be at least one caliber (Barrowman 2010). This result can be achieved by crafting the projectile to move the CoG forward ("dart stabilization") or adding tail fins to move the CoP aft.

Fins create aerodynamic lift at the tail. The farther back the fins are, and the greater their span, the more they shift back the center of pressure. The fletching on an arrow is effectively a fin, and it is responsible for an arrow's ability to hit the target point first. The tail of a weathervane is also a fin, which causes the weathervane to point into the wind.

The most obvious naval use of finned projectiles was in the torpedo, as well as in rockets and missiles, but there were occasional instances of "arrow shells" being manufactured.

During the Vietnam War, the "Swift Boats" made use of a muzzleloaded, smoothbore 81-mm mortar, mounted on a tripod. In trigger (lanyard) fire mode, this mortar could be used for low-elevation fire, ranging to over 1,000 yards (Stoner 2002). The ammunition it used included the M43, M362 and M374 high-explosive rounds, all finned. These were highly elongated, with the aftbody perhaps twice as long as the forebody and the span of the fins equaling the maximum body diameter. The body had a full-caliber obturating band, so there was no need for a sabot (Cooke 2006). In addition, experimental "arrow" shells were fired from 8-inch naval guns in 1968, achieving a maximum range of 72,000 yards. They were used by the USS *St. Paul* (CA-73) in attacking the Viet Cong in 1970 (navweaps.com 2022).

Gyroscopic (Spin) Stabilization

If a projectile that is already spinning is subjected to a torque, its axis of rotation will shift. However, the shift is not quite as one might expect. Suppose that its nose points above the direction of motion. "As soon as its nose rises, air pressure on the underside tries to push its nose farther upward." Now let us assume that the spin is clockwise (as viewed from the rear of the projectile). The combined effect of the spin and the applied torque is that the nose is pushed to the right. Once it's to the right of the trajectory, "air pressure tries to push it farther right," and "this causes downward" movement of the nose. That, of course, causes the nose to move to the left. The leftward movement results in an upward air pressure, bringing us back to where we began (BNP 1963, 189).

The overall result is that the nose has traced a clockwise circle around the trajectory. This circular movement is called precession, and it is analogous to the wobbling of a spinning top. (Since the shell is moving along the trajectory as this movement happens, the nose has actually spiraled around the trajectory.) The faster the spin rate, the slower the rate of precession, and the smaller the angle of the projectile axis from the trajectory tangent (this angle is called the yaw of repose, yaw here referring to that angle, regardless of whether it is in the horizontal plane).

It's important that when the projectile emerges from the muzzle, it's pointed correctly and is already spinning, so as to resist deviation. Imparting spin after the fact may stabilize it on the wrong trajectory.

The projectile must be spun sufficiently fast so the stability factor is greater than 1. For an essentially cylindrical projectile, the stability factor is inversely proportional to $d \times (0.75 \times d^2 + h^2)$, with d indicating diameter and h height (De Mestre 1990, 121; cylinder moments of inertia). Thus, high-caliber projectiles are harder to spin-stabilize, and there's a limiting length/diameter ratio for a given barrel and rifling twist. The stability factor is also proportional to the spin rate, which depends on the rifling of the gun barrel.

It is not unusual for designers to aim for a somewhat higher stability factor, such as 1.3 or 1.4. There are several reasons for this choice. First, the stability factor in part depends on atmospheric conditions. Second, air resistance to the spinning motion causes the spin rate to be reduced.

However, one must not over-stabilize the projectile (use too high a stability factor). If the projectile is spun too fast, the nose won't follow the trajectory; rather, it will keep pointing in the same direction, like a gyrocompass. And if so, it will not strike the target point-first.

The commonest method of imparting spin is by firing a projectile from a cannon with a rifled bore. The projectile must engage the rifling, which is usually done by means of a driving band (some older engagement methods are discussed in chapter 1). The length/diameter ratio may be as high as 5:1.

Air pressure on bent fins may be used to cause a finned projectile to rotate. The Zalinsky dynamite gun projectiles had a long tail with canted vanes on it; these would be expected to stabilize both like a fin by vaning and by inducing rotation. Spin may also be induced by internal channels or external grooves, or by internal thrusters, but I am not aware of any naval gun projectile examples. In general, these methods were found unsatisfactory (Fischer 1904, 198).

Spin-Drift

One of the downsides of spin stabilization is spin-drift. Because gravity is constantly pulling the projectile downward, it tends to spend more time with its nose above the line of trajectory than below (BNP 1963, 189). If it is spinning clockwise (as seen from behind), it will have a net rightward movement (drift), for the reasons explained in the previous section.

Ricochet Fire

This is the reflection of a shot by a surface. Shakespeare refers to the "bullet's crazing" (grazing), causing it to "break out into a second course of mischief, killing in relapse of mortality" (*Henry V*, Act IV, Scene iii). And William Bourne, in *The Art of Shooting in Great Ordnaunce* (1587), has a section titled "How and by what order the shot doth graze or glaunce upon lande or water," which recognizes that the ricochet happens only if the angle of incidence is shallow.

Ricochet occurs because the hydrodynamic lift exerted on the partially immersed projectile is sufficient at shallow entry angles to deflect it to a (slightly) upward exit trajectory. The critical angle depends on the projectile; Birkhoff proposed that it is 18 degrees divided by the square root of the ratio of the density of the projectile to the density of the medium (Johnson 1998). For an iron cannonball striking seawater, that's about 6.4 degrees (cp. Adam 2011, 111), but angles of 3–4 degrees (Douglas 1829, 108) or under 2 degrees (Beauchant 1828, 30) have been recommended.

Ricochet works best when the water is smooth. If there are waves, firing to leeward is more favorable than firing to windward, as the lee sides of waves are steeper (Douglas 1829).

There is also a minimum velocity for ricochet. For a spherical projectile, it is proportional to the square root of the radius (de Podesta 2007, equation 14), and for a 1-inch-diameter steel ball striking water, it is about 7 m/s.

It's really amazing how much ricocheting can increase range. By way of an extreme example, in 1797 the *Vesuvius* fired a 43.7-pound shot at a 1-degree elevation; its first graze was at 358 yards, but it ricocheted a total of 15 times, achieving a range of 1,843 yards (Douglas 1829, 209).

Table 10–4 relates elevation, charge, distance to first graze, and extreme range.

Table 10–4: Ricochet Ranges (Beauchant 1828, 20, 26)

Charge (lbs)	1-degree elevation		5-degree elevation	
	first graze	extreme range	first graze	extreme range
English 24 × 6.5, solid shot				
6	560	2,027	1,565	2,230
4	463	1,847	1,335	1,793
English 24 × 9.5, 5.5-inch shells				
3	277	1,424	1,182	1,733
2	213	1,139	836	1,670

The angle of incidence depends on the elevation of the gun, and the Union navy advised that elevation should not exceed 3 degrees. It also recommended limiting ricochet fire to ranges of 600–1,500 yards (U.S. Navy 1866, 87–88).

There are empirical formulae of uncertain reliability for estimating ricochet range (Abbot 1867, 59ff). There is, of course, some loss of energy at each bounce, so at least a one-third charge of powder was desirable for shooting at a large ship (Beauchant 1828, 31).

Rifled guns could not be used for effective ricochet fire. The fast-spinning projectiles "bound straight up in the air on touching the water and over the vessel. Some years ago we had an experiment made … and it was found that with round shot you could strike the water-line… whereas you could hardly touch it with rifle shot because you lost the ricochet" (Scott 1891, 25).

CHAPTER 11

The Art of Gunnery

Gunnery Errors

If there is a single trajectory by which the gun, fired at a particular instant, will hit the intended point of impact, then it follows that there are essentially three kinds of firing problems that result in a different point of impact: errors in traverse, in elevation, and in muzzle velocity. Errors in traverse result in a lateral error at the range of the target; errors in elevation result in a vertical error (relative to the side of a target ship) or a range error (relative to its deck); errors in muzzle velocity cause vertical and range errors directly, as well as indirect lateral errors (by making too much or too little allowance for wind deflection or ship motion during the time of flight).

All else being equal, if you increase the range, you decrease the accuracy. The horizontal extent of an angular error in bearing equals the range times the tan of the angle. The effect of an error in elevation is more complex, thanks to gravity, but the vertical or range error will still increase with range.

In 1940, the German *Scharnhorst*'s third salvo struck the carrier HMS *Glorious* at a range of about 26,000 yards. That same year, HMS *Warspite* scored a hit on the Italian battleship *Giulio Cesare* at about the same range (DiGiulian 2002). While these are the present records for successful long-range gunfire at sea, that they were possible was certainly the result of twentieth-century advances in the art of gunnery (and a bit of luck).

There are two ways of coping with errors: minimization and compensation. We can minimize variation in powder strength, shot size, and so forth. There are some errors that we can't avoid, but if they are of predictable magnitude and direction, we can compensate for them. For example, if spin causes a rifled projectile to drift 10 yards left at a range of 1,000 yards, we can aim enough to the right of the target so it will drift left onto it. Likewise, we can compensate for known wind, gun platform motion, and target motion.

Precision and Accuracy

Precision measures how closely the impacts are grouped together; accuracy, whether they hit the target. It's also helpful to recognize a concept that used to also be called accuracy but is now (ISO 5725 for the measurement community) called

198

"trueness": the distance of the mean point of impact to the desired point of impact. Both precision and accuracy are important.

It's possible to measure the precision of a gun (although this measurement assumes that you have minimized variation in ammunition, elevation and atmospheric conditions), but a gun doesn't have an inherent accuracy. Any reference here to the "accuracy" of a gun means the accuracy of that gun operated by a typical trained gun crew.

"Accuracy" is most often casually stated as the number of hits made on a target at a particular range; ideally, the records will also state the dimensions of the target.

The most useful method of quantifying either accuracy or precision is in terms of the mean error, laterally and vertically (or in range), of the points of impact from the desired point of impact (for accuracy) or from the mean point of impact (for precision), for a given range. One may also present the mean absolute error—the mean radial distance of the points of impact from the reference point. Unfortunately, most mean error data are from the mid-nineteenth century or later and thus don't help ascertain the accuracy and precision of naval gunnery at an earlier time.

There isn't much difference in the lateral deviation depending on the plane of measurement, but the deviation of range is quite different from the vertical deviation, equaling the latter multiplied by the cotangent of the angle of fall. While the vertical and horizontal deviations are loosely proportional to range, the deviation of range is not, since the angle of fall also changes. The range deviation remains "nearly the same for widely different ranges" and may indeed decrease slightly with range (Alger 1915, 253).

Nineteenth-Century Accuracy Data

At Metz, France, in 1740, a 24–10 on a 78-foot platform was given a 9-pound charge and elevated to 4 degrees. A series of shots was fired (Robins 1742, 238), and it's instructive to examine how much their ranges varied. The average was 835 toises (toise = 6.39 feet), but the minimum was 715 and the maximum 1,010. The standard deviation was 67.9.

In 1833–1849 British experiments, with naval 32-pounders loaded with double shot, at 300 yards, 26/28 shots struck a 10 × 6-foot target, but at 400 yards, only 8/28 did (*Experiments* 1854, 4).

For an 1850s American naval 32-pounder, "Firing at a vertical screen 40 feet wide by 20 feet high at a distance of 1,300 yards with a 32-pdr. of 57 cwt., only three out of 10 shots hit the target, two direct and one on ricochet. The average range to first splash was 1,324 yards with deviations [spread] from 1,238 yards to 1,383 yards" (Canfield 1968).

The Skill of the Gun Crew

Achieving precision is effectively a matter of minimizing the round-to-round variation in muzzle velocity, whereas attaining accuracy requires properly equipping and training gun crews.

There can be significant individual variations in accuracy among different gun crews operating different guns of the same type. In the Prize Firing of the British Mediterranean Fleet for 1899, the nine battleships with 12-inch guns scored an average of 33 percent hits on the standard target, but the best performer was 55 percent and the worst 11.7 percent. The same year, for the 4.7-inch quick-fire gun, the best performer was *Scylla* (80 percent), followed by *Vulcan* (51 percent) (Brassey 1904, 30–31). (*Scylla* was commanded by gunnery innovator Captain Percy Scott.)

Gunnery practice looked to improve crews' rate of fire as well as accuracy, and there is sometimes a tradeoff between the two.

Target Size and Accuracy

The larger the target, the easier it is to hit. The principal vertical target (hull side) is defined by the target ship's length on deck and freeboard. There may also be a substantial superstructure. The horizontal target (deck) is defined by the target's length and beam.

The angular width of the target, at a particular range, determines what degree of angular error in traverse can be tolerated.

For long-range shooting at ships, the "small angle" approximation works; the angular size is proportional to the range, so, at 1,000 yards, a 10-foot object is 0.19

On the USS *Rhode Island* (BB-17), "Crew members pose [with heads in shell holes] with a record target, displaying eight hits for eight shots fired in 51 seconds, following Atlantic Fleet gunnery practice, circa 1913. Photographed by Sargent. From the album of Francis Sargent; Courtesy of Commander John Condon, 1986. U.S. Naval History and Heritage Command Photograph." Courtesy of the Naval History and Heritage Command, Catalog No. NH 101079.

degrees. HMS *Victory* (1765), a British first rate, at 186 feet long, was one of the largest wooden sailing warships ever built. So the *Victory*, seen beam on, had an angular width at 1,000 yards of 3.55 degrees. The battleship *Iowa* (BB-61) had a waterline length of 860 feet (887.25 overall) (Dramiński 2020, 10) and thus more than four times the angular width of the *Victory*.

Danger Space

The concept of danger space takes into account, at a minimum, that the enemy target has height. As a result, misjudging the range to the front of the target may be harmless; the shot may hit the target lower down or higher up, but nonetheless it will still hit. The height considered is probably not the very top of the superstructure, but rather the freeboard of the main deck, or the height of the armored citadel.

The Royal Navy in 1910 computed danger space based on the height of the target, assumed to be 30 feet (Friedman 2013, 18). (The U.S. Navy used 20 feet [Alger 1915, 184].) Because a ship's profile rises above the water, it is possible for a shot projected for greater than the correct range (at sea level) to still hit the target somewhere on its superstructure. The taller the target, and the flatter the trajectory, the greater the effective "danger space" in which a mis-ranged shot could still strike the side of the target.

Since big guns could use lower elevations than small guns for a given range, the larger guns had an advantage. "At 4,500 yards, the 12 in/45 had a danger space of 130 feet … compared to 100 feet for the 6 in" (Friedman 2013, 18). As the range increases, the elevation must also increase, reducing the danger space. For the 12-inch/50 (muzzle velocity 2,567 fps), it was 572 yards at 2,000 yards and 33 yards at 12,000 yards (*ibid.*).

Obviously, the lower the profile of the enemy ship, the shorter the height-based danger space.

Some navies, at some periods, also considered that the target has a width (beam) and thus depth (in the line of fire). The USN's mid-twentieth-century definition of danger space was "for a given target and trajectory, the danger space is the greatest distance through which the target may be moved in the line of fire and still be intersected at some point by that trajectory" (NAVORD 1955, 17B11). It was assumed that the target's centerline was perpendicular to the line of fire, and narrowing at the extremities was ignored. The target's beam was added to the tabulated danger space in the appropriate row of the gun's range table.

The greater the beam, the greater the possibility of a deck hit. Moreover, as the range or beam increases, or the height decreases, a point is reached at which the range interval at which a deck hit is possible is greater than that at which a side hit could occur. Friedman (2013, 29) says that for the British 12-inch/45, the crossover occurred at 12,800 yards, for a target ship with a 30-yard beam.

A related concept—"hitting space"—is "the variation in sight bar range, at a fixed target distance, between the trajectory which intersects a given target at the waterline and the trajectory which intersects the top of the target" (NAVORD 1955,

17B11). In essence, in computing danger space, you mentally move the target and keep the trajectory stationary; in computing hitting space, you mentally change the range setting (thus, elevation) and keep the target stationary. At close battle ranges, the hitting space and danger space may be different (NAVORD 1955, Fig. 17B1).

Range Estimation

If the range were great enough that elevating the gun was necessary, then you had to have some way of determining what the range was so you could judge the correct elevation.

Purely Visual Methods

The gun captain might, through long experience, be able to estimate visually the range to the target and know the proper elevation to strike it.

Soldiers were taught that at 600 yards, a man's head was a small round ball, while at 225 yards, his face became distinguishable as a light-colored spot (Wingate 1876, 140); the eyes could be seen at 80 yards and the proverbial whites of the eyes at 30 (Upton 1875, 71). Presumably, sailors could similarly study the crew of an enemy ship, as well as the visibility of its gun ports, masts, and stays. For longer ranges, they could consider the apparent length or height of the enemy ship.

In land warfare, visual estimates supposedly had an error of 12–15 percent at a range of 600–1,200 yards (Hopkins 1915, 196). However, at sea, there isn't a succession of fixed reference points, such as trees and hills, which you can use to facilitate range estimation. In addition, weather conditions often will degrade visibility. According to William Fullam and Thomas Hart (1905, 459), at sea, "it is quite impossible to estimate ranges above 2000 yards with anything like sufficient accuracy."

Modern naval lookouts are told that until they are able to estimate range, they should describe it qualitatively: "close aboard," "hull up," "on the horizon," or "hull down." In addition, "the only readily available reference point … is the horizon," so they should know the height of their eye above the water and thus the range to the horizon (at 100 feet eye height, it is 23,000 yards) (U.S. Navy 2007, 22).

Trigonometric Methods

If you know the absolute dimension of any part of the target, such as the height of an enemy ship's mainmast, you can measure its angular size with the sextant, and calculate the range by trigonometry (or table lookup). Howard Douglas compiled a table of the heights of the parts of French ships of war (Douglas 1829, 214ff).

This calculation's usefulness was diminished by the increase in battle-ranges. Fullam and Hart complain that "it will be an easy matter for the enemy to alter his mast-head heights at the beginning of war … and … at battle-ranges, the angle subtended by even a very lofty mast must be measured with an extreme of accuracy which no instrument may be relied on to give" (1905, 461).

Another trigonometric method is to have observers stationed at the bow and stern of your ship sight the same object and report its bearing (Cooke 1875, 591). The accuracy of this method depends on the length of your ship, which serves as the baseline. It also required communication between the observers and wouldn't work if the target were ahead or astern (Friedman 2013, 23).

Alfred Ryder (1854, 8) advocated measuring the angle between the horizon and the enemy's waterline, preferably from a high place of observation. This method had the advantage that the geometric distance to the horizon was a function only of the height of the observer's eye above sea level.

Acoustical Methods

Just as you can estimate how far off a thunderstorm is by timing the interval from lightning flash to thunder rumble, you can count the seconds between the flash and the report of the enemy's guns. This process can be made somewhat more precise with an acoustic telemeter; a metal disc is caused to drop slowly through the liquid filling a calibrated tube when the flash is seen and stopped when the sound is heard. The calibration was based on the assumption that the disc moved at ½₅₀₀₀th the speed of sound, and the scale markings denoted 25-meter (roughly 27-yard) intervals. It was thought to be useful at up to 2,000 meters (a little over a mile) in favorable weather, and the accidental error (through delay in flipping the telemeter at start and finish) "does not generally exceed fifty meters; with practice this is diminished to twenty or twenty-five meters" (Cooke 1875, 592–94).

Optical Rangefinders

Optical rangefinders allow a single observer to simultaneously observe the same target from slightly different vantage points. The observer is behind the middle of the unit and the lenses, both facing forward, at either end. Each arm (essentially a horizontal periscope) of the unit has an optical system for bringing its lens' image to the eye of the observer. In one arm, that optical system also permits the observer to alter the line of sight of the lens. The greater the angle between the two lines of sight, the greater the range, and the device displayed the range based on the trigonometric relationship between the two. The accuracy of the rangefinder at a given range was proportional to the square root of the base length (Friedman 2013, 23).

In 1891, the Admiralty advertised for a rangefinder that would have an accuracy of 3 percent at 3,000 yards. The winning entry was the Barr-Stroud coincidence rangefinder. The 9-foot FQ2 (1906) was theoretically accurate to 1 percent (150 yards) at 15,000 yards, but in practice, refraction and heating of the tube degraded accuracy, with errors of 1,000–1,500 yards seen at ranges of 19,000–21,000 yards. A range could be taken in 8–12 seconds (Friedman 2013, 24; EB 1911, "Range-Finder").

The Barr-Stroud coincidence rangefinder was designed to show the top of the target through one lens and the bottom through the other. The operator looked for a vertical element in the target, the half-images of which would be brought into coincidence by adjusting the angles. To prevent similar rangefinders being used against them, the British "tried to break up the vertical lines of their masts and funnels with spirals around masts and then with triangular inserts (rangefinding baffles)" (Friedman 2013, 24).

Initially, the sight angle was changed by rotating a mirror, but this was replaced with either a fixed mirror combination or a pentaprism (in either case, reflecting at a 90-degree angle, down the arm), and the sight angle was adjusted by a "pair of compensator wedges" placed in one arm. A large change in the relative orientation of the wedges resulted in a small change in the sight angle, so this arrangement resulted in increased precision (NAVORD 1944, chapter 2).

An alternative design approach was taken by the Germans in 1893. This was the stereoscopic rangefinder, "in which each lens fed its image into one of the operator's eyes." The operator had to have perfect binocular vision, and if so, would see depth in the image and would move a marker "until it coincided with the target" (Friedman 2013, 25). By World War II, it was more widely used by the USN than the coincidence type, "since it is better suited to ranging on aircraft" (NAVORD 1944, 11A9).

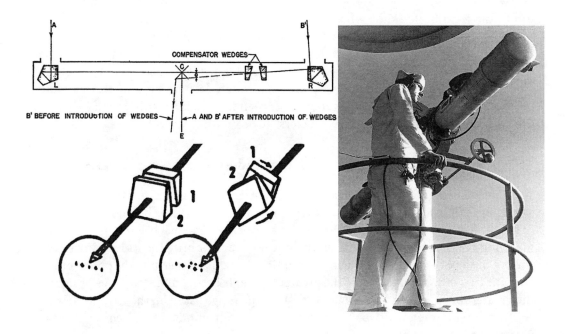

Top left: A schematic of a coincidence rangefinder (NAVORD 1955, Figure 16E9). Rays A and B are from the same target, which is at a finite distance (hence, the rays aren't parallel). They are reflected 90 degrees by the left (L) and right (R) pentaprisms, respectively. "C represents two 45° mirrors, one above the other." After suitable relative rotation of the compensator wedges, both rays impinge on eye E (actually, as separate half-images from the left and right arms, one above the other). Bottom left: The mode of action of the compensator wedges. In the "zero" position (for a target at "infinity"), "the first wedge bends the ray up; the second wedge bends the ray down; the result is no bending." When the wedges "have been rotated by exactly the same amount but in opposite directions," the up and down bends still cancel each out, but both wedges also bend the ray "a little to the right" (Figure 16E10). Right: A rangefinder (type unstated) in operation on an escort carrier during World War II. National Archives. Courtesy of the Naval History and Heritage Command, Catalog No. 80-G-K-16163.

Active Rangefinders

These devices "ping" the target with some kind of radiation—radio waves, sound or laser light—and measure the time to receive the reflection. If they are coupled with a scanning system, these technologies are called RADAR (radio detection and ranging), SONAR and LIDAR, respectively.

In 1938, the USS *New York* (BB-34) became the first warship to be equipped with radar (200 MHZ XAF set) capable of ranging as well as detection. It detected aircraft at up to 100 nautical miles, surface ships to 15, fall-of-shot splashes to 7 (Gebhard 1979, 180). The XAF set was "operated for nearly 3 months on an average of almost 20 hours a day," with only two breakdowns (from tube failures) (Howeth 1963, 487).

Radio waves travel at the speed of light, and range is determined from the time interval between emission of the pulse and receipt of the echo from the target. In World War II, this interval could be measured to one ten-millionth of a second (JCS 1943, 2).

Later World War II radar sets were optimized for specific purposes, such as searching for large ships (CXAM, SK), fire control, and long-range aircraft warning. With antennae at 130 feet, CXAM could reliably detect large ships at a maximum range of 25,000 yards. The range accuracy was ±200 yards, and azimuth accuracy ±3 degrees (JCS 1943, 14).

ASDIC and SONAR were both active systems employing sound. The heart of the

Left: Antenna of the XAF radar. Photograph taken in Washington Navy Yard, 1974 (Catalog NH 81483). The duralumin antenna was 17 feet square and nicknamed the "flying mattress" (Howeth 1963, 457). Right: View of the forward superstructure of the USS *New York* (BB-34). The XAF radar antenna, installed on top of the pilot house in 1938, is visible near the center of the image (Catalog NH 77350). Both images courtesy of the Naval History and Heritage Command.

British ASDIC device was a quartz crystal. Quartz crystals are piezoelectric, "contracting along one axis and expanding along another when subjected to an electric field" (Prendergast 1948). Thus, if subjected to an alternating field, they will oscillate, and that oscillation produces sound waves. If the oscillation is fast enough, the sound is supersonic, which increases its range and "eliminates much of the inherent ocean noises" (Howeth 1963, 472). The crystals are called transducers because they convert electrical energy to sound energy.

"HMS P59 received the world's first operational ASDIC set in late 1918." Its detection range was 2,500 to 3,000 yards (Hackmann 2018, 7).

American sonar was likewise developed over the interwar period (Prendergast 1948). In its 1940 incarnation, it relied on a "magnetostriction transducer comprising an array of nickel tubes driving a 1-foot steel plate mounted back to back with a Rochelle salt transducer inside a spherical housing." Magnetostriction is a change of shape in a ferromagnetic material (nickel) in response to a magnetic field. The Rochelle salt is piezoelectric, like quartz. It provided greater sensitivity, "but it was less reliable than the magnetostriction unit" (Massa 2017). Range recorders had been part of ASDIC, and they were incorporated into SONAR after the outbreak of World War II (Howeth 1963, 474).

LIDAR is a more recent development. There has been experimentation with its use to scan for mines and submarines (Uppal 2019).

The heart of LIDAR is a laser rangefinder; these devices have been in use for decades. The first working laser was built by Theodore Maiman and fired in 1960. Laser rangefinders were developed by the U.S. military "less than five years" later. They were first used on tanks (Neuenswander 2018).

Shipboard laser rangefinders may be ship-mounted or handheld. The U.S. Navy's 1992 ordnance manual does not make any reference to laser rangefinders, but that doesn't prove their absence. Its Mark 46 30-mm gun weapon system, introduced in 2005, uses a laser rangefinder and other devices to track "small, high speed surface targets" (U.S. Navy, Office of Information 2021). Some U.S. naval vessels carry a "compact laser designator," essentially a laser rangefinder that can also designate a target to a laser-guided projectile (Neuenswander 2018).

All of the above methods determine the geometric range of the observer to the target at the time of observation. Depending on host and target motion, the gun might have to be set to a different range.

Trial Shots and Bracketing

If all else fails, you may "try the range." Observing what proportion of the shot fired falls short of the target can be used to guide how to adjust the aim; if the proportion is much less than one half, the shots are on average overshooting.

Firing Ship Discrimination

The USN began using "splash colors" in 1930. Among the *Iowa*-class battleships (1940–1944), the color assignments were orange (*Iowa*), blue (*New Jersey*), red (*Missouri*) and green (*Wisconsin*) (DiGiulian 2023a).

The 1936 French armor-piercing shell had a ballistic cap that housed a dye bag, dispersed by a small bursting charge. This dye "served to color the shell splashes in order to facilitate spotting when operating with other ships…. The shells supplied to *Richelieu* contained a yellow dye; *Jean Burt* was assigned orange" (Jordan and Dumas 2009, 101).

The Japanese in World War II had them, too; in 1944, when an 8-inch Japanese shell "landed right off the [USS *Johnston's*] bow," it splashed "red dye" on the face of the *Johnston's* gunnery officer (U.S. Navy 1968, 556).

The dyed splashes were helpful even when a single ship was firing, as armor-piercing shells made a smaller, harder-to-spot splash than did high-explosive shells (Raven 2019).

Precision: Smoothbore versus Rifled Guns

Table 11–1 compares the precision of the "best shooting" smoothbore and rifled land artillery circa 1870.

Table 11–1: Precision, Smoothbore versus Rifled

	target range (yards) versus mean error (yards)			
	1,000 yards		*2,000 yards*	
	mean range error	*mean "reduced" deflection*	*mean range error*	*mean "reduced" deflection*
smoothbore	43	4.0	60	10
rifled	19	0.3	21	0.7

(Owen 1873, 334) ("Reduced" deflection means relative to the mean point of impact, not the point of aim.)

However, Charles Owen comments that up to 300–400 yards, the smoothbores are just as accurate as the rifled guns, and at very long ranges such that ricocheting is necessary, the smoothbores are superior because round shot ricochets more predictably (1873, 334–35).

Another source is Henry Abbot (1867), writing about the First Connecticut Artillery. With 32-pounder smoothbore seacoast guns, Fort Barnard achieved 20 feet mean deviation from center for a target 1,030 yards away. Fort Richardson didn't fare as well—28 feet at 950 yards (51). With the 30-pounder Parrott rifle, Fort Barnard reported 16 feet at 1,030 yards (117).

In 1870, three ironclads tested their big, rifled muzzleloaders on a rock 600 feet long and 60 feet high, 1,000 yards away, under favorable conditions, with the following results:

HMS *Hercules* (1868), 10-inch guns, 10 hits/17 shots
HMS *Captain* (1869), 12-inch guns, 4/11
HMS *Monarch* (1868) 12-inch guns, 9/12 (Brassey 1883, 284)

Note that this testing involved shooting at a stationary target much larger than a ship.

Windage, Balloting and Deviation

So what's the problem with smoothbore precision, and what was (or could have been) done about it? The principal cause of deviation is balloting—that is, the bouncing of the projectile as it passes down the bore as a result of windage.

In 1862, for smoothbores, the angular deviation of the line of departure (how the projectile actually left the bore) from the line of bore was reportedly not more than 5 minutes of arc vertically and 4.5 laterally (Benton 1862, 415). (One degree is sixty minutes of arc.)

However, there's also retained spin to be considered. This effect presumably occurs because the forward movement of the part of the ball touching the wall is retarded, imparting a rotation around it. The last bounce determines the final spin. With ordinary windage for a 24-pdr shell fired with 2.25 pounds of powder, the velocity of rotation was "30 feet" (assuming this was the tangential velocity of the rim in seconds, and the ball was 5.5 inches diameter, 1,251 rpm) (Benton 1862, 425). Topspin shortens the range and backspin increases it, while sidespin causes a curve to the left or right. This is the result of the "Magnus effect."

The lateral deflection of a spinning, moving ball was observed and first explained by Isaac Newton and Benjamin Robins. Heinrich Gustav Magnus demonstrated that a cylinder, rotating around its vertical longitudinal axis, exposed to a horizontal current of air, "will move [horizontally] in the opposite direction from the side which is moving toward the current of air from the blower" (Benton 1862, 429). The effect of the combination of the rotational and relative translational motion on the boundary layer of air surrounding a rotating sphere (or a rotating cylinder moving perpendicular to its spin axis) is to create a pressure difference between two sides and thus a net force (Borg 1985, 17–19).

Even without retained spin, if the ball was eccentric (meaning that the center of gravity didn't coincide with the geometric center), it deviated toward the side on which the center of gravity was located. John Dahlgren, using "service" 32-pounder shells, determined the location of the center of gravity of each and positioned them. He found that if the firing were such that a concentric shell would range 1,300 yards, with the eccentric center of gravity up, the travel was 1,415 yards; with it down, 1,264 yards; and inward, 1,360 yards (Benton 1862, 430).

Balloting is not a problem for rifled projectiles. While they necessarily experience spin, which in turn causes lateral drift (see chapter 10), that drift is predictable and can be compensated for, unlike that of spherical shot from smoothbores.

Other Sources of Error

Powder Conditions. Muzzle velocity increases with powder temperature. Figure a change of 2 fps per °F (NAVORD 1958, 17B4 Col. 10). It also decreases with increasing moisture content. A damp powder burns more slowly; a dry one, more rapidly. Powder that has been in storage a long time may deteriorate, resulting in a change in initial velocity (Alger 1915, 186).

Projectile Variation. Dahlgren (1856, 101–2), inspecting a heap of 32-pounder round shot "selected for service" (that is, they passed the two gauges, etc.), found that they varied in both diameter (6.22–6.28 inches) and weight (32.43–33.00 pounds). With ten such rounds, at 3 degrees of elevation, the mean range was 1,172 yards and the mean difference 18.4. If he used shot further selected so the diameter was limited to 6.24–6.26 inches (weight 32.43–32.47), the mean range was 1,195 yards and the mean difference only 10.3.

Variation in projectile weight has two opposing effects: a heavier projectile is accelerated less, in-bore, leaving with a lower muzzle velocity, and decelerated less in flight, giving it greater range for a given muzzle velocity.

In the case of a spherical projectile, there could also be defective casting—that is, "the center of gravity more or less removed from the center of the figure" (*Experiments* 1854, 151).

Jump and Droop. If the gun, when fired, has a positive elevation, the force of discharge causes the gun to rotate, bringing the muzzle higher ("jump"). However, the length and weight of the gun may cause the muzzle to droop, so the "line" of bore is not truly a straight line (Alger 1915, 167ff).

Air Density. Early twentieth-century range tables were calculated for a "standard atmosphere" of half-saturated air, 15°C, 29.53-inch pressure (Alger 1915, 189). Atmospheric pressure, temperature and humidity all affect air density and thus air resistance. For example, for Philip Alger's standard problem 12-inch gun, range 10,000 yards, if the barometer were 29.00" and the thermometer 96°F, the air would be 9 percent below standard density, and the range achieved would be 194 yards higher (189). A further complication is that temperature and humidity also affect the velocity of sound and thus the Mach number of the projectile for a given speed (Ingalls 1918, vii).

The effect of pressure and temperature can be determined by the ideal gas law, and that of humidity estimated by comparing the molecular weights of water vapor and dry air.

Pressure, temperature and humidity all vary from place to place and from time to time, and to take them into account, you need to be able to measure them. That measurement, of course, will be for where the gun is located and could be a bit different at the target (or in between).

The variation of air density with altitude is usually significant only for a high-trajectory fire. As an approximation, rather than actually measuring the variations, one can use the International Standard Atmosphere, which relates density to altitude (actually, to the geometric altitude corrected for the diminution of gravity with altitude).

Drift. The spin of the projectile fired from a rifled gun causes it to be deflected to one side; this drift increases with distance flown and is the net result of several forces (Denny 2011, 113ff).

Projectile Angle of Attack. Ballistic calculation methods often assume that either the projectile is spherical or, if elongated, its long axis is always tangential to the trajectory (zero angle of attack). In practice, it isn't. If it's a spin-stabilized projectile, the longitudinal axis will precess (rotate around) an equilibrium line, which itself is at an angle (the yaw of repose) to the direction of motion. The line points right for a right-hand spin. The yaw of repose thus is the average angle of attack. Air resistance increases as the angle of attack increases. The yaw of repose at apogee is perhaps 2 degrees for an elevation of 50 degrees, but it is 10 degrees or more for an elevation of 65–70 degrees (Pope 1985). For a statically stable non-spinning projectile, "the nose points slightly above the trajectory" (Carlucci and Jacobsen 2018, 309).

Wind. If we can measure the wind force and direction, then we can take it into account. Wind direction is easy—that's shown by a wind vane. Wind speed is determined with an anemometer. Of course, the anemometer will report the wind felt by the firing ship, and this effect will be the apparent wind felt by the ship (which is moving), rather than the true wind. So we must be able to convert the apparent wind on the ship to the true wind, and then that to the apparent wind felt by the projectile. This task requires knowing the speed and direction of the firing ship.

In 1910, the British Admiralty had a "gunnery calibration" form that called for recording data from an "anemometer and wind vane recorder." These were issued to "all ships down to and including 3d class cruisers and scouts" (Admiralty 1910, 967).

A 1917 report of the Superintendent of the United States Naval Observatory noted that a Kadel "buzzer type masthead anemometer" had been adopted as standard and was to be issued "to battleships for assisting in determining the initial sight-bar range and deflection for fire control" (USNO 1917, 201).

Wind is less consistent than the other atmospheric conditions; it can change in direction and strength while the projectile is in flight. And there's not much one can do about that other than look for telltales down-range of how the wind is behaving there. Also, in general, ballisticians consider only horizontal winds; updrafts and downdrafts are ignored.

Miscellaneous. At extreme ranges, gunners consider the Coriolis force caused by the rotation of the Earth (6-inch deflection at 1,000 yards), the decrease of gravitational force with altitude, and the curvature of the Earth.

Table 11–2 shows how changing conditions could create range and lateral errors. Do not make the mistake of assuming that the stated errors will hold true for other guns or projectiles (or other ranges); the underlying equations are highly nonlinear.

Table 11–2 Sample Range Errors and Deflections as a Result of Variations in Conditions, per Ballistics Tables, Standard Atmosphere

Problem A 3-inch, 13-pound shell, 1,150 fps, coefficient of form 1.00 normal range 2,000 yards			Problem C 4-inch, 33-pound shell, 2,900 fps, coefficient of form 0.67 normal range 3,000 yards			Alger 1915 page
condition	range error (yards) + overshot - undershot	deflection	condition	range error (yards)	deflection	
spin-drift		7.5			2.4	152
+25 fps	+49.8		+50 fps	+83.4		139
			+1 lb	-33.7		140
firing downwind, 8 knots wind	+16.5		firing downwind, 11 knots	+12.7		164

condition	range error (yards) + overshot - undershot	deflection	condition	range error (yards)	deflection	
Wind 6 kn from right		6.3 R	Wind 9 kn from right		5.7 R	"
Own motion 6 kn away	-14.7		Own motion 8 kn away	-11.5		165
Gun motion 8 kn left		23.6 L	Gun motion 9 kn left		15.7 L	"
Target motion 7 kn away	-21.4		Target motion 9 kn away	-17.3		"
Target motion 8 kn R		24.4 L	Target motion 10 kn R		19.2 L	"
P: 28.10" T: 5°F	-20.4		P: 29.00". T: 15°F	-64.9		206

Farnsworth Gun Error Computer. This was a mechanical device, constructed in 1915, for determining the errors in range and deflection attributable to wind, firing ship motion, target motion, powder temperature, and atmospheric density. It appears to have been a kind of circular slide rule with graphic representations of the values in the ballistics tables (Alger 2015, Appendix B).

CHAPTER 12

Accuracy at Sea

In this chapter, we will look at the relative effective range of early nineteenth-century land and sea artillery and the reasons why they were so different. We will also explore how effective range at sea was improved on.

In the late eighteenth and early nineteenth centuries, while one might open fire with a single gun at long range, broadside fire was delayed until the ships were close, under two cable lengths (400 yards) (Willis 2008, 141–42). Frederick Maitland, when captain of HMS *Bellerophon*, told Napoleon Bonaparte in 1815 that he would prefer to engage at half a cable length (100 yards) or less (Maitland and Dickson 1904, 96).

In 1867, an anonymous author argued that the introduction of the shell gun necessitated an increase in engagement range, since even if the chance of a hit at long range was small, a single shell could destroy a ship (Revolution 1867, 7).

"At Tsushima, in 1905, the range varied between about 4,000 and 6,00 yards. By 1910 the Navy was holding battle practices at 12,000 yards with reasonable accuracy. At the Dogger Bank engagement early in 1915, the opening range was between 18,000 and 20,000 yards … and at the end of World War I, fire control was efficient enough to cope with the ranges of about 24,000 yards possible with the maximum elevation of 15°." By World War II, the range limit was more than 40,000 yards (NAVORD 1944, 10A6).

Accuracy: Land versus Sea

The effective range of Napoleonic smoothbore field artillery (4–12-pounders) on land was 800–1,200 yards (Nosworthy 1996, 359ff). (The guns could probably range farther, but with open sights, aimed fire wouldn't be possible.) For a 12-pounder firing at a continuous screen six feet high, simulating a line of infantry, the Madras Artillery (1810–1817) reported that the 12-pounder achieved almost 80 percent hits at 300 yards, 60 percent at 900, and perhaps 25 percent at 1,200 (Hughes 1975, 37). Wilhelm Muller (1811, 195) reported that a 12-pounder achieved 45 percent hits on an embrasure 2.5 feet high and 8 wide at a range of 575 paces, and 18 percent at 1,300.

Why, then, was the engagement range of Napoleonic sea ordnance so low? Was it because the close range was needed to ensure penetration of the thick hull of a warship? Were naval guns of inferior precision? Or was accuracy much lower at sea than at land?

Firing from aboard a ship presented some difficulties that the land artillery didn't have to consider. Both the firing and the target ship were in motion, perhaps at different speeds on different courses, subject to change at any moment on account of the wind, damage, and tactical decisions, and thus the target range, bearing and aspect were in constant flux. (While a land target could be in motion, only charging cavalry were likely to be at a speed comparable to a sailing warship.)

In addition, if the sea wasn't smooth, the firing ship was rolling, pitching and yawing. Even if the two ships were still, estimating range was harder at sea than on land, as previously discussed. (It's also true that naval gun crews didn't practice firing at long-range targets, but that could be because of the other problems set forth above.)

There's evidence that ship motion was the principal problem. In 1847, the 74-gun *Leviathan* (or a canvas screen of equal size) was used as a target to test the accuracy of guns firing round shot, under ideal conditions (smooth water, light wind, both ships stationary), with the results shown in Table 12–1.

Table 12–1: Smoothbore Accuracy at Sea, Ideal Conditions

Shot Wt	Charge	Range (yards); % Hits			
		1,500	2,000	2,500	3,000
32	8	75	45	22	8
	10	75	45	25	11
68	14–15	"	"	"	"

(*Experiments 1854, 150*)

Those numbers can't be compared directly with those of field artillery, but they show acceptable accuracy at far beyond the then-normal naval battle range.

Effect of Ship Architecture

The calculation of the proper elevation of a gun is simplified if the axis of the trunnions is horizontal. However, decks of sailing ships had "sheer"—that is, they were curved parabolically upward toward the bow and stern. This shape reduced pitching and also made the ships less likely to take on water. Richard Meade suggests, "for a vessel of 200 feet length, a sheer or rise of about 2 feet at the bow and about 8 inches at the stern, but this is frequently exceeded" (1869, 144). Because of sheer, "the best firing on a ship is that done by her divisions which are quartered in the waist" (Simpson 1862, 346).

Another possible consideration is that a ship's sides aren't parallel; rather, they curve in toward the bow and the stern. For broadside guns near the bow and stern to point the same way as those amidships, they must be traversed, which we know to be a cumbersome process.

Effect of Roll, Pitch and Yaw

Let's look at the problem of firing ship motion more closely. If sailing on any course other than directly downwind, a sailing ship would be heeled over—that is, tilted from the vertical. In shooting, its gunners would have to compensate for this constant tilt. In addition, there would be continual yawing, pitching and rolling as a result of the action of the sea.

The yawing (left/right) of one's own ship would affect the relative target bearing and thus the necessary traverse. (The yawing of the target ship also makes it more difficult for a spotter to judge its heading.)

Rolling would change the required broadside gun elevation. A sailing ship would be heeled over by the wind (a constant roll angle), and the guns on the leeward side would need to increase elevation to compensate; the reverse would be true for the weatherly guns.

A ship could also be rolled back and forth by waves or swells. "A ship experiences its largest roll angles at or near its natural roll period" (Schonfeld 2021). In the 1920s, typical roll periods were five seconds for destroyers and seven seconds for battleships (Manning and Schumacher 1924, 90).

A typical rate of roll would be one degree a second. If the target range were 3,000 yards, the line of sight would sweep across 15 vertical feet in less than one-tenth of a second. But early twentieth-century German warships were "stiff," rolling at a rate of three degrees a second (Friedman 2013, 163). Thus the compensatory elevation adjustment would be changing continually, although the change would be slowest at the top and bottom of the roll.

For guns firing in locations other than on the beam, rolling would take the trunnion axis off the horizontal plane, so traversing the gun would also change its effective elevation, and elevating it would likewise change its effective train.

If a target ship were fleeing, and your ship trying to cut off its escape, chances were that your guns were firing obliquely rather than perpendicularly to your ship's centerline. If so, the trunnion axis would no longer be parallel to the ship's centerline, and roll changed not only elevation but also bearing—the latter was called "cross-roll." John Stevens (1834, 26) warned that the bow guns should therefore be pointed at the weathermost part of the enemy's hull.

Pitching would change the height of the gun, and therefore the proper elevation to account for ballistic drop at the target range, unless the gun happened to be on the pitch axis. More important, pitching would change the proper elevation for guns firing forward or backward, as well as the orientation of the axis of the trunnions of a broadside gun.

Timing the Roll

Gunners took roll into account. A ship rolled with a pendulum motion—fastest (but at constant speed) at mid-roll, paused (but accelerating or decelerating) at the top and bottom. Therefore, some gunners favored firing at the top or bottom of a roll. This decision had several consequences. First, it limited the rate of fire to the period (or half-period) of the roll. Second, the gunner had to anticipate when the top or bottom of the roll was approaching, and whether this was possible depended on the regularity of the roll.

For this reason, British and French nineteenth-century naval practice favored firing only on the rising motion, so that a shot intended for the hull would at worst hit the rigging (as opposed to missing the ship altogether) (Douglas 1829, 235ff). I must note that firing at the bottom of the roll was sometimes impractical, as that position meant that the ship was in the trough of the waves, so the shot might be delayed until later in the rise. The Americans, in contrast, fired at the "top of the sea," or on the falling motion (245).

The rising motion was slowest on the lee side, and the reverse was true on the weather side, but it wasn't always possible to take advantage of this (Stevens 1834, 21).

Henry Bessemer proposed (1873) a firing device that featured a "tumbling bob"—a slender triangular element positioned with the wide end up, resting against one of two flanking arms. One arm was insulated, while the other had an electrical contact, as did the bob. The whole assembly was itself mounted on a graduated quadrant, so it could be inclined at a specified angle to the frame of the quadrant, which corresponded to the desired true elevation at the time of firing. The idea was that with the bob resting against the insulated arm, the gunner would close one switch by pressing the firing button. When the ship rolled enough in the direction of the electrified arm so that the bob would fall over against it, the second and last contact would be closed and a firing signal delivered to the primer. Bessemer recognized that it would require a finite amount of time for the bob to change position, and that the launch of the projectile was also delayed by the "firing interval," so he provided a secondary movement for adjusting the neutral inclination to allow for this timing. It appears that Bessemer demonstrated a table model at the Royal Naval College, but his offer to fit a British warship with the device at his own expense fell on deaf ears (Vincent 1887, 507).

Firing Interval

The effect of the roll was exacerbated by the firing interval, as the gunner had to estimate where the line of bore would be when the projectile actually left the muzzle, as opposed to when he actuated the ignition mechanism. The longer and more variable the firing interval, the harder this was to do. The firing interval might be three-tenths of a second with electric firing (Fullam and Hart 1905, 222).

The change in the line of departure would depend on the period, phase and amplitude of the roll, but, looking at a range table for a 12-inch gun, if the correct range were 1,000 yards, for which the proper elevation was 23.4 degrees, and the effective elevation increased during the firing interval to 25.8 degrees, the shot would hit 100 yards farther away, and if it decreased to 21.1 degrees, it would fall 100 yards short (U.S. Navy, Bureau of Ordnance 1909, 2).

Roll Compensation

We are told that "one early device for correcting for the roll of the ship was a round shot suspended from a spar. The gunner watched this improvised pendulum swing with the roll of the ship, and just before it was parallel to the mast, he applied his slow match to the touch hole of the piece" (NAVORD 1958, 15A2). It is doubtful that any gunner actually proceeded in this manner, as it would require looking toward the mast (rather along the gun barrel at the enemy) just before firing.

Captain Philip Broke of HMS *Shannon* and Captain Samuel John Brooke-Pechell of HMS *San Domingo* appear to have been early proponents of using a pendulum in roll compensation. The pendulum, equipped with a graduated arc, was placed "in any convenient part of the ship" and the guns were equipped with tangent scales, so that once the inclination of the vessel was observed with the pendulum, the gun could be elevated or depressed as needed "to compensate for the heel of the ship" (Douglas 1820, 218–19). The reference to "heel" is important, as it is a constant angle of roll (maintained if the wind's speed and direction relative to the ship is constant). The pendulum would then hang vertically, as the only acceleration it felt was that of gravity (White 1900, 277). While not expressly stated, it may be assumed that an officer observed the pendulum and called out the angle of heel.

Let us examine more closely the ability of a pendulum device to serve as an instantaneous roll indicator. When a ship is being rolled by waves, the shipboard pendulum is not guaranteed to indicate the true vertical. The same is true of a spirit level or a mercury clinometer (White 1900, 282). First, there are vertical and horizontal accelerations due to the rotational motion. Second, there is a changing lateral acceleration from wave action. The wave moves the ship, which moves the point of support, the bob lagging behind (Mallock 1901, 34; Peabody 1904, 341).

The "resultant of the forces on an object on board ship when the ship is on a wave slope acts along the normal to the effective wave slope," and the pendulum error in indicating the roll angle is "directly proportional to the distance between its point of suspension and the centre of oscillation of the ship (near the centre of gravity)[.] The error is also inversely proportional to the square of the ship's period of roll" (Burger 1966).

If the pendulum has a short period, then, as discovered by William Froude, it will indicate the apparent vertical, perpendicular to the wave surface (Brown 2006, 61). The pendulum may be given a long period—say, "at least four times the ship's period so that there is no time for the pendulum to show an appreciable deflection. For all practical purposes it will indicate the true vertical" (Burger 1966), provided it is properly positioned. That is, the pendulum must hang from the center of oscillation (Attwood 1912, 231).

It is not practically implemented in the form of a common pendulum; its length would be too long. "The form actually used is a wheel with the center of gravity about 0.07 inches below the axis" (Peabody 1904, 342).

If the roll indicator were used simply to monitor the ship's stability, it could be placed near the center of oscillation. But for roll compensation of gun elevation, prior to the development of shipboard electronic communication, it was desirable that it be near the guns. Unfortunately, broadside guns are necessarily distant from the roll axis, and even centerline turrets are likely to be above the center of oscillation. So "one might expect an error of about 20% from a pendulum on the upper deck on an ironclad and of some 50% on a wooden battleship" (Brown 2006, 62).

An accurate method of determining the roll angle is to use a batten instrument referenced to the horizon. One form was a center-pivoted batten, with an angular scale, lined up horizontally with the horizon when the ship was "upright and at rest." The observer could either look along the batten, pointing it at the horizon, or look toward it, keeping the edge parallel to the horizon. Another form was to have two graduated vertical battens, on either side of the ship, and a fixed eyepoint between them. The observer would see where the line of the horizon bisected the batten on the lowered side. These devices, oriented differently, could alternately be used to determine pitch angle, and on occasion means were attached for recording the changes in inclination (White 1900, 287–90; Attwood 1912, 233).

Presumably, the observer could call out to the gunners either the current angle or when the batten line reached a predetermined angle. However, the principal purpose of the batten apparatus was probably to obtain the roll period and extreme inclinations of the ship, to guide future ship designs, and for that two observers were needed (White 1900; Ryder 1871, 58).

Sometime before 1855, the French "used a reflector to compare the indication of the pendulum with the real horizon; this combination was called *L'Horizon Ballistique*" (Friedman 2013, 292). Howard Douglas (1860, 445) indicated that this device was used by French gunners to adjust elevation.

In 1872, Froude designed a rather delicate automatic roll recorder that featured both short- and long-period pendula. The long-period one was an eccentrically mounted wheel "three feet in diameter and weighing 200 pounds," with a half-period of 34 seconds. The roll recorder was used in sea trials of the *Inflexible* (comm. 1881), the *Revenge* (1895) and the *Vivien*'s gyrostabilizer (1925). It was not used in a firing mechanism (Brown 2006, 62ff).

A "wave-motor" was proposed by John Rowe in 1888, "to automatically discharge the heavy guns of men-of-war when the vessel is on an even keel," and he received a U.S. patent in 1899. The patented version featured a cylindrical float submerged in liquid inside a cylindrical casing, both with horizontal axes. The sides of the float had spindles "passing in a watertight manner through the ends of the casing." The spindles communicated, through an adjustment disc (for setting the firing angle), with an electric firing mechanism, and for controlling a broadside gun, the device would be oriented so the spindles pointed fore and aft. Obviously, the float was a liquid-damped pendulum. However, the patent didn't discuss the required period of the device.

Arnulph Mallock's rolling indicator (1901) relied on liquid damping of a paddlewheel's motion to alter the period of an attached pendulum weight from four seconds to 30–40; this device was "issued to ships of the Royal Navy" (Attwood 1904, 233). The error resulting from mounting it away from the center of oscillation was "a small fraction of a degree" (Mallock 1901, 40).

Gyroscopic clinometers were proposed in the late nineteenth century, but at the time there was difficulty maintaining the speed of rotation (White 1900, 285).

Continuous Aim

Alternatively, with the right training and equipment, we can forget about timing the roll and just continuously adjust the aim.

In the late nineteenth century, if telescopic sights were available, they were used just to make the initial estimate of the range. The gunner dialed in the elevation but still waited for the roll to bring the aiming point into open sights. Accuracy was poor. Firing for five minutes each at a hulk 1,600 yards away, five British warships managed to score a grand total of two hits (Morison 1966).

In 1899, Percy Scott stunned the Royal Navy when his cruiser *Scylla* achieved 80 percent accuracy in a prize firing, about six times the normal performance. Rather than setting a fixed elevation for the estimated range and trying to time the roll, his gunners continuously aimed (i.e., adjusted the elevation of) their guns (Friedman 2013, 18).

While this approach was a procedural rather than a technological change, it was of course made possible by technological improvements, such as breechloading, rifling, elevating gears, and telescopic sights. Moreover, Scott did some technological fine-tuning. He changed the gear ratio on the elevating gear so that the gunner could follow the target during the roll. And he modified the mounting of the telescope sight so it wouldn't be pushed back (into the gunner's eye!) by the recoil (Morison 1966).

Scott's methods revolutionized naval gunnery; in 1905, a gunner "made fifteen hits in one minute at a target 75 by 25 feet at 1600 yards; half of them hit in a bull's eye 50 inches square" (Morison 1966).

However, the bigger the gun, the more difficult it was to move the gun fast enough to achieve "continuous aim"; the apparent limit at the time was 9.2-inch caliber (Friedman 2013, 20). In addition, 1,600 yards was about the practical limit without improved range estimation and prediction of target motion (72).

The Germans had difficulty practicing continuous aim because their ships had a high metacentric height and thus a quick roll. There were two solutions. In the short term, they used "a corrector, which took the time lag of firing and the roll rate into account." In the long term, the Austrian von Petravic gyro-firing mechanism, which held the sight on target by gyro, fired the guns electrically when the elevation was correct (Friedman 2013, 163).

Gun Platform and Ship Stabilization

Alternatively, ship designers could attempt to suppress the roll (and other perturbations).

Shifting Weight Stabilizers

The first such was Thornycroft's pendulum, which hydraulically shifted a weight within the hold to stabilize the entire ship (1892). However, it was too heavy to win

Admiralty acceptance (Bennett 1979, 97). Such stabilizers are "primarily useful for smaller vessels" (Smith and Thomas 1990, 12).

Gyroscopic Stabilizers

In 1889, Beauchamp Tower constructed and tested an apparatus for providing a steady naval gun platform. The position of the gyroscope affected the flow of pressurized water into four hydraulic cylinders on which the gun platform rested (White 1900, 294–96). The Admiralty tested it on two gunboats; it worked, but the weight was considered excessive.

In 1906, Ernst Otto Schlick showed that an 1,100-pound steam-driven "passive" gyroscope could reduce a torpedo boat's roll from 15 degrees each way to 1.5 degrees (Airey 1914, 49).

Gyroscopic stabilizers are classified as "passive" if "the precessional energy is obtained entirely from the roll energy of the ship." An experimental "active" gyroscope was installed in 1911 on the destroyer USS *Worden* (DD-16) (Haeberle 1923), and it was able to reduce the roll to "a maximum of five deg. in a boisterous seaway" (Skerrett 1915).

Fin Stabilizers

Fin stabilizers may be passive (set at a fixed angle, creating hydrodynamic drag), like the bilge keel (introduced in 1875), or active (with an angle of inclination that is gyroscopically controlled to one creating hydrodynamic lift).

Bilge keels were installed on, for example, the *Bismarck* and *Tirpitz*. Their disadvantage is that they increase hydrodynamic resistance and thus reduce ship speed (Garzke et al. 2019).

Active fin stabilizers are effective only when the ship is traveling. The Denny-Brown active fin stabilizers were used on British warships in World War II (Russell 1956, 23).

Tank Stabilizers

A tank stabilizer (anti-roll tank) operates even when the ship is at rest. Of course, the tanks take up space and add to the weight of the ship. Passive ones control liquid flow so it lags behind the roll. One version used a single partially filled tank with internal baffles; others (Frahm tanks) featured two wing tanks connected in some way, but with constricted flow between them. Active tank stabilizers use pumps, trading power for a faster response and the ability to cope with a broader range of wave frequencies (Smith and Thomas 1990, 5–11).

The first use of a tank stabilizer in a warship was in HMS *Inflexible*. The designers were not able to use two pairs of wing tanks as as Watts proposed in 1875. Watts claimed the simplified design reduced rolling by about 25 percent (Watts 1911, 203). But it did not impress the Admiralty. *Inflexible*'s tanks "were quite effective at small roll angles but were too small to help much at larger angles where bilge keels proved more effective" (Brown 2006, 229).

The German navy also experimented with Frahm roll tanks. On the battle-cruiser *Von der Tann* (commissioned 1910), they reduced rolling by only 33 percent. The tanks were repurposed as coal bunkers, and bilge keels were added (Dodson 2016). The tank stabilizer system on the 1930s-era German destroyers Z1-Z22 had similar problems (Brown 2019).

Fire Control Systems

The premodern fire control system was crude. The captain or another officer made the decision regarding when open to fire and conveyed it by a speaking horn. The individual gun captains would point and elevate their guns and, if commanded to "fire at will," would decide when to pull the lanyard.

The early twentieth-century increase in torpedo range to 1,500 yards at high speed and 3,500 at reduced speed provided considerable incentive for further increasing effective gun range, as "it was widely understood that a line of battleships would be a virtually unmissable target … [with] little or no underwater protection" (Friedman 2013, 22). That meant further improvements in fire control were necessary for the gun to regain primacy. In particular, it became necessary to account for own ship and target ship motion.

A fire control system must do three things:

1. collect the data regarding the target, the host ship, and the gun necessary for accurate targeting and transmit it to the "computer" (human or machine);
2. compute the firing solution and transmit firing orders to the gunners (or the guns themselves); and
3. execute the firing orders.

Steps 1–3 may be manual or automatic, and the communications may be by voice or electronic means.

Spotter Position

The spotter position affects the ability to obtain target data. A spotter inside a turret had a limited field of view, and it would be obscured by gun smoke. (Similar problems were experienced in the Age of Sail, when a gunner on a closed gun deck could see only what was visible through the gun port.)

The higher the spotter, the greater the distance to the horizon, but also the more the spotter was affected by the pitch and roll of the ship. In addition, the higher the position, the sturdier the "spotting top" had to be.

In the lead-up to World War I, British designers had a heated debate over whether the spotter needed to be below the level of the funnel, to avoid interference with funnel smoke (Friedman 2015, 120–21).

"The distance to the horizon for most spotting heights on capital ships is about 24,000 yards" (NAVORD 1944, 10A7).

"During World War I kite balloons … were towed by battleships at a height of from 1,000 to 3,000 feet, and carried a spotter who was in communication with the ship by telephone." This practice "limited the maneuverability of the ship," and "aircraft spotters took the place of balloon spotters" (NAVORD 1944, 10A7).

Fire Control Position

There was also the question of whether the spotting and computing functions should be concentrated in the same location. Doing so obviously facilitated oral communication of observations to the computers, but it would also put the computers in a more vulnerable position than if they were buried in the bowels of the ship. Ultimately, they were separated.

Fire Control: Collection of Targeting Data

Own Speed

In the early twentieth century, several methods existed for determining one's own speed. These methods were used primarily for navigation, but they could also be used in fire control.

First, there was the engine revolution counter. The ship designers would have predicted the correlation between the propeller rpm and the ship speed, and this correlation could have been refined during the ship's sea trials by running the ship over a measured course. Wave action could reduce the speed below that so predicted (Lockwood and Adamson 2018, 179).

Second, there was the "patent log," invented in the nineteenth century; this item had a propeller-like element that was rotated by the water rushing by. Some had mechanical or electrical means so that the number of rotations could be read from the taffrail without hauling in the device (EB 1911, "Log"). The patent log was still used by the Royal Navy in World War I (Goldrick 2015, 45). In 1940, the captain of the merchant ship *Rothesay Castle* was held liable for the ship's grounding, in part because he failed to use the patent log (Malcolm 2013).

Third, there was the pitometer log. This tool measures the total pressure of seawater in the direction of motion and perpendicularly to it, and it either measures the pressure difference or generates an equalizing pressure. The side pressure is just the hydrostatic pressure of the water, whereas the forward pressure is augmented by the motion, including a dynamic pressure proportional to the squared velocity (U.S. Navy 2013, 10–14). During World War II, this was the principal "own speed" input for USN fire control systems (NAVORD 1944, 17A5).

All of these methods measured the speed of the ship relative to that of the water, not its absolute speed. If the engines were at dead stop and the water current five knots, the ship would be moving at five knots across the Earth's surface, but the logs would register zero motion. (Modern GPS reports true speed.)

Own Course

The ship's heading is where the bow is pointed relative to north; the ship's course is its actual path through the water relative to north. The heading differs from the course by the leeway angle. Leeway could be estimated by studying the ship's wake; the leeway angle is the angle the wake makes with the keel. On October 12, 1944, the destroyer escort USS *Mason* reported that the convoy it was escorting was "averaging 15 degrees leeway" (Blackford 1996, 43).

Early modern sailors read their heading by comparing it to their magnetic compass, which pointed to magnetic north (or south). The magnetic compass reading requires correction for magnetic variation (caused by changes in the Earth's magnetic field) and deviation (caused by ferromagnetic materials on board). A gyrocompass finds true north. In World War II, USN fire control systems received heading data from the ship's gyrocompass (NAVORD 1944, 17A5).

Own Roll and Pitch

A gyroscope establishes a stable vertical. This is adjusted, as the ship sails, for the curvature of the Earth, so it corresponds to the local vertical. The deviation of the perpendicular to the deck plane from this stable vertical is determined and ultimately resolved into components in ("level angle") and across ("cross-level angle") the line of sight to the target, for use as adjustments.

Target Bearing

The target bearing is its angular position relative to the host ship's heading. With experience, target bearing can be estimated by eye within 5–10 degrees (U.S. Navy 2002, 3–13). Various training devices have been developed that allowed the student to view and judge a simulated ship under controlled conditions without knowing its relative bearing and then learn how good the estimate was (Brown 1945, 3–4).

In the early modern period, an azimuth (bearing) compass—a magnetic compass with sights—was used to determine the bearing of an object close to the horizon, for navigational purposes. The modern approach is to manufacture a separate bearing circle (alidade) that can be mounted over a magnetic or gyro compass. The sights may be simple or telescopic. The optical system may superimpose a view of a section of the compass on the telescope view.

Azimuths may be measured to an accuracy of 0.5 degrees in quiet water, 1 degree with the slightest roll, and 2 degrees or more at sea (Mixter et al. 1979, 45). Bearings taken when the compass is not in the horizontal plane are inaccurate. The bearing circle may include a bubble spirit level, and it may even be self-leveling via a pendulum element.

Target Range

Range estimation was addressed in chapter 11.

Target Speed and Course

In the modern U.S. Navy, target course is expressed as the "target angle"—the angle that the line of sight from the target ship to your ship makes to the target's bow (U.S. Navy 2007, 20). Norman Friedman (2013, 30) states that "at short ranges ... it was relatively easy to guess enemy course by how foreshortened the target looked." Observers trained themselves to estimate course by studying models of enemy ships, and they might be aided by instruments that measured the angular width of the enemy ship and calculated the angle it made to the line of bearing if the range and ship length were known.

Speed was initially estimated based on study of the enemy ship's bow wave and stern wake, and changes in range and bearing might also be considered (a ship overtaking you, on the same course, is clearly going faster than you) (U.S. Navy 2007, 22).

Ships were given dazzle camouflage (sometimes including a fake bow wave) to make it difficult to judge course and speed. But even without camouflage, in the early twentieth century, course was estimated by eye only to about a point (11.25 degrees) accuracy, and speed was typically 15–30 percent off (Friedman 2013, 45).

Once fire control had the benefit of a succession of range and bearing observations, the average target speed and course could be calculated. But this calculation was meaningful only if they had been essentially constant over the period in question.

Fall of Shot

Observation of missed shots may be used to correct the computed range and bearing.

Target Elevation and Altitude

For aerial targets, the fire control system also needed the aircraft's elevation angle ("position angle") as an input. Combined with the slant range, the aircraft altitude could be calculated. If it was flying level, the elevation would increase as it approached.

Environmental Conditions

Air pressure, temperature and humidity, and wind speed and direction will affect projectile trajectory. There are standard meteorological devices for measuring these variables. However, the wind that is felt by an anemometer on a ship is the apparent wind, not the true wind.

Additionally, shipboard sensors detect the near-surface values, not those characterizing the atmosphere through which a high trajectory passes. Conditions at higher altitudes may be reported by friendly aircraft or sampled by releasing sounding balloons (NAVORD 1944, 13B8, 13B14).

Gun Characteristics

The gun characteristics that affect fire control are relatively static and thus can be stored in a database and updated as needed.

Based on exterior ballistics models (corrected based on test firings), there was a range table for each gun, relating the trajectory characteristics to the gun's true elevation and the choice of projectile and charge.

The vertical and horizontal position of the gun was sometimes significantly different from the position of the observer whose measurements of target bearing and range were used in the computation. Not only would this discrepancy result in a displacement of the trajectory, but, if not accounted for, the magnitude and direction of the displacement would also be affected by the yaw, pitch and roll of the ship.

Each gun had limitations in terms of maximum elevation and depression, traversal without "wooding" (having its line of sight or fire blocked), and speed of elevation and traversal.

There was also a firing interval between when the firing order was received and when the projectile left the muzzle.

Ideally, the trunnion axis of the gun was parallel to the deck plane. If it wasn't, that would modify the effective elevation and train (NAVORD 1944, 13D5).

Guns also exhibited droop (downward curvature of the bore) and jump (an upward kick of the muzzle end), both of which changed the angle of departure of the projectile from the nominal angle of elevation of the gun.

The muzzle velocity was affected by the powder temperature (NAVORD 1944, 13B6) and barrel erosion (13B7).

Fire Control: Computation

Until the gun is fired, and during the "firing interval," the combined motions of the firing ship and the target ship cause the range and bearing of the target ship to continuously change. When the projectile leaves the muzzle, its velocity is the vector sum of the velocity imparted by the gun and the velocity of the ship. When the projectile is in flight, the firing ship's further motion is irrelevant, but the target's motion during the "time in flight" must have been anticipated in order for the projectile to strike its "advanced position."

Friedman (2013, 22) says, "Only once a ship's motion had been cancelled out did it really matter whether the range to the target was known." As a result of the relative motion of the ships, and late nineteenth-century warship speeds, the range could change at a rate of "200 yards or more per minute" (23).

The range to look up in the range tables is not the geometric range at the time the decision is made to fire, but rather the range at which the target is expected to be when the projectile descends low enough to strike it. If the firing ship and the target ship are moving at a constant direction and speed, the range will be changing at a "nearly constant" rate (Friedman 2013, 43), and the range to set is the sum of the geometric range and the product of the "range rate" and the sum of the firing interval and the time of flight. But the time of flight is itself a function of the range.

The problem of the combined motions of the gun and target could be solved by hand using the same traverse tables that were used for navigation. These were essentially precomputed trig tables for converting a distance on a course to a latitude and longitude change; you replaced "distance" with "speed" and interpreted "latitude" as rate of change parallel to the line of fire and "longitude" as the perpendicular rate.

Let us look at two "first generation" British mechanical fire control computing systems: the Dumaresq and the Vickers range clock.

The Dumaresq

During the early twentieth century, crude analog mechanical computers were used to consider the effect of gun and target motions on the proper range and bearing setting. One such device was the "Dumaresq," invented in 1902–1904 and variations of which were used in World War I (Friedman 2013, 29ff).

The Dumaresq subtracted the firing ship's velocity (direction and speed) from the enemy ship's velocity, resolving the difference into components along the line of bearing (the range rate) and perpendicular to it (the deflection rate). First, the inner ring was rotated to the enemy's bearing relative to your bow. Then the outer ring was rotated to your own heading. A slider was mounted on an overhead bar supported by the outer ring, and this slider was moved "aftward" to show your speed forward, thus subtracting it. A ring hung down from the slider, which was rotated to show the enemy heading. This ring had a slider bar, and the slider was moved to show the enemy speed. A pointer hung down from that slider, marking a point on a graph that indicated the corresponding range and deflection rates (yards/minute).

Unfortunately, period rangefinders were not sufficiently accurate to make good estimates of range rates, which, after all, were the differences between range measurements made at short time intervals (*ibid.*). As for bearing rates, the trouble was that ships yawed back and forth a great deal, so the bearing rate output was very "noisy" (44).

Vickers Range Clock

The Dumaresq yielded range and deflection rates, but for firing orders, the range and deflection angle at a specified future time was needed. To obtain those numbers, one must integrate the rates.

On the Vickers "range clock" (1903), a wheel spun at constant speed, and a spherical roller connected to an output shaft was held against it; the closer to the rim it was, the faster it turned. The roller was set to a position based on the computed range rate, and the outputs were the current true range (black hand) and the adjusted range for targeting (red hand). The latter would be entered into the range tables. Unfortunately, the range rate wasn't constant even if speeds and courses were maintained. Later models included adjustments for time or flight and wind (Friedman 2013, 1854).

Ford Rangekeeper

The Ford rangekeeper essentially combined the functionalities of the Dumaresq and the Vickers range clock into a single analog computer (Mindell 2004, 36–37). "The first one was installed in the battleship *Texas* in 1917" (Wildenberg 2015). The rangekeeper, of course, continued to evolve.

Fire Control: Communication and Automation

The targeting data had to be timely communicated to the computers, and the results to the gunners. This communication could be done by voice (through a sound pipe or over a phone or radio) or by an electrical signal from one machine to another. The concerns were transmitting the data accurately and without disruption by enemy action.

After the firing solution was computed, it had to be conveyed to the guns. One way of doing this was to transmit the required offsets to receivers at the guns. The pointer and trainer would subsequently elevate and traverse the gun until its scales matched the numbers on the receivers. The gun could then be fired either by the director or locally.

In later practice, the gun was automatically elevated and traversed in response to the orders from the centralized fire control system.

World War II Director Fire Control System: An Example

A "director" is a device for controlling "the elevation, training and firing of a group of guns." On, say, a battleship, the director could be large enough so that the personnel operating the device are seated inside it (NAVORD 1944, Fig. 18A4). It has been called a "master gun" (10A5), but it can't actually fire a shot itself.

On a World War II USN battleship, the main battery had two primary directors, both Mark 38s (NAVORD 1944, 18A2), "the forward one being about 120 feet above the waterline, the after one about 75 feet" (10B3). Each was staffed by a spotter, trainer, pointer (leveler), cross-leveler, rangefinder operator, parallax range setter and stand-by rangefinder operator (18A5). The main battery plotting room lay, protected, below deck. This room contained the Mark 8 rangekeeper (computer), Mark 41 stable vertical (element), and the range receiver (18A2).

A simplified description of the director fire operation follows: The target was designated, by relative bearing, by the fire control tower and communicated electrically to the primary director for the guns that were to engage that target. The fire control tower contained an auxiliary (Mark 40) director and an auxiliary computer.

The director was turned to the designated target bearing. Range information was provided by the rangefinder, which on the Mark 38 was a 26.5-foot stereoscopic rangefinder with a range transmitter (NAVORD 1944, 18A3). The spotter, using a 12-power periscope, "estimate[d] target angle, target speed, and wind conditions

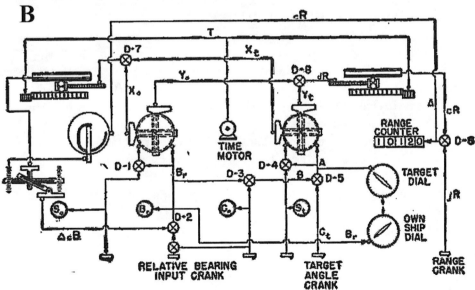

(A) Rangekeeper operator correcting range (BNP 1956, 288). The operator would have compared the computed present range (a counter reading) to the observed range. (B) Mechanical schematic of a rangekeeper (BNP 1951, 146–47). The integrators are in the upper corners. The sliding device in the lower left represents a multiplier. There are also differential gears (X in a circle), two component solvers, a computing cam, dials and hand cranks. The hand of the operator in (A) is presumably on the "range crank."

and telephones these values to plot so they may be entered into the range keeper" (18A5).

The 1944 naval manual makes no reference to radar, possibly for security reasons. On the USS *Iowa*, a Mark 8 (FH) radar, providing range and bearing information, was mounted on top of the Mark 38 directors in 1943 (Dramiński 2020, 24–25).

The rangekeeper, taking these and other inputs into account, generated expected future target relative bearings as train angles for the director. Computations were made relative to the "main battery reference point," which was usually the auxiliary director in the fire control tower (NAVORD 1944, 18A2).

The trainer looked for the target through his telescope, mounted on the hub. If the crosshairs stayed on the target, then the rangekeeper solution was a good one, and the director train drive was left under rangekeeper control. If they drifted off, the trainer used handwheels to correct the train angle, and this angle, corrected for parallax with respect to the main-battery reference point, was transmitted to the rangekeeper (NAVORD 1944, 18A5).

The leveler and cross-leveler turned "their handwheels to keep their crosswires on the horizon." This action caused the director to generate the level and cross-level angles, which corrected for the ship's roll and pitch. If they couldn't observe the horizon, then they "matched pointers on dials actuated by a stable element" in the plotting room (NAVORD 1944, 18A4).

The rangekeeper calculated a gun-elevation order that "consists of level angle added to the sight angle corrected for the effect of trunnion tilt," and a gun-train order that "is director train combined with the computed sight deflection corrected for the effect of trunnion tilt" (NAVORD 1944, 18A7). These orders were sent to the turrets as indications (to be matched by the turret crew) or automatic settings (to drive servos). In either case, these orders were corrected at the turret for the difference in line of sight between the turret and the reference point (18A4). The corrected values were expressed as angular offsets from the line of sight (16A8).

"Using a director system it is possible to reduce the amount of pointing and training by laying the guns at predetermined angles and firing them as ship roll and pitch bring the guns into the required position" (NAVORD 1944, 16A6).

The rangekeeper activated a time-of-flight buzzer just before a salvo was expected to strike, to warn the spotter to be alert and observe the fall of shot. The spotter then phoned in the outcome to the plotting room, and the firing solution was corrected as needed.

Chapter 13

Beyond the Gun

A warship could be armed with weapons other than guns. The choices included flamethrowers ("Greek fire"), rockets, missiles, torpedoes and depth charges. In addition, a ship could be turned into a projectile.

Rams

Rams are known, from artwork, to have been introduced no later than around 850 BCE (Casson 1991, 76). The advantage of the ram was its ability to inflict underwater damage on the enemy warship. The sine qua non was the ability to maneuver to face the enemy's beam and to achieve a high enough speed to strike it before the target could turn away (in both respects, regardless of wind direction). This method was feasible with the ancient oared warship, given a sufficient number of rowers.

Once the enemy vessel was rammed, it was important that the attacker be able to back away, lest it be boarded by the enemy's marines or rammed by another enemy ship while encumbered. The original, pointed ram could get stuck. It was eventually replaced by an improved ram with "a blunt, roughly square face with three transverse fins." Its purpose wasn't to punch a hole in the enemy hull, but rather to loosen the latter's seams (Casson 1991, 89), causing it to take on water. One example from the second century BCE was a bronze casting that weighed more than a thousand pounds (135).

Ramming attacks were extremely rare in the Age of Sail. The ships of this period were not designed for ramming because their reliance on the wind made the necessary maneuvering and acceleration difficult. Since they were not intended to ram, their bows were weak, relative to their sides, and so ramming was more likely to damage the attacker. In addition, during the approach, the enemy's broadside would be fired down the would-be rammer's throat.

However, steam power (and armor) made ramming more attractive. Waterline armor could be extended at the bow to form a ram. CSS *Virginia* successfully rammed the USS *Cumberland* in 1862. Ramming was also used successfully by the Union at the First Battle of Memphis (1862) and by the Austrians at the Battle of Lissa (1866) (Clowes 1894).

That said, ramming was only rarely productive. "Most rammers had insufficient

A Currier and Ives lithograph depicting the sinking of the USS *Cumberland* by CSS *Virginia* on March 8, 1862. Courtesy of the Beverly Robinson Collection, U.S. Naval Academy Museum, Annapolis, Maryland. Courtesy of the U.S. Naval History and Heritage Command, Catalog No. NH-64088-KN.

power and maneuverability, and most rammees seemed able to alter course, often only just in time, to make the blow a glancing rather than a perpendicular one" (Hill 2000, 36). Statistics confirm this view, at least when the rammee had freedom to maneuver (see Table 13–1).

Table 13–1: Ramming Statistics, 1861–1879

Rammee	Nil	Slight Damage	Serious Damage	Disabled	Sunk	Total
under steam with sea room	26	5	1			32
under steam, narrow waters	9	9	3	2	9	32
unmanageable or at anchor	1	4	1		4	10
Total	36	18	5	2	13	74
Effect on Rammer	56	13	3	1	1	74

(Clowes 1894, 92–93)

The ramming of submarines by surface ships was considerably more effective. During World War I, at least sixteen German or Austrian submarines were sunk by ramming (as compared to twenty-one apiece by gunfire and depth charges). In four cases, a merchant vessel accomplished this feat (ONI 1918, 6). Admittedly, the number of failed attempts is not stated.

Ramming could be "effective even against a submerged submarine at periscope depth, which for German submarines meant that the upper part of the pressure hull was only about 10 or 12 feet below the surface, with the conning tower less than that." HMS *Dreadnought*, which drew 29 feet, rammed and sank *U-29* in 1915 (Farquharson-Roberts 2014, 180).

While there were more anti-submarine assets available in World War II, "twenty-seven U-boats were rammed [by British ships] with some degree of success in 1940–43, and in about half of these cases ramming was the major cause of sinking" (Lavery 2016, 239).

The downside was that ramming could result in damage to the rammer, such as loss of sonar underwater fittings (Gardner 1999, 106) or an injured bow. The latter might take seven to eight weeks to repair (Owen 2006, 140). (Some "destroyers were fitted with reinforced bows" [Osborne 2005, 60].) Occasionally, the rammer sank, as in the case of HMS *Fairy* (in 1918) (Henry 2006). HMS *Harvester* was disabled after ramming *U-444* in 1943 and then torpedoed and sunk by *U-432* (Helgason 2023). Subsequently, ramming by British warships was "officially discouraged" (MacIntyre 2019).

Fireships

A fireship—an expendable vessel filled with combustible materials—was used by Sicily against Athens in the Battle of the Great Harbor (413 BCE), and there were other instances of fireship use during the ancient and medieval periods (CANI 2017).

Probably the most famous use of fireships was against the Spanish Armada. They did not actually harm any of the Spanish ships, but the Spanish "cut their cables" (thus losing their anchors) and fled in great disorder (Lewis 1960, 154). A half-century later, Zheng Zhilong, using large, seemingly normal junks as fireships, humiliated a Dutch squadron at the Battle of Liaoluo Bay (1633) (Andrade 2016, 205–6). But the most decisive use of fireships in Chinese history was at the Battle of Poyang Lake (1363), which led to the creation of the Ming Dynasty (Andrade 2016, 64).

Fireships were "the subject of an early arms control proposal, when the Dutch proposed a mutual renunciation of fireships just before the second Dutch war." Ironically, the Earl of Sandwich, who was "chiefly instrumental in rejecting the proposal," perished when his first-rate flagship *Royal James* was destroyed by the Dutch fireship *Vrede* in 1672 (Davies 2008, 60).

Fireships continued to be deployed from time to time up through the nineteenth century—that is, until the replacement of wood with iron made them ineffectual.

During the eighteenth century, a distinction could be drawn between "temporary" fireships (which were typically old ships, or prizes, hastily converted into fireships) and "permanent" ones (which were built for such use). The first British "permanent" fireships were two-deckers, classified as fifth rates. Their construction was first authorized in 1689. The lower deck ports, held open, would create a draft, and these "were fitted with lids hinged at the bottom … so that they could not be closed by fire burning through the tackles that held the lid. Aft on the same deck was a large sallyport through which the final skeleton crew could escape into a boat," towed behind it. "On the deck above a lattice-work was constructed as a false platform on which combustibles could be stored, while large chimneys were fitted through the upper deck to increase the circulation of air." Under the 1703 Establishment, a typical crew was 45 men, as opposed to 115 for a normal fifth-rate ship. The fireships also had fewer, lighter guns (Winfield 2010, 1600).

The arrangement of the incendiary materials and fusing was intended to cause the entire ship to catch fire simultaneously. Another concern was protecting the incendiary material from sea spray.

Below deck, iron chambers, charged with gunpowder, were positioned to blow open the ports. Troughs and cross-troughs were laid down in the "fire-room," and reeds and bavins (bundles of wood), previously dipped in incendiary composition, were tied down in them. Curtains, also so dipped, were hung from the beams. Fire barrels containing the composition were placed strategically around the fire room. Fire-trunks conducted the flame to the shrouds above deck. All of these materials were connected with quick-match (Steel 1812, 398; Simmons 1812, 152–53).

Theophilus Beauchant describes methods of creating a "temporary fire ship" (1828, 137–44). He also comments, "It is not so much against the hull, as the rigging and sails of an enemy, the fire should be directed. Experience has proved that the best fire ship composition will take some hours to burn through the deck and sides of a vessel. Attention should therefore be given to creating as much flame aloft as possible; and the yards should be secured by chains, that they may support it. Curtains … should be nailed to fore and after parts of the yards" (144–45).

Toward the same end, Robert Simmons describes placing fire-boxes, filled with the incendiary composition, above deck in various locations: "It was found that two men with lighted port-fires can set fire to the whole of the leaders on the deck, bowsprit, catheads, outriggers, etc. in less than a minute…. The leaders are laid in painted canvas hose" (1812, 153–54).

The fireship had to be steered by a skeleton crew, which ideally abandoned ship just before impact. Since that timing exposed them (and their escape boat) longer to gunshot, they were often tempted to ignite the powder train early. "At the battles off La Rochelle in 1628, at least seven English fireship captains were court-martialled for this offense," and, in 1667, the Dutch sentenced one captain to death by firing squad, while three others were dishonorably discharged (Kirsch 2009).

Fireships were most useful in constricted waters, where the target ships would have difficulty in maneuvering out of harm's way. On rivers, an upstream attacker might be able to deploy a crewless fireship, since the current would carry the fireship down and evasive action was limited.

"Hellburners" (Explosion Vessels)

These are the less common siblings of the fireship, carrying explosives rather than incendiaries. They were first used in 1585 at the siege of Antwerp (Officers 1881, 280).

Italy used explosive-laden motorboats to damage the moored heavy cruiser HMS *York* in 1941 (Bagnasco 2023, 57).

The Japanese navy's *Shinyo* motorboats had bow-mounted explosives, whereas those used by the army were supposed to drop a depth charge with a six-second time fuse and make a U-turn (still effectively a kamikaze mission). The navy expected a "10 percent hit rate," but the actual success was even more limited (Hackett and Kingsepp 2011).

Explosive vessels still have relevance, as they are capable of damaging steel-hulled vessels. Even a small boat laden with high explosives could do substantial damage if it detonated nearby, as in the case of the 2000 attack on the USS *Cole* (DDG-67), which created a hole 40 feet in diameter (Gartner and Segura 2021, 163).

Most recently, Ukraine used unmanned surface vessels to attack the Russian Black Sea Fleet (Ozberk 2022). Such vessels may follow a set course, be remote-controlled, or (if they have suitable sensors) be autonomously guided to their target.

Flamethrowers

Byzantine warships carried pumps that could project a flammable liquid ("Greek fire"). While it was a short-range weapon, it likely would have discouraged the enemy from attempting to ram or board the Byzantine *dromon*, thus limiting them to arrow and ballista fire. The composition of Greek fire, as well as the flamethrower apparatus, remained a state secret and thus has been the subject of speculation for centuries. It seems likely that the composition was petroleum based, and John Haldon (2006) was able to construct a full-scale working device that could plausibly have been constructed in the seventh century.

The Byzantines appear to have abandoned Greek fire after the twelfth century, possibly because of loss of access to petroleum sources (Haldon 2006, 316). However, incendiaries could still be projected by catapults and ballistae. Later, guns became available for firing "carcasses" and heated shot.

The naval flamethrower made a brief, limited return in World War II. Essentially, it was intended to provide merchant ships with a means of persuading German dive bombers to drop their bombs from a higher altitude, out of the flame's reach.

The flamethrower was first developed for airfield defense, and Lagonda Car Company came up with a device that burned "a mixture of diesel oil and tar" and projected a flame "thirty feet in diameter" for "about a hundred yards" (Pawle 2009, 45). "Fired vertically," from the trawler *La Patrie*, "the length of the flame was increased by its own heat," reaching "an altitude of at least four hundred feet" (46).

Nonetheless, the initial tests of the naval version were somewhat problematic. The first pilot, who knew what to expect, wasn't fazed. The second test was with "a pilot who had no previous knowledge of the flame-gun." He nonetheless nonchalantly took his wing through the flames. They might have abandoned the project at that point, had he not confessed that his prewar job was driving "cars through sheets of plate-glass and walls of fire for a stunt firm" (Pawle 2009, 47).

Some flamethrowers "were mounted in coasters plying between the Thames and the Forth." The devices were problematic—they had high fuel consumption (eight gallons per second); their high pressures created maintenance issues; and they could spray fuel all over the deck. Nonetheless, "the average height of attack soon lifted far above two hundred feet," possibly because the Luftwaffe was concerned by intelligence reports of the new weapon (Pawle 2009, 48).

Rockets, Unguided

Rockets are self-propelled projectiles with very slow burning propellants. Rockets were first used in naval combat by Chinese warships in the twelve century (Denny 2011, 28). Their first use in Europe appears to have been by the French in the fifteenth century, in siege warfare. Several early modern books describe rocket construction, including Biringuccio's *Pyrotechnics* (1540), the anonymous *Book of Cannons and Fireworks* (1561), Pavelourt's *Brief Instructions on Matters of French Artillery* (1597), and Lorrain's *Pyrotechnics* (1630).

The "rockets' red glare" in "The Star-Spangled Banner" refers to the British shipborne Congreve rockets, intended for attacking land targets. Their flight was crudely stabilized by a long (15-foot) stick (the rocket proper was 3.5 feet long). They weren't very effective against Fort McHenry, but a Congreve rocket assault had been much more successful against the softer target of Copenhagen, destroying three-quarters of the city in 1807.

In the Second Battle of Chuanbi (1841), during the Opium War, "the very first rocket fired from the *Nemesis* was seen to enter the large junk against which it was directed … and almost instantly it blew up with a terrific explosion." The Qing abandoned the rest of their warjunks in dismay (Andrade 2016, 254).

In the early nineteenth century, naval rockets were typically launched from boats or by a landing party rather than from a warship deck. They could be given different payloads; carcass rockets were used against towns and shell rockets against troops or shore batteries. Extreme range was 2,000–3,500 yards (Beauchant 1828, 95ff). Effective ranges were more like 800–1,200 yards, but rockets did have the advantage of a high rate of fire—perhaps ten per minute (Wise 1979, 31).

William Hale's "rotary" rockets (patented in 1844) were spin-stabilized (see chapter 10) as a result of the combined action of fins and secondary exhaust nozzles; the United States used these rockets in the Mexican War. There was a launcher ("Machine Rocket, War, Naval") designed for seaborne use; it looks to me like an elevatable tube that would mount outboard. The Hale rockets were made in two sizes, 9 and 24 pounds, with the former having a maximum effective range of 1,200 yards (EB 1911, "Rocket").

Mousetrap, a USN anti-submarine rocket with a hydrostatic fuse, was placed in service in 1942. It was typically used by light vessels to test the suspected presence of a submarine before depth charges were deployed (Christman 1971, 131–33).

Rockets were also used for shore bombardment by the American "brown water" navy, including World War II landing boats and subsequent amphibious fire support ships (Hoppe 2021).

The principal advantage of a rocket is that the launch device does not feel any recoil. Momentum is conserved in that the backward movement of the exhaust gases

A 1945 image of a naval LSMR ("Landing Ship Medium, Rocket") showing an array of loaded rocket launchers. Image is believed to be of the LSM(R) 190, carrying 4-inch fin-stabilized aircraft rockets (MacKay 2016, 32). National Archives. Courtesy of the Naval History and Heritage Command, Catalog No. USN 700732.

compensates for the forward movement of the rocket. Consequently, the launch device (and the ship!) can be a lot lighter than what would be the case if it had to absorb the recoil that would be necessary to propel a projectile of the same power to the same range from a conventional gun. (It is because of that lack of recoil that a shoulder-fired rocket launcher, the bazooka, is possible.)

Another advantage relates to impact velocity. A rocket can be engineered to achieve a higher impact velocity than an equivalent shell (shell mass corresponding to rocket payload, artillery charge to rocket propellant). The shell stops accelerating when it leaves the muzzle, so from that time on its speed decreases, thanks to aerodynamic drag. However, the rocket is still burning fuel after launch, and whenever this propulsive force exceeds the drag force, its speed will increase. For any given time to impact, the rocket may be given a fuel fraction sufficient to ensure that its impact speed will be greater than that of the equivalent shell (Denny 2011, 142).

The great disadvantage of the rocket is that it is inaccurate. While spin stabilization definitely improved accuracy, variation in burn rate can also be a problem, especially with solid propellants. The first solution to the accuracy problem was to fire rockets in large numbers. Another solution was to give the rocket a guidance system, which turned it into a missile.

Missiles

The first missiles used in warfare were the German V-1 flying bomb and V-2 rocket of World War II. A missile is a rocket with a guidance system. There are two basic kinds of guidance systems: remote and autonomous.

With remote guidance, the missile receives signals from an operator. One possibility is a radio control system; in this setup, the missile must carry a radio receiver, and jamming is possible. Another possible remote guidance system is by electric wire; the wire remains attached to the missile after launch, and reels out as it flies, and the gunner steers it by signals sent down-wire.

Bear in mind that effective remote guidance requires that the operator be able to visualize the target and its relationship to the rocket—and the rocket, at least, is moving very quickly.

An autonomous guidance system is carried entirely by the missile. In an "open loop" system, it is just following preprogrammed instructions. It can follow a complex course, but there is no adaptation to circumstances. In "closed loop," it can sense the environment and respond to what it senses.

It should be obvious, but all the guidance in the world is of no use unless the missile has the ability to adjust its flight. This can take a number of forms, such as adjustable tail fins, moveable vanes in the exhaust chamber, a gimbaled engine, or side thrusters.

Of course, if the designer must make room for guidance and maneuver systems, there is that much less space for payload and propellant. Firing many cheap, inaccurate rockets is sometimes more effective than firing a small number of missiles. The value of guidance and maneuver increases with range to target (and target value).

A Terrier anti-aircraft missile was fired experimentally from the battleship USS *Mississippi* in 1954. The "world's first guided missile cruiser," the USS *Boston* (CAG-1), was a *Baltimore*-class heavy cruiser refitted in 1955 with Terriers (BSJ 1956). The first ship equipped with surface-to-surface missiles (SSMs) was probably the Russian destroyer *Bedovyi*, which began missile trials in 1952 (Mawdsley 1992). The first

SSM engagement, between Israeli and Syrian missile boats, was the Battle of Latakia during the 1973 Yom Kippur War (Grant 2011, 342).

A "cruise missile" reaches its target as a result of the combination of jet propulsion and aerodynamic lift. The USN's first cruise missile submarine was the converted USS *Tunny,* carrying a Regulus missile, and its first launch was in 1953 (Yenne 2018, 66). The USS *Halibut* (commissioned in 1960) was the first American nuclear submarine with cruise missiles. In 1967, the Israeli destroyer *Eilat* was sunk by a Styx cruise missile fired by an Egyptian Komar fast-attack craft (Hind 2008).

The term "ballistic missile" refers to a missile that, after a phase of powered flight, continues toward its target just like a normal unpowered artillery shell, experiencing the same exterior ballistics.

The Soviet Union added two missile launch tubes to a diesel-powered submarine and carried out a test launch of a Scud tactical ballistic missile from it in 1955 (Bukharin 2004, 237). Moreover, the original missile sub class, the Project V-611, had to surface for five minutes in order to launch (283). It was not until 1960 that the Soviet submariners had the ability to launch missiles while submerged (289).

Diesel submarines had to recharge their batteries every day or two, and they were more vulnerable to discovery when they came to the surface or to snorkel depth to do so. The USS *George Washington* (SSBN-598), launched in 1959, was the first nuclear-powered ballistic missile submarine; it test launched a Polaris missile in 1960 while submerged (NHHC 2023).

Missiles may be launched from vertical launch tubes (on deck or in the sail) or from torpedo tubes. The latter has the advantage of not adding new structures to the submarine design but limits it to the torpedo tube dimensions (in the USN, 21 inches diameter and 246 inches long) (Werrell 1985, 153).

Torpedoes

Torpedoes, in essence, are explosive projectiles that are fired at a target (or carried to it) and caused to explode underwater. That way, you may sink the enemy craft outright, which is much more difficult to do with a single shot hitting the target above water.

Spar Torpedoes

The spar torpedo was carried by a boat or submersible; essentially it is an explosive charge at the end of a long spar (reminding one of the adage "He who sups with the Devil must carry a long spoon"). Making it long enough to safeguard the attacker, but not so long as to render the attacker unable to maneuver, was a problem. In 1864, the Confederate submersible *Hunley* sank the USS *Housatonic,* but pressure waves caused by the blast may have killed the *Hunley*'s crew (Lance 2020, 124).

One proposal was that after the spar contacted the target, the torpedo would be detached from the spar and be left behind in the target's hull; the attacker would then reverse course and set off the torpedo with a spooled-off lanyard from a safe distance. But judging that distance was still tricky. A lanyard-detonated spar torpedo was used by a Union steam launch to destroy the CSS *Albemarle*, but the force of the explosion filled the launch with water, forcing its abandonment (Bradford 1882, 23–25; Coggins 2012, 149).

While a submersible has the advantage when it comes to stealth, spar torpedoes were more frequently delivered by small, high-speed surface attack boats. Spar torpedo boats were successfully used by the French against the Chinese in the Battle of Foochow (1884) and the Battle of Sheipu (1885) (Sleeman 1889, 338).

Towed Torpedoes

The Harvey towing torpedo was towed on a line off a ship's quarter. The towing ship would run past the target so it would strike the tow line; the torpedo would then swing around and hit the target. Its range was limited by the length of the tow line. It was adopted by Russia in 1869 and England in 1870, and experimented with by the United States, but abandoned after self-propelled torpedoes became available (Sleeman 1889, 229; Duke 2023, 7–8).

Locomotive (Self-Propelled) Torpedoes

The greatest disadvantages of the early locomotive torpedoes were their short range and low speed, which were far inferior to those of cannon shells, let alone rockets. Many methods of torpedo propulsion were investigated.

Flywheel. In the Howell torpedo (1870–1898), a 132-pound flywheel was spun up to 10,000–12,000 rpm by a tube-mounted steam turbine. This arrangement acted both to drive the propeller shaft and (with the flywheel axis horizontal and perpendicular to the torpedo axis) to act as a gyroscope to keep the torpedo on course. The kinetic energy stored in a flywheel is proportional to the density and to the squares of the rotational speed and the diameter. Energy storage was limited by the strength/density ratio of the available materials. The design appears to have maxed out at 1,000 yards and 30 knots (Bull 2004, 272).

Compressed air. The Whitehead torpedo was propelled by internal compressed air that drove a piston engine, which in turn drove the propeller. The original torpedo had a single propeller, but the *Encyclopedia Britannica* 1911 article refers to twin propellers. If these are contra-rotated, it will defeat the tendency of a single prop torpedo to turn in a circle.

Some historical perspective may be helpful. The first Whitehead torpedo (1866) had a range of almost 330 yards at less than 6 knots. A decade later, it could reach 545 yards at 18 knots (Ireland and Grove 1997, 41). The 1894 Mark I had a range of 800 yards, at 26.5–27.5 knots (Jolie 1978).

John Ericsson experimented (1873) with a torpedo that had compressed air supplied through a hose from a shore station, rather than carried onboard. Its range was limited by the length of the hose (800 feet), and it made only 3 knots (Jolie 1978; King 1894, 65).

Winched wire. The Brennan torpedo (1876–1906) was used for shore defense. On board, there were two drums wound with wire. When the torpedo was launched, shore-based engines drew out these wires. The drums were connected to twin contra-rotated propellers. The shore operator steered the torpedo by controlling the speeds of the two engines. If the drums rotated at different rates, the rudder was shifted accordingly. The speed was 20–27 knots, depending on the gauge of the wire, and "the operator was able to hit a floating fruit basket at 2000 yards" (Mitchell n.d.). One problem was that the wire was thick and thus "required a mass of wire so large that it was inconvenient and even dangerous aboard a ship" (Weir 2019, 123).

Combustion. One option is internal combustion; the torpedo burns alcohol or kerosene, and the combustion gases drive a piston or turbine. Or you can use external combustion; the combustion chamber is cooled with water ("wet heater"), which is flashed into steam. The Bliss-Leavitt Mark 7 steam torpedo (1912) ran 600 yards at 35 knots (Newpower 2006, 18–19). The deck-launched U.S. Mark 15 steam torpedo had three speeds, ranging from 26.5 knots (15,000 yards) to 45 knots (6,000 yards) (NAVORD 1957, 12A5).

The source of oxygen for combustion was typically compressed air. Since air contains nitrogen, which is not consumed, the torpedo would leave a trail of nitrogen gas bubbles. It was recognized at a very early stage that pure oxygen would be better than compressed air; the weight of the nitrogen would be eliminated, and the torpedo would be wakeless. So what's the catch? Well, if the oxygen torpedo exploded on the host ship, that would do tremendous damage. And this outcome was a real risk; oil and grease in the oxygen pipes could ignite spontaneously. On top of that, it is difficult to lubricate the moving parts of the torpedo properly without increasing oil and grease exposure.

"The Japanese began experimenting with oxygen-driven torpedoes about 1924, but gave up after numerous explosions and failures." Then, somewhat farcically, in 1927, faulty intelligence led them to believe that the British were well on their way to producing a workable oxygen torpedo, and they decided that they needed one too. It took the Japanese until 1933 to complete the development of the type 93 "long lance" oxygen torpedo. Part of the solution was beginning the ignition with air and only gradually changing over to oxygen. They also took many precautions against inadvertent oxygenation of the lubricants (Evans and Peattie 2012, 267).

Rocket. If expanding gases are jetted out the rear of the torpedo, rather than used to drive (via a piston, crankshaft and transmission) a propeller, you have a rocket torpedo. Rocket torpedoes tend to have high speeds (making them difficult to evade) but reduced range and accuracy.

A Major Hunt lost his life experimenting with a rocket torpedo in 1862 (King 1881). Rocket torpedoes were demonstrated by Francis Barber (1873) and Patrick Cunningham (1893), but they exhibited short range and erratic trajectories (Kirby 2000).

The "V (Jet) Torpedo" (1938–1942) was an experimental British design, essentially a standard torpedo "with the reciprocating engine removed and the number of burners increased from one to four" and the propeller replaced by a "convergent/divergent nozzle." As a simpler design, it was expected to be cheaper to manufacture. Unfortunately, in a 1942 test, it traveled for only 800 yards at 23 knots. While it was thought that replacing compressed air with oxygen would have improved the performance to an acceptable level, the project was terminated (Kirby 2000).

In the 1950s, the British tested various CAMROSE designs, one of which had a thrust of 2,600 pounds, which was expected to provide 60 knots underwater. In the final design, 1,150 yards at 35 knots, from 435 pounds of ammonium nitrate-guanidine nitrate RC pressed propellant, was hoped for. On one run, a CAMROSE notoriously left the water and endangered a hotel (Kirby 2000).

There was also experimentation with a rocket-assisted torpedo. Essentially a ballistic rocket carried a homing torpedo to the general vicinity of the target, and the torpedo took over from there. However, the rocket proved too inaccurate (Friedman 2004, 280).

Nonetheless, the Russians did deploy the APR-2E, an air-dropped homing torpedo with a rocket motor and solid propellant, with speeds up to 70 mph and a 1,640-yard range. The later APR-3E had some kind of hybrid propulsion system that also featured a water jet (RF 2016).

A more recent twist is the Russian *Shkval*, a supercavitating torpedo (1995). A cavitator cone at the nose creates a gas cavity. Ventilation ducts convey rocket exhaust into the bubble, enlarging it until it envelops the entire torpedo ("supercavitation"). This result reduced drag, allowing the torpedo to achieve a speed of 230 mph in water. It took 17 years for this torpedo to reach operational status, and at least the original version was only capable of a straight run without disrupting the gas envelope (Ashley 2001; Polmar and Moore 2004, 304; Branfill-Cook 2014, 73).

Electric cable. In one embodiment, the Sims-Edison torpedo (1889) carried about two miles of cable. This device had an inner core that carried the steering current (a polarized relay used electromagnets to pull on adjustable tiller rods) and an outer core carrying the main current feeding the electric motor. Its speed was over 20 mph. Tests showed that it could be launched from a ship (King 1881).

Electric battery. General John Foster patented a torpedo driven by a primary battery in 1872 (King 1894ars). But it took decades to develop batteries with high enough capacity and power per unit weight for practical torpedo use. Bear in mind that torpedoes require a lot of power but just for a short time, the necessary power being proportional to the cube of the speed.

In theory, all you need is a primary battery, since the torpedo is destroyed by use against an enemy. In practice, you need a rechargeable battery, since a limited number of torpedoes can be carried and "most torpedo firings … are practice shots" (Dell et al. 2007, 91).

Electric torpedoes are primarily submarine weapons; while they are slow and relatively short range, they do not leave a wake (Branfill-Cook 2014, 55).

The Mark 18, the USN's principal electric torpedo in World War II, ran 4,000 yards at 29 knots on lead-acid battery power. Charging the batteries resulted in production of hydrogen gas, which had to be vented or burned off so it didn't accumulate and cause an explosion. The batteries also had to be preheated to maintain efficiency and required frequent maintenance (U.S. Navy, Bureau of Ordnance 1943, 5, 26, 33, 34, 38).

"Since the 1970s, warshot torpedoes have been propelled principally by zinc-silver-oxide or magnesium-silver chloride reserve batteries" (Dell et al. 2007, 91).

Rocket-assisted torpedo. The post–World War II ASROC is a ballistic missile that delivers an acoustic homing torpedo to the vicinity of the submarine, thus increasing its effective range (Jolie 1978, 121). In the RUM-139A version, it is vertically launched, and "the range is controlled … by motor cutoff and airframe separation at a precalculated point in the trajectory. The … torpedo … is decelerated and stabilized by a parachute system before it enters the water" (Parsch 2004). After detection of water entry, the torpedo engine activates.

Torpedo Shape

Early torpedoes had pointed noses. Tests showed that the modern blunt nose created less drag (by about a knot), and a torpedo with a long, cylindrical midbody and hemispherical nose could hold more explosive and propellant (Jolie 1978).

Such a shape will have laminar (low-drag) flow only over the nose. There was

The USS *Concord* (CL-10) fires "a torpedo from her port side upper torpedo tubes, circa the early or middle 1920s." Note the cigar shape of the torpedo, with a long cylindrical midbody, a slightly rounded forebody and a tapered aftbody bearing fins. Courtesy of the U.S. Naval History and Heritage Command, Catalog No. NH 55317. The *Concord* was an *Omaha*-class light cruiser, in commission 1923–1945 (Wikipedia).

experimentation in the twentieth century with extended laminar flow shapes. One such shape has a long, pointed forebody and a short, funnel-like aftbody. But it can't be launched from a standard torpedo tube, laminar flow is degraded by a micron-size surface irregularity, and the observed region of laminar flow is less than predicted (Kirby 2000).

Maintaining Set Depth

In general, you want the torpedo to remain underwater; it's less vulnerable to enemy fire, a given explosive charge causes much more damage if the explosion is underwater, and the hull is likely to be weakest below the waterline (and any armor belt).

If you are trying to hit the side of the enemy ship, the ideal running depth would probably be half the draft of the latter, thus allowing for the most vertical error. By contrast, if you want to set off an explosion under the bottom of the ship, then you would set the depth to be several feet below the enemy keel. The latter strategy requires a proximity fuse, and you run the risk that the torpedo will pass under the enemy without exploding.

Some early torpedoes maintained a fixed depth by rigidly connecting a float above the torpedo, but the float made the torpedo easier to spot (Branfill-Cook 2014, 51).

Controlling depth requires a depth sensor and a feedback mechanism that inclines the diving planes accordingly. Robert Whitehead's December 1866 torpedo had a hydrostatic valve in which a rubber diaphragm separated the face of a piston from the water. The piston was spring-loaded. If the torpedo was too deep, the hydrostatic pressure would be greater than that exerted by the spring, and the diaphragm (and thus the piston) would be forced inward. The piston was connected by rods to the diving plane (horizontal rudder), which would be adjusted to cause the torpedo to glide upward. When the hydrostatic pressure equaled the spring pressure, the piston would return to the neutral position, and so would the diving plane. Obviously, the reverse would occur if the torpedo were running shallow (Burke 2017, 30, 32).

Unfortunately, if the feedback mechanism is responsive just to depth, then it will tend to overshoot the target value, and the torpedo will "porpoise" through the water, as did Whitehead's torpedo. Whitehead's 1868 torpedo solved this problem by adding a pitch sensor. This device was a vertical pendulum that was connected to the diving plane in such a way that if they were pitched three degrees or more for upward (or downward) movement, it would send it a down-elevator (or up-elevator) signal. This negative feedback slowed down the approach to the desired depth and thus inhibited overshooting. The depth error was reduced to ±6 inches (Burke 2017, 32–33; Branfill-Cook 38; Sears 1898, 92).

One difficulty was that while the torpedo was accelerating, the pendulum, instead of hanging vertically (neutral position), would lag behind, thus impelling the torpedo to dive. Whitehead therefore added a locking gear that caused the diving plane mechanism to ignore the diaphragm and pendulum until "the engine has made a prescribed number of revolutions" (Leavitt 1893, 7); this included a rudder index that controlled the position in which the rudder was locked (Sears 1898, 97).

Maintaining Set Course

Here we are concerned with the ability of the torpedo to maintain a set (straight or curved) course after launch, rather than whether it can alter course after launch to counter the target's evasive maneuvers.

Barber's early torpedo had a twisted surface, apparently in hopes of achieving spin stabilization. This idea did not catch on. Both Howell and Whitehead torpedoes had tail fins to provide some directional stability, but it wasn't enough for operational needs; a more active feedback control system was needed.

The Howell torpedo had good directional stability. It used a pendulum to sense the "heel" (lean) of the torpedo and adjust the rudder accordingly; the gyroscopic effect of the flywheel also helped (Jolie 1978).

The Whitehead torpedo's track was pretty erratic, which limited its utility until he incorporated Obry's gyroscope. This device "reached its maximum speed of 2,400 rpm in something less than half a second," and at 800 yards, the lateral deviation with gyroscopic control was just 8 yards (without it, 24 yards) (Tailyour 1999).

A gyroscope capable of curving the torpedo's path was apparently proposed by Washington Chambers around 1900, and a proof-of-concept was achieved by John Moore in 1902 (Epstein 2014, 27). The basic idea was that during the firing procedure, the crew set the "gyro angle"—the angle between the direction in which the torpedo tube was pointing and the direction that they wanted the torpedo to go. The gyro would be spun up to point in the latter direction. After the torpedo traveled a set distance ("reach") in a straight line—this could be sensed by a pedometer-like device connected with the propeller shaft—the gyro would be unlocked, enabling the linkage between it and the rudder. If the gyro angle were zero, then the torpedo self-corrected any course deviations, resulting in a straight-line track out of the firing position of the tube. If it weren't zero, the torpedo would steer into a course that was the original spin-up direction, resulting in a "curved shot." This was very convenient if the tubes were fixed or had a limited angle of train (NAVORD 1944, 20A3).

A rudder malfunction could cause a torpedo to circle back. "There are at least thirty documented cases of circular runs by torpedoes fired by US submarines at enemy vessels in World War II," and both the USS *Tullibee* and the USS *Tang* were thus "hoist[ed] by their own petard" (Patoway 2019). The solution was to condition explosion on a minimum distance or time of run (and for the submarine to descend quickly after firing).

Pattern-running torpedoes took curved fire a step further. They could circle or execute a spiral, a zigzag, or a loop (actually, a series of broad 180-degree turns) after a straight run to take them amid a convoy. Pattern-running torpedoes were used by Royal Navy submarines in World War I and by German submarines in World War II (Friedman 2011, 325–26; Florek 2017).

Post-Launch Guidance

The Howell and Whitehead torpedoes were uncontrolled. Obviously, that meant they could not respond to evasive action on the part of the enemy, although one could fire a salvo on diverging courses and hope that at least one torpedo hit. The possible solutions to this problem were remote guidance and autonomous guidance.

Remote Guidance

The first remotely guided torpedo was perhaps the wire-guided Brennan torpedo (1878). For such a weapon to be practical, the operator must know where it is at all times. The Brennan torpedo was fitted with an indicator mast so it could be spotted from above. Of course, that meant the enemy could spot it, too, but the operator knew where and when to look. The alternative was to equip the torpedo with sensors and have it relay information to the operator. However, that option wasn't practical in the late nineteenth century.

Radio-controlled torpedoes were proposed by Von Siemens in 1906, but the weight and size of the transmitter-receiver had to be small to be accommodated by the torpedo, and the radio signals had to penetrate the water. The radio wave penetration depth depended on the salinity and temperature of the water, as well as the frequency of the radio wave.

Autonomous Guidance

These torpedoes home in on the target, either passively or actively (the latter "ping" the target). The method of sensing the prey varies.

Passive acoustic torpedoes home in on the target's engine noise, whereas active ones can also detect the reflection off the hull of sound emitted from the torpedo. A wooden hull will provide a return.

The world's first acoustic homing torpedo was the German G73/T4 "Falke" (1943). For its sensors to work properly, the firing submarine had to stop its engines, and the torpedo itself couldn't run faster than 20 knots. The American aircraft-launched Mark 24 "FIDO" (1943) and the submarine-launched Mark 27 "Cutie" had four crystal microphones amidships, one in each quadrant. The amplified left/right voltage difference, combined with a voltage based on rudder position, drove the rudder while the top/down one, combined with voltages based on depth and pitch, drove the elevator. Both FIDO and Cutie ran on electric batteries at 12 knots (Miller 2011; Pelick 1996; Brood 2004).

Wake-homing torpedoes attempt to detect the turbulence of the target's wake, zigzag across it, and then follow it in. Optical wake detection was demonstrated in 1947 and acoustic (sonar) wake detection in 1953 (Pelick 1996a). The first mass-produced torpedo of this type was probably the Soviet Type 53–65, introduced in 1965 (Branfill-Cook 2014, Appendix).

Deployment

The earliest deployment mechanism was the drop frame, which held the torpedo horizontally; it was literally dropped into the water, where, ideally, it would start moving in the right direction.

This device was replaced by the torpedo tube, placed above or below water. If above water, it might be a trainable deck mount or fixed into the hull. The deck mount allowed the attacker to shoot one way while moving another, but it required a large deck area. Fixed tubes could be in the bow (preferred), in the stern (vulnerable to wake interference), or even amidships (not aimable).

A danger with the above-water tube is that an enemy shot or shell might strike it, detonating the torpedo. That outcome may sound improbable, but it happened to the *Almirante Oquendo* at the Battle of Santiago (1898). With early torpedoes, there was also concern that impact with the water could damage the mechanism.

If tubes are built into the hull, whether above or below water, they potentially weaken it.

The underwater tube also poses an increased risk of flooding.

There's a fair amount of mechanical complication associated with a submerged torpedo tube. It must have a breech door at one end and a muzzle door at the other; the two operate together somewhat like an airlock on a spacecraft. The tube is drained of water for loading and filled for firing.

Initially, expelling the torpedo was accomplished mechanically, with a push rod, but this method could damage its rudder, and so the rod was replaced, first with a compressed-air gun and then with a propellant (gunpowder, cordite) charge (EB 1911, "Torpedo"). Modern torpedo tubes use compressed-air discharge for most torpedoes; electric torpedoes "swim out" under their own power. A further problem is making sure that the torpedo isn't buffeted unduly by water currents as it leaves the tube. One expedient was to extrude a tube with grooves that would guide the torpedo until it was clear (*ibid.*).

Detonation

Torpedo payload is limited by the length and diameter of the torpedo and the portion that must be reserved for the propulsion system. That in turn depends on the mode of propulsion and the range and speed sought. The original Whitehead torpedo (1868) had a 60-pound charge (Sleeman 1889, 174). The 14.2-inch-diameter, 11-foot-long 1890 Howell flywheel torpedo weighed 580 pounds, with a 100-pound warhead. The short (140-inch, 845-pound) and long (197-inch, 1,160-pound) 17.7-inch-diameter Mark I Whitehead torpedoes delivered 118 and 220 pounds of explosive, respectively (Jolie 1978). In World War II, the USN torpedoes carried "400 to 800 pounds" of "TNT or torpex" (NAVORD 1944, 9B5). The current USN heavyweight Mark 48 torpedo carries 650 pounds of PBXN-103, "equivalent to about 1200 lbs…. TNT" (navweaps.com 2021a).

Early torpedoes exploded on contact; magnetic and acoustic proximity fuses were introduced in World War II.

Depth Charges

Depth charges were first used for anti-submarine warfare in World War I (Polmar and Allen 2012, 241; the latter is the principal source for this section). The fuse controlled the depth at which the explosion occurred. An early fuse design, used on the British Type A depth charge, "operated by a fixed-length lanyard attached to a float that 'pulled the pin' when the bomb sank to the required depth. Unfortunately, the lanyard frequently became tangled and set off the charge prematurely." Type B used a "dissolving chemical pellet" (McKee 1993, 56).

The first hydrostatic fuse was tested in September 1914. The water would press against a diaphragm, and, when the pressure was great enough, it would overcome a resistance and actuate the charge. (Compare the depth control on the Whitehead torpedo.) A 1917 refinement adjusted the depth setting to 40–150 feet by having a turning key expose "various sized flooding holes." British World War I depth charges had a maximum depth of 150 feet, whereas the limit in World War II was 700. The World War II USN experimented with proximity fuses, including one with an "acoustic echo-operated pistol," but they were "little used" (McKee 1993, 56).

The first depth charges used guncotton. This method was superseded by TNT and Amatol later in World War I. In World War II, Monol and Torpex were also used. The type A charge was only 32.5 pounds, whereas Type D was 300. "The Type D danger circle to submarines was considered to be about 140 feet" (McKee 1993).

The "classic" drum-shaped depth charges were released by rolling them off a stern rack. The number that could be carried was limited initially by production and later by ship stability and related considerations. Since the weight was concentrated on the stern, it would have increased the ship's tendency to pitch unless there was a compensatory reduction in gun and torpedo armament (*ibid.*).

The Mark X of World War II, which carried a ton of high-explosive material, was torpedo shaped (for faster sinking to target deep targets) and fired from a torpedo tube. But "these monsters seldom worked" (*ibid.*).

World War II depth charges could also be thrown ahead of the ship by spigot mortars (see next section).

The sinking rate could be increased by attaching weights, as on the World War II Mark VII heavy depth charge, to address faster-diving U-boats. It could also be reduced by a parachute-like device, for shallow water use (*ibid.*).

Spigot Mortars

These mortars constitute a rather radical offshoot of the gun; indeed, I consider them rocket launchers. There is no gun barrel. Instead, the projectile sits on a rod (the spigot) attached to a baseplate. The projectile has a tubular tail that acts somewhat like a conventional gun barrel in that it confines the propellant gases. The propellant is in a container within the projectile itself.

The World War II "Hedgehog" was an anti-submarine spigot mortar battery, hurling 24 mortar rounds in a set pattern ahead of the ship. Their range (250–280 yards) was great enough that they could be fired while the submarine was still far enough away to be detectable by sonar (Lanzendörfer 2003). They were contact fused. That had the advantage that if they missed the sub, they didn't explode and disturb the sonar (Tucker 2011, 345). (For the "Squid" system, see chapter 5.)

CHAPTER 14

Hull Penetration and Damage

Hull Penetration Physics

Solid shot penetrates a hull (or armor) by virtue of its kinetic energy ($0.5 \times m \times v^2$, where m is projectile mass and v is impact velocity). The ballistic limit velocity is the greatest impact velocity the target can withstand without being perforated.

The projectile does work by deforming and penetrating the armor and, in the process, dissipates its kinetic energy until it comes to a rest inside the target, perforates it, or ricochets off it. (It may also do work by deforming itself.)

If each "slice" of hull or armor resists the projectile independently of the rest of the armor, then penetration will be proportional to the kinetic energy and thus to the square of the impact velocity (and linearly to the mass). However, if each "slice" resists in proportion to the entire thickness still facing the projectile, the penetration will be linearly proportional to the impact velocity (and to the square root of the mass) (Okun 2017).

Another consideration is the effect of the armor on the projectile. If the projectile suffers "progressive damage that gradually reduces penetration ability," this will also result in a less-than-quadratic dependence of penetration on impact velocity. This situation created the incentive to harden projectile noses with chilled cast iron or even steel; in addition, the ogive shape was found to be the most effective (Owen 1873, 273). However, plate quality typically decreased as thickness increased (Okun 1998).

Explosive shells do damage by virtue of the heat and pressure of the expanding gases, along with the kinetic energy of the shell fragments and splinters carried with them. The damage caused by an explosion is quite dependent on whether the blast is in the open or confined and the speed at which the debris is moving.

Plunging Fire and Oblique Impact

Normally, the velocity of the projectile decreases as it gains range, due to air resistance. However, if the shot is fired with a high inclination, then, on the descending portion of its trajectory, its speed will increase as a result of gravity (Beauchant 1828, 46). The only premodern naval armament to which this point would apply are the mortars of bomb ketches and boat howitzers. The maximum possible impact velocity due to "plunging fire" is the "terminal velocity" (the velocity at which the air resistance equals the gravitational force).

At the end of the descending portion of a high inclination shot, the impact trajectory will be nearly vertical. This is good for penetrating the (horizontal) deck of a target warship, less so for piercing its sides (assuming the latter are themselves vertical or even flared outward, as on modern ships).

If the shot strikes the target obliquely and continues on course, then there's naturally a greater effective thickness to penetrate (Beauchant 1828, 49), the effective thickness becoming the actual thickness divided by the cosine of the angle of obliquity (0 degrees for square hits). Alternatively, we may argue that the projectile turns in toward the plate, and the energy available for penetration is based on the component of the velocity that is perpendicular to the target surface. Since energy is proportional to velocity squared, that would make the penetration inversely proportional to the square of the cosine of the angle of obliquity (Admiralty 1880, 248–51).

However, the actual physical phenomenon is rather more complicated. If the angle of obliquity exceeds a critical value, the projectile ricochets rather than penetrates (Vayig and Rosenberg 2021). That value depends on the projectile nose shape, hardness, length/diameter ratio, and striking velocity, as well as armor type and thickness, but usually lies in the range of 30–70 degrees (Cronkhite and Chester 1893, 243; Admiralty 1880, 248; Brassey 1889, 364).

The curved hulls of the early modern wooden warship, with bilge and tumblehome, thus were able to deflect shot in a way that a "wall-sided" hull couldn't. Some early ironclads (CSS *Virginia*) had sloped sides to deflect low-trajectory shot, and deflection is also the *raison d'être* for preferring a domed turret to a cylindrical one, and cylindrical to block. However, this is a compromise, as impact would be closer to perpendicular if the projectile were fired at long range (thus, rising and falling on a steeper trajectory) (Brown 2023).

On the USS *Iowa*, the internal belt armor was inclined outward at 19 degrees as a defense against plunging (long-range) fire with armor-piercing projectiles (Dramiński 2020, 12, 103).

Wooden Ship Hull Thicknesses

Until the mid-nineteenth century, warships trusted in their longitudinal wooden planking to fend off cannonballs. While elm was used for the keel and lower strakes, the above-water timbers were usually made of oak, with other woods used for ships constructed outside of Europe (e.g., teak in India).

The thicker the hull, the more resistant it was to attack. In the *Seaman's Grammar* (1627), John Smith states, "If you would have a ship built of 400 tuns, she requires a plank of 4 inches; if 300 tuns, 3 inches; small ships 2 inches, but none less" (13). According to a Dutch shipbuilding rule formulated by Nicolaes Witsen, the thickness of the inside of the stem (stern) was one inch for every ten feet of the ship's length (between outsides of stem and stern), and the planking of the hull one quarter of that thickness. So for a 160-foot length, the required planking would be four inches. By another rule, this one from Cornelis van Yk, the thickness was based on the "length class" of the ship, ranging from 2 inches for 40–60 feet to 4.5 inches for 140–160 feet (Hoving and Wildeman 2012, 56, 250ff).

It seems likely that these rules were for merchantmen, and warships were stouter. The 36-gun *Dartmouth* (1655), essentially a Dunkirk frigate, had framing timbers of 8-inch "moulding" (thickness) (Kenchington 1993, 33).

The *Vasa* was the largest Swedish warship when it was built in 1628. "The hull consists of three layers, and is approximately 40 cm [16 inches] thick." It was made of European oak (*Quercus robur*) (Ljungdahl 2006).

About a decade after the Napoleonic Wars, warship hulls had thicknesses of 10–26 inches, depending on warship size and the place of measurement (see Table 14–1).

Table 14–1: Hull Thickness of Early Nineteenth-Century British Warships (Beauchant 1828, 132ff)

Thickness, Oak (inches)	At Load Line	At Upper Deck
10		10-ton brig
11		18-ton brig
12	10-gun brig	
14	18-gun brig	28-gun ship
15		frigate
16		60-gun ship
18	28-gun ship	third rate
20	frigate	second rate
21		first rate
23	60-gun ship	
24	third rate	
26	second rate	
28	first rate	

(For mid-nineteenth-century French warships, see Dahlgren 1856, 183.)

A number of American Civil War gunboats were timberclads, notably the USS *Conestoga*, *Lexington* and *Tyler*. The timber armor was intended for protection against small-arms fire and consequently was 5 inches thick (Smith 2008, 59).

Solid Shot versus Wood Targets: Experimental Penetration Data

In tests conducted by John Greaves (1602–1652) at Woolwich in 1651, a target was set up at a range of 200 yards. The target consisted of three butts, each 19 inches thick (13 of oak and the rest of elm), with 14 yards between the first pair and 8 between the second. Results are listed in Table 14–2.

Table 14–2: Reported Penetration, Mid–Seventeenth-Century Solid Shot versus Wooden Targets

Gun	Weight	Length	Shot	Powder	Performance
demi-cannon	3,500		32	8–10	pierced the first two butts and struck in the third
"	3,600		32	7	pierced the first two butts
whole culverin	5,300	11 feet, 1 inch	18	8–10	three shots passed through the first two butts, of which just one entered gently into the third
"	3,580	10 feet	18	8–9	four shots pierced the first two butts, of which one penetrated seven inches into the third, and another pierced it completely
demi-culverin			9	4	passed through one butt and entered the second
demi-culverin 2⅛-inch bore			9	4	one shot passed through both butts and the other almost passed through the second

(Greaves 1737, 470)

In 1742, Benjamin Robins reported that at 30 yards, an 18-pounder penetrated 14.5–15.5 inches of oak with a 1-pound charge, nearly 33 inches with 3 pounds, and 37–46 inches with 6 pounds (Robins, 310).

In an 1810 British trial, a 24-pounder with only a 4-pound (one-sixth) charge (probably of cylinder powder) fired 21 rounds double-shotted at a 5-foot, 2-inch-thick butt of fir, 100 yards away. Ten of the balls penetrated the butt completely and traveled another 50 yards beyond it; another ten penetrated it partially, to an average depth of four feet, and one ball missed. While fir has perhaps half the resistance of oak, this was still an impressive performance, and one can imagine what a 32- or (the admittedly phased-out) 42-pounder would do to even a ship of the line, especially with a greater charge (Beauchant 1828, 22, 45; Morriss 2010, 221).

In 1814, American experiments with a 32-pounder (11-pound charge) resulted in penetration in white oak of 60 inches at 100 yards and 54 inches at 150 yards (Haswell 1853, 234).

John Dahlgren conducted experiments in which, at 1,000 yards, a 32-pounder penetrated 25 inches of white oak, and a 64-pounder, 37 inches (Broun 1862, 59).

In tests conducted by HMS *Excellent* in 1838, at 1,200 yards, firing at the *Prince George*, even an 18-pounder (6-pound charge) achieved an average 25.5 inches of penetration. A 24 × 9.5 (8-pound charge) and a 32 × 7.5 (6-pound) both passed through 30 inches, a 32 × 9.5 (one-third charge) 34 inches, a 68 × 9 (10–12-pound) 35 inches, and a 68 × 5.3 carronade (5.5-pound charge) 30 inches (Royal Engineers 1852, 101). In 1853, at a range of 1,200 yards, their 68-pounder with a 16-pound charge penetrated 45 inches into the old 74-gun *York*, and their 32-pounder with a 10-pound charge achieved 30 inches (*Experiments* 1854, 2).

Most of these tests involved "flat fire" against vertical targets, and thus the impacts would have been close to perpendicular. Sloped armor would have had enhanced resistance against such fire.

Prediction of Wooden Hull Penetration

Leonhard Euler and Benjamin Robins proposed a solid shot penetration formula of the form

$$z = 0.5 \, wv^2/gR$$

with w indicating weight (pounds); v, striking velocity (fps); g, gravity (32 ft/s^2); and R, resistive force—R is the cross-sectional area (square feet) of the projectile times 912,190 for oak or 475,070 for fir (Douglas 1829, 124; PC 1838, 495). The underlying assumption is that the resistance is constant and proportional to the cross-sectional area.

Jean Poncelet suggested that penetration is limited by a combination of constant resistance and resistance proportional to the squared instantaneous velocity (Bulson 1997, 142). He also assumed that the resistance was proportional to the diameter squared (Douglas 1860, 55).

Tests were carried out (1835–1844) at Gavre and Metz and resulted in the following Poncelet-type formula (LaFay 1850, 462) for penetration z (cm) in oak (456) as a function of predicted striking velocity u (m/s), diameter of shot a (cm), and specific gravity (SpG) of shot:

$$z = 2.306 \times a \times SpG \times \log_{10} (1 + 0.00001 \, u^2)$$

The striking velocity would in turn depend on the projectile mass and caliber, along with the range, elevation and muzzle velocity; the latter would depend on the projectile characteristics and the powder charge. The formula would need to be modified if the projectile broke through, as then it isn't reduced to zero velocity.

While sources vary (and wood is heterogeneous), the U.S. Army suggested that one "multiply the penetration in oak by 1.3 for the penetration in elm, by 1.8 for white pine, and by 2 for poplar" (2022, 398). Although the denser woods appear to be more resistant, the advantage of oak over fir (1.8 or even 2.0) is greater than their relative densities (1.4) (Simmons 1837, 32).

Calculation of Impact Parameters

Applying the quoted hull penetration formulae requires knowing the striking velocity of the projectile. By the methods of exterior ballistics, one may calculate, given the muzzle velocity, gun elevation and target range, and the projectile's mass, diameter and drag function, the striking velocity and angle of the projectile.

Unfortunately, there are no modern data on the drag of spherical projectiles of the size used in pre-twentieth-century naval warfare.

In the mid-nineteenth century, air resistance per unit frontal area was typically assumed (per Poncelet's fit to Hutton's data) to be proportional to $v^2 (1 + v/k)$, where, for spherical projectiles at "service velocities," k = 1,427 feet with v fps (Benton 1862, 403–4). That would make the drag coefficient proportional to the parenthesized term.

Later, Nikolai Mayevski suggested that the drag on a spherical projectile was proportional to v^2 for velocities greater than 1,233 fps and to $v^2 (1 + v^2 / k^2)$, with k = 612.25 feet, for lesser velocities (Ingalls 1886, 28).

The striking velocity was often calculated by a formula that assumed a flat trajectory with air resistance and without gravity (Lafay 1850, 461; Benton 1862, 408). Jules Lafay adjusted a parameter based on the diameter of the projectile, which may have provided some accommodation to Reynolds number effects.

By way of example, a Canon de 30, firing a 15.1-kg (Lafay 1850, 450) ball with an 8-kg charge, had a muzzle velocity of 485 mps (1,591 fps). This yielded the predicted impact velocities and penetrations shown in Table 14–3.

Table 14–3: Predicted Impact Velocity and Oak Penetration

	Range			
	Metric Units (m)		*Imperial Units (ft)*	
	1,000	*2,000*	*3,285*	*6,562*
impact velocity (mps, fps)	290	190	951	623
penetration (m, ft)	0.88	0.42	2.89	1.34

(Lafay 1850, 462–63)

Stout as Oak

Wooden warships could shrug off an enormous number of hits with solid shot.

In 1800, the 74-gun British *Foudroyant* was locked in battle with the 80-gun French *Guillaume Tell*, so close that "her spare anchor just escaped catching in the mizzen rigging of the *Guillaume Tell*." The *Foudroyant* fired 1,200 32-pdr, 1,240 24-pdr, 118 18-pdr and 200 12-pdr shot at its adversary, which had already fought the 64-gun *Lion* and the frigate *Penelope* earlier that morning. After several hours, the *Guillaume Tell* was completely dismasted and forced by rolling to close its lower gunports, and therefore struck its colors, but it wasn't sunk, and it was towed to port and refitted for British service (Douglas 1860, 210; Wikipedia, "HMS Malta [1800]").

Then there was the 1813 capture of USS *Chesapeake* (36 guns) by HMS *Shannon* (38). The *Chesapeake* "was struck by twenty-five 32-pounder shot, twenty-nine 18-pounder shot, three hundred and six grape-shot, and two 9-pounder shot," and for its sins, the *Shannon* received "thirteen 32-pounder shot, twelve 18 pounder shot, one hundred and nineteen grape-shot, and fourteen bar-shot" (Preble 1879, 17). The cannonade was at a distance of a ship's width (40 feet), and yet some shots stuck in the enemy's sides, without perforating the hull (for exact locations, see Douglas 1860, 78ff). Both ships suffered substantial damage to their rigging. The bombardment of the *Chesapeake* disabled five of its guns, but the casualties among its gun crews probably had a greater effect on its effective firepower. A total of 47 were killed and 99 wounded on the *Chesapeake* (Preble 1879, 17, 25ff).

Splinter Generation

There are numerous statements in nineteenth-century literature to the effect that the shot would ideally just penetrate the hull; this impact apparently maximized the generation of splinters (Douglas 1860, 66ff). Howard Douglas (67) therefore urged reducing the standard powder charge from one-third to one-sixth of shot weight.

This idea has been confirmed by modern experiments with scaled-down replicas; splinter generation was greater when the hull absorbed 91 percent of the shot's kinetic energy than when it removed 54 percent (Kahanov et al. 2012, 2912; Hocker 2017). The explanation is that splintering is caused by bending-induced fracture, and higher-velocity projectiles punch through by shearing, with little bending (Cotterell 2010, 354).

Mythbusters episode 71 would have us believe that sailors were killed only by direct hits from cannonballs, splinters not being given enough force to be lethal. While I don't doubt that being hit with a cannonball was worse, splinters could definitely do serious damage. On the *Penelope* (in 1854), "one man was struck across the face by a heavy splinter, which buried itself in his brain" (Marquis 1898, 577), and at the Battle of Lake Erie, Lieutenant Stokes of *Queen Charlotte* was struck senseless by a splinter (Bancroft 1912, 2).

Explosive Shells versus Wooden Hulls

Explosive shells of a sort were used in early modern warfare. These were, however, fired on high-angle trajectories from mortars and, therefore, not very useful for targeting a ship in motion.

Henri Joseph Paixhans built an 8,131-pound "bomb cannon" for firing an 86.25-pound spherical shell on a relatively flat trajectory. The fuse ignited when the gun was fired. In 1824, he fired twelve shots at the 80-gun *Pacificateur* at a distance of 640 yards. To ensure that the target would survive the test, it was cleared of combustible materials and dampened. The results were as follows:

> shot 1: made breach of 8.5 inches diameter in the ship's side, which was 29 inches thick, tore off two feet of the inner plank, made a 2–3 foot square hole in the orlop deck, and all told "shattered to atoms about 160 square feet of wood-work."
>
> shot 2: carried two large pieces of plank off the quarter deck, knocked 3–4 foot, 9.5 inch thick splinter off the main mast, tore off a 130 pound mast band and drove it into the opposite bulwark....
>
> shot 3: tore off a 200 pound oaken knee, and its splinters knocked down 40 figures [wooden test dummies!].

There were nine more shots, one of which made "a breach of several feet in height and width in the side of the ship." Paixhans concluded that "the horizontal projection of bombs must make great ravages in a vessel, and may, by a single shot, endanger her safety" (Paixhans 1838, 12–14, 29ff, 40).

Fast forward to the Battle of Sinope in 1853. It wasn't surprising that the

Russians won; the Ottomans were badly outgunned. What was noteworthy was that two Ottoman frigates were blown up by Russian shell guns within fifteen minutes (Dahlgren 1856, 303), whereas the Russian flagship was "struck by 84 cannon balls without major damage" (Mikaberidze 2011, 837).

Clad in Iron (or Steel)

It is a matter of some academic controversy whether the Korean "turtle ships" of the sixteenth century were iron plated. Ch'oe (2006, 94) firmly asserts that the *geobukseon*, first introduced in the 1592 naval battle of Dangpo, was an ironclad version of the traditional Korean battleship. Ch'oe's principal source for the structure of the *geobukseon* is the *Yi Chumgmugong Jeonso* (1795), written in praise of the Korean commander at Dangpo, Admiral Yi.

The doubt arises from three points. First, why would they bother, given that the attacking Japanese warships had few cannons? Second, would they have been able to produce sufficient iron? Third, why didn't Admiral Yi mention the iron plating in his own writing? (Yi said only that the hull featured iron spikes.)

Ironclad Construction

An ironclad could have a wooden hull (*La Gloire*, 1859) or an iron one (HMS *Warrior*, 1860). Iron-hulled ships also have framing, both transverse (ribs of metal) and longitudinal (stringers paralleling the keel). The bottoms and sides ("shell") are formed by metal plates that are riveted to the frame and to adjacent plates. In 1911, the plates were typically 20–40 feet long, 5–7 feet wide, and ¼ to 1 inch thick (EB 1911, "Shipbuilding"). If the plates were steel, they were usually mild steel.

An iron warship would have armor plate protecting the shell. The armor plate could have wood backing (teak was popular) separating it from the shell (EB 1911, "Shipbuilding"). There might also be an inner skin of iron as a further splinter shield (Farrow 1895, 123). Additional armor might be disposed inside the hull to protect vital areas.

Armor Fabrication

Ordinary cast iron, which was much cheaper than wrought iron, was tested but found wanting because of its brittleness. A few round shots, at point-blank range, destroyed a 4-foot-thick block (Holley 1865, 629). Nor was it practical to attach cast iron face plates to a wrought iron foundation; the bond failed (NAVORD 1937, s1201).

The first experiments on the ability of wrought iron to resist shot were carried out by Robert and Edward Stevens and communicated to the U.S. government in 1841. They reported that iron was sixteen times as resistant as oak (Holley 1865, 624).

But some experiments at Woolwich in 1845 were nonetheless discouraging. The thin (e.g., ⅝-inch) plates tested were "shivered to fragments" and produced "numerous dangerous splinters." By 1859, it was recognized that a wooden backing increased the value of the armor (Beeler 2001, 34).

All else being equal, the thicker the plate, the better. However, it might not be possible at a particular point in time to make plate greater than a given thickness. For example, in 1854–1858, the maximum plate thickness was 4.5 inches; even then, quality was irregular. The problem was that the rolling mills couldn't handle this thickness, and thus the plate had to be shaped by hammering (Garrison 1892, 346).

A greater armor thickness could be achieved by lamination (fastening several thin plates together), which was done with American Civil War ironclads. For example, the USS *Monitor*'s turret had eight thicknesses of 1-inch iron (Garrison 1892, 346). The laminates could be made of just metal sheets or of metal alternating with wood. However, laminated armor was very vulnerable to perforation by pointed projectiles (Browne 1898, 5).

I believe that the thickest wrought iron armor was that of HMS *Inflexible* (1881)—two layers totaling 24 inches (Cotterell 2010, 365).

In 1876, tests demonstrated that, insofar as resisting perforation was concerned, steel was superior to wrought iron by a ratio of about 1.3:1. However, steel was susceptible to through-cracking, and consequently, in 1877, Charles Cammell and J.D. Ellis introduced compound armor, in which a steel face place was melted (Cammell)

An 1898 photograph, originally on a tinted postcard, of the USS *Nahant* (1862–1904), a "*Passaic*-class ironclad monitor" (Wikipedia). The "dents in the ship's turret armor were caused by Confederate gunfire during the Civil War, some thirty-five years earlier." Copyrighted by Waldon Fawcett, circa 1898. Courtesy of the U.S. Naval History and Heritage Command, Catalog No. NH 100797-KN.

or cemented (Ellis) onto a wrought iron foundation. In 1887, T.J. Tressider found it possible to harden the steel face by "chilling the heated surface of a plate by means of jets of water under pressure" (EB 1911, "Armour Plates").

By 1880–1890, homogeneous steel plate could be made adequately resistant to through-cracking and was considered equivalent to composite plate of equal thickness for resisting perforation, perhaps 25 percent more effective than wrought iron (NAVORD 1937, s1204). In 1891, H.A. Harvey reported how to face-harden an all-steel plate. The same process also toughened the back of the plate; carbon content was greatest at the face and decreased as you went deeper (NAVORD 1937, s1206). The Harvey and Tresidder processes were combined ("Harveyized armor") and found to give steel twice the resistance of wrought iron (EB 1911, "Armour Plates").

The first nickel steel armor plate was manufactured in 1889 (NAVORD 1937, s1205). Experimentation with addition of chromium began in the 1880s, and the

Photograph of results of a Krupp test of Cammell's steel-faced wrought iron plate (Brassey 1889, Plate III, Figure 2); 304-pound projectiles were fired by an 8.26-inch gun, striking velocity 1,807 fps. The plate was 15.55 inches thick, on backing of oak 7.87 inches thick. The projectiles marked C and D penetrated the plate completely, making the holes marked A and B, and were recovered essentially intact. (The other holes, one with a projectile embedded in it, are from an earlier test of the same plate with other guns and projectiles.) Thomas Brassey commented that the plate "has held well together under heavy punishment; but the question arises whether it would not be better to sacrifice this ... in order to keep the projectiles out" (363). That would mean increasing hardness at the expense of toughness.

problems of making large nickel-chrome steel ingots were resolved in 1892–1893 (NAVORD 1937, s1207). Nickel steel armor rendered compound armor obsolete, making possible reduction in armor thickness and thus increased speed or armored area (Breyer 1973, 39). Typical alloying levels were 2–5 percent nickel and 1–2 percent chromium (EB 1911, "Armour Plates").

For thicker plates (5+ inches), "Krupp cemented" (KC) armor was favored, and the early version was 15 percent more effective than Harveyized armor (increased by World War II to 40 percent) (battleshipbean 2017). Early Krupp armor was made using a gaseous hydrocarbon in the cementation furnace, but later a solid hydrocarbon was used. The cemented steel plate was "decrementally hardened" by heating and quenching. Once the resulting hardening was 30–40 percent deep, the plate was sprayed with water "at first on the superheated side and a moment layer on both sides." The result was a plate that was hard in front and tough in the rear (NAVORD 1937, s1207).

Steel may be cast or forged; casting is cheaper and more suitable to producing complicated forms (turrets), but forged steel is freer from flaws and thus more resistant.

Explosive Shells versus Metal Armor

Unfortunately (at least from the attacker's point of view), surface explosions mostly went "splat!" on armor. Experiments at Woolwich (1856) showed that "plates of ⅝ths inch thick prevented any shells then known from passing through and exploding inside the ship" (Murray 1861, 24; for later experiments, see Alger 1900). For shells that partially penetrated thinner plates, most of the force of the explosion took the path of least resistance—that is, back up the cavity carved by the projectile.

Naturally, the more powerful the shell, the greater the thickness it could shatter, but a good rule of thumb was that armor thicker than one-third the caliber of the shell could protect the ship from a high-explosive shell (Brassey 1904, 366).

Armor-Piercing Shells versus Metal Armor

Hence the development of the armor-piercing shell. Against somewhat thicker armor—up to, say, half a caliber—the semi-armor-piercing projectile was more effective (Brassey 1904, 367). Beyond that, an armor-piercing shell was required. Its development inspired the advances in armor design discussed earlier.

There are several different modes of penetration. In *discing*, the plate first "dishes" (bulges backward), and then the bulge breaks free as a disc. In *punching* (plugging), the projectile shears a disc of diameter slightly greater than that of the projectile and pushes it backward, thus shearing the disc behind it, and so on until a cylindrical plug is forced out the back of the plate. In *petalling*, the plate flows away from the point of the projectile, forming concentric ridges, and tensile stresses crack the plate radially, forming "petals" that are peeled away. This damage exposes the next layer of the plate to the same attack, and so on until the plate is perforated.

More than one mechanism might be in play simultaneously, and it appears that which is favored depends on the shape and hardness of the projectile, as well as its impact speed (Dean et al. 2009).

Charles Owen (1873, 143) stated that penetration is inversely proportional to the diameter of the projectile. George Stone (1994, 9–12) argues that with both flat-nosed and conical projectiles striking armor plate, the penetration should be proportional to the initial kinetic energy per unit surface area and thus inversely proportional to diameter squared. William Fullam and Thomas Hart (1905, 436) relate the effort of discing (which they call punching) to the circumference of the projectile and that of punching (which they call wedging) to its frontal area.

Damage can occur even without complete penetration. The impact can cause cratering (digging a pit on the front of the plate), rendering the affected area more vulnerable to a second shot, or spalling (fragmentation of the back), which might cause injury to the crew or interior. In addition, repeated impacts can cause racking—shaking the armor loose from its fastenings. Racking was best achieved by heavy, large-diameter projectiles with low velocity (Owen 1873, 274).

Numerous formulae exist (Okun 2017), because armor and armor-piercing projectiles have co-evolved. If these formulae are compared, the dependence of

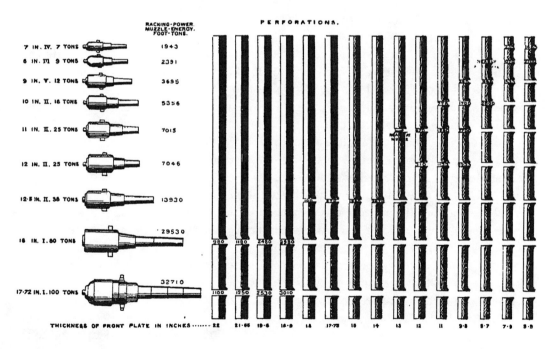

This figure (Brassey 1889, Plate V) shows the expected ability of various British muzzleloaders to perforate wrought iron armor on a direct hit, depending on the muzzle energy (half mass times square of muzzle velocity), the front plate armor thickness, and the range. The guns increase in muzzle energy as you move down, and the armor thickness decreases as you move right. "Maximum ranges of perforation less than 3000 yards are named" in the figure (e.g., the last gun penetrates 22 inches at 1,100 yards). All of the armor was assumed to be backed with 18 inches of wood. Plate VI gave similar information for British breechloaders, and VII and VIII for French and German guns, respectively.

penetration on striking velocity varied from V^1 to $V^{1.539}$, so it was not linearly proportional to the total kinetic energy ($\propto V^2$). Penetration was inversely proportional, but usually not quite linearly, to projectile diameter.

Armor Distribution

When armor was first introduced, most naval engagements were at close range, and the guns projected shot on nearly flat trajectories. Hence, it was the sides of the ships that needed protection. The only early exception was on ships of the "Monitor" type, which had very low freeboard and therefore needed either deck armor or an armored "breastwork" (Brassey 1904, 108ff).

When engagement ranges increased, even more conventional ships had to face plunging fire; thus, they benefited from deck armor. Moreover, if the warship was engaged in support of troops ashore, it could be exposed to deck-piercing fire from land (from mortars or ordinary cannons in elevated positions) (Smith 2008, 44, 241, 384, 461). (Ship designers didn't have to worry about aerial bombardment until the early twentieth century.)

As guns became more powerful, armor had to be made thicker, and compromises had to be made. Figure that every square foot of 1-inch-thick plate is about 40 pounds (Friedman 2007, 13).

On the early "broadside ironclads," the armor ran from "the upper deck down to 5 or 6 feet below the waterline" (Brassey 1904, 106). Even that was a compromise; on a warship of 75-foot beam, a 10-degree roll would be sufficient to expose the unarmored portion, and if the ship had already been cruising for several months, it would be riding high (because of consumption of ammunition, provisions and fuel) and a lesser inclination would be enough.

Designers found it necessary to limit the vertical extent of the armor. Belt armor extended from a few feet above the average waterline to a few feet below it, covering the areas that would be intermittently submerged and exposed as a result of wind and wave action. The purpose was to safeguard the buoyancy of the ship. The vertical extent of the belt varied considerably. On the Argentine corvette *Almirante Brown* (1880, 4,200 long tons displacement), amidships, it extended from 13.5 feet above to 4 feet below the waterline (Samuda 1881, 2). In contrast, an 1886 article on the British navy reported that five armored cruisers (5,000 tons displacement) were under contract, with belt armor specified to run from 1.5 feet above to 4 feet below the waterline (Reed 1886, 355).

To save weight, the lower and upper edges of the belt armor could taper out (on the *Almirante Brown*, the upper edge tapered down to 3 feet at bow and stern), or the belt could cover only part of the waterline (two-thirds on the *Almirante Brown*).

Naturally, it was also important to armor the ship's battery, so as to preserve its fighting ability. In some ships, only the main guns were armored, the assumption being that the secondary guns wouldn't be targeted at the long ranges at which armor was most effective; only the enemy's main guns would be in action, and they had to take out their counterparts.

Weight could be reduced by confining the armor longitudinally to a "central citadel," of perhaps one-third to one-half the ship's length, leaving the ends unprotected. This approach still protected the armament, because the "broadside ironclads" had been replaced by ones with just a few big guns in turrets or barbettes, and those could be positioned close together amidships. The propulsion system could be placed below the waterline, and the ends could be finely divided by bulwarks and packed with cork so that many hits would be needed to substantially reduce their buoyancy (Hovgaard 1920, 43ff).

Warships could also have armored "conning towers," although the increased protection they offered was offset by their limitation of the commander's field of view (Power 1993, 88).

Armored bulkheads are of some importance in limiting the damage caused by a shell that penetrates the main armor and explodes inside the battery. The explosion of a 12-inch shell on the *Hiyei* put men 80 feet away out of action (Brassey 1904, 351). If each gun has its own compartment, protected internally by bulkheads, then an explosion in a turret won't kill the crews of all the guns that the ship carries.

Non-Metallic Armor

Supposedly, at the 1815 Battle of New Orleans, cotton bales were used to protect American ships from British fire (Crawford 1924, 140). The British eventually decided to put this idea to the test, although they used wool instead of cotton. At 100 yards, a 68-pounder with a service charge put its shot through 11 feet of wool and 12 feet of solid earth besides (Barry 2022, 216).

Coal-burning steamships have used coal bunkers as a secondary defense. It was determined that "roughly speaking, 2 feet of coal is equivalent to one inch of iron" (Browne 1888, 341).

Underwater Explosions

In 1891, a single Whitehead torpedo hit was sufficient to sink the Chilean navy ironclad *Blanco Encalada* within a few minutes (Newpower 2006, 15).

Not only is the warship's armor likely to be weakest below the waterline, but an underwater explosion is also likely to cause more damage than a surface one. This difference can be seen by comparing the above- and below-waterline damage from the 2000 attack on the USS *Cole*.

Underwater explosions have a multitude of nasty effects (Webster 2007; Keil 1961; Sulfredge et al. 2005; SEH 1992; Reid 1996, 4). When an explosion occurs underwater, a shock wave radiates outward, initially much faster than the speed of sound in water (5,000 fps) but dropping quickly to that speed and carrying about 53 percent of the energy (Reid 1996, 4). Some of this energy is lost as the wave moves through the water.

Besides striking the ship, the shock wave hits the sea surface and bottom and is partially reflected. The reflected waves may also strike the ship, with a strength dependent on the depths of the explosion and the bottom, creating a pressure load. Depending on the shape of the bottom, the bottom-reflected wave may be focused or spread out.

Interference occurs between the direct wave and the surface-reflected wave, causing cavitation—that is, a cavity in the water. The cavitation region will close, creating a new pressure wave (cavitation pulse) and consequent "reloading." Usually, reloading is insignificant if the charge is at a range greater than twice the charge depth.

The explosion also forms a highly compressed, superheated gas bubble, carrying about 47 percent of the released energy (Reid 1996). This bubble expands (more slowly than the initial shock wave or the reloading), inertia carrying it beyond the point at which the internal pressure equals the water pressure. The water then forces it to contract. The bubble goes through a series of oscillations of declining amplitude. The peak pressure from the first "bubble pulse" is 10–15 percent that of the shock wave, but it is of much longer duration (Reid 1996, 6). Variation in pressure leads to variation in the vertical velocity of the ship's girder along its length, straining it and perhaps even breaking the back of the ship. If the frequency of the ship's response to the shock wave and bubble pulses matches the resonant frequency, hull girder vibrations build up ("whipping"), making failure more likely (Webster 2007, 30).

The gas bubble is buoyant and thus rises toward the surface; it also will tend to migrate toward the ship. If it collapses against the ship, it forms a high-speed jet of water (this is the result of the water at the bottom moving faster, because of pressure difference, than the water at the sides or top of the bubble). This jet can puncture the hull or catapult the ship upward ("kickoff"), and of course the ship ultimately slams back down. Because of these effects, an "underbottom" explosion is, all else being equal, more dangerous than an explosion on the surface (Webster 2007).

In addition to stressing the hull, the various shocks may result in the flight of inadequately secured equipment and in shock damage to secured equipment. And naturally the rupture of the ship hull creates shrapnel that can do damage.

It should be evident from the foregoing recital of potential woes why there was interest in inflicting underwater explosions on the enemy, whether by torpedoes, mines or "diving shells."

The U.S. Hydrographic Office reported that the explosion of "300 pounds of TNT would almost certainly cause pressure hull rupture and therefore presumed lethal damage when the center of detonation is within 25 feet of the pressure hull of a U.S light-hulled submarine (SS284 and previous)." At 25–50 feet, there would still be permanent hull deformation and serious machinery damage (USHO 1949, 15-12).

So far, we have been looking at non-contact explosions. For contact explosions, a traditional formula (Keil 1956) for hull plate rupture is that the explosion from a charge of TNT-equivalent weight W (kg) will make a hole of radius R (m) in plate of thickness t (m), if the weight exceeds the critical value $2.72 \times t$, and the radius is then 0.0704 times the square root of W/t (Rajendran and Narasimhan 2001).

The explosive charges for a torpedo were perhaps ten times the size of those for an armor-piercing shell, so torpedoes were more worrisome.

Port side of the USS *Salinas* (AO-19), showing "bulged and ripped plating, raised and cracked decks caused by first torpedo hit," October 30, 1941. Courtesy of the Naval History and Heritage Command, Catalog No. NH108570. Cropped by author.

Ideally, an enemy submarine would be destroyed before it fired, by gunfire, ramming, depth charges, or anti-submarine rockets, torpedoes or friendly aircraft bombs.

The first lines of defense against dumb torpedoes, once launched, were taking evasive action and destroying the torpedo by defensive fire (e.g., a rapid-firing gun).

Their effectiveness depended on the range at which the torpedo was detected (visually or, later, by sonar). If the ship were confronted with a homing torpedo, evasive action was ineffectual, but decoys could be used, achieving either a soft kill (the torpedo would run out of fuel as it followed the decoy) or a hard one (the decoy would explode when the torpedo came close enough).

Another possible defense against torpedoes was the iron mesh torpedo net (rather like chain mail). The net was hung on wooden or steel booms and would catch the torpedo, causing it to detonate at a safe distance from the ship. Nets were used primarily on ships at anchor, especially at night. One successful example was on the battleship *Sebastopol* in 1904 (Hovgaard 1920, 474). They gradually became less effective as torpedo mass and speed increased, and some torpedoes were also equipped with net cutters. By the end of World War I, ship-mounted torpedo nets were abandoned (475).

Torpedo nets did reappear in World War II (and thereafter), but the required standoff distance was much greater, so the Type T "individual ship protection net" was "held off about 60 feet from the sides of the ship by special spars" (NAVORD 1957, 14E4). This option was used only when the ship was moored.

These measures weren't foolproof, so ships were designed to survive some underwater explosions. Layered protection, with thin, flexible membranes dividing the protective area into "concentric" compartments, worked better than simple armor—the latter would have been prohibitively heavy, and rigid armor would transmit the shock. An air-filled compartment would allow the gas to expand freely, reducing the overpressure, but it wouldn't stop fragments. A liquid-filled compartment was less helpful for reducing overpressure, but more so for retarding fragments; the liquid could be fuel or seawater (Czarnecki 2001).

Conclusion

The first scientist (or engineer) known to have entered the service of Mars was Archimedes, who created war machines for the defense of Syracuse against the Roman navy. Many more were to follow. Roger Bacon experimented with gunpowder formulations. Galileo Galilei and Isaac Newton wrote about ballistics (and Galileo was consulted in 1593 by the Venetian Arsenal regarding how best to propel larger galleys mounting heavier artillery). Benjamin Robins measured muzzle velocities, and Thomas Rodman, gun bore pressure; Antoine Lavoisier in France and William Congreve in England improved the art of black powder manufacture; Paul Vielle, Alfred Nobel, Frederick Abel and James Dewar developed early forms of smokeless powder.

But even when no scientist was consulted by the authorities in the design of naval armament and armor, or the development of the art of gunnery, science lay at the foundation of their navies' success (or failure). The laws of physics and chemistry controlled the burning of every charge of gunpowder and the movement of every projectile.

In this book, I have tried to show, by a series of functionally organized vignettes, the influence of science and technology—the "cold equations"—on naval offense and defense. I hope you have found them of interest.

Appendix:
Ballistics of Spherical Projectiles

Since we are interested in the performance of smoothbore naval artillery, it would be beneficial to predict the ballistics of spherical projectiles. While there have been many modern experimental studies of aerodynamic drag on spheres, these have primarily been directed to small spheres and thus to a relatively limited range of Reynolds numbers (Bailey and Hiatt 1971; Krumins 1972; Parmar 2010).

The critical Reynolds number for a smooth sphere is "about 250,000" (McCoy 2012, 77) and is reduced to 100,000 for "very rough spheres" (78). We can calculate the velocity and Mach number corresponding to the critical Reynolds number for different-size smooth spheres. We may also calculate the Reynolds (Re) numbers for a typical early nineteenth-century muzzle velocity of 1,600 fps (Mach 1.45) (all calculations in Table Appx1 assume International Standard Atmosphere, sea level, conditions).

**Table Appx1: Mach and Reynolds Numbers
for Spherical Shot of Various Diameters at Various Velocities**

Spherical Shot		At Crit Re (2.5e5)		At Velocity 1,600 fps (Mach 1.45)
Shot Wt (lbs)	Shot Diam (in)	Velocity (fps)	Mach	Re
	9/16	838.56	0.76	4.77e5
	1.5	314.46	0.28	1.27e6
3	2.775	169.98	0.15	2.35e6
6	3.498	134.85	0.12	2.97e6
9	4	117.92	0.11	3.39e6
12	4.403	107.13	0.10	3.73e6
18	5.040	93.59	0.08	4.27e6
24	5.547	85.04	0.08	4.70e6
32	6.105	77.26	0.07	5.18e6

The 9/16th and 1.5-inch spheres are the largest used in modern testing. And it is only for the 9/16th sphere that the velocity corresponding to the critical Reynolds number is borderline transonic.

If the muzzle velocity is in the range of 1,200–1,700 fps, all of the spherical shot will initially be traveling at supersonic speed, and Mach number will control the drag coefficient. If it is fired on a relatively flat trajectory, the atmospheric parameters underlying the Reynolds and Mach numbers will remain relatively unchanged, and those numbers will decline in lockstep with the velocity as it is slowed by air resistance. It is likely that for cannon-size projectiles, at the striking velocities at which they would have a meaningful chance of penetrating a warship's hull (see chapter 14), the Reynolds number will still be in the turbulent flow regime, but the Mach number may be transonic or even subsonic.

If the flow around a sphere is subsonic and laminar, the boundary layer separates "just ahead of the point at which the maximum diameter of the sphere occurs." If it is subsonic and turbulent, the point of separation moves aft, which "significantly reduces the base drag" (McCoy 2012, 77). Thus, Reynolds number effects must be considered if a significant part of the flight is in the subsonic-turbulent flow regime, which seems likely to have been the case with premodern or nineteenth-century naval ordnance.

Donald G. Miller and Allan B. Bailey (1979) reviewed resistance data from Charles Hutton (ballistic pendulum, 1787–1791), Isidore Didion (ballistic pendulum, 1839–1840), Nikolai Mayevski (chronograph, 1868) and Francis Bashforth (chronograph, 1868), and they concluded that Bashforth's data (projectiles 3–9 inches in diameter, muzzle velocities of 220–700 mps) were consistent with more modern data in the flight regimes where they overlapped. Hence, they combined Bashforth's data with the latter to obtain a picture (their Fig. 4) of the variation of C_D for spheres at Mach numbers 0.1–1.8 and Reynolds numbers 10^4 to 10^7.

If C_D is plotted against Mach number, at Mach numbers 0.85 up, those with diameters in the range 12.5–200 mm all showed the same behavior: the drag increased with Mach number, albeit with declining slope (Miller and Bailey 1979, Fig. 10). But at lower Mach numbers, there was a definite Reynolds number effect, "as much as a factor of 2 in C_D" (462), for the 50-mm spheres. With the smaller spheres, C_D was nearly constant at around 0.5 at Mach 0.2–0.6, and then it rose sharply.

For 100-mm spheres, there is something of a mixed message. Miller and Bailey's 1979 article shows that C_D was below 0.2 at Mach 0.3, increased linearly to around 0.45 at Mach 0.7, and then increased more rapidly to Mach 0.85 (*ibid.*). But Robert McCoy later said that there were "anomalous subsonic effects" attributable to Reynolds number for "4-inch diameter spheres" (2012, 76).

Attempts have been made to consider both Mach number and Reynolds number in calculating the drag coefficient for a sphere (Collins, "Cannonball Aerodynamic Drag"; Yager 2014), but they remain problematic given the limitations of the published data on which they rely. Hence, we cannot readily use modern ballistics models to reconstruct the behavior of historical spherical shot, since the drag function can't be properly corrected for the Reynolds number effect over the entire flight.

Bibliography

Abbreviations

AHA	Alexander Historical Auctions	**MM**	*Mechanics Magazine*
ANJ	*Army and Navy Journal*	**MSIUS**	Military Service Institution of the United States
BNP	U.S. Navy, Bureau of Naval Personnel	**NAVORD**	U.S. Navy, Bureau of Naval Personnel, *Naval Ordnance and Gunnery*
BNW	U.S. Navy, Bureau of Naval Weapons	**NHHC**	Naval History and Heritage Command
BPHS	Baker Perkins Historical Society	**NMM**	National Maritime Museum
BSJ	U.S. Navy, Bureau of Ships	**NMRN**	National Museum, Royal Navy
CANI	Classical Association of Northern Ireland	**OBoM**	Ontario Bureau of Mines
CSGB	Chemical Society (Great Britain)	**ONI**	U.S. Navy, Office of Naval Intelligence
DANFS	*Dictionary of American Naval Fighting Ships*	**PC**	*Penny Cyclopedia*
EB	*Encyclopaedia Britannica*	**RF**	*Russian Firearms*
FAS	Federation of American Scientists	**SEH**	Bartholomew et al., *U.S. Navy Salvage Engineer's Handbook*
FHTD	Firearms History, Technology & Development	**Society**	Society for the Encouragement of Arts, Manufactures and Commerce
INMM	*Illustrated Naval and Military Magazine*		
IT	Iron Trade		
JCS	Joint Chiefs of Staff	**USHO**	U.S. Hydrographic Office
MFMM	Mel Fisher Maritime Museum	**USJ**	*United Service Journal*
MGRG	Medieval Gunpowder Research Group	**VNEM**	*Van Nostrand's Engineering Magazine*
MIT	Massachusetts Institute of Technology	**WRG**	Warbirds Resource Group

Abbot, Henry L. 1867. *Siege Artillery in the Campaigns Against Richmond*. Government Printing Office.

Adam, Craig. 2011. *Essential Mathematics and Statistics for Forensic Science*. Wiley.

Addiscott, Tom M. 2005. *Nitrate, Agriculture and the Environment*. CABi Pub.

Admiralty, Lord Commissioners of the. 1880. *Manual of Gunnery for Her Majesty's Fleet, 1880*. HM Stationery Office.

Admiralty, Lord Commissioners of the. 1910. *The Navy List for January 1910*. HM Stationery Office.

Aikman, Charles Morton. 1894. *Manures and Principles of Manuring*. W. Blackwood and Sons.

Airey, John. 1914, May. "Engineering Aspects of the Gyroscope with Special Reference to Stabilizing Problems." *The Michigan Technic*, 27(1): 42–54.

Akhavan, Jacqueline. 2004. "Explosive Power and Power Index." http://www.globalspec.com/reference/55654/203279/explosive-power-and-power-index.

Albrecht, William A. 1981. "Bat Guano and Its Fertilizing Value." University of Missouri College of Agriculture, *Agricultural Experiment Station, Bulletin*, 180.

Alder, Ken. 2010. *Engineering the Revolution: Arms and Enlightenment in France, 1763–1815*. University of Chicago Press.

Alexander Historical Auctions. 2021, Dec. 9. "18th Century Chain Shot." https://www.alexautographs.com/auction-lot/18th-century-chain-shot_03246C395F.

Alford, Leon Pratt. 1917. *Manufacture of Artillery Ammunition*. McGraw-Hill.

Alger, Philip R. 1900, June. "High Explosives in Naval Warfare." *Proceedings of the U.S. Naval Institute*, 26(2): 245.

Alger, Philip R. 1905, Sept. "Recoil." *Proceedings of the U.S. Naval Institute*, 31(3): 677–92.

Alger, Philip R. 1908, Sept. "The Firing Interval." *Proceedings of the U.S. Naval Institute*, 34(3): 1023. https://www.usni.org/magazines/proceedings/1908/september/firing-interval.

Alger, Philip R. 1911, June. "The Le Duc Velocity Formula." *Proceedings of the U.S. Naval Institute*, 37(2): 138. https://www.usni.org/magazines/proceedings/1911/june/le-duc-velocity-formula.

Alger, Philip R. 1915. *The Groundwork of Practical Naval Gunnery*. U.S. Naval Institute.

Allen, E.J. 2018, Feb. "Approximate Ballistics Formulas for Spherical Pellets in Free Flight." *Defence Technology*, 14(1): 1–11.

Allen, Thomas B., and Roger MacBride Allen. 2009. *Mr. Lincoln's High-Tech War*. National Geographic.

Allsop, Derek, and Glenn Foard. 2007, Nov. "Case Shot: An Interim Report on Experimental Firing and Analysis to Interpret Early Modern Battlefield Assemblages." In Tony Pollard and Iain Banks, *Scorched Earth: Studies in the Archaeology of Conflict*, 111ff. Brill.

Amiable, Ren. 2006. "Scientific Reasoning and the Empirical Approach at the Time of the European Invention of Smokeless Powder." In Brenda J. Buchanan, *Gunpowder, Explosives and the State: A Technological History*, 343–55. Ashgate.

Ammen, Rear Admiral Daniel. 1883. *The Navy in the Civil War*. Volume II: *The Atlantic Coast*. Charles Scribner's Sons.

Anderson, Romola, and Roger Charles Anderson. 1963 [1927]. *The Sailing-Ship: Six Thousand Years of History*. Norton.

Andrade, Tonio. 2016. *The Gunpowder Age: China, Military Innovation, and the Rise of the West in World History*. Princeton University Press.

Antonicelli, Aldo. 2013. "The Compression Carriage or Hardy Carriage." *The Mariner's Mirror*, 99(3): 323–24. DOI: 10.1080/00253359.2013.815994.

Armstrong, Lord William George, and Josiah Vavasseur. 1888. "The Application of Hydraulic Power to Naval Gunnery." *Transactions of the Institution of Naval Architects*, 29: 8–25.

Army and Navy Journal. 1863, Sept. 12. "Parrott Guns." *Army and Navy Journal*, 1: 37.

Arora, V.K. 2010. "Proximity Fuzes: Theory and Techniques." DESIDOC. http://drdo.gov.in/drdo/pub/monographs/Introduction/Proximity_Fuzes.pdf.

Asfaw, Yohannes T. 2008. *Structural Design and Analysis of an Existing Aerodynamically Optimised Mortar Shell*. M.S. thesis, Addis Ababa University.

Ashley, Stephen. 2001, May 1. "Warp Drive Underwater." *Scientific American*, 284(5): 70–79.

Atkinson, Stephen. 2019, May 4. "Artifact of the Month: Bar Shot." https://www.qaronline.org/blog/2019-05-04/artifact-month-bar-shot.

Attwood, Edward L. 1904. *War-Ships: A Textbook on the Construction, Protection, Stability, Turning, of War Vessels*, 5th ed. Longman, Green.

Bagnasco, Erminio. 2023. *Italian Assault Craft, 1940–1945: Human Torpedoes and Other Special Attack Weapons*. Pen & Sword.

Bailey, Allan B., and J. Hiatt. 1971, Mar. *Free-Flight Measurements of Sphere Drag at Subsonic, Transonic, Supersonic and Hypersonic Speeds for Continuum, Transition and Near-Free-Molecular Flow Conditions*. https://apps.dtic.mil/sti/tr/pdf/AD0721208.pdf.

Baker, Major R., et al. 1841, Mar. 1. "Documents Relating to the Improvement of the System of Artillery." In H.R. Rep. 229, National Foundry (27th Cong, 3d Sess.), 1843, Feb. 23, 242ff.

Baker Perkins Historical Society. n.d. "The Origins of the Founders of Baker Perkins." http://www.bphs.net/EarlyHistory/Origins/index.htm.

Baldwin, Michael. 2014, June. "Sulfur in the Solent." Chemistry World. https://www.chemistryworld.com/opinion/june-2014/7620.article.

Ball, Alpheus Messerly. 1964, Sept. *Solid Propellants Part One*. U.S. Army Materiel Command, Engineering Design Handbook, Explosives Series. AMCP 706-175.

Ballou, Lt. Cmdr. Sidney. 1924, Sept. "Condition

of the American Navy." *Proceedings of the U.S. Naval Institute*, 50(9) (Whole No. 259): 1509–17.

Bancroft, George. 1912. "Oliver Hazard Perry and the Battle of Lake Erie." *Rhode Island History. Book 2*. http://digitalcommons.providence.edu/ri_history/2.

Barlow, W.R. 1874. *Treatise on Ammunition*. HM Stationery Office.

Barnett, Edward de Barry. 1919. *Explosives*. Bailliere, Tindall and Cox.

Barrowman, James. 2010. "Calculating the Center of Pressure of a Model Rocket." Centuri Eng'g Co., Inc. (Technical Information Report 33). https://ftp.demec.ufpr.br/foguete/bibliografia/TIR-33_Calculating_the_Center_of_Pressure_of_a_Model_Rocket.pdf&usg=AOvVaw2PPXvcGEFkB7dEzd00JUNd&opi=89978449.

Barry, Patrick. 2022. *Shoeburyness and the Guns: A Philosophical Discourse*. Bod Third Party Titles.

Barthel, Thomas. 2021. *Opening the East River: John Newton and the Blasting of Hell Gate*. McFarland.

Bartholomew, Captain Charles A., et al. 1992, May 1. *U.S. Navy Salvage Engineer's Handbook*. Volume 1: *Salvage Engineering*. S0300-A8-HBK-010.

Bashforth, Francis. 1871. *Tables of Remaining Velocity, Time of Flight, and Energy of Various Projectiles Calculated from the Results of Experiments Made with the Bashforth Chronograph, 1865–1870*. E. & F.N. Spon.

Bashforth, Francis. 1873. *A Mathematical Treatise on the Motion of Projectiles, Founded Chiefly on the Results of Experiments Made with the Author's Chronograph*. Asher & Co.

Bashforth, Francis. 1881. *A Mathematical Treatise on the Motion of Projectiles, Founded Chiefly on the Results of Experiments Made with the Author's Chronograph*. Asher & Co.

Batchelor, John, and Ian Hogg. 1972. *Artillery*. Charles Scribner's Sons.

Bateman, Alan M. 1950. *Economic Mineral Deposits*. John Wiley & Sons.

battleshipbean. 2017, Dec. 20. "Armor Part 1." https://www.navalgazing.net/Armor-Part-1.

battleshipbean. 2018, June 27. "Rangefinding." https://www.navalgazing.net/Rangefinding.

battleshipbean. 2019, Apr. 17. "Shells Part 2." https://www.navalgazing.net/Shells-Part-2.

Baylay, Colonel F.G. 1888. "Precis of Lydd Experiments, August and September, 1884." *Journal of the Royal Artillery*, 15: 1. https://archive.org/details/in.ernet.dli.2015.279134/mode/2up.

BBC. 2009. "Queen Elizabeth's Lost Guns" (broadcast). https://www.youtube.com/watch?v=Z36JKhrvv7o.

Beauchant, Lieutenant T.S. 1828. *The Naval Gunner*. Longman & Co.

Bebie, Jules. 1943. *Manual of Explosives, Military Pyrotechnics and Chemical Warfare Agents: Composition Property Uses*. Macmillan.

Beeler, John Francis. 2001. *Birth of the Battleship: British Capital Ship Design, 1870–1881*. Chatham.

Bell, Jack. 2003. *Civil War Heavy Explosive*

Ordnance: A Guide to Large Artillery Projectiles, Torpedoes and Mines*. University of North Texas Press.

Bellamy, Martin. 2006. *Christian IV and His Navy: A Political and Administrative History of the Danish Navy, 1596–1648*. Brill.

Benjamin, Delmar, and Steve Wolf. 1993. *Gee Bee*. Zenith Imprint.

Bennett, Stuart. 1979. *A History of Control Engineering, 1800–1930*. Peter Peregrinus.

Bentham, Lady Mary S. 1854, Aug. 25. "On Mounting Ordnance on the Principle of Non-Recoil." *Journal of the Society of Arts*, 2(92): 691–92.

Bentham, Lady Mary S. 1855, Aug. "On Mounting Ordnance on the Non-Recoil Principle." *The Artizan*, 13: 193–94.

Bentham, Mary S. 1862. *The Life of Brigadier-General Sir Samuel Bentham, KSG*. Longman, Green, Longman and Roberts.

Bentham, Brigadier-General Sir Samuel. 1828. "Essay I, Efficiency of the Material." In *Naval Essays*, 31–90. Longman, Rees, etc.

Benton, Captain J.G. 1862. *A Course of Instruction in Ordnance and Gunnery*. D. Van Nostrand.

Bernhard, Anne. 2010. "The Nitrogen Cycle: Processes, Players, and Human Impact." *Nature Education Knowledge*, 3(10): 25. https://www.nature.com/scitable/knowledge/library/the-nitrogen-cycle-processes-players-and-human-15644632/.

Berube, Claude G., and John A. Rodgaard. 2005. *A Call to the Sea: Captain Charles Stewart of the USS Constitution*. Potomac Books.

Bessemer, H. 1873. "On the Accurate Firing of Naval Ordnance by Means of the Vessel's Motion." *Journal of the Royal United Service Institution*, 17: 888.

Bidder, George Parker. 1861, Apr. 23. "The National Defences." *Minutes of Proceedings of the Institution of Civil Engineers*, 20: 391.

Biringuccio, Vannoccio (transl. Cyril Stanley Smith and Martha Teach Gnudi). 1990 [1959]. *The Pirotechnia of Vanoccio Biringuccio: The Classic Sixteenth-Century Treatise on Metals and Metallurgy*. Dover.

Blackford, Mansel G. 1996. *On Board the USS Mason: The World War II Diary of James A. Dunn*. Ohio State University Press.

Blackwood, J.D., and F.P. Bowden. 1952, July 8. "The Initiation, Burning and Thermal Decomposition of Gunpowder." *Proceedings of the Royal Society A*, 213: 285–306.

Blake, Nicholas, and Richard Lawrence. 2005. *The Illustrated Companion to Nelson's Navy*. Stackpole Books.

Bobic, Nikola, et al. 2017. "The Gelatinization of Nitrocellulose by Primary Stabilizers." *Advanced Technologies*, 2(2): 31–37.

Bond, Paul Stanley, and Michael Joseph McDonough. 1916. *Technique of Modern Tactics: A Study of Troop Leading Methods in the Operations of Detachments of All Arms*. George Banta Publishing Co.

Borg, John E. 1985. *Magnus Effect—An Overview of Its Past and Future Practical Applications*. Volume 1. Contract #N00024-83-C-5350. Naval Sea Systems Command.

Boudriot, Jean (transl. Roberts, David H.). 1987. *Bonhomme Richard, 1779*. Published by Author.

Bourne, William. 1587. *The Art of Shooting in Great Ordnaunce*. https://quod.lib.umich.edu/e/eebo/A16508.0001.001/1: 3?rgn=div1;view=fulltext.

Boxer, Captain Edward Mourrier. 1859. *Treatise on Artillery Prepared for the Use of the Practical Class, Royal Military Academy*, Section I, Part I. HM Stationery Office.

Bracebridge, J.E. Compton. 1894. "Disappearing Gun Mountings." *Operations of the Division of Military Engineering of the International Congress of Engineers*, 773–99.

Braddock, John. 1832. *A Memoir on Gunpowder: In Which Are Discussed the Principles Both of Manufacture and Proof*. J.M. Richardson.

Bradford, Lt. Cmdr. Royal Bird. 1882. *Notes on the Spar Torpedo*. U.S. Torpedo Station.

Brady, George S., et al., 1996. *Materials Handbook, 14th ed*. McGraw-Hill.

Braithwaite, R. 2009, Oct. *32 Gun Frigate HMS Southampton Stability Analysis*.

Branfill-Cook, Roger. 2014. *Torpedo: The Complete History of the World's Most Revolutionary Naval Weapon*. Naval Institute Press.

Brassey, Thomas A. 1883. *The British Navy: Its Strength, Resources and Administration, 2d ed.* Vol. III, Part III (Opinions on the Shipbuilding Policy of the Navy). Longmans, Green, and Co.

Brassey, Thomas A. 1886. *The Naval Annual, 1886*. J. Griffin and Co.

Brassey, Thomas A. 1889. *The Naval Annual, 1888–9*. J. Griffin and Co.

Brassey, Thomas A. 1904. *The Naval Annual, 1904*. J. Griffin and Co.

Brassey, Thomas A. 1921. *Brassey's Naval and Shipping Annual*. William Clowes and Sons, Limited.

Brassington, Rob. 2008. "HMS *Colossus*, 1882–1906; Models and Animations of the Main Armament." http://www.dreadnoughtproject.org/tech/colossus/gunhistory.php.

Brassington, Rob. 2008a. "HMS *Colossus*, 1882–1906: Gunpowder." http://www.dreadnoughtproject.org/tech/colossus/gunpowder.php.

Brassington, Rob. 2008b. "Loading Drill in the Turret." http://www.dreadnoughtproject.org/tech/colossus/loading3.php.

Bretscher, Ulrich, n.d. "The Recipe for Black Powder." http://soggybiscuits.icu/recipe.html.

Bretscher, Ulrich. 2009, Sept. 12. "Charcoal." http://soggybiscuits.icu/charcoal.html.

Breyer, Siegfried. 1973. *Battleships and Battle Cruisers, 1905–1970*. Doubleday.

Brick, Gregory Arthur. 2013, Aug. *The Nitrate Deposits of Rock Crevices in the Upper Mississippi Valley*. Ph.D. dissertation, University of Missouri.

Brodine, Charles, Jr., et al. 2007. *Ironsides! The Ship, the Men, and the Wars of the USS Constitution*. Fireship Press.

Brood, Mike. 2004. "The 'Cutie.'" https://web.archive.org/web/20170818023308.

Broun, W. Leroy. 1862. *Notes on Artillery*. West & Johnston.

Brown, D.K. 2023. *The Grand Fleet: Warship Design and Development, 1906–1922*. Pen & Sword.

Brown, David K. 2006. *The Way of a Ship in the Midst of the Sea: The Life and Work of William Froude*. Periscope.

Brown, G.I. 2011. *Explosives: History with a Bang*. History Press.

Brown, M.E., and R.A. Rugunanan. 1989. "A Temperature-Profile Study of the Combustion of Black Powder and Ts Constituent Binary Mixtures." *Propellants, Explosives, Pyrotechnics*, 14: 69–75.

Brown, Robert. 2019. *German Destroyers*. Pen & Sword.

Brown, Ruth. 2001. "Concealed Plugs and Rotten Trunnions: David Tanner and His Problems with Gunfounding in the American War of Independence." *Historical Metallurgy*, 35(2): 81–86.

Brown, Lt. William B. 1945, Oct. 6. *The Relative Bearing and Target Angle Trainer*. Medical Research Laboratory Report 77, U.S. Submarine Base, New London.

Browne, Captain C. Orde. 1870. *Ammunition: A Descriptive Treatise*. Part II—Ammunition for Rifled Ordnance. HM Stationery Office.

Browne, Captain C. Orde. 1888. "Short History and Description of Armour and Its Attack by Artillery." *Minutes of Proceedings of the Royal Artillery Institution*, 15: 303–49.

Bruce, Robert V. 1989 [1956]. *Lincoln and the Tools of War*. University of Illinois Press.

Bruff, Captain Lawrence Laurenson. 1896. *A Text-Book of Ordnance and Gunnery: Prepared for the Use of Cadets of the U.S. Military Academy*. J. Wiley & Sons.

Bruff, Captain Lawrence Laurenson. 1903. *A Text-Book of Ordnance and Gunnery: Prepared for the Use of Cadets of the U.S. Military Academy, 2d ed*. J. Wiley & Sons.

Buchanan, Brenda J. 2006. *Gunpowder, Explosives and the State: A Technological History*. Taylor and Francis.

Buchanan, Brenda J. 2014. "Gunpowder Studies at ICOHTEC." *Icon*, 20(1): 56–73.

Bucknill, John Townsend. 1889. *Submarine Mines and Torpedoes as Applied to Harbour Defence*. Wiley.

Budge, Kent G. 2014. "Bombs." The Pacific War Online Encyclopedia. http://pwencycl.kgbudge.com/B/o/Bombs.htm.

Bukharin, Oleg. 2004. *Russian Strategic Nuclear Forces*. MIT Press.

Bull, Stephen. 2004. *Encyclopedia of Military Technology and Innovation*. Bloomsbury Academic.

Bull, Stephen. 2008. *"The Furie of the Ordnance": Artillery in the English Civil Wars*. Boydell Press.

Bulson, P.S. 1997. *Explosive Loading of Engineering*

Structures: A History of Research and a Review of Recent Developments. CRC Press.

Bunyard, Katrina. 2019. *The Development of the Naval Truck Gun Carriage: History, Archaeology, and Design.* Master's thesis, East Carolina University.

Burger, M. 1966. "Rolling of Ships." In W. Burger and A.G. Corbett, *Ship Stabilizers: A Handbook for Merchant Navy Officers*, Chapter 3. Pergamon.

Burke, Arthur E. 2017. "Torpedoes and Their Impact of Naval Warfare." Naval Undersea Warfare Center Division. https://apps.dtic.mil/sti/pdfs/AD1033484.pdf.

Caiella, J.M. 2018, Apr. "Armaments & Innovation—The Davis Gun." *Naval History Magazine*, 32(2). https://www.usni.org/magazines/naval-history-magazine/2018/april/armaments-innovation-davis-gun.

Califf, First Lieutenant Joseph M. 1889. "The Development of the Modern High-Power Rifled Cannon." *Railroad & Engineering Journal*, 63(4): 159; 63(5): 207; 63(6): 257; 63(8): 360; 63(9): 401; 63(10): 453.

Campbell, John, and N.J.M. Campbell. 1985. *Naval Weapons of World War Two.* Conway Maritime Press.

Campbell, N.J.M. 1978. "Technical Topics: Cordite." *Warships*, 2(6): 136–38.

Canfield, Eugene B. 1968. "Civil War Naval Ordnance." From *Dictionary of American Fighting Ships*, Volume III. Navy Department, Office of the Chief of Naval Operations, Naval History Division, Washington, D.C.

Cantwell, Brian J. 2002. *Introduction to Symmetry Analysis.* Cambridge University Press.

Carlisle, Rodney P. 2002. *Powder and Propellants: Energetic Materials at Indian Head, Maryland, 1890–2001.* University of North Dakota Press.

Carlucci, Donal E., and Sidney S. Jacobsen. 2018. *Ballistics: Theory and Design of Guns and Ammunition, 3d ed.* CRC Press.

Carman, W.Y. 2015 [1955]. *A History of Firearms from Earliest Times to 1914.* Taylor & Francis.

Carroll, Elise. 2020, Feb. 1. "Artifact of the Month: Cheap Shot." https://www.qaronline.org/blog/2020-02-01/artifact-month-langrage.

Casson, Lionel. 1991. *The Ancient Mariners: Seafarers and Sea Fighters of the Mediterranean in Ancient Times, 2d ed.* Princeton University Press.

Chapelle, Howard Irving. 1935. *History of American Sailing Ships.* Bonanza Books.

Chapelle, Howard Irving. 1949. *The History of the American Sailing Navy: The Ships and Their Development.* W.W. Norton and Company.

Chapelle, Howard Irving. 1988 [1930]. *The Baltimore Clipper: Its Origin and Development.* Dover.

Chemical Society (Great Britain). 1916. "Sir Andrew Noble..." (Obituary Notice). *Journal of the Chemical Society*, 109: 432–34.

Ch'oe, Wan-Gi. 2006. *Traditional Ships of Korea.* Ewha Womans University Press.

Christman, Albert B. 1971. *History of the Naval Weapons Center, China Lake, California, Vol. I: Sailors, Scientists, and Rockets: Origins of the Navy Rocket Program and of the Naval Ordnance Test Station, Inyokern.* Naval History Division.

Churchill, Awnsham, John Churchill, and John Locke. 1704. *A Collection of Voyages and Travels.* Volume III: *Awnsham and John Churchill.* ("Sir William Monson's Naval Tracts" are at 155–60.)

Clarke, Major G. Sydenham. 1890. *Fortification: Its Past Achievements, Recent Development, and Future Progress.* John Murray.

Classical Association of Northern Ireland. 2017, Dec. 31. "Not Just the Spanish Armada—Some Uses of Fire Ships in the Ancient World." https://classicalassociationni.wordpress.com/2017/12/31/not-just-the-spanish-armada-some-uses-of-fire-ships-in-the-ancient-world/.

Clemmow, C.A. 1928, June 11. "IX. a Theory of Internal Ballistics Based on a Pressure-Index Law of Burning for Propellants." *Philosophical Transactions of the Royal Society of London*, 228: 345–82.

Cline, Donna. 2004. *Trajectories*, Parts 1–4, consisting of Part 1: "Vacuum" (2003); Part 2: "'Atmosphere': The 'Point Mass' Trajectory: Flat-Fire Approximate Method" (2004); Part 3: "'Atmosphere': The 'Point Mass' Trajectory: The Siacci Method 'Ballistic Coefficient'" (2002); Part 4: "'Atmosphere': The 'Point Mass' Trajectory: Numerical Integration Method" (2004). http://www.angelfire.com/poetry/u31240468/AeroBallistics.pdf.

Clowes, W. Laird. 1894. "The Ram in Action and in Accident." *Proceedings of the U.S. Naval Institute*, 20(1) (Whole No. 69): 85–108.

Coggins, Jack. 2012 [1962]. *Arms and Equipment of the Civil War.* Dover.

Collins, A.R. n.d. "Benjamin Robins on Ballistics." https://www.arc.id.au/RobinsOnBallistics.html.

Collins, A.R. n.d. "British Cannonball Sizes." http://arc.id.au/Cannonballs.html.

Collins, A.R. n.d. "Cannonball Aerodynamic Drag." https://arc.id.au/CannonballDrag.html.

Collins, A.R. n.d. "Royal Ordnance in 1637." http://arc.id.au/Ordnance1637.html.

Collins, A.R. n.d. "Smooth Bore Cannon Ballistics." https://www.arc.id.au/CannonBallistics.html.

Colomb, Vice Admiral Philip Howard. 1898. *Memoirs of Admiral the Right Honble. Sir Astley Cooper Key....* Methuen & Co.

Cooke, Augustus Paul. 1875. *Text-Book of Naval Ordnance and Gunnery.* 2 vols. John Wiley & Sons.

Cooke, Augustus Paul. 1880. *A Text-book of Naval Ordnance and Gunnery.* 2 vols. John Wiley & Sons.

Cooke, Gary W. 2006. "81mm Mortar Ammunition and Fuzes." http://www.inetres.com/gp/military/infantry/mortar/81mm.html.

Corbett, Julian Stafford. 1898. *Papers Relating to*

the Navy during the Spanish War, 1585–1587. Navy Records Society.

Cotterell, Brian. 2010. *Fracture and Life*. Imperial College Press.

Coulthard, Sally. 2021. *The Barn: The Lives, Landscape and Lost Ways of an Old Yorkshire Farm*. Head of Zeus.

Courtney, Elya, et al. 2015, Oct. 26. *Experimental Tests of the Proportionality of Aerodynamic Drag to Air Density for Supersonic Projectiles*. BTG Research.

Coutts, H.B. Money. 1908. *Famous Duels of the Fleet and Their Lessons*. W. Blackwood.

Crain, Colonel J.K. 1922. "Tendencies in Ammunition Design." *Army Ordnance*, 3: 252–255.

Cramp, Charles. 1894. "Discussion: The Disappearing Gun Afloat." *Proceedings of the U.S. Naval Institute*, 21 (Part 4): 867–96.

Crawford, Kent R. 2021. "The Last Years of the Black Powder Era." *Voennyi Sbornik*, 9(2): 70–75. DOI: 10.13187/vs.2021.2.70.

Crawford, Morris de Camp. 1924. *The Heritage of Cotton: The Fibre of Two Worlds and Many Ages*. G.P. Putnam's Sons.

Crawford, R.J., and James L. Throne. 2001. *Rotational Molding Technology*. Elsevier Science.

Cressy, David. 2013. *Saltpeter: The Mother of Gunpowder*. Oxford University Press.

Creuze, Augustin Francis Bullock. 1846. *Treatise on the Theory and Practice of Naval Architecture*. Adam & Charles Black.

Cronkhite, Adelbert, and James Chester. 1893. *Gunnery for Non-Commissioned Officers*. J. Wiley & Sons.

Culmann, F.I. (transl. Captain Alfred Mordecai). 1836. "On the Manufacture of Military Projectiles." *Journal of the Franklin Institute*, 18 (New Series): 8–17 (July); 82–90 (August); 145–53 (September).

Culver, Major Richard Otis, Jr., and Captain Raymond Michael Burns. 1972, Dec. *Velocity and Pressure Effects on Projectiles Due to Variation of Ignition Parameters*. M.S. thesis, Naval Postgraduate School.

Cummins, Joseph. 2009. *The War Chronicles: Front Flintlocks to Machine Guns*. Fair Winds Press.

Cunningham, H.D. 1864. "The Application of Steam Power to the Working of Heavy Guns." *Journal of the Royal United Service Institution*, 8: 67–81.

Curtin, Lt. Cmdr. Roland I., and Lt. Cmdr. Thomas L. Johnson. 1915. *Naval Ordnance: A Text-book Prepared for the Use of the Midshipmen of the United States Naval Academy*. United States Naval Institute.

Czarnecki, Joseph. 2001, Jan. 31. "Torpedo Defense Systems of World War II." http://www.navweaps.com/index_tech/tech-047.htm.

Dahlgren, John Adolphus Bernard. 1853. *Ordnance Memoranda: Naval Percussion Locks and Primers, Particularly Those of the United States*. A. Hart.

Dahlgren, John Adolphus Bernard. 1856. *Shells and Shell-Guns*. King & Baird.

Dahlgren, John Adolphus Bernard. 1856a. *Boat Armament of the U.S. Navy, 2d ed*. King & Baird.

Dahlgren, John Adolphus Bernard. 1861, Aug. 6 (issue date). U.S. Patent No. 32,983. "Cast Iron Ordnance."

Dakin, Douglas. 2022. *The Greek Struggle for Independence, 1821–1833*. University of California Press.

Daly, Colin H. 2003. "Thick Walled Cylinders." http://courses.washington.edu/me354a/Thick%20Walled%20Cylinders.pdf.

Davies, J.D. 2008. *Pepys's Navy: Ships, Men & Warfare, 1649–1689*. Seaforth Publishing.

Davis, Charles Gerard. 1984. *American Sailing Ships: Their Plans and History*. Dover.

Davis, Charles Gerard. 1989 [1933]. *The Built-Up Ship Model*. Dover.

Davis, Tenney L. 1943. *The Chemistry of Powder and Explosives*. Volume II. Angriff Press.

Dawson, Commander William. 1872. *Naval Guns, and Mounting and Working Heavy Guns at Sea*. W. Mitchell and Co.

Dean, J., et al. 2009, Oct. "Energy Absorption during Projectile Perforation of Thin Steel Plates and the Kinetic Energy of Ejected Fragments." *International Journal of Impact Engineering*, 36(10–11): 1250–58.

Deane, John. 1858. *Deane's Manual of the History and Science of Fire-arms*. Longman, Brown, etc.

Deering, W.H. 1889, Nov. 1. "Recent Inventions in Gunpowder and Other Explosives." *Notes on the Construction of Ordnance No. 51*. Government Printing Office.

Delgado, James P. 2019. *War at Sea: A Shipwrecked History from Antiquity to the Twentieth Century*. Oxford University Press.

Dell, R.M., et al. 2007. *Understanding Batteries*. Royal Society of Chemistry.

De Mestre, Neville. 1990. *The Mathematics of Projectiles in Sport*. Cambridge University Press.

Denny, Mark. 2011. *Their Arrows Will Darken the Sun: The Evolution and Science of Ballistics*. Johns Hopkins University Press.

Denny, Mark. 2011a, Feb. "Depth Control of the Brennan Torpedo." https://ieeexplore.ieee.org/abstract/document/5687826.

Deogracias, Major Alan J., II. 2003. *The Battle of Hampton Roads: A Revolution in Military Affairs*. Master's thesis, U.S. Army Command and General Staff College.

de Podesta, Michael. 2007, Sept. "Bouncing Steel Balls on Water." *Physics Education*, 42(5): 466–77.

DeRose, Charles E., and Peter F. Intrieri. 1970, Aug. "Chap. 3, Model and Sabot Design and Launching Techniques." In Thomas N. Canning et al., *Ballistic-Range Technology*. North Atlantic Treaty Organization, Advisory Group for Aerospace Research and Development.

de Tousard, Louis. 1809. *American Artillerist's Companion*. 2 vols. C. and A. Conrad.

de Villehuet, Jacques Bourdé, and Jean

Nicolas Jouin de Sauseuil. 1788. *Le Manœuvrier.* S. Hooper.

Dias Júnior, Ananias Francisco, et al. 2016, Oct.–Dec. "Higroscopicity of Charcoal Produced in Different Temperatures." https://www.scielo.br/j/cerne/a/RTQ9qvNk4zX673N3p8XtpGS/?lang=en#.

Dictionary of American Naval Fighting Ships, Volume 3. 1968. Government Printing Office.

DiGiulian, Tony. 2002, Aug. 22. "Longest Gunfire Hit on an Enemy Warship." http://www.navweaps.com/index_tech/tech-006.php.

DiGiulian, Tony. 2022a, Nov. 2. "Naval Propellants: A Brief Overview." http://www.navweaps.com/index_tech/tech-100.php.

DiGiulian, Tony. 2023. "Definitions and Information about Naval Guns: Part 1—Weapons and Mountings." http://www.navweaps.com/Weapons/Gun_Data.htm.

DiGiulian, Tony. 2023a. "Definitions and Information about Naval Guns: Part 2—Ammunition, Fuzes, Projectiles and Propellants." http://www.navweaps.com/Weapons/Gun_Data_p2.php.

DiGiulian, Tony. 2023b. "Definitions and Information about Naval Guns. Part 3—Miscellaneous Definitions." http://www.navweaps.com/Weapons/Gun_Data_p3.php.

Ding, Dayu, and Tadao Yoshida. 2012. "Combustion Properties of Grain Black Powder Used as a Lifting Charge of Fireworks." *Science and Technology of Energetic Materials,* 73(4): 109–14.

Dodson, Aidan. 2016. *The Kaiser's Battlefleet: German Capital Ships, 1871–1918.* Pen & Sword.

Douglas, Major General Sir Howard. 1820. *A Treatise on Naval Gunnery.* John Murray.

Douglas, Major General Sir Howard. 1829. *A Treatise on Naval Gunnery, 2d ed.* John Murray.

Douglas, Major General Sir Howard. 1860. *A Treatise on Naval Gunnery, 5th ed., rev.* John Murray.

Downie, Neil A. 2006. *Exploding Disk Cannons, Slimemobiles, and 32 Other Projects for Saturday Science.* Johns Hopkins University Press.

Dramiński, Stefan. 2020. *The Battleship USS* Iowa. Osprey Publishing.

Duke, Audrey. 2023, May 15. *The Quest to Achieve "One Accurate Shot": U.S. Navy Torpedo Development and Testing, 1896–1917.* Graduate certificate in maritime history, U.S. Naval War College.

Dyer, A.B. 1868. *Proceeding of a Court of Inquiry… Against A.B. Dyer, Chief of Ordnance.* Part II. Government Printing Office.

Earle, Lieutenant Commander Ralph. 1914, July. "The Development of Our Navy's Smokeless Powder." *Proceedings of the U.S. Naval Institute,* 40(152). https://www.usni.org/magazines/proceedings/1914/july/development-our-navys-smokeless-powder.

Eger, Christopher. 2021, Sept. 22. "Warship Wednesday, Sept. 22, 2021: Behold, the Destroyerzooka." https://laststandonzombieisland.com/tag/destroyer-305mm-recoilless-rifle/.

Egerton, T. 1801. *The Little Bombardier and*

Pocket Gunner. http://www.napoleon-series.org/research/abstract/military/army/britain/artillery/c_ammo.html.

El-Sayed, Ahmed F. 2016. *Fundamentals of Aircraft and Rocket Propulsion.* Springer London.

Elkin, Dolores, et al. 2007. "Archaeological Research on HMS Swift: A British Sloop-of-War Lost Off Patagonia, Southern Argentina, in 1770." *International Journal of Nautical Archaeology,* 36(1): 32–58.

Ellacott, Samuel Ernest. 1970. *The Seaman. Book 2.* Abelard-Schuman.

Ellet, Alexander. 1946. *Summary Technical Report of Division 4, NRDC, Volume 3, Summary, Photoelectric Fuzes and Miscellaneous Projects.* https://apps.dtic.mil/sti/tr%2Fpdf/AD0221589.pdf.

Encyclopaedia Britannica. 1888 [1894]. 9th edition. 24 vols. A. & C. Black.

Encyclopaedia Britannica. 1911. 11th edition. 29 vols. Horace Everett Hooper.

Engineer. 1896, Nov. 13. "The Navies of the World." *The Engineer,* 82: 486–87.

Engineers Edge. 2023 (accessed). "Densities of Metals and Elements Table." https://www.engineersedge.com/materials/densities_of_metals_and_elements_table_13976.htm.

Epstein, Katherine C. 2014. *Torpedo: Inventing the Military-Industrial Complex in the United States and Britain.* Harvard University Press.

Evans, David C., and David Peattie. 2012. *Kaigun: Strategy, Tactics, and Technology in the Imperial Japanese Navy.* Naval Institute Press.

Evans, Nigel F. 2014, June 6. "British Artillery in World War 2: Effect and Weight of Fire." nigelef.tripod.com/wt_of_fire.htm.

Exmundo, Jex. 2022, Nov. 3. "Railguns: All You Need to Know about the Weapon That Uses Electromagnetic Force." https://interestingengineering.com/innovation/railgun.

[Experiments] Anonymous. 1866. *Experiments with Naval Ordnance. HMS Excellent. 1866.* Harrison & Sons.

Experiments in Her Majesty's Ship Excellent, Under the Supervision of Captain Sir Thomas Hastings, VB and Chaptain HD Chads, CB. 1854.

Ezell, Edward C. 1962, July. "The Early Development of Propellant Gun Powders; the Development of Mammoth Powder, 1858–1872." https://digital.hagley.org/MS1645_018.

Falconer, William, and William Burney. 1815. *An Universal Dictionary of the Marine.* T. Cadell & W. Davies.

Falkenau, Arthur. 1898, Apr. "Some Applications of High Explosives in Warfare." *Proceedings of the Engineers' Club of Philadelphia,* 15(2): 108.

Farquharson-Roberts, Mike. 2014. *A History of the Royal Navy: World War I.* Bloomsbury.

Farrow, Edward S. 1885. *Farrow's Military Encyclopedia.* 3 vols. Published by the author.

Farrow, Edward S. 1895. *Farrow's Military Encyclopedia.* 3 vols. Military Naval Publishing Company.

Federation of American Scientists. 2023 (accessed). *Fundamentals of Naval Weapons Systems.* Weapons and Systems Engineering Department, U.S. Naval Academy. https://man.fas.org/dod-101/navy/docs/fun/index.html.

Ffoulkes, Charles John. 2011 [1937]. *The Gun-Founders of England: With a List of English and Continental Gun-Founders from the XIV to the XIX Centuries.* Cambridge University Press.

Firearms History, Technology & Development Blog. 2016, June 19. "Manufacture of Sulfur—II." http://firearmshistory.blogspot.com/2016/06/manufacture-of-sulfur-ii.html.

Firearms History, Technology & Development Blog. 2016a, June 21. "Manufacture of Sulfur—III." http://firearmshistory.blogspot.com/2016/06/manufacture-of-sulfur-iii.html.

Fischer, H.B. 1904, Apr. "The Development of Projectiles." *Yale Scientific Monthly,* 10(7): 196–200.

Fitzpatrick, Richard. 2006, Mar. 29. "Air Drag." https://farside.ph.utexas.edu/teaching/329/lectures/node42.html.

Fleet, United States. 1943, Feb. *Operating Instructions for the Five Inch, 38 Caliber, Gun Crews.* Government Printing Office.

Fletcher, Clive A.J. 2012. *Computational Techniques for Fluid Dynamics: Specific Techniques for Different Flow Categories.* Springer Berlin Heidelberg.

Florek, Maciek. 2017. "Torpedo Fire Control System and Fat Torpedoes." Torpedo Vorhaltechner Project. http://www.tvre.org/en/torpedo-fire-control-system-and-fat-torpedoes.

Fonvielle, Chris E., Jr. 2001. *The Wilmington Campaign: Last Departing Rays of Hope.* Stackpole Books.

Fox, Frank L. 2009. *The Four Days' Battle of 1666: The Greatest Sea Fight of the Age of Sail.* Pen & Sword.

Frey, James. 2009, Fall. "The Indian Saltpeter Trade, the Military Revolution, and the Rise of Britain as a Global Superpower." *The Historian,* 71(3): 507–54.

Friedman, Norman. 2004. *The U.S. Destroyers: An Illustrated Design History.* Naval Institute Press.

Friedman, Norman. 2011. *Naval Weapons of World War One.* Seaforth.

Friedman, Norman. 2013. *Naval Firepower: Battleship Guns and Gunnery in the Dreadnought Era.* Pen & Sword.

Friedman, Norman. 2014. *Naval Anti-Aircraft Guns and Gunnery.* Pen & Sword.

Friedman, Norman. 2015. *The British Battleship: 1906–1946.* Naval Institute Press.

Friedman, Norman, and A.D. Baker III. 2008. *British Destroyers & Frigates: The Second World War and After.* Seaforth.

Fullam, William Freeland, and Thomas Charles Hart. 1905. *Text-Book of Ordnance and Gunnery.* United States Naval Institute.

Gagnon, Bernard. 2015, Apr. 30. "RBL 7 Inch Armstrong Gun in Fort No. 1, Lévis, Québec, Canada." https://commons.wikimedia.org/wiki/File: Fort_No_1,_L%C3%A9vis_-_Canon_Armstrong_02.jpg.

Garbett, Captain H. 1897. *Naval Gunnery: A Description and History of the Fighting Equipment of a Man-of-War.* George Bell and Sons.

Gardiner, Robert. 1992. *The First Frigates: Nine Pounder and Twelve Pounder Frigates, 1748–1815.* Conway Maritime Press.

Gardiner, Robert, and Richard Unger. 1994. *Cogs, Caravels and Galleons: The Sailing Ship, 1000–1650.* Conway Maritime Press.

Gardner, W. 1999. *Decoding History: The Battle of the Atlantic and Ultra.* Palgrave Macmillan UK.

Garrison, F. Lynwood. 1892. "The Development of American Armor-Plate." *Journal of the Franklin Institute,* 133: 337–56 (May); 133: 421–53 (June); 134: 20–42 (July).

Garry, Jim. 2012. *Weapons of the Lewis and Clark Expedition.* University of Oklahoma Press.

Gartner, Scott Sigmund, and Gary M. Segura. 2021. *Costly Calculations: A Theory of War, Casualties, and Politics.* Cambridge University Press.

Garzke, William H., et al. 2019. *Battleship Bismarck: A Design and Operational History.* Pen & Sword.

Garzke, William J., and Robert O. Dulin. 1985. *Battleships: Axis and Neutral Battleships in World War II.* Naval Institute Press.

Gebhard, Louis A. 1979. *Evolution of Naval Radio-electronics and Contributions of the Naval Research Laboratory.* NRL Report 8300. Naval Research Laboratory.

Glete, Jan. 1993. *Navies and Nations: Warships, Navies and State Building in Europe and America, 1500–1860.* Almqvist & Wiksell International.

Glete, Jan. 2010. *Swedish Naval Administration, 1521–1721: Resource Flows and Organisational Capabilities.* Brill.

Glover, Gareth. 2021. *Nelson's Navy in 100 Objects.* Pen & Sword.

Gluchoff, Alan. 2011. "Artillerymen and Mathematicians: Forest Ray Moulton and Changes in American Exterior Ballistics, 1885–1934." *Historia Mathematica,* 38: 506–47.

Golas, Peter J. 1999. Volume 5 (Chemistry and Chemical Technology), Part XIII (Mining). In Joseph Needham, *Science and Civilisation in China.* Cambridge University Press.

Goldrick, James. 2015. *Before Jutland: The Naval War in Northern European Waters, August 1914–February 1915.* Naval Institute Press.

Goodwin, Peter. 2019. *Nelson's Arctic Voyage: The Royal Navy's First Polar Expedition 1773.* Bloomsbury.

Gover, John. 1805, Dec. 19. British Patent 2803. "Improvements in the Construction of Gun-Carriages." Abstract in *Abridgments of the Specifications Relating to Fire-arms and Other Weapons, Ammunition, and Accoutrements: A.D. 1588,* 41 (1859).

Grant, R.G. 2011. *Battle at Sea: Years of Naval Warfare.* D.K. Publishing.

Greaves, John. 1737. "An Account of Some Experiments for Trying the Force of Great Guns." *Miscellaneous Works of Mr. John Greaves*, Volume II. Birch. [First published by Stubbs in *Philosophical Transactions of the Royal Society of London*, 173: 1090, July 1685.]

Greene, Jack, and Alessandro Massignani. 1998. *Ironclads at War: The Origin and Development of the Armored Warship, 1854–1891*. Da Capo Press.

Greenhalgh, Michael. 2019. *Plundered Empire: Acquiring Antiquities from Ottoman Lands*. Brill.

Grey, Charles, and George Fletcher MacMunn. 1932. *The Merchant Venturers of London: A Record of Far Eastern Trade & Piracy During the Seventeenth Century*. HF&G Witherby.

Grubb, Sir Howard, et al. 1902, Feb. 5 (issue date). British Patent 22,127. Issued on application filed Dec. 5, 1900. "Improvements in Sighting Devices for Guns."

Gruntman, Mike. 2004. *Blazing the Trail: The Early History of Spacecraft and Rocketry*. American Institute of Aeronautics and Astronautics.

Guilmartin, John Francis, Jr. 1982. "The Guns of the Santissimo Sacramento." www.angelfire.com/ga4/guilmartin.com/Santissimo.html.

Guilmartin, John Francis, Jr. 2003. *Gunpowder & Galleys*. Conway Maritime Press.

Guilmartin, John Francis, Jr. 2007, July. "The Earliest Shipboard Gunpowder Ordnance: An Analysis of Its Technical Parameters and Tactical Capabilities." *Journal of Military History*, 71: 649–69.

Gurstelle, William. 2007. *Whoosh, Boom, Splat*. Three Rivers Press.

Guthrie, William P. 2003. *The Later Thirty Years War: From the Battle of Wittstock to the Treaty of Westphalia*. Bloomsbury Academic.

Gutzman, Philip. 2010. *Vietnam: Navy and Riverine Weapons*. lulu.com.

Hackborn, William W. 2006. "The Science of Ballistics: Mathematics Serving the Dark Side." Canadian Society for the History and Philosophy of Mathematics (CSHPM), 2006 Annual Meeting, York University, Toronto. https://www.researchgate.net/publication/319459791_The_Science_of_Ballistics_Mathematics_Serving_the_Dark_Side.

Hackett, Bob, and Sander Kingsepp. 2011, Nov. 26. "Battle Histories of Japan's Explosive Motorboats." http://www.combinedfleet.com/ShinyoEMB.htm.

Hackmann, Willem. 2018 (pdf creation). *Asdic to Sonar and the Cross-over to the Science of Underwater Acoustics*. https://acoustics.ac.uk/wp-content/uploads/2018/08/D1_WHackmann_History.pdf.

Haeberle, Lt. F.E. 1923, Sept. "Ship Stabilization." *Proceedings of the U.S. Naval Institute*, 49(9) (Whole issue 247): n.p. https://www.usni.org/magazines/proceedings/1923/september/ship-stabilization.

Hager, Thomas. 2009. *The Alchemy of Air: A Jewish Genius, a Doomed Tycoon, and the Scientific Discovery That Fed the World but Fueled the Rise of Hitler*. Three Rivers Press (Crown).

Haldon, John. 2006. "'Greek Fire' Revisited: Recent and Current Research." In Elizabeth Jeffreys, *Byzantine Style, Religion and Civilization: In Honour of Sir Steven Runciman*, 290–325. Cambridge University Press.

Hall, Alfred Rupert. 1952. *Ballistics in the Seventeenth Century: A Study in the Relations of Science and War with Reference Principally to England*. Cambridge University Press.

Hall, Andy. 2012, Oct. 21. "Moving the Big Guns on Alabama." https://deadconfederates.com/2012/10/21/moving-the-big-guns-on-alabama/.

Hamilton, Donny L. 1997. "Ceramic Firepots." https://liberalarts.tamu.edu/nautarch/reportlist/crl-reports-conservation-of-ceramic-firepots/.

Hamilton, Douglas Thomas. 1916. *High-Explosive Shell Manufacture*. Industrial Press.

Hamilton, Douglas Thomas. 1916a. *Cartridge Manufacture*. Industrial Press.

Hamilton, William R. 1888, Oct. "American Machine Cannon and Dynamite Guns." *The Century Illustrated Monthly Magazine*, 36: 885–93. https://www.victorianvoices.net/ARTICLES/CENTURY/Century1888B/C1888B-Guns.pdf.

Harbron, John D. 1988. *Trafalgar and the Spanish Navy*. Conway Maritime Press.

Haswell, Charles Haynes. 1853. *Engineers' and Mechanics' Pocket-Book....* Harper & Brothers.

Hawkins, Captain Wilford J. 1912. "Twenty Years Progress in Powders, Projectiles, Fuses, and Primers." *Journal of the United States Artillery*, 38: 142–66.

Hayes, Thomas Jay. 1938. *Elements of Ordnance: A Textbook for Use of Cadets of the United States Military Academy*. J. Wiley & Sons.

Hazlett, James C., et al. 1988. *Field Artillery Weapons of the Civil War*. University of Delaware Press.

Head, M.A. 1989, Dec. "The Loss of HMS Natal Due Internal Explosion—1915." *Naval Historical Review*. https://navyhistory.au/the-loss-of-hms-natal-due-internal-explosion-1915/.

Hearings Before the Committee on Naval Affairs of the House of Representatives on Estimates Submitted by the Secretary of the Navy 1908–9. 60th Cong., 1st Sess. Government Printing Office.

Heath, Captain Frank (Chief of Ordnance, U.S. Army). 1892. "Appendix 33: Test of Merriam's Base Precussion Fuze." In *Annual Report of the Chief of Ordnance to the Secretary of War for the Fiscal Year Ended June 30, 1892*. Government Printing Office.

Hebert, Luke. 1849. *The Engineer's and Mechanic's Encyclopædia*. Thomas Kelly.

Heidler, David Steven, et al. 2002. *Encyclopedia of the American Civil War: A Political, Social, and Military History*. W.W. Norton & Co.

Helgason, Guðmundur. 2023. "Allied Warships: HMS Harvester (H19)." https://uboat.net/allies/warships/ship/4231.html.

Hempstead, Colin A., and William E. Worthington. 2005. *Encyclopedia of 20th-Century Technology*. Volume 2. Routledge.

Henderson, James. 2011. *Frigates—Sloops & Brigs*. Pen & Sword.

Henderson, Lieutenant R.W. 1904, Apr. "The Evolution of Smokeless Powder." *Proceedings of the U.S. Naval Institute*, 30(2): 110. https://www.usni.org/magazines/proceedings/1904/april/evolution-smokeless-powder.

Henry, Chris. 2006. *Depth Charge: Royal Naval Mines, Depth Charges & Underwater Weapons, 1914–1945*. Pen & Sword.

Hess, Earl J. 2022. *Civil War Field Artillery: Promise and Performance on the Battlefield*. Louisiana State University Press.

Hickey, Donald R. 2012. *The War of 1812: A Forgotten Conflict, Bicentennial Edition*. University of Illinois Press.

Hidden, Enoch, and S. Sawyer. 1842, Apr. 29 (issue date). U.S. Patent 2,594. "Improvement in Cannon-Locks."

Hill, Carol A. 1981, Mar. "Origin of Cave Saltpeter." *Journal of Geology*, 89(2): 252–59.

Hill, Richard. 2000. *War at Sea in the Ironclad Age*. Smithsonian Books.

Hime, Lt. Henry William Lovett. 1870. "The Field Artillery of the Great Rebellion; Its Nature and Use." *Minutes of Proceedings of the Royal Artillery Institution*, 6: 283–302.

Hime, Lt. Col. Henry William Lovett. 1904. *Gunpowder and Ammunition, Their Origin and Progress*. Longmans, Green.

Hime, Lt. Col. Henry William Lovett. 1915. *The Origin of Artillery*. Longmans, Green and Company.

Hind, Andrew. 2008, Oct. "The Cruise Missile Comes of Age." *Naval History Magazine*, 22(5). https://www.usni.org/magazines/naval-history-magazine/2008/october/cruise-missile-comes-age.

Hirschel, Ernst Heinrich, et al. 2012. *Aeronautical Research in Germany: From Lilienthal Until Today*. Springer Berlin Heidelberg.

Hobson, Assistant Naval Constructor Richmond Pearson. 1895, July. "The Disappearing Gun Afloat." *Proceedings of the United States Naval Institute*, 21: 599–656.

Hocker, Fred. 2017. "Ships, Shot and Splinters: The Effect of 17th-Century Naval Ordnance on Ship Structure." ISBSA Conference 14 Proceedings, 193–200.

Hogg, Ian V. 2016. *German Secret Weapons of World War II: The Missiles, Rockets, Weapons, and New Technology of the Third Reich*. Skyhorse Publishing.

Hogg, Oliver Frederick Gillilan. 1970. *Artillery: Its Origin, Heyday, and Decline*. Archon Books.

Holley, Alexander Lyman. 1865. *A Treatise on Ordnance and Armor*. D. Van Nostrand.

Holman, James. 1834. *A Voyage Round the World*. Volume II. Smith, Elder and Co.

Hopkins, Albert Allis. 1915. *The Scientific American War Book: The Mechanism and Technique of Warfare*. Munn.

Hoppe, Jon. 2021, June. "Rocket Ships." *Naval History Magazine*, 35(3): n.p. https://www.usni.org/magazines/naval-history-magazine/2021/june/rocket-ships.

Hore, Peter. 2019. *The World Encyclopedia of Battleships*. Lorenz Books [Anness Publishing].

Hoskins, Sara. 2003, Dec. *16th Century Cast-Bronze Ordnance in the Museu De Angra Do Heroismo*. M.A. thesis, Texas A&M.

Hough, Richard. 2003. *Dreadnought: A History of the Modern Battleship*. Periscope.

Hovgaard, William. 1920. *Modern History of Warships*. E. & F.N. Spon.

Hoving, A.J., and Diederick Wildeman. 2012. *Nicolaes Witsen and Shipbuilding in the Dutch Golden Age*. Texas A&M University Press.

Howard, Robert A. 1975, Summer. "Black Powder Manufacture." *IA: The Journal of the Society for Industrial Archaeology*, 1(1): 13–28.

Howard, Robert A. 2006. "Realities and Perceptions in the Evolution of Black Powder Making." In Brenda J. Buchanan, *Gunpowder, Explosives and the State: A Technological History*, 21–41. Taylor and Francis.

Howeth, Captain L.S. 1963. *History of Communications-Electronics in the United States Navy*. Government Printing Office.

Hughes, Basil Perronet. 1975. *Firepower: Weapons Effectiveness on the Battlefield, 1730–1850*. Scribner.

Hunt, F.R.W., and C.E. Wright. 1922. "A Solution of the Principal Internal-Ballistic Problem for Long Elliptic Cords." *Minutes of Proceedings of the Royal Artillery Institution*, 48: 443–55.

Hunt, Walter F. 1915. "The Origin of the Sulphur Deposits of Sicily." *Economic Geology*, 10: 543–79.

Hutchinson, C.M. 1917. *Saltpetre: Its Origin and Extraction in India*. Bulletin No. 68, Agricultural Research Institute, Pusa. Calcutta: Government Printing.

Hutton, Charles. 1812. *Tracts on Mathematical and Physical Subjects, etc.* Volume III. London.

Hutton, Charles. 1812a. *A Course of Mathematics*. 2 vols. London.

Illustrated Naval and Military Magazine. 1885, Aug. 1. "The Moncrieff System of Disappearing Gun Carriages." *Illustrated Naval and Military Magazine*, 3(14): 120–24.

Ingalls, Colonel James Monroe. 1886. *Exterior Ballistics in the Plane of Fire*. D. Van Nostrand.

Ingalls, Colonel James Monroe. 1912. *Interior Ballistics*. John Wiley & Sons.

Ingalls, Colonel James Monroe. 1918. *Ingalls' Ballistics Tables*. Government Printing Office. (Originally computed 1893, revised under direction of the Ordnance Board, 1917.)

Inman, James. 1828. *An Introduction to Naval Gunnery*. W. Woodward.

Ireland, Bernard. 2000. *Naval Warfare in the Age of Sail: War at Sea, 1756–1815*. Norton.

Ireland, Bernard, and Eric Grove. 1997. *Jane's War at Sea 1897–1997, 100 Years of Jane's Fighting Ships*. HarperCollins.

Iron Trade. 1924, June 12. "How English Test Big Forgings." *Iron Trade Review*, 74: 1557–59.

James, William. 1816. *An Inquiry Into the Merits of the Principal Naval Actions, Between Great Britain and the United States....* Self-published.

James, William. 1826. *The Naval History of Great Britain*. 6 vols. https://sites.rootsweb.com/~pbtyc/Naval_History/Index.html.

Jane, Frederick Thomas. 1904. *The Imperial Japanese Navy*. W. Thacker & Co.

Jarrett, D.N. 2005. *Cockpit Engineering*. Ashgate Pub.

JBMBallistics. n.d. Untitled list of CD vs. Mach number for $^9/_{16}$th inch sphere, obtained from Robert L. McCoy, U.S. Army Ballistics Research Laboratory, believed to correspond in part to data in Charters, 1945, "The Aerodynamic Performance of Small Spheres from Subsonic to High Supersonic Velocities." *Journal of the Aeronautical Sciences*, 12: 468–76. https://jbmballistics.com/ballistics/downloads/downloads.shtml.

JBMBallistics/G1. n.d. Untitled list of CD vs Mach number for a standard G1 projectile. https://jbmballistics.com/ballistics/downloads/text/mcg1.txt, cited under "More Drag Functions." https://jbmballistics.com/ballistics/downloads/downloads.shtml.

Jeffers, William N., Jr. 1850. *A Concise Treatise on the Theory and Practice of Naval Gunnery*. D. Appleton & Company.

Johnsen, Frederick A. 2018. *Testbeds, Motherships & Parasites: Astonishing Aircraft from the Golden Age of Flight Test*. Specialty Press.

Johnson, W. 1998. "The Ricochet of Spinning and Non-spinning Spherical Projectiles, Mainly from Water, Part I: Some Historical Contributions." *International Journal of Impact Engineering*, 21: 15–24; "Part II: An Outline of Theory and Warlike Applications," 21: 25–34.

Johnston, James J., and James J. Johnston. 1990, Summer. "Bullets for Johnny Reb: Confederate Nitre and Mining Bureau in Arkansas." *Arkansas Historical Quarterly*, 49(2): 124–67.

Joint Chiefs of Staff. 1943, Aug. 1. "U.S. Radar: Operational Characteristics of Radar Classified by Tactical Application." FTP 217. https://www.history.navy.mil/research/library/online-reading-room/title-list-alphabetically/u/operational-characteristics-of-radar-classified-by-tactical-application.html.

Jolie, E.W. 1978, Sept. 15. "A Brief History of U.S. Navy Torpedo Development." NUSC Technical Document 5436. https://maritime.org/doc/jolie/index.php.

Jones, Charles R. 1978, Jan. "Weapon Effects Primer." *Proceedings of the U.S. Naval Institute*, 104(1): 899. https://www.usni.org/magazines/proceedings/1978/january/weapon-effects-primer.

Jones, R.N., et al. 1965, Feb. *Engineering Design Handbook, Ballistics Series: Interior Ballistics of Guns*. U.S. Army Materiel Command, AMCP 706-150.

Jordan, John. 2015. *Warship 2015*. Bloomsbury.

Jordan, John, and Robert Dumas. 2009. *French Battleships, 1922–1956*. Seaforth.

Josten, Louis J. 1921. "Manufacture of Fourteen- and Sixteen-Inch Cupro–Nickel Rotating Projectile Bands by Centrifugal Casting Machine Process." *Proceedings of the U.S. Naval Institute*, 47: 28.

Kahanov, Y., et al. 2012. "Akko 1 Shipwreck: The Effect of Cannon Fire on the Wooden Hull." *Journal of Archaeological Science*, 39: 1993–2002.

Kaiho, Tatsuo. 2014. *Iodine Chemistry and Applications*. Wiley.

Kaiserfeld, Thomas. 2006. "Saltpetre at the Intersection of Military and Agricultural Interests in Eighteenth-Century Sweden." In Brenda J. Buchanan, *Gunpowder, Explosives and the State: A Technological History*, 142–57. Taylor and Francis.

Kaiserfeld, Thomas. 2009 (pdf creation date). "From Mapping to Mixing: Political Recognition of Expertise from the Allotment System to the Public Promotion of Manufactories." https://www.kth.se/polopoly_fs/1.108212.1550158196!/Menu/general/column-content/attachment/Kaiserfeld.pdf.

Kakaliagos, A., and N. Ninis. 2018. "Orban's Gun Ballistics and Assessment of Historical Evidence Concerning the Bombardment of Constantinople Walls in 1453." *Procedia Structural Integrity*, 10: 179–86.

Keil, A.H. 1961, Nov. 1. "The Response of Ships to Underwater Explosions." Department of the Navy, David Taylor Model Basin, Report 1576.

Keliher, Macabe. 2003. *Out of China, Or, Yu Yonghe's Tales of Formosa: A History of 17th Century Taiwan*. SMC Publishing.

Kelly, Jack. 2004. *Gunpowder: Alchemy, Bombards, and Pyrotechnics: The History of the Explosive That Changed the World*. Basic Books.

Kemiss, William. 1874. *Treatise on Military Carriages and Other Manufactures of the Royal Carriage Department*. HM Stationery Office.

Kenchington, Trevor. 1993, Jan. "The Structures of English Wooden Ships: William Sutherland's Ship, Circa 1710." *The Northern Mariner*, 3(1): 1–43. http://www.cnrs-scrn.org/northern_mariner/vol03/tnm_3_1_1-43.pdf.

Kennedy, Donald R. 1990. *History of the Shaped Charge Effect: The First 100 Years*. D.R. Kennedy & Associates.

Kennish, William. 1837. *A Method for Concentrating the Fire of a Broadside of a Ship of War*. John Bradley.

Kettell, Thomas P. 1864. "Fire-Arms." In *Eighty Years Progress in the United States*. L. Stebbins.

Kinard, Jeff. 2007. *Artillery: An Illustrated History of Its Impact*. Bloomsbury Academic.

King, James Wilson. 1881. *The War-ships and Navies of the World*. A. Williams & Co.

King, Lt. Col. W.R. 1894. "Controllable Torpedoes Operated from Shore Installations." In Major Clifton Comly, *Operations of the Division of Military Engineering of the International Congress of Engineers*, Sen. Doc. 119 (53rd Cong, 2d Sess.), 59–67. Government Printing Office.

Kirby, Geoff. 2000. *The Development of Rocket-Propelled Torpedoes*. http://www.geoffkirby.co.uk/rocket-torpedoes.pdf.

Kirsch, Peter. 2009. *Fireship: The Terror Weapon of the Age of Sail*. Pen & Sword.

Konstam, Angus. 2008. *Tudor Warships (1): Henry VIII's Navy*. Bloomsbury.

Konstam, Angus. 2017. *Big Guns: Artillery on the Battlefield*. Casemate.

Konstam, Angus. 2018. *British Ironclads, 1860–75: HMS Warrior and the Royal Navy's "Black Battlefleet."* Bloomsbury.

Konstam, Angus. 2019. *European Ironclads, 1860–75: The Gloire Sparks the Great Ironclad Arms Race*. Bloomsbury.

Kosanke, B.J., et al. 2012. *Encyclopedic Dictionary of Pyrotechnics (and Related Subjects)*. Journal of Pyrotechnics, Incorporated.

Kramer, Gerald. 1996. "Das Feuerwerkbuch: Its Importance in the Early History of Black Powder." In Brenda J. Buchanan, *Gunpowder, Explosives and the State: A Technological History*, 45–56. Taylor and Francis.

Krause, Keith. 1995. *Arms and the State: Patterns of Military Production and Trade*. Cambridge University Press.

Krooth, Richard. 2004. *A Century Passing: Carnegie, Steel and the Fate of Homestead*. University Press of America.

Krumins, Maigonis V. 1972, Jan. 18. "A Review of Sphere Drag Coefficients Applicable to Atmospheric Density Sensing." Naval Ordnance Laboratory. https://apps.dtic.mil/sti/citations/AD0742768.

Kutney, Gerald. 2007. *Sulfur: History, Technology, Applications & Industry*. ChemTec Publishing.

Lacombe, Paul, and Charles Boutell. 1870. *Arms and Armor in Antiquity and the Middle Ages*. D. Appleton & Company.

Lafay, Capt. J. 1850. *Aide-Memoire D'Artillerie Navale*. J. Correard.

Lambert, Andrew. 1987. *Warrior: Restoring the World's First Ironclad*. Conway Maritime Press.

Lambert, Andrew. 2012. *The Challenge: Britain Against America in the Naval War of 1812*. Faber & Faber.

Lance, Rachel. 2020. *In the Waves: My Quest to Solve the Mystery of a Civil War Submarine*. Dutton.

Landmann, Isaac. 1801. *The Principles of Artillery*. T. Egerton.

Landsberg, P.G. 2000, July. "Underwater Blast Injuries." *Trauma & Emergency Medicine*, 17(2): n.p. http://scuba-doc.com/underwater-blast-injuries/.

Langstrom, Bjorn. 1961. *The Ship: An Illustrated History*. Doubleday & Co.

Lanzendörfer, Tim. 2003. "Anti-Submarine Projector Mks 10 & 11 (Hedgehog)." In "The Pacific War: The U.S. Navy." http://www.microworks.net/pacific/armament/mk10&11_hedgehog.htm.

Lappalainen, Mirkka. 2021. "Manufacturing Saltpetre in Finland in the Late 16th and Early 17th Centuries." In Petri Talvitie and Juha-Matti Granqvist, *Civilians and Military Supply in Early Modern Finland*, 161–176. Helsinki University Press.

Laughton, Sir John Knox. 1907. *Letters and Papers of Charles, Lord Barham, Admiral of the Red Squadron, 1758–1813*. Volume I. Navy Records Society. [Note: Lord Barham was Charles Middleton.]

Lavery, Brian. 1987. *The Arming and Fitting of English Ships of War, 1600–1815*. Conway Maritime Press.

Lavery, Brian. 1989. "Carronades and Blomefield Guns: Developments in Naval Ordnance, 1778–1805." In Robert D. Smith, ed., *British Naval Armaments*. Royal Armouries, Conference Proceedings 1.

Lavery, Brian. 2016. *Churchill's Navy: The Ships, People and Organisation, 1939–1945*. Bloomsbury.

Lavery, Brian. 2021. *Anson's Navy: Building a Fleet for Empire, 1744–1763*. Pen & Sword.

Leavitt, F.M. 1893, Jan. "The Whitehead Torpedo." *Stevens Indicator*, 10(1): 1–9.

Lewis, Michael. 1960. *The Spanish Armada*. Macmillan.

Lipscombe, Trevor, and Carl Mungan. 2012, Apr. "The Physics of Shot Towers." *Physics Teacher*, 50(4): 218.

Little, Benerson. 2005. *The Sea Rover's Practice: Pirate Tactics and Techniques, 1630–1730*. Potomac Books.

Ljungdahl, Jonas. 2006. *Structure and Properties of Vasa Oak*. Licentiate thesis, Department of Aeronautical and Vehicle Engineering, Royal Institute of Technology, Stockholm, Sweden.

Lockwood, Charles A., and Hans Christian Adamson. 2018. *Tragedy at Honda*. Lulu.com.

Lombard, Jean Louis. 1797. *Traité du Mouvement des Projectiles, Appliqué au Tir des Bouches a Feu*. Dijon: L.N. Frantin.

López-Martín, Francisco Javier. 2007, June. *Historical and Technological Evolution of Artillery from Its Earliest Widespread Use Until the Emergence of Mass-Production Techniques*. Ph.D. thesis, London Metropolitan University.

Lossing, Benson J. 2010. *Pictorial History of the Civil War*. Volume 3. Applewood Books.

Lundgren, Robert, and Nathan Okun. 2022. "Analysis of Damage: USS *South Dakota* at the Naval Battle of Guadalcanal." http://www.navweaps.com/index_lundgren/South_Dakota_Damage_Analysis.php.

MacDougall, D.P., and N.M. Newmark. 1946, May. *Explosives and Terminal Ballistics*. Headquarters Air Materiel Command.

MacIntyre, Captain Donald. 2019 [1956]. *U-Boat Killer*. Eumenes Publishing.

MacKay, Ron, Jr. 2016. *The U.S. Navy's "Interim" LSM(R)s in World War II: Rocket Ships of the Pacific Amphibious Forces*. McFarland.

Maitland, Sir Frederick Lewis, and William Kirk Dickson. 1904. *The Surrender of Napoleon*. W. Blackwood and Sons.

Malcolm, Ian M. 2013. *Shipping Company Losses of the Second World War*. History Press.

Mallet, Robert. 1862. *On Muzzle Swiveling and Hydraulic Mounting*. Patent Offices.

Mallock, A. 1901. "An Instrument for Measuring the Rolling of Ships." *Transactions of the Institution of Naval Architects*, 43: 34–47.

Manganiello, Stephen C. 2004. *The Concise Encyclopedia of the Revolutions and Wars of England, Scotland, and Ireland, 1639–1660*. Scarecrow.

Manning, Lt. Cmdr. George Charles, and Lt. Theodore Leon Schumacher. 1924. *Principles of Naval Architecture and Warship Construction*. United States Naval Institute.

Manning, Harold G. 1919. "Practical Interior Ballistics." *Journal of the United States Artillery*, 51: 414, 424, 494.

Manucy, Albert C. 1985 [1949]. *Artillery Through the Ages: A Short Illustrated History of Cannon, Emphasizing Types Used in America*. National Park Service.

Manwayring, Sir Henry. 1644. *The Sea-Mans Dictionary...* London: John Bellamy.

Marquis of Dufferin and Ava. 1898, Nov. 17. "My First Cruise." *The Youth's Companion*, 72: 577.

Marriott, Leo, and Jonathan Forty. 2017. *Heavyweights: The Military Use of Massive Weapons*. Chartwell Books.

Marshall, Arthur. 1915. *Explosives: Their Manufacture, Properties, Tests and History*. P. Blakiston's Son & Co.

Martin, Colin, and Geoffrey Parker. 1999. *The Spanish Armada, rev ed*. Manchester University Press.

Martin, Commander Tyrone G. 2015, Dec. "Armaments & Innovations—The First Shell Gun." *Naval History Magazine*, 29(6). https://www.usni.org/magazines/naval-history-magazine/2015/december/armaments-innovations-first-shell-gun.

Marx, Robert F. 1987 [1963]. *Shipwrecks in the Americas*. Dover.

Marzetta, Dante R. 1946, Jan. 30. "Shell Forging Methods for Army High Explosive Shells." Carnegie Institute of Technology.

Massa, Frank. 2017, Aug. "Sonar Transducers: A History." https://www.massa.com/wp-content/uploads/2017/08/Frank_Massa-Sonar_Transducers-A_History.pdf.

Massachusetts Institute of Technology. 2011. "Archimedes's Steam Cannon." http://designed.mit.edu/gallery/data/2011/homepage/experiments/steamCannon/ArchimedesSteamCannon.html.

Mauskopf, Seymour H. 1999. "'From an Instrument of War to an Instrument of the Laboratory: The Affinities Certainly Do Not Change': Chemists and the Development of Munitions, 1785–1885." *Bulletin for the History of Chemistry*, 24: 1–15.

Mauskopf, Seymour H. 2006. "Pellets, Pebbles and Prisms: British Munitions for Larger Guns, 1860–1885." In Brenda J. Buchanan, *Gunpowder, Explosives and the State: A Technological History*, 303–39. Taylor and Francis.

Mawdsley, Evan. 1992. "The World's First Guided-Missile Ship?" *Warship International*, 29(1): 48–53.

McCaul, Edward B., Jr. 2005. *Rapid Technological Innovation: The Evolution of the Artillery Fuze During the American Civil War*. Ph.D. dissertation, Ohio State University.

McConnell, David. 1988. "British Smooth-bore Artillery: A Technological Study to Support Identification, Acquisition, Restoration, Reproduction, and Interpretation of Artillery at National Historic Parks in Canada." Environment Canada.

McCoy, Major Curtis L. 1992. "Is a Liquid Propellant Gun a Viable Option for the Future Main Battle Tank in the United States Army?" https://apps.dtic.mil/sti/citations/ADA258887.

McCoy, Robert L. 1981, Feb. "McDrag—A Computer Program for Estimating the Drag Coefficients of Projectiles." Tech Report ARBRL-TR-02293. U.S. Army Armament Research and Development Command, Ballistic Research Laboratory.

McCoy, Robert L. 2012. *Modern Exterior Ballistics: The Launch and Flight Dynamics of Symmetric Projectiles*. Schiffer Military History.

McDermott, James. 2005. *England and the Spanish Armada: The Necessary Quarrel*. Yale University Press.

McEvily, Arthur J. 2002. *Metal Failures: Mechanisms, Analysis, Prevention*. Wiley.

McGrath, Captain James P., III. 2018, Oct. 31. "What Do You Call It? The Politics and Practicalities of Warship Classification." https://cimsec.org/what-do-you-call-it-the-politics-and-practicalities-of-warship-classification/.

McKee, Fraser M. 1993, Jan. "An Explosive Story: The Rise and Fall of the Common Depth Charge." *The Northern Mariner/Le Marin du Nord*, 3(1): 45–58.

McLaughlan, Ian. 2014. *The Sloop of War, 1650–1763*. Seaforth Publishing.

McLeod, A.B. 2012. *British Naval Captains of the Seven Years' War: The View from the Quarterdeck*. Boydell Press.

McNeese, Tim. 2003. *America's Civil War*. Lorenz Educational Press.

McSherry, Patrick. 2023. "Dynamite Cruiser VESUVIUS." http://www.spanamwar.com/vesuvius.htm.

Meade, Cmdr. Richard Worsam. 1869. *A Treatise on Naval Architecture and Ship-Building*. J.P. Lippincott & Co.

Mechanics Magazine. 1832, Oct. 18. Volume 18, Issue 479.

Mechanics Magazine. 1848. "On the Mounting of

Ordnance on the Non-Recoil Principle—Compiled from the Papers of the Late Brig. Gen. Sir Samuel Bentham." Volume 49, Issue 1325: 634–38.

Medieval Gunpowder Research Group. 2002, Sept. "The Ho Experiments, Part 1." Report No. 1.

Medieval Gunpowder Research Group. 2003, Aug. "The Ho Experiments, Part 2." Report No. 2.

Medieval Gunpowder Research Group. 2004, Aug. "The Saltpetre Extraction Experiment."

Medieval Gunpowder Research Group. 2006, Sept. "Sulphur from Iceland."

Medieval Gunpowder Research Group. 2006a, Nov. "Saltpetre from India."

Medieval Gunpowder Research Group. 2007, Apr. "Sulphur from Sicily."

Medieval Gunpowder Research Group. 2013, Sept. "Making Saltpetre, Part 1."

Medieval Gunpowder Research Group. 2014, Aug. "Making Saltpetre, Part 2."

Medieval Gunpowder Research Group. 2015, Sept. "Sulphur, Refining." https://ahc.leeds.ac.uk/downloads/download/35/ho_medieval_gunpowder_research_group.

Mehl, Hans. 2002. Naval Guns: Years of Ship and Coastal Artillery. Chatham.

Mehler, Natascha. 2015. "The Sulphur Trade of Iceland from the Viking Age to the End of the Hanseatic Period." In Irene Baug et al., Nordic Middle Ages—Artefacts, Landscapes and Society: Essays in Honour of Ingvild Øye on Her 70th Birthday, 193–212. University of Bergen.

Meide, Chuck. 2002, Nov. "The Development and Design of Bronze Ordnance, Sixteenth Through Nineteenth Centuries." College of William and Mary.

Meigs, John Forsyth. 1902. "Late Developments in Ordnance and Armor." Transactions of the Society of Naval Architects and Marine Engineers, 9: 201.

Meigs, Lieutenant John Forsyth, and Lieutenant R.R. Ingersoll. 1887. Text-Book of Ordnance and Gunnery: Naval B.L.R. Guns, 2d ed. Isaac Friedenwald.

Mel Fisher Maritime Museum. 1986. "Split Shot." Accession 1986.008.0826a. https://melfisher.info/Detail/objects/3184. (Also note artifacts with tag number 50549 and 51858 in the artifact database, searchable here: https://www.melfisherartifacts.com/.)

Mellor, David Paver. 1958. "Chapter 16—Ammunition and Explosives." In Australia in the War of 1939–1945. Series 4—Civil, Volume 5—The Role of Science and Industry. Australia War Memorial.

Merriam, Henry P. 1893. "A New Percussion Fuze." Journal of the United States Artillery, 2: 59–65.

Microworks.net. n.d. "The Proximity (Variable-Time) Fuze." http://microworks.net/pacific/equipment/vt_fuze.htm.

Mihajlović, Igor. 2014. "4.2. The Ordnance." In Carlo Beltrame et al., Sveti Pavao Shipwreck: A 16th Century Venetian Merchantman from Mljet, Croatia. Oxbow Books.

Mikaberidze, Alexander. 2011. Conflict and Conquest in the Islamic World: A Historical Encyclopedia. Volume 1. ABC-CLIO.

Miles, E. 1841. An Epitome, Historical and Statistical, Descriptive of the Royal Naval Service of England. Ackermann and Company.

Military Service Institution of the United States. 1905. "The Grubb Gun-Sight." 37: 552–56.

Millar, John Fitzhugh. 1986. Early American Ships. Thirteen Colonies Press.

Miller, Donald G., and Allan B. Bailey. 1979. "Sphere Drag at Mach Numbers from 0–3 to 2–0 at Reynolds Numbers Approaching L0[7]." Journal of Fluid Mechanics 93 (part 3): 449–64.

Miller, Lt. Col. H.W. 1921. A Report on the Characteristics, Scope of Utility, Etc. of Railway Artillery. Volume 1. Ordnance Department, Doc. 2034. Government Printing Office.

Miller, Captain Richard H. 2011, Nov. "'FIDO': The First Acoustic Torpedo Developed by the U.S." Officer Review: The Military Order of the World Wars, 51: 4.

MilliporeSigma. 2023. "Solubility Table of Compounds in Water at Temperature." https://www.sigmaaldrich.com/US/en/support/calculators-and-apps/solubility-table-compounds-water-temperature.

Mindell, David A. 2004. Between Human and Machine: Feedback, Control, and Computing Before Cybernetics. Johns Hopkins University Press.

Mitchell, Peter. n.d. "The Brennan Torpedo." http://www.submerged.co.uk/brennan.php.

Mixter, George Webber, et al. 1979. Primer of Navigation: With Problems in Practical Work and Complete Tables. Van Nostrand Reinhold.

Moncrieff, Alexander. 1868. Moncrieff's Protected Barbette System. Royal Artillery Institution.

Morgan, Frederick Cyril. 1884. Handbook of Artillery Materiel. W. Clowes and Sons.

Morgan, Lt. Stokeley. 1894. "Electric Firing on Board Ship: Electric Primers and Firing Attachments. Proc. U.S. Naval Institute. 20: 783-8.

Morison, Elting E. 1966. "Gunfire at Sea: A Case Study of Innovation." In Men, Machines, and Modern Times, 17–44. MIT Press. [Previously published as Morison, Elting E. 1960, Apr. "A Case Study of Innovation." Engineering and Science Monthly, 13(7): 5–10.]

Morris, Charles. 1898. The American Navy: Its Ships and Achievements. Hutchinson & Company.

Morriss, Roger. 2014. The Foundations of British Maritime Ascendancy: Resources, Logistics and the State, 1755–1815. Cambridge University Press.

Morriss, Roger. 2020. Science, Utility and British Naval Technology, 1793–1815: Samuel Bentham and the Royal Dockyards. Taylor & Francis.

Muir, Malcolm, Jr. 1996. Black Shoes and Blue Water: Surface Warfare in the United States Navy, 1945–1975. Naval Historical Center.

Muldoon, Robert A. 1977, Mar. Projectile Motion and Loads Versus Travel in Gun Tube. Army Materials and Mechanics Research Center.

Muller, Wilhelm. 1811. *Elements of the Science of War*. Volume II. Longman.

Multhauf, Robert P. 1971, Apr. "The French Crash Program for Saltpeter Production, 1776–94." *Technology and Culture*, 12(2): 163–81.

Murray, Andrew. 1861. *The Theory and Practice of Ship-Building*. Edinburgh: Adam and Charles Black.

Najendran, R., and Krishnaiyengar Narasimhan. 2001, Apr. "Damage Prediction of Clamped Circular Plates Subjected to Contract Underwater Explosion." *International Journal of Impact Engineering*, 25(4): n.p.

National Maritime Museum, Greenwich London. 2023 (accessed). "Wolverine (1798); Warship; Sixth Rate; Sloop; 12 Guns." Model ID SLR0596. https://www.rmg.co.uk/collections/objects/rmgc-object-66557.

National Museum, Royal Navy. 2012, May 12 (access date). "HMS Victory." https://web.archive.org/web/20120501012624.

Naval History and Heritage Command. 2023, Jan. 11. "USS George Washington (SSBN-598)." https://www.history.navy.mil/browse-by-topic/ships/submarines/george-washington-ssbn-598.html.

navsource.org. 2023. "USS VESUVIUS (Dynamite Cruiser)." http://navsource.org/archives/04/vesuvius/vesuvius.htm.

navweaps.com. 2008. "Zalinsky Pneumatic 'Dynamite' Guns." http://www.navweaps.com/Weapons/WNUS_Zalinsky.htm.

navweaps.com [DiGiulian, Tom]. 2021, July 3. "United States of America: Electromagnetic Rail Gun." http://www.navweaps.com/Weapons/WNUS_Rail_Gun.php Proposal.

navweaps.com [DiGiulian, Tom]. 2021a, Sept. 8. "Torpedoes of the United States of America: Post–World War II." http://www.navweaps.com/Weapons/WTUS_PostWWII.php.

navweaps.com. 2022. "United States of America: 8"/55 (20.3 cm) Marks 12 and 15." http://www.navweaps.com/Weapons/WNUS_8-55_mk12-15.php.

navweaps.com. 2022a. "20 Mm Phalanx Close-in Weapon System (CIWS)" http://www.navweaps.com/Weapons/WNUS_Phalanx.php.

navweaps.com. 2023. "United Kingdom: ASW Weapons." http://www.navweaps.com/Weapons/WAMBR_ASW.php.

navweaps.com. 2023a. "United States of America: 16"/50 (40.6 cm) Mark 7." http://www.navweaps.com/Weapons/WNUS_16-50_mk7.php.

Nelson, Arthur. 2001. *The Tudor Navy: The Ships, Men and Organisation, 1485–1603*. Conway Maritime Press.

Nelson, Vice Admiral Horatio. 1845. *The Dispatches and Letters of Vice Admiral Lord Viscount Nelson: January 1802 to April 1804*. H. Colburn.

Neuenswander, Lt. Col. David. 2018 (pdf creation date). *Joint Laser Interoperability: Tomorrow's Answer to Precision Engagement*. Maxwell Air University. https://www.airuniversity.af.edu/Portals/10/ASPJ/journals/Chronicles/neuenswander.pdf.

Neutrium. 2013, Nov. 5. "Thermal Conductivity of Metals and Alloys." https://neutrium.net/heat-transfer/thermal-conductivity-of-metals-and-alloys/.

Newhouse, Paul. 2022, Aug. 2. "A Primer on Shaped Charges." https://smallarmsreview.com/a-primer-on-shaped-charges/.

Newpower, Anthony. 2006. *Iron Men and Iron Fish: The Race to Build a Better Torpedo during World War II*. ABC-CLIO.

Nichols, Harry James. 1948, May 18 (issue date). U.S. Patent 2,441,897 (filed Oct. 25, 1932). "Method of and Apparatus for Exploding Armor Piercing Projectiles."

Noble, Sir Andrew. 1906. *Artillery and Explosives: Essays and Lectures Written and Delivered at Various Times*. E.P. Dutton and Company.

Noble, Captain Andrew, and Frederick Augustus Abel. 1875, Jan. 1. "II. Researches on Explosives. Fired Gunpowder." *Philosophical Transactions of the Royal Society of London*, 165: 49–155.

Nolan, Cathal J. 2006. *The Age of Wars of Religion, 1000–1650: An Encyclopedia of Global Warfare and Civilization*. Volume 1. Greenwood Press.

Norton, Robert. 1628. *The Gunner Shewing the Whole Practise of Artillery*. Humphrey Robinson.

Nosworthy, Brent. 1996. *With Musket, Cannon and Sword: Battle Tactics of Napoleon and His Enemies*. Sarpedon.

NPS18th. National Park Service. 2015. "Manual of Instruction for the Safe Use of Reproduction 18th Century Artillery in Historic Weapons Demonstrations."

NPS19th. National Park Service. 2022. "Manual of Instruction for the Safe Use of Reproduction 19th Century Artillery in Historic Weapons Demonstrations."

Nye, Nathaniel. 1648. *The Art of Gunnery*. W. Leak.

"Officer of the Royal Artillery." 1884[?]. "Weapons of War—III. Gunpowder." *The Technical Educator*, Volume I, 154–55. Cassell & Co.

"Officers and Others of Recognized Authority...." 1881. *A Naval Encyclopaedia*. L.R. Hamersly & Co.

Officers of the U.S. Navy. 1910. *Ordnance and Gunnery: A Text-Book Prepared for the Use of the Midshipmen of the United States Naval Academy*. United States Naval Institute.

Officers of the U.S. Navy. 1921. *Naval Ordnance: A Textbook Prepared for the Use of the Midshipmen of the United States Naval Academy*. United States Naval Institute.

Okun, Nathan. 1998, June 1. "Major Historical Naval Armor Penetration Formulae." www.combinedfleet.com/formula.htm.

Okun, Nathan. 1998a, Dec. 10. "Miscellaneous Naval-Armor-Related Formulae." www.combinedfleet.com/miscarmor.htm.

Okun, Nathan. 2004, Oct. 4. Summary of

NAVTECMISEU Technical Report #191–45 "Standard German Projectile Fuzes" (Aug. 1945). http://www.navweaps.com/index_nathan/germanWWIIFuzes.php.

Okun, Nathan. 2017. "Major Historical Naval Armor Penetration Formulae." http://www.navweaps.com/index_nathan/Hstfrmla.php.

Ontario Bureau of Mines. 1893. *Second Report of the Bureau of Mines 1892*. Warwick & Sons.

Oppenheim, Michael. 1896. *A History of the Administration of the Royal Navy and of Merchant Shipping in Relation to the Navy*. J. Lane.

Oppenheim, Michael. 1913. *The Naval Tracts of Sir William Monson*. 6 vols. Navy Records Society.

Ordnance, Chief of (Brigadier-General S.V. Benét). 1878. "Appendix S-2, Trial of Fuses." In *Annual Report of the Chief of Ordnance to the Secretary of War for the Fiscal Year Ended June 30, 1878*. Government Printing Office.

Osborne, Eric W. 2005. *Destroyers: An Illustrated History of Their Impact*. Bloomsbury.

Ott, Nathaniel G. 2010, July. *Battlecruisers at Jutland: A Comparative Analysis of British and German Warship Design and Its Impact on the Naval War*. Senior honors thesis, Ohio State University.

Owen, Charles Henry. 1873. *The Principles and Practice of Modern Artillery, 2d ed*. John Murray.

Owen, Charles Henry, and Thomas Longworth Danes. 1861. *Elementary Lectures on Artillery, 3d ed*. Royal Artillery Institution.

Owen, Gregory L. 2006. *The Longest Patrol: A U-Boat Gunner's War*. iUniverse.

Ozberk, Tayfun. 2022, Oct. 30. "Analysis: Ukraine Strikes with Kamikaze USVs—Russian Bases Are Not Safe Anymore." https://www.navalnews.com/naval-news/2022/10/analysis-ukraine-strikes-with-kamikaze-usvs-russian-bases-are-not-safe-anymore/.

Paixhans, Lt. Col. Henri Joseph. 1838. *An Account of the Experiments Made in the French Navy for the Trial of Bomb Cannon, Etc*. Dorsey.

Parker, G.W. 1977. "Projectile Motion with Air Resistance Quadratic in the Speed." *American Journal of Physics*, 48(7): 606.

Parkerson, A.C. 1898. *How Uncle Sam Fights: Modern Warfare—How Conducted*. R.H. Woodward.

Parliament. 1778. *The Parliamentary Register*. J. Almon.

Parsch, Andreas. 2004. "Lockheed Martin (Loral) RUM-139 VL-Asroc." http://www.designation-systems.net/dusrm/m-139.html.

Partington, J.R. 1999. *A History of Greek Fire and Gunpowder*. Johns Hopkins University Press.

Patowary, Kaushik. 2019, Oct. 20. "The Submarine Sunk by Her Own Torpedo." https://www.amusingplanet.com/2019/10/the-submarine-sunk-by-her-own-torpedo.html.

Patterson, G.W. 1911, June. "Sarrau's Velocity Formula, Modified for Smokeless Powder." *Proceedings of the U.S. Naval Institute*, 37(2) (Whole Issue 138): 531–34. https://www.usni.org/magazines/proceedings/1911/june/sarraus-velocity-formula.

Patterson, G.W. 1912, Sept. "The Le Duc Ballistic Formulae." *Proceedings of the U.S. Naval Institute*. https://www.usni.org/magazines/proceedings/1912/september-0/le-duc-ballistic-formulae.

Pawle, Gerald. 1957. *The Secret War 1939–45*. William Sloane Associates.

Pawle, Gerald. 2009. *Wheezers and Dodgers: The Inside Story of Clandestine Weapon Development in World War II*. Seaforth.

Peabody, Cecil Hobart. 1904. *Naval Architecture*. J. Wiley & Sons.

Peake, James. 1897 [1867]. *The Elementary Principles of Naval Architecture*. Crosby Lockwood and Son.

Pegler, Martin. 2011. *Out of Nowhere: A History of the Military Sniper, from the Sharpshooter to Afghanistan*. Bloomsbury.

Pelick Tom. 1996, Jan. "FIDO—The First U.S. Homing Torpedo." https://archive.navalsubleague.org/1996/fido-the-first-u-s-homing-torpedo.

Pelick, Tom. 1996a, July. "Post WWII Torpedoes—1945 to 1950." https://archive.navalsubleague.org/1996/post-wwii-torpedoes-1945-to-1950.

Peng, Chao, et al. 2022, July. "A Database for Deliquescence and Efflorescence Relative Humidities of Compounds with Atmospheric Relevance." *Fundamental Research*, 2(4): 578–87.

Penny Cyclopedia, Volume 11 (1838). Charles Knight.

Perkins, E.W. 1952. *Investigation of the Drag of Various Axially Symmetric Nose Shapes of Fineness Ratio 3 for Mach Numbers from 1.24 to 3.67*. NACA RM A52H28.

Perley, C. 1865, Dec. 12 (issue date). U.S. Patent 51,475. "Operating Ordnance."

Peterson, Harold Leslie. 1969. *Round Shot and Rammers: An Introduction to Muzzle-Loading Land Artillery in the United States*. Bonanza.

Pilkey, Walter D. 1997. *Peterson's Stress Concentration Factors, 2d ed*. John Wiley & Sons.

Poche, David, and Peter George. n.d. "Solid Shot Essentials: A Guide to the Authentic and Non-Authentic." http://www.pochefamily.org/books/SolidShotEssentialsMod.html.

Pol, M.H., et al. 2009. "Analysis of Normal Penetration of Ogive Nose Projectiles into Thin Metallic Plates." *World Academy of Sci., Eng'g & Technol.*, 50: 235.

Polmar, Norman, and Kenneth J. Moore. 2004. *Cold War Submarines: The Design and Construction of U.S. and Soviet Submarines*. Brassey's.

Polmar, Norman, and Thomas B. Allen. 2012 [1991]. *World War II: The Encyclopedia of the War Years, 1941–1945*. Dover.

Pope, R.L. 1985. "Breakdown of the Modified Point Mass Model for High Elevation Trajectories." Tech. Mem. WSR L-0396-TM.

Porter, Captain David. 1823. "A Voyage in the South Seas in the Years 1812, 1813, and 1814." In *New Voyages and Travels*, Volume VIII, Part V. Sir Richard Phillips & Co.

Power, Hugh Irvin. 1993. *Battleship Texas.* Texas A&M University Press.

Preble, George Henry. 1879. *The Chesapeake and Shannon, June 1, 1813.* J.P. Lippincott & Co.

Prendergast, Maurice. 1948, Aug. "Sonar and Asdic, Anti-submarine Sisters." *Proceedings of the U.S. Naval Institute,* 74(8): 546. https://www.usni.org/magazines/proceedings/1948/august/sonar-and-asdic-anti-submarine-sisters.

Puype, J.P. 2000. "Three-Wheeled Gun Carriages." *Royal Armories Yearbook,* 5: 106–16.

Quartsein, John V. 2006. *A History of Ironclads: The Power of Iron Over Wood.* History Press.

Raines, C.W. 1903. *Year Book for Texas.* Volume II. Gammel-Statesman Publishing.

Rains, George. 1861. *Notes on Making Saltpetre from the Earth of the Caves.* New Orleans: Daily Delta Job Office.

Rajendran, R., and K. Narasimhan. 2001, Apr. "Damage Prediction of Clamped Circular Plates Subjected to Contact Underwater Explosion." *International Journal of Impact Engineering,* 25(4): 374–86.

Ramsey, Hobert Cole. 1918. *Elementary Naval Ordnance and Gunnery.* Little, Brown and Company.

Rao, K.S. Bhaskara, and K.C. Sharma. 1982, Apr. "Art in Internal Ballistics." *Defence Science Journal,* 132(2): 157–74. https://core.ac.uk/reader/333721670.

Raven, Alan. 2019. *British Cruiser Warfare: The Lessons of the Early War, 1939–1941.* Pen & Sword.

Rawson, Edward K., and Robert H. Woods. 1898. Series I—Volume 7. *North Atlantic Blockading Squadron from March 8 to September 4, 1862.* Official Records of the Union and Confederate Navies in the War of the Rebellion. H. Rep. Doc. 559 (55th Cong, 2d Sess.). Government Printing Office.

Reed, Sir Edward. 1886, Feb. "The British Navy." *Harper's New Monthly Magazine,* 72(429): 333–56.

Reed, Sir Edward James. 1869. *Our Iron-Clad Ships.* J. Murray.

Reid, Warren D. 1996. *The Response of Surface Ships to Underwater Explosions.* DSTO-GD-0109. DSTO Aeronautical and Maritime Research Laboratory.

Rendel, George Whitewick. 1874. "Gun-Carriages and Mechanical Appliances for Working Heavy Ordnance." *Minutes of Proceedings of the Institution of Civil Engineers,* 38: 85–140.

[Revolution] Anonymous. 1867. *The Revolution in Naval Warfare.* Harrison and Sons.

Rice, Richard E. 2006. "Smokeless Powder: Scientific and Institutional Contexts at the End of the Nineteenth Century." In Brenda J. Buchanan, *Gunpowder, Explosives and the State: A Technological History,* 355–62. Ashgate.

Rielly, Robin L. 2013. *American Amphibious Gunboats in World War II: A History of LCI and LCS(L) Ships in the Pacific.* McFarland.

Rinker, Robert A. 1999. *Understanding Firearm Ballistics: Basic to Advanced Ballistics: Simplified, Illustrated, and Explained.* Mulberry House.

Roberts, Elizabeth. 2010. *"Freedom, Faction, Fame and Blood": British Soldiers of Conscience in Greece.* Sussex Academic Press.

Roberts, William. 1996. "That Imperfect Arm: Quantifying the Carronade." *Warship International,* 33(3): 231–40.

Robertson, Frederick Leslie. 1921. *The Evolution of Naval Armament.* Constable & Co., Ltd.

Robins, Benjamin. 1742. *New Principles of Gunnery.* A new edition, "Corrected and Enlarged with the Addition of Several Notes by Charles Hutton" (1805). F. Wingrave.

Robinson, John. 2014 [1922]. *The Sailing Ships of New England, 1607–1907.* Europäischer Hochschulverlag.

Roden, E.K. (nominally by International Correspondence Schools). 1911. *The Mariner's Handbook, 2d ed.* International Textbook Company.

Rodger, N.A.M. 1996. "The Development of Broadside Gunnery, 1450–1650." *The Mariner's Mirror,* 82(3): 301–24. DOI: 10.1080/00253359.1996.10656604.

Rodger, N.A.M. 1997. *The Safeguard of the Sea: A Naval History of Britain, 660–1649.* W.W. Norton.

Rodger, N.A.M. 2004. *The Command of the Ocean: A Naval History of Great Britain, 1649–1815.* W.W. Norton.

Rodman, Captain T.J. 1861. *Reports of Experiments on the Properties of Metals for Cannon, and the Qualities of Cannon Powder, with an Account of the Fabrication and Trial of a 15-Inch Gun.* Charles H. Crosby.

Romer, Justice. 1894, Mar. 14. Opinion in *Nobel's Explosives Company, Limited V. Anderson, Reports of Patent, Design and Trademark Cases,* 11(8): 115–29 (High Court of Justice, Chancery Division).

Rose, James E. 1980. "The Role of Charcoal in the Combustion of Black Powder." Report No. 1980-5016AH. https://cdn.hackaday.io/files/8963383472992/1980_The_Role_of_Charcoal_in_the_Combustion_of_Black__Powder_Jim_Rose_IPS_proceedings.pdf.

Ross, David. 2015. *The World's Greatest Battleships: An Illustrated History.* Amber Books.

Rossi, Cesare, Flavio Russo and Ferruccio Russo. 2009. *Ancient Engineers' Inventions: Precursors of the Present.* Springer.

Rowe, John A. 1889. "A New Wave-Motor." *Transactions of the North-East Coast Institution of Engineers and Shipbuilders,* 7(5): 105–22.

Rowe, John A. 1899, Aug. 1 (issue date). U.S. Patent 629,819. "Apparatus for Automatically Discharging Guns of War Ships."

Rowland, Lt. Cmdr. Buford, and Lt. William B. Boyd. 1953. *U.S. Navy Bureau of Ordnance in World War II.* Government Printing Office.

Rowlinson, J.S. 2016. *Sir James Dewar, 1842–1923: A Ruthless Chemist.* Taylor & Francis.

Royal Armouries. n.d. "Chain Shot 1700–1799" (Object XX.65). https://collections.royalarmouries.org/object/rac-object-16908.html.

Royal Armouries. n.d. "Gun—Breech Loading Iron Swivel Gun" (Object XIX.3). https://collections.royalarmouries.org/object/rac-object-34046.

Royal Engineers, Corps of. 1852. *Aide-Mémoire to the Military Sciences*. Volume 3: *Paleontology to Zig-Zag*. John Weale.

Royal Museums Greenwich. n.d. "'Vesuvius' (1776) Bomb Vessel." ID ZAZ5779. https://www.rmg.co.uk/collections/objects/rmgc-object-85570.

Royal Museums Greenwich. 2018, Nov. 8. "How Long Did It Take to Sail Across the Atlantic?" https://www.rmg.co.uk/stories/blog/library-archive/18th-century-sailing-times-between-english-channel-coast-america-how.

Rumford, Count. 1870. "An Account of Some Experiments Upon Gunpowder," and "Experiments to Determine the Force of Fired Gunpowder." In *The Complete Works of Count Rumford*, Volume I. American Academy of Arts and Sciences.

Russell, Michael S. 2015. *The Chemistry of Fireworks*. Royal Society of Chemistry.

Russell, Lt. Ronald B. 1956, Sept.–Oct. "Antirolling Devices." *The Engineer's Digest* (U.S. Coast Guard), 100: 22–24.

Russian Firearms. 2016, Mar. 5 (Wayback Machine capture date). "APR-2E, APR-3E and APR-3ME Airborne Antisubmarine Missiles." *Russian Firearms: Specifications, Photos, Pictures*. https://web.archive.org/web/20160305002433.

Ryder, Captain Alfred Phillipps. 1854. *Methods of Ascertaining the Distance from Ships at Sea, 2d ed.* W. Woodward.

Ryder, Rear Adm. Alfred Phillipps. 1871. "Forms for Registering the Angles of Rolling and Heeling for the Information of the Construction Department at the Admiralty." *Royal United Services Institution Journal*, 15: 58–67.

Sabin, C.M. 1956, Nov. *The Effects of Reynolds Number, Mach Number, Spin Rate and Other Variables on the Aerodynamics of Spheres at Subsonic and Transonic Velocities*. Ballistic Research Laboratories, Memorandum Report No. 1044.

Salisbury, Winfield W. 2007. "Proximity Fuse Jamming." http://www.smecc.org/proximity_fuze_jamming_-_w_w__salisbury.htm.

Samuda, J. D'A. 1881. "The Almirante Brown Argentine-Cased Corvette, and the Effect of Steel Hulls and Steel-Faced Armor on Future War-Ships." *Transactions of the Institution of Naval Architects*, 22: 1–11.

San Miguel, Anthony. 1971, July. *Design Criteria for Inert or Consumable Polymer Cartridge Materials*. Naval Weapons Center Technical Publication 5208.

Sarrau, M.E. 1884, Jan. "Researches on the Effects of Powder (1874–1878)." *Proceedings of the U.S. Naval Institute*, 10(1) (Whole No. 28): 1–170.

Sasse, Ronald A. 1981, Mar. "The Influence of Physical Properties on Black Powder Combustion." Technical Report ARBRL-TR-02308. U.S. Army Ballistic Research Laboratory. https://ntrl.ntis.gov/NTRL/dashboard/searchResults/titleDetail/ADA100273.xhtml.

Schaefer, J.C. ("Fr. Frog"). 2015, Sept. 22. "Ballistic Coefficient Tables." http://www.frfrogspad.com/bcdata.htm.

Schafer, Dagmar. 2011. *The Crafting of the 10,000 Things: Knowledge and Technology in Seventeenth Century China*. University of Chicago Press.

Schmidt-Rohr, Klaus. 2015. "Why Combustions Are Always Exothermic, Yielding About 418 KJ Per Mole of O_2." *Journal of Chemical Education*, 92: 2094–99.

Schnug, Ewald, et al. 2018, Sept. "Guano: The White Gold of the Seabirds." DOI:10.5772/intechopen.79501.

Schonfeld, Christian. 2021, May 14. "Understanding Your Yachts' Roll Period." https://www.dockwalk.com/technology/understanding-roll-periods.

Schuyler, Lieutenant G.L. 1915, May. "An Application of the Le Duc Ballistic Formula." *Proceedings of the U.S. Naval Institute*. https://www.usni.org/magazines/proceedings/1915/may/application-le-duc-ballistic-formula.

Scientific American. 1885, Dec. 5. "Moncrieff Gun Carriages for Russian Ironclads." 53: 359–60.

Scott, Lloyd N. 1920. *Naval Consulting Board of the United States*. Government Printing Office.

Scott, Rear Admiral R.A.E. 1891. Communication appended as discussion to "Future Policy of War-Ship Building." *Transactions of the Royal Institution of Naval Architects*, 32: 21–39.

Seaforces. 2023 (accessed). "Mark-8 Naval Gun." https://www.seaforces.org/wpnsys/SURFACE/BAE-Mark-8-gun.htm.

Sears, Lt. W.J. 1898. "A General Description of the Whitehead Torpedo." *Proceedings of the U.S. Naval Institute*, 24(1) (Whole No. 85): 89–110.

Seel, Fritz. 1984. "Sulfur in History: The Role of Sulfur in 'Black Powder.'" In A. Muller and B. Krebs, eds., *Sulfur, Its Significance for Chemistry, for the Geo-, Bio-, and Cosmosphere and Technology*, 55–66. Elsevier.

Sephton, James. 2011. *Sovereign of the Seas: The Seventeenth-Century Warship*. Amberley Publishing.

Sicking, Louise. 2004. *Neptune and the Netherlands: State, Economy, and War at Sea in the Renaissance*. Brill.

Silverstone, Paul H. 2006. *The Sailing Navy, 1775–1854*. Routledge.

Simmons, Robert. 1812. *The Sea-Gunner's Vade Mecum*. Steel and Co.

Simmons, Captain T.F. 1837. *Ideas as to the Effect of Heavy Ordnance Directed Against and Applied by Ships of War*. F. Pinkney.

Simpson, Edward. 1862. *A Treatise on Ordnance and Naval Gunnery*. D. Van Nostrand.

Simpson, Edward. 1873. *Report on a Naval Mission to Europe*. Government Printing Office.

Skaarup, Harold A. 2012. *"Shelldrake": Canadian Artillery Museums & Gun Monuments*. iUniverse.

Skerrett, Robert G. 1915, Dec. 18. "The Active Gyroscope as a Ship Stabilizer." *Scientific American*, 113(25): 533, 547.

SKYbrary. 2023. "Centre of Pressure." https://skybrary.aero/articles/centre-pressure.

Sladen, Joseph. 1879. *Principles of Gunnery: Rifled Ordnance*. Mitchell.

Sleeman, Charles William. 1889. *Torpedoes and Torpedo Warfare*. Griffin.

Slover, Gene. 2023. "Gun Barrel Construction." https://www.eugeneleeslover.com/USNAVY/GUN-BARL-CONSTRUCTION-1.html.

Smeaton, John. 1797. *Reports of the Late Mr. John Smeaton, FRS*. Volume 1. S. Brooke.

Smith, Bolling W. 1998, Aug. "Seacoast Artillery Fuzes." *Coast Defense Study Group Journal*, 12(3): 32.

Smith, Geoff. n.d. "Saltpetre in Medieval Gunpowder: Calcium or Potassium Nitrate?" https://www.academia.edu/10603252/Calcium_Gunpowder.

Smith, Geoff. 2009, May. "On the Absence of Wood Ash from the Firework Book; An Un-reported Reaction. Calcium Gunpowder Continued." https://www.academia.edu/10603448/On_the_absence_of_wood_ash_from_the_Firework_Book_an_un_reported_reaction_Calcium_gunpowder_continued&nav_from=d873c0df-4083-4d15-a145-f1927ca4eb81&rw_pos=0.

Smith, Geoff. 2013, Mar. "Medieval Gunpowder Chemistry, the Firework Book Revisited." https://www.academia.edu/12138350/Medieval_Gunpowder_Chemistry_The_Firework_Book_Revisited&nav_from=64c98370-754e-48a2-a4fa-8a7991dc057d&rw_pos=0.

Smith, Geoff. 2019. "Serpentine Gunpowder and the Guns That Used It." *Journal of the Ordnance Society*, 26: n.p.

Smith, Geoff. 2020. "Saltpetre: The Soul of Gunpowder." *Journal of the Ordnance Society*, 27: n.p.

Smith, Geoff. 2021. "Sulphur: The Trigger of Gunpowder." *Journal of the Ordnance Society*, 28: n.p.

Smith, Geoff. 2021a, Sept. 5 (pdf creation date). "Charcoal: The Fuel of Gunpowder." https://www.academia.edu/51292275/Charcoal_the_fuel_of_Gunpowder.

Smith, Lloyd. 2001. "Heavy American Mortars in WWII." http://www.g2mil.com/Heavy-Mortars.htm.

Smith, Myron J., Jr. 2008. *The Timberclads in the Civil War: The Lexington, Conestoga and Tyler on the Western Waters*. McFarland.

Smith, T.C., and W.L. Thomas III. 1990, Sept. *A Survey of Ship Motion Reduction Devices*. Departmental Report DTRC/SHD-1338-01, Ship Hydromechanics Department, David Taylor Research Center. https://apps.dtic.mil/sti/pdfs/ADA229278.pdf.

Smith, Thomas. 1628. *The Complete Souldier, Containing the Whole Art of Gunnery..., 2d ed.* Volume 1. R. Dawlman.

Smyth, William Henry. 1867. *The Sailor's Word-Book*. Blackie and Son.

Snow, Richard. 2017. *Iron Dawn: The Monitor, the Merrimack, and the Civil War Sea Battle That Changed History*. Scribner.

Society for the Encouragement of Arts, Manufactures and Commerce. 1836. "No. VIII. Recoil Carriage for Pivot Guns." *Transactions of the Society for the Encouragement of Arts, Manufactures and Commerce*, 50: 73–79 and plate 2.

Sondhaus, Lawrence. 2012. *Naval Warfare, 1815–1914*. Taylor & Francis.

Song, Chaoming, et al. 2008, May 29. "A Phase Diagram for Jammed Matter." *Nature*, 453: 629–32.

Spears, John Randolph. 1897. *The History of Our Navy from Its Origin to the End of the War with Spain, 1775–1897*. Volume 4. C. Scribner's Sons.

Spencer, Hugh H. 1946. "Azon and Razon." In Hugh H. Spencer, *Guided Missiles and Techniques*, Volume 1, 27–47. Summary Technical Report of Division 5, National Defense Research Committee.

Stafford, Charles W., and Giles F. Ward. 1864. *Memorial to the Senate and House of Representatives on the History of the Stafford Projectiles in Connection with the Government and Its Officials*. Philip & Solomons.

Stahlbuhk, Amelia. 2015, July 25. "Calcium Nitrate." https://www.saltwiki.net/index.php/Calicum_nitrate (citing Robie, R.A., B.S Hemingway, and J.A. Fisher. 1978. "Thermodynamic Properties of Minerals and Related Substances at 298.15 K and 1 Bar Pressure and Higher Temperatures." *U.S. Geological Survey Bulletin*, 1452).

Staunton, Capt. P.M. 1901, Mar. 15. "Capped Armour-Piercing Projectiles." *Engineering: An Illustrated Weekly Journal*, 71: 336–39.

Steel, David. 1801. *The Ship-master's Assistant and Owner's Manual, 9th ed.* David Steel.

Steel, David. 1812. *The Elements and Practice of Naval Architecture, Or, a Treatise on Ship-Building..., 2d ed.* Steel & Co.

Stevens, Captain John Harvey. 1834. *Some Description of the Methods Used in Pointing Guns at Sea*. John Murray.

Stille, Mark. 2012. *Imperial Japanese Navy Battleships 1941–45*. Bloomsbury.

Stille, Mark. 2020. *British Battleship vs Italian Battleship: The Mediterranean 1940–41*. Bloomsbury.

Stone, George W. 1994, Oct. *Projectile Penetration Into Representative Targets*. Sandia National Laboratories.

Stoner, Bob. 2002. "Ordnance Notes, Mk 2 Mod 0 and Mod 1 .50 Caliber MG/81mm Mortar." http://pcf45.com/misfire/mortar.html.

Stoney, William E., Jr. 1954, Feb. 5. *Transonic Drag Measurements of Eight Body-Nose Shapes*. NACA RM L33K17. https://ntrs.nasa.gov/citations/19930087953.

Strauss, Lieutenant Joseph. 1896, July. "Telescopic Sights for Guns." *Proceedings of the U.S. Naval Institute*, 22(3) (Whole Issue 79): 587–97. https://www.usni.org/magazines/proceedings/1896/july/telescopic-sights-guns.

Strauss, Lieutenant Joseph. 1901, Oct. "Smokeless Powder." *Proceedings of the U.S. Naval Institute*, 27/4/100 (online); 27(4) (Whole Issue 100): 733–38. https://www.usni.org/magazines/proceedings/1901/october/smokeless-powder.

Sturek, Walter B. 1975, Dec. *Three-Dimensional Boundary Layer Research as Applied to the Magnus Effect on Spinning Projectiles*. U.S. Army Ballistics Research Laboratories (BRL) Memorandum Report 2572.

Sulfredge, C. David, et al. 2005, Jan. "Calculating the Effect of Surface or Underwater Explosions on Submerged Equipment and Structures." Oak Ridge National Laboratory.

Suliman, Mohamed Allaa Yousef, et al. 2009, May 26–28. "Computational Investigation of Base Drag Reduction for a Projectile at Different Flight Regimes." Aerospace Sciences & Aviation Technology, paper ASAT-13-FM-05.

Sweet, Frank W. 2005. *Six Gems of Forgotten Civil War History: Essays That Did Not Make It into the Dissertation, but Were Too Much Fun to Discard*. Backintyme.

Symonds, Craig L. 2012. *The Civil War at Sea*. Oxford University Press.

Tailyour, Lieutenant Commander Patrick. 1999, Oct. "Torpedo Development." https://archive.navalsubleague.org/1999/torfedo-development.

Tanner, Joseph Robson. 1903. *A Descriptive Catalogue of the Naval Manuscripts in the Pepysian Library at Magdalene College, Cambridge*. Volume 1. Publication of the Navy Records Society, Volume XXVI.

Temming, Maria. 2021, Apr. 22. "X-Ray Scans Explain How the 'Brazil Nut Effect' Works." https://www.sciencenews.org/article/brazil-nut-effect-mixed-nuts-xray-scan-physics.

Tennent, Sir James Emerson. 1864. *The Story of the Guns*. Longman, Green, etc.

Testo, Alex. 2016. "The Grand Battery—The Latest Evidence." https://projecthougoumont.com/the-grand-battery-the-latest-evidence/.

Thompson, Mark. 2009. *The White War: Life and Death on the Italian Front, 1915–1919*. Basic Books.

Thomson, Harry C., and Lida Mayo. 1955. "Chapter 5: Artillery." In *United States Army in World War II: The Technical Services: The Ordnance Department. Procurement and Supply*. http://tothosewhoserved.org/usa/ts/usatso02/chapter05.html.

Toll, Ian W. 2008. *Six Frigates: The Epic Story of the Founding of the U.S. Navy*. W.W. Norton.

Tschappat, William Harvey. 1917. *Text-Book of Ordnance and Gunnery*. John Wiley & Sons.

Tucker, Spencer C. 1973, Aug. "The Carronade." *Proceedings of the U.S. Naval Institute*, 99(8): 846. https://www.usni.org/magazines/proceedings/1973/august/carronade.

Tucker, Spencer C. 1992, Sept. "Technical Report—The Dahlgren Boat Howitzer." *Naval History Magazine*, 6(3). https://www.usni.org/magazines/naval-history-magazine/1992/september/technical-report-dahlgren-boat-howitzer.

Tucker, Spencer C. 1997, Mar. "The Carronade." *Nautical Research Journal*, 15–23.

Tucker, Spencer C. 2008. *The Encyclopedia of North American Colonial Conflicts to 1775: A–K*. ABC-CLIO.

Tucker, Spencer C. 2009. *A Global Chronology of Conflict: From the Ancient World to the Modern Middle East*. ABC-CLIO.

Tucker, Spencer C. 2011. *World War II at Sea: An Encyclopedia*. ABC-CLIO.

Tucker, Spencer C. 2015. *Instruments of War: Weapons and Technologies That Have Changed History*. ABC-CLIO.

Tucker, Spencer C. 2020. *Weapons and Warfare: From Ancient and Medieval Times to the 21st Century*. ABC-CLIO.

Tucker, Spencer C., and Priscilla Mary Roberts. 2005. *World War I Encyclopedia*. Volume 1. ABC-CLIO.

Tucker, Spencer. 2013, May. "Armaments and Innovations—The Soda-Bottle-Shaped Shell Guns." *Naval History Magazine*, 27(3): n.p. https://www.usni.org/magazines/naval-history-magazine/2013/may/armaments-and-innovations-soda-bottle-shaped-shell-guns.

Tunis, Edwin. 1954. *Weapons: A Pictorial History*. Johns Hopkins University Press.

Turnbull, Stephen. 2018. *The Art of Renaissance Warfare: From the Fall of Constantinople to the Thirty Years War*. Pen & Sword.

United Service Journal. 1832. "Captain Pole's Gun Carriage." *United Service Journal and Naval and Military Magazine*, Part III: 516–17.

United Service Journal. 1836, Oct. "Correspondence from the Principal Ports and Stations." *United Service Journal and Naval and Military Magazine*, Part III: 262ff.

U.S. Army. 1922, June. *American Coast Artillery Materiel*. Ordnance Department, Doc. 2042. Government Printing Office.

U.S. Army. 1990, Jan. "Mark 19 Model 3 40-mm Heavy Machine Gun." *Army*, 40(1): 52–53.

U.S. Army. 2022 [1861]. *The Ordnance Manual for the Use of the Officers of the United States Army*. Verlag.

U.S. Army, Department of the Army, Military Explosives. 1989. TM 9-1300-213.

U.S. Army, Materiel Command. 1964, Feb. *Gun Tubes*. Research and Development of Materiel. Engineering Design Handbook. Gun Series. AMCP 706-252.

U.S. Hydrographic Office. 1949, Jan. 1. "War Damage Report No. 58, Submarine Report: Depth Charge, Bomb, Mine, Torpedo and Gunfire Damage Including Losses in Action, 7 Dec. 1941 to 15 Aug. 1945." Section 15 (Behavior of Underwater Non-Contact Explosions): http://www.

ibiblio.org/hyperwar/USN/rep/WDR/WDR58/WDR58-15.html; Section 16 (Hull Damage and Strength): http://www.ibiblio.org/hyperwar/USN/rep/WDR/WDR58/WDR58-16.html.

U.S. Navy. 1866. *Ordnance Instructions for the United States Navy.* Part III, Ordnance and Ordnance Stores. Government Printing Office.

U.S. Navy. 1880. *Ordnance Instructions for the United States Navy.* Part III, Ordnance and Ordnance Stores. Government Printing Office.

U.S. Navy. 1918. *Gunnery Instructions, U.S. Navy 1913.* Government Printing Office.

U.S. Navy. 1923, Sept. *Ammunition: Instructions for the Naval Service 1923.* Ordnance Pamphlet 4. Government Printing Office.

U.S. Navy. 1968. *Dictionary of American Naval Fighting Ships.* Volume III. Government Printing Office.

U.S. Navy. 1992. Harris, L.S. *Principles of Naval Ordnance and Gunnery.* NAVEDTRA 12970. Government Printing Office.

U.S. Navy. 2002, Feb. *Basic Military Requirements.* NAVEDTRA 14325. Government Printing Office.

U.S. Navy. 2007, Feb. *Lookout Training Handbook.* NAVEDTRA 12968-D. Government Printing Office.

U.S. Navy. 2013. *The Book of Basic Machines: The U.S. Navy Training Manual.* Skyhorse Publishing.

U.S. Navy, Bureau of Naval Personnel. 1937. *Naval Ordnance and Gunnery.* Government Printing Office.

U.S. Navy, Bureau of Naval Personnel. 1944. Polk, Lt. Cmrd. Orval H., et al. *Naval Ordnance and Gunnery.* NAVPERS 16116. Government Printing Office.

U.S. Navy, Bureau of Naval Personnel. 1955. *Naval Ordnance and Gunnery, Volume 2: Fire Control.* NAVPERS 10798. Government Printing Office.

U.S. Navy, Bureau of Naval Personnel. 1957. *Naval Ordnance and Gunnery, Volume 1: Naval Ordnance.* (Chapters 1–14.) NAVPERS 10797-A. Government Printing Office.

U.S. Navy, Bureau of Naval Personnel. 1958. *Naval Ordnance and Gunnery, Volume 2: Fire Control.* NAVPERS 10798-A. Government Printing Office.

U.S. Navy, Bureau of Naval Personnel. 1963. *Fire Control Technician 2.* Navy Training Course. NAVPERS 10174-A. Government Printing Office.

U.S. Navy, Bureau of Naval Personnel. 1964. *Gunner's Mate G 3 & 2.* Government Printing Office.

U.S. Navy, Bureau of Naval Personnel. 1965. *The 5"/38 Gun.* NAVPERS 10111.

U.S. Navy, Bureau of Naval Weapons. 1963. *Weapon System Fundamentals: Vol. 2, Analysis of Weapons.* NAVWEPS OP 3000.

U.S. Navy, Bureau of Ordnance. 1909. Oct. *12-Inch Range Table.* Ordnance Pamphlet 293. Government Printing Office.

U.S. Navy, Bureau of Ordnance. 1913. *Steel for Ordnance Purposes.* Ordnance Pamphlet 401. Government Printing Office.

U.S. Navy, Bureau of Ordnance. 1941, Oct. *16-Inch Range Table 25000 F.S. Initial Velocity.* Ordnance Pamphlet 770. Government Printing Office.

U.S. Navy, Bureau of Ordnance. 1943, Apr. *U.S. Navy Torpedo Mark 18 (Electric).* Ordnance Pamphlet 946. Government Printing Office.

U.S. Navy, Bureau of Ordnance. 1946, May 15. *VT Fuzes for Projectiles and Spin-Stabilized Rockets.* Ordnance Pamphlet 1480. Government Printing Office.

U.S. Navy, Bureau of Ordnance. 1947, May 28. *U.S. Explosive Ordnance.* Volume 1. Ordnance Pamphlet 1664. Government Printing Office.

U.S. Navy, Bureau of Ships. 1956, Jan. "Guided Missile Cruiser Joins Fleet." *Bureau of Ships Journal,* 4(9): 9.

U.S. Navy, Navy Department. 1918, May 25. *The Ship and Gun Drills.* Edward N. Appleton.

U.S. Navy, Office of Information. 2021, Sept. 20. "MK 46-30 Mm Gun Weapon System." https://www.navy.mil/Resources/Fact-Files/Display-FactFiles/Article/2220690/mk-46-30-mm-gun-weapon-system/.

U.S. Navy, Office of Naval Intelligence. 1918, Oct. *Antisubmarine Tactics.* Government Printing Office.

U.S. War Department. 1914. *Coast Artillery Drill Regulations, United States Army, 1914.* Government Printing Office.

Uppal, Rajesh. 2019, June 4. "Countries Developing Underwater LIDAR Imaging Systems for Rapid Wide-Area Anti-Mine and Anti-Submarine Operations." https://idstch.com/military/navy/lidar/.

Upton, Emory. 1875. *Infantry Tactics, Double and Single Rank, Adapted to American Topography and Improved Fire-arms.* Appleton.

Valin, Christopher J. 2010. *Fortune's Favorite: Sir Charles Douglas and the Breaking of the Line.* Fireship Press.

Van Duzer, Lieutenant L.S. 1901, September. "Professional Notes." *Proceedings of the U.S. Naval Institute,* 27(3): 587ff.

Van Nostrand's Engineering Magazine. 1871. "Gunpowder—Its Nature and Action as Exemplified by Recent Researches." *Van Nostrand's Engineering Magazine,* 4: 299–307.

Vasselin, Roger. 1915. "Tungsten Projectiles." *Antiaircraft Journal,* 44: 372.

Vayig, Yaniv, and Zvi Rosenberg. 2021, Aug. 8. "The Penetration and Ricochet of Ogive-nosed Rigid Projectiles Obliquely Impacting Metallic Targets." *International Journal of Protective Structures,* 13(1): n.p.

Verbeek, J.R. 2013 (pdf creation). "'Screws,' or Tricks of Trade: Secret Repairs of Solid Cast Cannon by Jan Verbruggen." *Smoothbore Ordnance Journal.* https://www.napoleon-series.org/military-info/OrdnanceJournal/Issue6/SOJ-6-6_C18th_Gunfounding.pdf.

Very, Edward Wilson. 1880. *Navies of the World.* J. Wiley & Sons.

Vincent, D'Arcy George. 1887. "Torpedoes, Naval Gunnery, and National Defence, Part V." *Colburn's United Service Magazine and Naval Military Journal*, 168: 496–507.

Voelcker, Tim. 2013. *Broke of the Shannon and the War of 1812.* Seaforth Publishing.

Volo, Dorothy Denneen, and James M. Volo. 2001. *Daily Life in the Age of Sail.* ABC-CLIO.

Volo, Dorothy Denneen, and James M. Volo. 2003. *Daily Life during the American Revolution.* ABC-CLIO.

von Maltitz, Ian. 2001, Winter. "Our Present Knowledge of the Chemistry of Black Powder." *Journal of Pyrotechnics* __(14): 27–39.

von Maltitz, Ian. 2003. *Black Powder Manufacturing, Testing & Optimizing.* American Fireworks News.

Vos, Roelof, and Saeed Farokhi. 2015. *Introduction to Transonic Aerodynamics.* Springer Netherlands.

Wakely, Andrews, and John Adams. 1787. *The Mariner's Compass Rectified, Etc.* Mount and Page.

Walker, J. Bernard. 1918, Apr. 20. "Velocity and Range of Guns." *Scientific American*, 118: 360.

Walton, Steven Ashton. 1999. *The Art of Gunnery in Renaissance England.* Ph.D. thesis, University of Toronto.

Warbirds Resource Group. 2017. "Introduction to Fuzes." http://www.warbirdsresourcegroup.org/LRG/fuzeintro.html (citing *German Explosive Ordnance*, Army Tech. Manual TM 9-1985-2).

Ward, James Harmon. 1845. *An Elementary Course of Instruction in Ordnance and Gunnery.* Carey and Hart.

Ward, James Harmon. 1861. *Elementary Instruction in Naval Ordnance and Gunnery.* D. Van Nostrand.

War Office (British). 1879. *Manual of Siege and Garrison Artillery Exercises.* HM Stationery Office.

War Office (British). 1902. *Treatise on Ammunition.* HM Stationery Office.

Watts, Anthony John. 1994. *The Royal Navy: An Illustrated History.* Naval Institute Press.

Watts, Sir Philip. 1911. Comment. In H. Frahm, "Result of Trials of the Anti-Rolling Tanks at Sea," 202–7. *Transactions of the Institution of Naval Architects*, 53: 183–201.

Webster, Keith G. 2007, Jan. 29. *Investigation of Close Proximity Underwater Explosion Effects on a Ship-like Structure Using the Multi-material Arbitrary Lagrangian Eulerian Finite Element Method.* M.S. thesis, Virginia Polytechnic Institute.

Weir, William. 2006. *50 Military Leaders Who Changed the World.* Fall River Press.

Weir, William. 2019. *50 Weapons That Changed Warfare.* Permuted Press.

Welles, Gideon. 1865, Dec. 4. *Report of the Secretary of the Navy.* Government Printing Office.

Werrell, Kenneth P. 1985, Sept. *The Evolution of the Cruise Missile.* Air University Press.

Wertime, Theodore A. 1961. *The Coming of the Age of Steel.* University of Chicago Press.

Whisonant, Robert C. 2001, Nov. "Geology and History of Confederate Saltpeter Cave Operations in Western Virginia." *Virginia Minerals*, 47(4): 33–42.

White, Peter. 2010. *Crime Scene to Court: The Essentials of Forensic Science.* Royal Society of Chemistry.

White, Sir William Henry. 1900. *A Manual of Naval Architecture.* J. Murray.

Whittaker, Colin W., and Frank O. Lundstrom. 1934, July. *A Review of the Patents and Literature on the Manufacture of Potassium Nitrate with Notes on Its Occurrence and Uses.* U.S. Department of Agriculture, Misc. pub. 192. USDA.

Wildenberg, Thomas. 2015, Oct. "The Revolutionary Rangekeeper." *Naval History Magazine*, 29(5): n.p. https://www.usni.org/magazines/naval-history-magazine/2015/october/revolutionary-rangekeeper.

Wilds, George W. 1986. *Seaman.* NAVEDTRA 10120-J1. Government Printing Office.

Wilhelm, Thomas. 1881. *A Military Dictionary and Gazetteer.* L.R. Hamersly & Co.

Williams, D.J., and W. Johnson. 2000. "A Note on Casting Iron Cannon Balls: Ideality and Porosity." *International Journal of Impact Engineering*, 24: 429–33.

Willis, Sam. 2008. *Fighting at Sea in the Eighteenth Century: The Art of Sailing Warfare.* Boydell Press.

Wilson, Herbert Wingley. 1896. *Ironclads in Action: A Sketch of Naval Warfare from 1855 to 1895.* Volume 2. Little, Brown and Company.

Winfield, Rif. 2010. *British Warships in the Age of Sail, 1603–1714: Design, Construction, Careers and Fates.* Pen & Sword.

Wingate, George Wood. 1876. *Manual for Rifle Practice.* W.C. & F.P. Church.

Wise, Terence. 1979. *Artillery Equipments of the Napoleonic Wars.* Osprey Publishing.

Worden, Edward Chauncey. 1911. *Nitrocellulose Industry.* 2 vols. Constable and Company.

Worden, Edward Chauncey. 1921. *Technology of Cellulose Esters: A Theoretical and Practical Treatise....* Volume 1, Part 1. D. Van Nostrand.

Wu, Bin, et al. 2008, June. "Heat Transfer in a 155 Mm Compound Gun Barrel with Full Length Integral Midwall Cooling Channels." *Applied Thermal Engineering*, 28: 881–88. https://www.sciencedirect.com/science/article/abs/pii/S1359431107002426.

Yager, Robert J. 2014, June. *Calculating Drag Coefficients for Spheres and Other Shapes Using C++.* U.S. Army Research Laboratory.

Yenne, Bill. 2018. *The Complete History of U.S. Cruise Missiles: From Kettering's 1920s' Bug & 1950's Snark to Today's Tomahawk.* Specialty Press.

Young, Major C.G. 1920. "Notes on Fuze Design."

Journal of the United States Artillery, 53(1) (Whole No. 167): 484–524.

Zabecki, David T. 1999. *World War II in Europe: An Encyclopedia*. Volume 1. Garland Pub.

Zalinski, Captain Edmund Lewis. 1888. "The Naval Uses of the Pneumatic Torpedo Gun." *Proceedings of the U.S. Naval Institute*, 14(1) (Whole No. 44): 9–55. https://www.usni.org/magazines/proceedings/1888/january/naval-uses-pneumatic-torpedo-gun.

Author's Preexisting Work

As noted on the copyright page, portions of this book were previously published in the *Grantville Gazette*, which ceased publication in July 2022. That online magazine presented fiction set in and nonfiction relating to the fictional literary universe created by the late Eric Flint's alternate-history sci-fi novel *1632*. In that novel, a new timeline is created when a fictional West Virginia town (Grantville) is moved from the year 2000 to Thuringia, Germany, during the Thirty Years' War. The nonfiction considered the limited knowledge and resources that would have been available to the townspeople and proposed how they might cope. Naturally, the fictional aspects have been omitted from the present work.

Cooper, Iver P. 2013, Jan. "Naval Armament and Armor, Part 1: Big Guns at Sea." *Grantville Gazette*, 45.

Cooper, Iver P. 2013, Mar. "Naval Armament and Armor, Part 2: Ready, Aim, Fire." *Grantville Gazette*, 46.

Cooper, Iver P. 2013, May. "Naval Armament and Armor, Part 3: Hitting the Target." *Grantville Gazette*, 47.

Cooper, Iver P. 2013, July. "Naval Armament and Armor, Part 4: Implements of Destruction." *Grantville Gazette*, 48.

Cooper, Iver P. 2013, Sept. "Naval Armament and Armor, Part 5: Thrust and Parry." *Grantville Gazette*, 49.

Index

Abel, Frederick 53–54, 74, 164, 265
Adams, John 63
Adams, W. Bridges 129
air defense 133–34, 137, 150–51
ammunition: bag 20, 99, 101, 143; explosive train 98–99; fixed (case, cartridge) 20, 99, 101, 103, 154; loading 17, 134, 142–45; rounds 99–; sabot 16, 80–81, 87, 99, 103–5; storage, gunpowder 103–4; storage, projectiles 101–2, 104; *see also* fuses
Archimedes 78, 265
armor 231; distribution 260–1; metal 255–8; non-metallic 261; underwater protection (vs. torpedoes) 264; *see also* gun mounts, turrets and barbettes; hull penetration
Armstrong, William 16–17, 21, 45–6, 81, 125, 137
artillery *see* guns; weapons, miscellaneous

Bacon, Roger 265
ballistic pendulum 73, 173–4, 185–6, 268
ballistics, exterior: aerodynamics and air resistance 11, 21, 79, 86–87, 95, 106, 183–84, 188–95, 248, 252; ballistics tables 190–91; early history 183–84; flight stabilization 20, 104, 125, 193–96; impact parameters, calculation of 252–3; speed measurement (of projectiles) 185; spherical projectiles 267–8; trajectory calculation 187–91, 248–9; *see also* gunnery; guns; windage
ballistics, internal: 161–2; barrel thickness and 9, 168–70; bore length, optimal 17, 175–76; combustion

physics 165–68; grain size and shape 165–69; heat and heat dissipation 171–72; high-low pressure guns and 173; powder charge, optimal 17, 176; pressure measurement 162–5, 172; pressure vessel, gun as 7, 20, 162; velocity at muzzle, experimental determination of 173–75; velocity at muzzle, prediction of 79, 83, 167–8, 177–82; velocity in-bore, experimental determination of 176; *see also* guns; windage
ballistics, terminal *see* hull penetration
ballistite 74; *see also* gunpowder, smokeless
bar shot *see* projectiles: shot, disabling
barbettes *see* gun mounts
Bashforth, Francis 185, 190, 193, 268
Bate, John 62
battles: Algiers, bombardment of (1682) 87; Antwerp, siege of (1585) 232; Cadiz, siege of (1812) 79; Chuambi, Second Battle of (1841) 234; Copenhagen (1807) 234; Dangpo (1592) 255; Dogger Bank (1915) 133, 212; Finisterre, Second Battle of (1747) 135; Foochow (1884) 238; Fort McHenry (1814) 234; Four Days Battle (1666) 83; Glorious First of June (1794) 82; Great Harbor (413BCE) 231; Hampton Roads (1862) 31; Jutland (1916) 101; Kagoshima, bombardment of (1863) 16; Lake Erie (1813) 254; La Rochelle (1628) 232; Latakia (1973) 237; Liaoluo Bay (1633) 231; Lissa (1866) 20, 31, 229;

Memphis, First Battle of (1862) 229; New Orleans (1815) 261; Poyang Lake (1363) 231; Quiberon Bay (1759) 153; Salona (1821) 82; Santiago (1908) 245; Sheipu (1885) 238; Shimonoseki Strait (1864) 46; Sinope (1853) 87, 254; Spanish Armada (1588) 83; Toulon (1744) 135; Tsushima (1905) 212
Bentham, Samuel 32, 117, 119–21
Bernoulli, Daniel 187
Berthelot, Marcellin 54
Bessemer, Henry 215
Biringuccio, Vannoccio 40–41, 43, 59, 62–64, 94–95, 175, 234
Bomford, George 164
Bonaparte, Napoleon 1, 212
Borgard, Albert 11, 170
Bourne, William 67–68, 73, 196
Brazil nut effect 70
broadside *see* warships, design of, horizontal distribution of guns
Broke, Captain Philip 152–3, 216
Brooke-Pechell, Captain Samuel John 216

canister shot *see* projectiles: shot, case
cannon *see* guns
Cavalli, Giovanni 20
Cecil, Robert 59
chain shot *see* projectiles: shot, disabling
Chance, Alexander 56
Chance, C.F. 56
Chevreul, Michael 53
Claus, Carl Friedrich 56
Coles, Captain Cowper Phipps 35
Collado, Luis 9, 13, 186
Congreve, Sir William 116, 234, 265